THE POSSIBILITY OF KNOWLEDGE

THE POSSIBILITY OF KNOWLEDGE

NOZICK AND HIS CRITICS

Edited by

Steven Luper-Foy
Trinity University

ROWMAN & LITTLEFIELD
PUBLISHERS

ROWMAN & LITTLEFIELD

Published in the United States of America in 1987
by Rowman & Littlefield, Publishers
(a division of Littlefield, Adams & Company)
81 Adams Drive, Totowa, New Jersey 07512

Copyright © 1987 by Rowman & Littlefield

Library of Congress Cataloging-in-Publication Data

The Possibility of knowledge.

   Includes part 3 of Robert Nozick's Philosophical
explanations and 12 critical essays about Nozick's work.
   Bibliography: p. 323.
   Includes indexes.
   1. Knowledge, Theory of. 2. Skepticism.
3. Nozick, Robert. I. Luper-Foy, Steven.
II. Nozick, Robert. Philosophical Explanations.
1986.
BD161.P728   1987   121   86–20445
ISBN 0-8476-7446-0
ISBN 0-8476-7447-4

90 89 88 87
6 5 4 3 2 1

Printed in the United States of America

CONTENTS

PREFACE

Interest in skepticism is once again strong. No doubt there are many reasons for this revival, among them the decline of verificationism, which had led many philosophers to dismiss as "pseudoproblems" vast areas of important inquiry including the issue of skepticism. But another major reason for the revival is the novel approach to skepticism and knowledge that Nozick offers in his book *Philosophical Explanations.* His fascinating view is complex and highly controversial, and the body of literature to which it has given rise is already large.

Nozick's opponents, skeptics, challenge our confident claim to know the nature of the world around us. A typical skeptical argument begins with the assertion that it would be wildly exaggerated to say that you know that you are *not* in the following situation. In this scenario, you are a mere brain in a vat on a planet far from earth, and scientists there are using electrochemical means to produce in you exactly the same experiences you now have. How can you possibly tell that you are not in this situation or others that, were you in them, would seem exactly like your actual situation? But if you grant that you do *not* know you are not in this skeptic's scenario, then there is a short argument for the conclusion that you know virtually nothing. Presumably the following principle (the Principle of Entailment) is true: if you know one thing and believe a second thing by deducing it from what you know, then you know the second thing as well. But notice what would happen if you were to claim that you know, say, that you are on earth (or that you are reading, or that you have hands and a body, and so on). Using the above Principle of Entailment, we could conclude that you know you are *not* in the skeptic's scenario, since being on earth *entails* that you are not on a distant planet. Since we have said that you *cannot* claim to know you are not in the skeptic's scenario, then we must conclude that you do not know that you are on earth. You do not know you are reading or even that you have a body.

Those who reject this skeptical argument tend to be antiskeptics; that is, they argue that it is obvious that you *do* know you are on earth (and have a body, etc.), and so, using the Principle of Entailment, you can conclude that you *do* know that you are not in the skeptic's scenario. You know you are not a brain in a vat and that you are not being deceived by alien scientists. If the antiskeptic's argument is sound, then obviously the skeptic's is not. On the other hand, if the skeptic's argument is sound, the antiskeptic's is flawed. At least one of the two arguments must be rejected, but which?

This unhappy standoff is broken by Nozick. He has found an account of knowledge that allows him to reject the arguments of *both* the skeptic and the antiskeptic. This is possible because he is able to reject an innocent-looking assumption present in both arguments: the Principle of Entailment. Throwing out this principle, however, leads Nozick to adopt an extremely surprising view. On his account, you *do* know you are on earth, but you do *not* know that you are not on a planet far from earth being deceived by alien scientists.

In this book, Nozick's epistemological writings are confronted by twelve critical essays. Part 3 of *Philosophical Explanations* is reprinted here virtually in its entirety. The critical essays that follow have been prepared specifically for this volume. In several of these, the claim is that Nozick has not succeeded in rebutting the skeptic. Some offer fresh accounts of skepticism and its flaws. Others criticize Nozick's externalist accounts of knowledge and evidence. Still others welcome externalism but attempt to replace Nozick's accounts of knowledge and evidence with more plausible analyses.

I am indebted to Robert Nozick for his encouragement and for discussion of his epistemology as well as for his permission to reprint the relevant part of his essay. Harvard University Press is due thanks for the same reason. My editors at Rowman & Littlefield have been patient and helpful; they are due thanks, as are the contributors to this volume for their work. Finally, I thank Rebecca C. Reyes for the excellent work she has done preparing the manuscript.

INTRODUCTION

Steven Luper-Foy

We would all like to suppose that our beliefs concerning the nature of the world have been acquired in a reasonably reliable manner. Unfortunately, it is far from obvious that there *are* ways to discover the facts about the world with *any reliability at all.* There are enormously powerful skeptical arguments to the effect that if we ever arrive at an accurate world-view, it will be a sheer coincidence. Typically, skeptics point out that there is a vast number of possible situations in which the sources on which we rely in order to form our beliefs would be completely misleading. Consider a particularly worrisome example. Our beliefs about the world are all based in one way or another on sensory information; it is the *source* for our beliefs about the world. Hence the possibility that our sensory source is misleading is very disturbing. But there *are* situations in which this information would lead us to adopt a completely inaccurate picture of our circumstances. Just imagine that we are brains in vats on a planet completely different from earth, and that scientists there are feeding us our present misleading sensory information. With more ingenuity we could describe situations in which we are even more radically deceived, ones in which the planets and other sorts of objects with which we are familiar do not exist even though our sensory input is as it is now. In view of these possibilities, how can we claim to know the truth of any claim based on sensory experience?

Still, the fact that there are situations in which our belief sources would be unreliable only shows that *conceivably* our sources are unreliable. And it is one thing to point out that our sources of belief could *conceivably* be unreliable, and quite another to provide reasonable grounds for thinking that they *are* unreliable. Skeptics owe us an

I thank David Shatz and John Murphy for helpful comments on an earlier draft of this introductory essay.

account of how they get from the fact that we can conceive of situations in which our sources would be misleading to the conclusion that in the *actual* situation our sources are unreliable. They need to fill in the details of the argument by which they challenge our claim to know that our beliefs about the world are true.

In his book *Philosophical Explanations*,[1] Robert Nozick offers a plausible explanation of the reasoning involved in skepticism. He also offers a striking and novel reply to the skeptic, a reply that has already inspired a great deal of discussion among philosophers. Drawing on the analysis of knowledge that he develops, he is able to challenge a key assumption on which skeptics rely.

Nozick's analysis of knowledge, leaving out some qualifications, is this: I know that my belief that p is true just in case:

(1) p is true;

(2) I believe that p through method M;

(3) If p weren't true and I were to use M to arrive at a belief whether (or not) p, then I wouldn't believe, via M, that p; and

(4) If p were true and I were to use M to arrive at a belief whether (or not) p, then I would believe, via M, that p.

Given that I believe correctly that p, Nozick says of me that when (3) and (4) hold, I *track the fact that* p.

Conditions (3) and (4) employ the use of subjunctive conditionals. Nozick declines to provide an analysis of the truth conditions for subjunctives, except to say that a subjunctive conditional of the form,

If p were true, q would be true

is true just in case q is true throughout the *p-neighborhood* of the actual world (680–81, note 8).[2] The p-neighborhood is the set of possible worlds in which p is true that are close to the actual world. A fully acceptable explication of the closeness relation, however, has not yet been provided. (In the bibliography at the end of this book, I provide a list of useful works dealing with the semantics of subjunctives.)

Consider the way Nozick's analysis functions. Condition (3) is met if in normal circumstances I arrive at my belief that a table is before me on the basis of my present sensory information. It is met, at least, when my method of belief formation is to infer that a table is before me if I am confronted with the appearance of a table, and to infer that no table is there if I am confronted with the appearance of a tableless room. For if there *were* no table before me, I would not be appeared to in a table way, and so applying my method would lead me to believe that no table is before me rather than that one is there. On this construal of my method, I also meet condition (4): if a table were before me and I were to apply my method to form a belief, it would be the belief that a table is there.

Unfortunately, this analysis is seriously flawed; fortunately, the flaw can be removed, at least in part. The problem is that Nozick's analysis functions properly only when applied to two-sided methods — that is, those capable of yielding both yes and no verdicts concerning the truth of a belief.[3] For example, the method which led to my belief that a table is before me was two-sided. But suppose that my method had been to infer that a table is before me if I am confronted with the appearance of a table, so that my method is incapable of recommending the belief that there is no table before me. Then I cannot meet condition (3) using my method. To satisfy the antecedent of (3), I would have to arrive at a belief concerning the table using my method. Given that it is one-sided, I could only believe that a table is there using my method, and then I could not satisfy (3)'s consequent. In general, I can never meet (3) using a method which one-sidedly indicates that my belief is true.

The opposite problem arises in connection with condition (4). To satisfy its antecedent when I am using my one-sided method, I *must* believe that a table is before me, and then I cannot help but satisfy its consequent. Thus I cannot help but meet (4) using methods which one-sidedly indicate that my belief is true.

Revised versions of (3) and (4) will help:

(3) If p were false, I would not believe that p via M;

(4) If p were true and I applied M, then I would believe that p via M.

On this account, which loosens up the antecedents of Nozick's old conditions, I can know a table is before me even when I use my one-sided method.

It is important to note that even the new analysis will work properly only if certain assumptions are made concerning methods of belief formation. As Richard Fumerton, David Shatz, and Steven Luper-Foy have pointed out, it is possible to construe methods in either an internalist sense or in an externalist sense.[4] Suppose that I believe that a table is before me because I see it there; what is my method of belief here? An externalist approach would construe my method as a causal chain including such events as the stimulation of my retinas by light from my table, nerve impulses, brain activity, and so on. On this construal, however, I would know that a table is before me even if I have taken a drug which induces hallucinations of tables so long as I veridically perceive a table. Yet surely I know no such thing under these conditions. Nonetheless, conditions (3) and (4) are met simply because if I were to hallucinate, it would not be the externalist method that would lead me to a false belief about my table; instead, it would be a method involving table hallucinations. On an internalist interpretation, the method leading to my belief concerning my table would be described solely in terms of my perceptual states and my beliefs and relations among them. On *this* approach, I would *not* know that a table is before me if I have taken the drug, for my method might well lead me to a false belief about my table.

To the extent that Nozick deals with this issue, he does so by emphasizing internalist specifications of methods, so that any two methods are identical if and only if the percepts involved in them are identical (184–85). However, this reply has struck many as inadequate. First, as Lawrence BonJour and Richard Fumerton indicate, it is puzzling that an externalist like Nozick adopts internalist specifications of methods. Second, Nozick cannot (and does not) insist that methods be given an *exclusively* internalist specification, for we could arrive at knowledge through accurate devices that directly implant beliefs into our brains; since these devices would not produce perceptual states, then no internalist specification of the method of belief formation would be available.[5] Hence Nozick owes us an account of when methods are to be specified "from the inside" and when "from the outside."

On Nozick's account, suitably revised, people can know many of the sorts of thing they typically claim to know. I can know, for example, that I have two hands and that my brain is inside my cranium. My present sensory evidence is best explained by the hypotheses that I have two hands and that my brain is in my skull. The inferences I have based on this sensory evidence can be thought of as the methods through which I have arrived at my beliefs concerning my hands and brain. If I did not have two hands (or if my brain were not in my skull) then the character of my experience would be different from the way it is, and so I would not have been led to believe I had two hands (or that my brain is in my skull) on the basis of my present experience. Condition (3) of Nozick's analysis is met; so is (4): had I two hands, and were I to arrive at a belief concerning whether or not I have two hands on the basis of my present sensory information, the belief to which I would be led would be that I have two hands.

Though I can, on Nozick's view, know such things as that I have two hands and that my brain is in my cranium, I *cannot* know many of the sorts of things of which skeptics insist I am ignorant. Do I, for instance, know that I am not a brain in a vat being stimulated by scientists in such a way as to have my present experiences? I cannot know this, on Nozick's view, for his third condition is violated. If it were *false* that I am not a brain in a vat (that is, if I *were* a brain in a vat), then I would *still* have those sensory experiences I take to indicate that I am not in a vat.

Admitting that I cannot know that my brain is not deceived by scientists who have taken it out of my skull and placed it in a vat appears inconsistent with the claim that I can know that my brain is in my skull where it ought to be. Indeed, there seems to be a proof that ignorance of the former entails ignorance of the latter, and on Nozick's interpretation, skepticism consists primarily in this purported proof (though he sketches other sorts of skeptical arguments as well). The proof rests on the following Principle of Entailment: If I know that *p* and I believe that *q* by deducing *q* from *p*, then I know that *q*. Using this principle, skeptics can show that not knowing that my brain has not been transferred to the skeptic's vat is inconsistent with knowing that my brain is in my skull. The proof is a *reductio ad absurdum* and starts with the assumption that I do not know that my brain is not in a vat.

(1) I do not know that my brain has not been removed and placed in the skeptic's vat.

(2) Suppose that I *did* know that my brain is in my skull.

(3) It follows that it has not been removed; seeing this, I can arrive at the belief that my brain has not been removed and placed in the skeptic's vat by deducing it from the fact that my brain is in my skull, a fact I know to hold by assumption.

(4) Given the Principle of Entailment,

(5) It would follow that I know that my brain has not been transferred to the skeptic's vat.

(6) But this is something I do *not* know, we have seen. Hence I do not know that my brain is in my skull after all.

Similar reasoning can be used by skeptics to challenge the epistemic status of our other claims about the world. On their view, to be ignorant of not being in a given skeptical scenario is to be ignorant of being in any corresponding *anti*skeptical scenario, that is, any situation that is incompatible with being in the skeptical scenario at hand.

Having laid out this powerful skeptical argument, Nozick proceeds to attack it at what would seem to be its least vulnerable point: he rejects the Principle of Entailment. For on his account, knowing that *p* is true need not put us in a position to know that the logical consequences of *p* are true even when we deduce them from *p*. Hence skeptics cannot conclude that I would know that my brain is not in a vat if I knew that it is in my cranium, and the argument through which they hope to challenge our knowledge claims fails. Skeptics are only partly right: I *can*-

not know that my brain has not not been transferred from my skull to the skeptic's vat, but I *can* know that it is in my skull. I cannot know that I am not in skeptical scenarios even though I can know that I am in corresponding antiskeptical scenarios.

Nozick's rebuttal to skepticism is a fascinating one, and repays careful study. However, the reaction of most philosophers to it has been one of skepticism, and while Nozick shows enormous ingenuity in anticipating the consequences of his rejection of the Principle of Entailment, many would be sympathethic to Shatz's quip that Nozick is just drawing his *modus ponens* before others have a chance to draw their *modus tollens*.[6] Moreover, if the rejection of skepticism depends on the rejection of the Entailment Principle, then perhaps we would be better off adopting skepticism. Most of the papers in this volume say at least something about whether Nozick has given a plausible case against the Entailment Principle. Ernest Sosa goes so far as to argue that the manner in which the tracking account handles the Principle of Entailment generates incoherent outcomes. To know that I am sitting by a fire, I must be firmly convinced that I am. Moreover, to be robustly convinced that I am by a fire I must be completely convinced that I am not a deceived brain in a vat, and the degree of conviction of the two beliefs must match. However, on Nozick's account, I must also think that for all I know I am a deceived brain in a vat, and on an intuitive conception of knowledge such a thought is in tension with a strong conviction that I am not a brain in a vat. Putting all of these beliefs together forces me to maintain an incoherent state of mind.

The great initial plausibility of the Principle of Entailment has made Nozick's view difficult to swallow. Still, it is not as if Nozick were the first philosopher to reject a seemingly obvious epistemic principle. Fred Dretske rejected the Entailment Principle some years before Nozick, and for similar reasons.[7] Remarks by J. L. Austin easily could be expanded into a rejection of this principle as well.[8] And Nelson Goodman reacted to Carl Hempel's raven paradoxes in a way that questioned an obvious epistemic principle.[9]

Hempel had suggested that an item which satisfies the antecedent and consequent of a generalization ought (with certain exceptions) to be considered a confirming instance of it. He also adopted a principle called the Equivalence Condition, which holds that what confirms a statement also confirms any equivalent statement. But Hempel noted that this conception of confirmation (*Hempel-confirmation*, as it might be called) generates paradoxical results. Consider the following three equivalent statements:

(a) All ravens are black.

(b) All nonblack things are nonravens.

(c) All things that are either ravens or nonravens are either nonravens or black.

Any nonblack nonraven, including yellow jellybeans and green slime, satisfies the antecedent and consequent of (b) and so Hempel-confirms (a). Moreover, any nonraven satisfies the antecedent and consequent of (c), so that a muddy shoe Hempel-confirms (a).

Hempel swallowed these seemingly paradoxical results. But Goodman's discussion of the raven paradoxes (as extended by Israel Scheffler[10]) suggests a different approach, one which leads to the rejection of the Equivalence Condition. The crucial point Goodman noted was that items which Hempel-confirm statements may *also* Hempel-confirm the *contraries* of those statements. We just saw that any nonravens Hempel-confirm (a); the same nonravens Hempel-confirm the contrary of (a), namely,

(d) All ravens are nonblack things,

which is equivalent to

(e) All things that are either ravens or nonravens are either nonravens or nonblack things.

Any nonraven satisfies the antecedent and consequent of (e) and so Hempel-confirms (d). Contrast black ravens: these Hempel-confirm (a) but *not* its contrary (d). Do we want to adopt a notion of confirmation like Hempel's, given which an item that is a confirming instance of a statement might *also* be a confirming instance of its contrary? It would seem best to prefer a notion of *selective confirmation* which allows as confirming instances of a statement only items which in a given sense confirm that statement and *not* its contrary. For example, we could say that an item *Goodman-confirms* a statement just in case it Hempel-confirms that statement *without* Hempel-confirming its contrary. This criterion would lead us to consider a black raven but not a nonraven as a Goodman-confirming instance of (a).

However, this conception of Goodman-confirmation will also lead us to reject the Equivalence Condition. Whereas a black raven Goodman-confirms (a), it does *not* Goodman-confirm (b) even though (b) is equivalent to (a). For black ravens Hempel-confirm the contrary of (b), namely

(f) All nonblack things are ravens,

because they satisfy the antecedent and consequent of an equivalent of (f), namely,

(g) All things that are either black or nonblack are either black or ravens.

The above discussion shows that very plausible reasons can be adduced for rejecting the seemingly obvious Equivalence Condition. Nonetheless, the reasoning is not conclusive, for one can come up with accounts of selective confirmation which *sustain* the Equivalence Condition.

The rejection of the Equivalence Condition has important implications for our discussion of Nozick. For the case Goodman and Scheffler make against the Equivalence Condition could be extended against other epistemic principles. It obviously undermines principles which entail the Equivalence Condition, such as the principle that evidence for p is evidence for anything logically entailed by p. Again, abandoning this second principle would probably lead us to reject the Evidential Principle of Entailment, which holds that if I am justified in believing that p, and believe that q by deducing q from p, then I am justified in believing that q as well. And rejecting the Evidential Principle of Entailment is at least as counterintuitive as rejecting the Principle of Entailment.

The rejection of plausible epistemic principles is not without precedent, but has Nozick really given us good reason to reject the Principle of Entailment? There are powerful considerations to the contrary. David Shatz and Steven Luper-Foy point out that slightly altered versions of Nozick's analysis would *sustain* this principle, so that the altered versions are more plausible analyses than the original (though of course there could be further problems with both). Shatz's suggestion is that Nozick construe *inferring from known facts* as a method of belief formation. He suggests that if we arrive at a belief, say q, by deducing it from another p which we know to be true, then we can say that p is arrived at through a two-step process that combines coming-to-know that p with deducing q from p. Allowing such methods, Shatz points out, puts me in a position to know that my brain has *not* been transferred to the scientists' vat by deducing that fact from my knowledge that my brain is in my skull. For if my brain *were* in the scientists' vat rather than in my skull, then I would not know that it is in my skull, and hence would not believe that my brain is not in the scientists' vat using the method of inferring (or deducing) my belief from my knowledge that my brain is in my skull. In general, anytime I track p and believe that q by deducing q from p, then I track q via the method of inferring q from known p. This is because of the fact that when p entails q, the falsity of q entails that I do not know p; hence the falsity of q entails that I have not inferred q from known p.

Luper-Foy points out a few more alterations of Nozick's analysis that sustain the Principle of Entailment. One approach is simply to add a further condition to his tracking account, one strong enough to sustain the Entailment Principle. Alternatively, it suffices to replace Nozick's third condition with its contraposition:

If I believed that *p* via method M, then *p* would be true. We can leave the rest of Nozick's account as is. The resulting analysis, loosely a version of reliabilism, sustains the Principle of Entailment, for the account requires not just that *p* be true in all of the close worlds in which I believe that *p* via M, but also that the logical *consequences c* of *p* be true in all of those worlds. Hence if I deduce *c* from *p* after arriving at the belief that *p* through a method that meets the new account, I will have arrived at the belief that *c* through a method which meets the account as well.

In other respects, the new analysis has about the same results as Nozick's; essentially, it differs only when applied to skeptical scenarios such as the situation of my brain being in a vat. My belief that my brain is in my skull, not in the hands of scientists who are stimulating it to produce my present experiences, has no trouble meeting the new version of (3): in the close situations in which I take this belief to be the best explanation of my present experiences, my brain is not in a vat. (Of course, these observations presuppose that the world is roughly the way we think it is.)

At one point Nozick says that his conditions differ from reliabilist conditions in that the one requires that tracking occur in a different *direction* than the other. Luper-Foy's claim that the contrapositive of Nozick's third condition is more plausible than the original can be restated in terms of direction: Nozick has gotten the *direction* of the tracking relation backwards (266). (As I will explain later, Richard Foley makes the same charge about Nozick's account of *evidence*.) Nozick's own condition requires that our belief via a method track the truth or falsity of that in which we believe. The contraposition, on the other hand, requires that the truth or falsity of that in which we believe track our belief via our method.

If we retain the Principle of Entailment, we must reject Nozick's reply to the skeptic. In fact, if either of the transformed versions of Nozick's analysis is an accurate account of knowledge, it is rather difficult to understand how skeptical worries ever arose. For on the new account, knowing such things as that I have two hands and that my brain is in my skull rather than in a scientist's vat is straightforward. To explain the appeal of skepticism, we must look elsewhere. The papers of Lawrence BonJour, Alan Goldman, Shatz, Klein, and Luper-Foy offer alternative accounts of skepticism, ones which Nozick's discussion does not deal with.

Nozick's account of skepticism is in trouble if we cleave to the Principle of Entailment, and there are additional worries about Nozick's defense of his brand of partial skepticism. Shatz points out that contrary to the impression Nozick seeks to give, it is not so obvious that Nozick's claims about skepticism are the product of an independently motivated analysis of knowledge. Instead, Nozick's approach to knowledge is at least largely determined by independently accepted views concerning skepticism. Thus whereas Nozick would reject Shatz's and Luper-Foy's suggestions for altering his account of knowledge, ultimately the reason he would do so seems to be simply that he believes that we do *not* know that skeptical scenarios do not hold and is willing to tinker with his analysis in any way necessary to secure that result.

Should we conclude that Nozick ought not be read as defending his partial skepticism on the basis of his tracking account of knowledge, but rather as defending his tracking analysis on the basis of his partial skepticism? Even this reading is in trouble, Shatz says, since Nozick's account could not be defended on the grounds that it handles skepticism in an intuitively plausible manner. The claims Nozick makes concerning skepticism are as often as not very counterintuitive. It may seem plausible to say, with the skeptic, that I do not know I am not a deceived brain in a vat; but is it also plausible to add, as Shatz shows Nozick must, that I *do* know that I am not in a vat and that I am not being deceived by scientists? Again, is it plausible to say *both* that I do not know that I am not dreaming that a table is before me *and* that I know that I am not dreaming?

BonJour and Goldman press another criticism of Nozick's discussion of skepticism: at best, Nozick has shown that even though it is conceivable that we are in some skeptical scenario, it is still *possible* that we know facts about the world. He has not given us any reason to suppose that we actually possess knowledge, so for all we know, we do not. Goldman goes further: he claims that on Nozick's account we *cannot* know that we possess knowledge. To *know* we know that a claim such as 'I have a hand' is true, we must know that we meet Nozick's conditions as applied to that claim. But we could meet those conditions only if none of the especially global skeptical scenarios holds, ones in which I have no hands. However, that these scenarios do not hold is precisely the sort of thing I cannot know on Nozick's account, and "if we cannot know that the skeptic's worlds are not actual . . . , then we surely cannot know that they are distant from the actual world."[11]

Stephen Barker criticizes Nozick's discussion of skepticism on rather different grounds. As Barker reads him, Nozick understands knowledge in terms of the tracking metaphor which originally described the relationship between hunters and (tracks left by) their quarry. Applying this metaphor results in the suggestion that a knower's belief states concerning some matter are and would be adjusted in a relevant range of possible circumstances so as to conform to the truth about that matter. Nozick's third and fourth conditions are designed to capture this idea of tracking. However, they do not always succeed, Barker charges, and when they do not we should resort to the metaphor of tracking for help. In particular, Nozick's conditions do not capture what would be involved in my tracking the fact that I am not a brain in a vat. Once we are clear about what would be involved, Barker suggests, we will see that it is not impossible for some shrewd individuals to track, and know, that they are not brains in vats.

Peter Klein provides yet another critique of Nozick's approach to skepticism. According to him, Nozick has mislocated the flaw in the skeptical argument which Nozick discusses. Klein says that Nozick is wrong to reject the Entailment Principle. The real problem with the skeptical argument Nozick attacks is that it begs the question. Given the Entailment Principle, skeptics are in no position to use the claim that we do not know that we are not in skeptical scenarios to show that we do not know that things are true which are incompatible with being in such scenarios. If we know at least one thing that *is* incompatible, just one *anti*skeptical scenario, then, as G. E. Moore pointed out, the tables could be turned on the skeptic: since we know that the antiskeptical scenario holds then given the Entailment Principle, we can know that skeptical scenarios do not hold. Hence skeptics can show that we are ignorant of the fact that we are not in skeptical scenarios only *after* demonstrating our ignorance of being in antiskeptical scenarios.

Let me now put aside criticisms of Nozick's explanation of skepticism and discuss some doubts about the accuracy of Nozick's analysis of knowledge, justified belief, and evidence. One worry, expressed by BonJour, Fumerton, and Luper-Foy, is that on Nozick's view we can know the truth of claims we infer from others even though it is irrational for us to believe those claims. It would be irrational for me to decide that the lights in the other room are on, on the basis of the fact that the coin I just tossed landed heads-up, or that they are off because it landed heads-down. But if, unknown to me, someone is looking on and seeing to it that the lights are on whenever my coin toss is heads and off when my toss is tails, then I track the fact that the lights are on. This example also shows that on Nozick's account completely unreliable mechanisms of belief formation are capable of yielding knowledge in certain circumstances.

In various papers BonJour has offered criticisms of externalist accounts of knowledge; in his present essay, he extends these criticisms to Nozick's account.[12] BonJour terms 'externalist' any analysis that "holds that the conditions required for knowledge in addition to true belief concern facts about the relation between belief and world which need not (and normally will not) be within the cognitive grasp of the believer. . . ."[13] On an externalist view, BonJour points out, it is possible to know the truth of a claim that we have no reason to believe. The fact that we have no grounds for a claim makes believing it irrational, according to BonJour. Since Nozick's view is externalist, this complaint arises for him. Thus Leroy the telepath can know the mental state of his mother using his accurate telepathic powers even if he has no reason whatever for thinking that he has telepathic powers and even if he has very good reason to doubt that he has such powers. All we need suppose is that he is an extremely reliable telepath in the case of his mother; we need not suppose that his powers work in the case of anyone else. Goldman, incidentally, would flatly deny BonJour's view concerning Leroy. Speaking of a medium who suddenly acquired the ability infallibly to foretell the future, Goldman claims that she "would have to be said to know the future . . . from the time that her predictions began to be right."[14]

Another problem faced by Nozick's account of knowledge is that it too easily allows us to know necessary truths. As he himself points out, it is difficult to say whether we meet his third condition when our belief is that some necessary truth holds. When (3) is applied to a necessary truth, its antecedent involves the denial of a necessary truth and so is impossible to meet; at best we can say that (3) is met *vacuously* when applied to necessary truths. Thus the burden of deciding whether or not we know such truths falls entirely on Nozick's fourth condition, so that after arriving at the belief (for example) that $2 + 2 = 4$ through some method, I know that my belief is true just in case I believe that $2 + 2 = 4$ in all of the close worlds to the actual world in which I apply my method so as to reach a verdict about whether or not $2 + 2 = 4$.

However, *any* one-sided method will then count as a method through which I can know that $2 + 2 = 4$ (and any other necessary truth). Fumerton dramatizes this point by asking us to consider the consequences of indiscriminately believing true (and never false) any mathematical proposition we entertain. This one-sided method will yield knowledge of any mathematical truth on Nozick's analysis. Similarly, indiscriminately believing *any* proposition we entertain enables us to know any necessary truth which crosses our mind.

Conditions (3) and (4) are too weak to handle knowledge of necessary truths, we just saw. Nozick's account can be criticized for excessive strength as well. Jonathan Vogel claims that Nozick's third condition makes knowledge through the use of inductive inference far too difficult; many examples of inductive knowledge do not meet this condition. For example, it seems plausible to say that I may know, through an inductive inference, that the ice cubes in a glass which, hours ago, I left standing in the sun on a sweltering day have melted even though I have not gone back and looked. But Vogel argues that Nozick's third condition is not met. Even if the cubes had not melted, I might well still have my present evidence, and it might still have led me to believe they had melted.

Nozick does not limit himself to a discussion of knowledge. He also investigates the nature of evidence and justified belief. In the course of discussing the latter, Nozick adopts the view that justified belief is belief through the most reliable appropriate method that is available to the person at hand (265). Thus justified, true belief need not be knowledge; indeed, my belief may be justified even if the method through which it is acquired or sustained has a degree of reliability less than one-half, so long as that method is more reliable than others that are available to me.

How plausible is this reliabilist conception of justified belief? Luper-Foy has argued that it is too strong: I can justifiably believe that on my wall is hanging a painting I produced a few years ago after looking over and seeing it there — no further verification is necessary.[15] Yet a more reliable method is *available* to me: I could perform a range of tests of authenticity to determine whether it is a forgery, for example. It might also be pointed out that Nozick's account is too weak. It appears to entail a very implausible sort of *anti*skepticism (a sort which is in tension with Nozick's other claims about skepticism): supposing that I have done my best to determine that some claim (for example, that I am not a brain in a vat) is true, then I am justified in thinking that it is true, even if my best is extremely unimpressive. My best cannot fail to be adequate.

George Pappas criticizes Nozick's account of justified belief on other grounds. He points out that a certain sort of memory phenomenon which Ulrich Neisser calls "flashbulb memory" cannot be dealt with in terms of a reliabilist account of justified belief. Since Nozick adopts a version of the reliabilist theory of rational belief, flashbulb memory is a problem for him, too. Flashbulb memory occurs when a fact, such as the fact that Jones is a pianist, is suddenly recalled after being forgotten for a time. During periods in which such facts are forgotten by us, we do not know that they hold, according to Pappas. But we do know (and justifiably believe) that such facts hold the instant they are recalled.

The problem discussed by Pappas and elsewhere by Richard Feldman[16] is that reliabilists face grave difficulties in describing the process involved in flashbulb memory. They are committed to saying that the flashbulb memory process is reliable if (as they must) they grant that this process secures us knowledge and justified belief. But how should the process be described? If we describe it broadly, say as memory itself, then it is too hard to attain justified belief through flashbulb memory. For even if my memory is in general unreliable I can still secure justified belief (and knowledge) through flashbulb memory, according to Pappas. On the other hand, if we describe the process too narrowly, say as the unique event of suddenly recalling such and such, then it will be too *easy* to secure justified belief. To describe the process as a unique event is to make it trivially reliable, reliable in a sense in which a lucky guess is reliable; but such guesses certainly are not justified beliefs.

In his discussion of the nature of evidence, Nozick makes interesting claims about our evidence that typical skeptical situations do not hold. One striking claim is that just as we cannot know that we are not in skeptical scenarios so, according to Nozick, we cannot have strong *evidence* that we are not in such situations. On Nozick's view, e is *strong* evidence for h just in case the following subjunctive conditionals are satisfied:

(a) If h were true, then e would be true.

(b) If h were false, then e would be false.

And e is *weak* evidence for h just in case:

(a) If h were true, then e would be true.

(c) If h were false, then e *might* be false (that is, it is false that: were h false, e would be true).

On this account, no (intrinsic) facts about my sensory information constitute strong or even weak evidence that I am not a brain in a vat. For if I were, I would have precisely the same sensory information as I have now; the facts about my information would still hold.

Of course, it does not follow that I *cannot* have evidence against my being a brain in a vat. Just as one can give knowledge-yielding methods of belief formation an internalist or an externalist interpetation, so, as Fumerton points out, one can give evidence an internalist or an externalist reading. If, for example, the fact that I now have a veridical perception of a table can count as evidence, then it will be strong evidence indeed that I am not a brain in a vat being deceived about the table.

But suppose that we interpret evidence internalistically, so that I have no evidence that my brain is in my skull and not in the skeptic's vat. Nonetheless, even on an internalist approach to evidence, I *can* have strong (and weak) evidence that my brain is in my skull. For in the close worlds in which my brain is *not* in my skull, I would not have any sensory information at all, and so any facts about my current sensory information are strong and weak evidence that my brain is in my skull.

Thus Nozick's view of evidence is inconsistent with a principle that is analogous to the Principle of Entailment, namely, the Evidential Principle of Entailment:

If e is (strong) evidence for h, and h entails p, then e is (strong) evidence for p.

While my sensory information provides strong evidence for the fact that my brain is in my skull, and while my brain's being in my skull entails that my brain has not been transferred from my skull to a vat on a distant planet, nonetheless sensory information (internalistically construed) does not provide strong evidence that my brain is not in a vat.

Earlier it was pointed out that reversing the direction of the tracking relation specified by Nozick's account of knowledge would result in a more plausible analysis, one that sustains the Principle of Entailment. After offering several criticisms of Nozick's account of evidence, Richard Foley suggests that the same move be made for evidence. Nozick's own approach requires that evidence track the truth and falsity of that for which it is evidence. But it is more plausible, claims Foley, to say that evidence must be tracked *by* the truth or falsity of that for which it is evidence. Thus e is strong evidence for h just in case:

If e were true, then h would be true.

This account of strong evidence sustains the Evidential Principle of Entailment. For if h is true in all of the close worlds in which e is true, then so are all of the logical consequences of h.

Like Foley, Paxson also offers a range of criticisms of Nozick's account of evidence. As an alternative to Nozick's account, Paxson suggests that e is evidence for h just in case

$\text{prob}(e, h) > \text{prob}(e, \text{not-}h)$.

Thus Paxson sides with Nozick vis-à-vis the direction of tracking, analyzing evidence in terms of the probabilities of e given h and e given not-h, and not in terms of the probabilities of h given e and h given not-e.

As by now will be apparent, the essays in this volume offer a wide variety of criticisms of Nozick's epistemology. I have grouped the essays under two headings: those that deal primarily with some aspect of Nozick's accounts of knowledge, justification, or evidence, and those that deal mainly with Nozick's approach to skepticism. Many discuss both aspects of his work, so to some extent the classification is artificial. At the end of the book the reader will find a list of additional works which deal with Nozick's essay and some of his themes.

NOTES

1. Cambridge: Harvard University Press, 1981, chap. 3.
2. Parenthetical references are to *Philosophical Explanations,* ibid.
3. I developed this criticism in "The Epistemic Predicament: Knowledge, Nozickian Tracking, and Skepticism," *Australasian Journal of Philosophy* 62 (1984): 26–49.
4. I did so in "The Epistemic Predicament," op. cit.
5. See "The Epistemic Predicament," op. cit.
6. Shatz believes that the quip can be traced to David Kaplan, but possibly beyond.
7. In "Epistemic Operators," *Journal of Philosophy* 67 (1970): 1007–23.
8. I owe this point to Barry Stroud; see *The Significance of Philosophical Skepticism* (Oxford: Clarendon Press, 1984), 44–45.

Austin claims that "if you have asked 'How do you know it's a goldfinch?' then I may . . . set out . . . those features of the situation which enable me to recognize it . . . ." "If you say 'That's not enough,' then you must have in mind some more or less definite lack." However, ". . . . enough is enough. . . . It does *not* mean, for example, enough to show it isn't a *stuffed* goldfinch." See Austin's essay "Other Minds," *Philosopical Papers,* 2d ed. (Oxford: Oxford University Press, 1961), 83–84.

9. Carl Hempel's discussion appears in chapter 1 of his *Aspects of Scientific Explanation and Other Essays in the Philosophy of Science* (New York: The Free Press, 1965); Goodman's discussion is in his *Fact, Fiction and Forecast* (Cambridge: Harvard University Press, 1955), especially 71–72.
10. Scheffler develops Goodman's discussion in *The Anatomy of Inquiry* (Indianapolis: Bobbs-Merrill, 1963), especially section 6 of part III.
11. Goldman, 182.
12. E.g., see BonJour's essay "Externalist Theories of Empirical Knowledge," *Midwest Studies in Philosophy* 5 (1980): 53–73; as well as his book *The Structure of Empirical Knowledge* (Cambridge: Harvard University Press, 1985).
13. BonJour, 297.
14. Goldman, 182.
15. See "The Reliabilist Theory of Rational Belief," *The Monist* 68 (1985): 214.
16. Richard Feldman, "Reliability and Justification," *The Monist* 68 (1985).

part one

KNOWLEDGE AND SKEPTICISM

KNOWLEDGE AND SKEPTICISM

Robert Nozick

I. KNOWLEDGE

Conditions for Knowledge

Our task is to formulate further conditions to go alongside

(1) p is true

(2) S believes that p.

We would like each condition to be necessary for knowledge, so any case that fails to satisfy it will not be an instance of knowledge. Furthermore, we would like the conditions to be jointly sufficient for knowledge, so any case that satisfies all of them will be an instance of knowledge. We first shall formulate conditions that seem to handle ordinary cases correctly, classifying as knowledge cases which are knowledge, and as nonknowledge cases which are not; then we shall check to see how these conditions handle some difficult cases discussed in the literature.[6]

The causal condition on knowledge, previously mentioned, provides an inhospitable environment for mathematical and ethical knowledge; also there are well-known difficulties in specifying the type of causal connection. If someone floating in a tank oblivious to everything around him is given (by direct electrical and chemical stimulation of the brain) the belief that he is floating in a tank with his brain being

The portions of *Philosophical Explanations* contained herein are reprinted by permission of the publisher and the author (Cambridge: The Belknap Press of Harvard University Press, © 1981 by Robert Nozick), pp. 182–209, 211–68, 280–83, and accompanying notes. All references to Philosophical Explanations in this volume refer to page numbers in the Harvard University Press edition.

stimulated, then even though that fact is part of the cause of his belief, still he does not know that it is true.

Let us consider a different third condition:

(3) If p weren't true, S wouldn't believe that p.

Throughout this work, let us write the subjunctive 'if-then' by an arrow, and the negation of a sentence by prefacing "not-" to it. The above condition thus is rewritten as:

(3) not-p → not-(S believes that p).

This subjunctive condition is not unrelated to the causal condition. Often when the fact that p (partially) causes someone to believe that p, the fact also will be causally necessary for his having the belief — without the cause, the effect would not occur. In that case, the subjunctive condition 3 also will be satisfied. Yet this condition is not equivalent to the causal condition. For the causal condition will be satisfied in cases of causal overdetermination, where either two sufficient causes of the effect actually operate, or a back-up cause (of the same effect) would operate if the first one didn't; whereas the subjunctive condition need not hold for these cases.[7] When the two conditions do agree, causality indicates knowledge because it acts in a manner that makes the subjunctive 3 true.

The subjunctive condition 3 serves to exclude cases of the sort first described by Edward Gettier,[*] such as the following. Two other people are in my office and I am justified on the basis of much evidence in believing the first owns a Ford car; though he (now) does not, the second person (a stranger to me) owns one. I believe truly and justifiably that someone (or other) in my office owns a Ford car, but I do not know someone does. Concluded Gettier, knowledge is not simply justified true belief.

The following subjunctive, which specifies condition 3 for this Gettier case, is not satisfied: if no one in my office owned a Ford car, I wouldn't believe that someone did. The situation that would obtain if no one in my office owned a Ford is one where the stranger does not (or where he is not in the office); and in that situation I still would believe, as before, that someone in my office does own a Ford, namely, the first person. So the subjunctive condition 3 excludes this Gettier case as a case of knowledge.

The subjunctive condition is powerful and intuitive, not so easy to satisfy, yet not so powerful as to rule out everything as an instance of knowledge. A subjunctive conditional "if p were true, q would be true," p → q, does not say that p entails q or that it is logically impossible that p yet not-q. It says that in the situation that would obtain if p

---

[*]"Is Justified True Belief Knowledge?" *Analysis* 1963, 121–23.

were true, q also would be true. This point is brought out especially clearly in recent 'possible-worlds' accounts of subjunctives: the subjunctive is true when (roughly) in all those worlds in which p holds true that are closest to the actual world, q also is true. (Examine those worlds in which p holds true closest to the actual world, and see if q holds true in all these.) Whether or not q is true in p worlds that are still farther away from the actual world is irrelevant to the truth of the subjunctive. I do not mean to endorse any particular possible-worlds account of subjunctives, nor am I committed to this type of account.[8] I sometimes shall use it, though, when it illustrates points in an especially clear way.*

The subjunctive condition 3 also handles nicely cases that cause difficulties for the view that you know that p when you can rule out the relevant alternatives to p in the context. For, as Gail Stine writes, "what makes an alternative relevant in one context and not another? . . . if on the basis of visual appearances obtained under optimum conditions while driving through the countryside Henry identifies an object as a barn, normally we say that Henry knows that it is a barn. Let us suppose, however, that unknown to Henry, the region is full of expertly made papier-mâché facsimiles of barns. In that case, we would not say that Henry knows that the object is a barn, unless he has evidence against it being a papier-mâché facsimile, which is now a relevant alternative. So much is clear, but what if no such facsimiles exist in Henry's surroundings, although they once did? Are either of these

---

*If the possible-worlds formalism is used to represent counterfactuals and subjunctives, the relevant worlds are not those p worlds that are closest or most similar to the actual world, unless the measure of closeness or similarity is: what would obtain if p were true. Clearly, this cannot be used to explain when subjunctives hold true, but it can be used to represent them. Compare utility theory which represents preferences but does not explain them. Still, it is not a trivial fact that preferences are so structured that they can be represented by a real-valued function, unique up to a positive linear transformation, even though the representation (by itself) does not explain these preferences. Similarly, it would be of interest to know what properties hold of distance metrics which serve to represent subjunctives, and to know how subjunctives must be structured and interrelate so that they can be given a possible worlds representation. (With the same one space serving for all subjunctives?)

One further word on this point. Imagine a library where a cataloguer assigns call numbers based on facts of sort F. Someone, perhaps the cataloguer, then places each book on the shelf by looking at its call number, and inserting it between the two books whose call numbers are most nearly adjacent to its own. The call number is derivative from facts of type F, yet it plays some explanatory role, not merely a representational one. "Why is this book located precisely there? Because of its number." Imagine next another library where the person who places books on the shelves directly considers facts of type F, using them to order the books and to interweave new ones. Someone else might notice that this ordering can be represented by an assignment of numbers, numbers from which other information can be derived as well, for example, the first letter of the last name of the principal author. But such an assigned number is no explanation of why a book in this library is located between two others (or why its author's last name begins with a certain letter). I have assumed that utility numbers stand to preferences, and closeness or similarity measures stand to subjunctives, as the call numbers do to the books, and to the facts of type F they exhibit, in the second library.

circumstances sufficient to make the hypothesis (that it's a papier-mâché object) relevant? Probably not, but the situation is not so clear."[9] Let p be the statement that the object in the field is a (real) barn, and q the one that the object in the field is a papier-mâché barn. When papier-mâché barns are scattered through the area, if p were false, q would be true or might be. Since in this case (we are supposing) the person still would believe p, the subjunctive

(3) not-$p \rightarrow$ not-(S believes that p)

is not satisfied, and so he doesn't know that p. However, when papier-mâché barns are or were scattered around another country, even if p were false q wouldn't be true, and so (for all we have been told) the person may well know that p. A hypothesis q contrary to p clearly is relevant when if p weren't true, q would be true; when not-$p \rightarrow q$. It clearly is irrelevant when if p weren't true, q also would not be true; when not-$p \rightarrow$ not-q. The remaining possibility is that neither of these opposed subjunctives holds; q might (or might not) be true if p weren't true. In this case, q also will be relevant, according to an account of knowledge incorporating condition 3 and treating subjunctives along the lines sketched above. Thus, condition 3 handles cases that befuddle the "relevant alternatives" account; though that account can adopt the above subjunctive criterion for when an alternative is relevant, it then becomes merely an alternate and longer way of stating condition 3.[10]

Despite the power and intuitive force of the condition that if p weren't true the person would not believe it, this condition does not (in conjunction with the first two conditions) rule out every problem case. There remains, for example, the case of the person in the tank who is brought to believe, by direct electrical and chemical stimulation of his brain, that he is in the tank and is being brought to believe things in this way; he does not know this is true. However, the subjunctive condition is satisfied: if he weren't floating in the tank, he wouldn't believe he was.

The person in the tank does not know he is there, because his belief is not sensitive to the truth. Although it is caused by the fact that is its content, it is not sensitive to that fact. The operators of the tank could have produced any belief, including the false belief that he wasn't in the tank; if they had, he would have believed that. Perfect sensitivity would involve beliefs and facts varying together. We already have one portion of that variation, subjunctively at least: if p were false he wouldn't believe it. This sensitivity as specified by a subjunctive does not have the belief vary with the truth or falsity of p in all possible situations, merely in the ones that would or might obtain if p were false.

The subjunctive condition

(3) not-$p \rightarrow$ not-(S believes that p)

tells us only half the story about how his belief is sensitive to the truth-value of p. It tells us how his belief state is sensitive to p's falsity, but not how it is sensitive to p's truth; it tells us what his belief state would be if p were false, but not what it would be if p were true.

To be sure, conditions 1 and 2 tell us that p is true and he does believe it, but it does not follow that his believing p is sensitive to p's being true. This additional sensitivity is given to us by a further subjunctive: if p were true, he would believe it.

(4) $p \rightarrow$ S believes that p.

Not only is p true and S believes it, but if it were true he would believe it. Compare: not only was the photon emitted and did it go to the left, but (it was then true that): if it were emitted it would go to the left. The truth of antecedent and consequent is not alone sufficient for the truth of a subjunctive; 4 says more than 1 and 2.[11] Thus, we presuppose some (or another) suitable account of subjunctives. According to the suggestion tentatively made above, 4 holds true if not only does he actually truly believe p, but in the "close" worlds where p is true, he also believes it. He believes that p for some distance out in the p neighborhood of the actual world; similarly, condition 3 speaks not of the whole not-p neighborhood of the actual world, but only of the first portion of it. (If, as is likely, these explanations do not help, please use your own intuitive understanding of the subjunctives 3 and 4.) /

The person in the tank does not satisfy the subjunctive condition 4. Imagine as actual a world in which he is in the tank and is stimulated to believe he is, and consider what subjunctives are true in that world. It is not true of him there that if he were in the tank he would believe it; for in the close world (or situation) to his own where he is in the tank but they don't give him the belief that he is (much less instill the belief that he isn't) he doesn't believe he is in the tank. Of the person actually in the tank and believing it, it is not true to make the further statement that if he were in the tank he would believe it — so he does not know he is in the tank.[12]

The subjunctive condition 4 also handles a case presented by Gilbert Harman.[13] The dictator of a country is killed; in their first edition, newspapers print the story, but later all the country's newspapers and other media deny the story, falsely. Everyone who encounters the denial believes it (or does not know what to believe and so suspends judgment). Only one person in the country fails to hear any denial and he continues to believe the truth. He satisfies conditions 1 through 3 (and the causal condition about belief) yet we are reluctant to say he knows the truth. The reason is that if he had heard the denials, he too would have believed them, just like everyone else. His belief is not sensitively tuned to the truth, he doesn't satisfy the condition that if it were true he would believe it. Condition 4 is not satisfied.[14]

There is a pleasing symmetry about how this account of knowledge relates conditions 3 and 4, and connects them to the first two conditions. The account has the following form.

(1)

(2)

(3) not-1 → not-2

(4) 1→ 2

I am not inclined, however, to make too much of this symmetry, for I found also that with other conditions experimented with as a possible fourth condition there was some way to construe the resulting third and fourth conditions as symmetrical answers to some symmetrical looking questions, so that they appeared to arise in parallel fashion from similar questions about the components of true belief.

Symmetry, it seems, is a feature of a mode of presentation, not of the contents presented. A uniform transformation of symmetrical statements can leave the results nonsymmetrical. But if symmetry attaches to mode of presentation, how can it possibly be a deep feature of, for instance, laws of nature that they exhibit symmetry? (One of my favorite examples of symmetry is due to Groucho Marx. On his radio program he spoofed a commercial, and ended, "And if you are not completely satisfied, return the unused portion of our product and we will return the unused portion of your money.") Still, to present our subject symmetrically makes the connection of knowledge to true belief especially perspicuous. It seems to me that a symmetrical formulation is a sign of our understanding, rather than a mark of truth. If we cannot understand an asymmetry as arising from an underlying symmetry through the operation of a particular factor, we will not understand why that asymmetry exists in that direction. (But do we also need to understand why the underlying asymmetrical factor holds instead of its opposite?)

A person knows that p when he not only does truly believe it, but also would truly believe it and wouldn't falsely believe it. He not only actually has a true belief, he subjunctively has one. It is true that p and he believes it; if it weren't true he wouldn't believe it, and if it were true he would believe it. To know that p is to be someone who would believe it if it were true, and who wouldn't believe it if it were false.

It will be useful to have a term for this situation when a person's belief is thus subjunctively connected to the fact. Let us say of a person who believes that p, which is true, that when 3 and 4 hold, his belief *tracks* the truth that p. To know is to have a belief that tracks the truth.

Knowledge is a particular way of being connected to the world, having a specific real factual connection to the world: tracking it.

One refinement is needed in condition 4. It may be possible for someone to have contradictory beliefs, to believe p and also believe not-p. We do not mean such a person to easily satisfy 4, and in any case we want his belief-state, sensitive to the truth of p, to focus upon p. So let us rewrite our fourth condition as:

(4) $p \rightarrow$ S believes that p and not-(S believes that not-p).[15]

As you might have expected, this account of knowledge as tracking requires some refinements and epicycles. Readers who find themselves (or me) bogged down in these refinements should move on directly to this essay's second part, on skepticism, where the pace picks up.

Ways and Methods

The fourth condition says that if p were true the person would believe it. Suppose the person only happened to see a certain event or simply chanced on a book describing it. He knows it occurred. Yet if he did not happen to glance that way or encounter the book, he would not believe it, even though it occurred. As written, the fourth condition would exclude this case as one where he actually knows the event occurred. It also would exclude the following case. Suppose some person who truly believes that p would or might arrive at a belief about it in some other close situation where it holds true, in a way or by a method different from the one he (actually) used in arriving at his belief that p, and so thereby come to believe that not-p. In that (close) situation, he would believe not-p even though p still holds true. Yet, all this does not show he actually doesn't know that p, for actually he has not used this alternative method in arriving at his belief. Surely he can know that p, even though condition 4, as written, is not satisfied.

Similarly, suppose he believes that p by one method or way of arriving at belief, yet if p were false he wouldn't use this method but would use another one instead, whose application would lead him mistakenly to believe p (even though it is false). This person does not satisfy condition 3 as written; it is not true of him that if p were false he wouldn't believe it. Still, the fact that he would use another method of arriving at belief if p were false does not show he didn't know that p when he used this method. A grandmother sees her grandson is well when he comes to visit; but if he were sick or dead, others would tell her he was well to spare her upset. Yet this does not mean she doesn't know he is well (or at least ambulatory) when she sees him. Clearly, we must restate our conditions to take explicit account of the ways and methods of arriving at belief.

Let us define a technical locution, S knows, via method (or way of believing) M, that p:

(1) p is true.

(2) S believes, via method or way of coming to believe M, that p.

(3) If p weren't true and S were to use M to arrive at a belief whether (or not) p, then S wouldn't believe, via M, that p.

(4) If p were true and S were to use M to arrive at a belief whether (or not) p, then S would believe, via M, that p.

We need to relate this technical locution to our ordinary notion of knowledge. If only one method M is actually or subjunctively relevant to S's belief that p, then, simply, S knows that p (according to our ordinary notion) if and only if that method M is such that S knows that p via M.

Some situations involve multiple methods, however.

First Situation: S's belief that p is overdetermined; it was introduced (or reinforced) by two methods, each of which in isolation would have been sufficient to produce in S the belief that p. S's belief that p via one of these methods satisfies conditions 1–4. However, S's belief that p via the second method does not satisfy conditions 1–4, and in particular violates condition 3.

A case of this sort is discussed by Armstrong.[16] A father believes his son innocent of committing a particular crime, both because of faith in his son and (now) because he has seen presented in the courtroom a conclusive demonstration of his son's innocence. His belief via the method of courtroom demonstration satisfies 1–4, let us suppose, but his faith-based belief does not. If his son were guilty, he would still believe him innocent, on the basis of faith in his son. Thus, his belief that p (that his son is innocent) via faith in his son violates condition 3. Looking at his belief alone, without mention of method, his belief that p violates the third condition (namely, if p were false S wouldn't believe that p), which made no mention of method.

Second Situation: S's belief that p via one method satisfies conditions 1–4. However, if p were false, S would not use that method in arriving at a belief about the truth value of p. Instead, he would use another method, thereby deciding, despite p's falsity, that p was true. S's actual belief that p is in no way based on the use of this second method, but if p were false he would believe p via the second method. (However, if p were false and S were to decide about its truth value by using the first method, then S would not believe that *p*. To be sure, if *p* were false S wouldn't decide about it by using that first method.) The truth value of *p* affects which method S uses to decide whether *p*.

Our earlier example of the grandmother is of this sort. Consider one further example, suggested to me by Avishai Margalit. S believes a certain building is a theater and concert hall. He has attended plays and concerts there (first method). However, if the building were not a theater, it would have housed a nuclear reactor that would so have altered the air around it (let us suppose) that everyone upon approaching the theater would have become lethargic and nauseous, and given up the attempt to buy a ticket. The government cover story would have been that the building was a theater, a cover story they knew would be safe since no unmedicated person could approach through the nausea field to discover any differently. Everyone, let us suppose, would have believed the cover story; they would have believed that the building they saw (but only from some distance) was a theater.

S believes the building is a theater because he has attended plays and concerts inside. He does not believe it is a theater via the second method of reading the government's cover story plus planted spurious theater and concert reviews. There are no such things. However, if it weren't a theater, it would be a nuclear reactor, there would be such cover stories, and S would believe still (this time falsely and via the second method) that the building was a theater. Nonetheless, S, who actually has attended performances there, knows that it is a theater.

To hold that a person knows that *p* if there exists at least one method M, satisfying conditions 1-4, via which he believes that *p*, would classify the father as knowing his son is innocent, a consequence too charitable to the father. Whereas it seems too stringent to require that all methods satisfy conditions 1-4, including those methods that were not actually used but would be under some other circumstances; the grandmother knows her grandson is well, and the person who has attended the concerts and plays knows the building is a theater. It is more reasonable to hold he knows that *p* if all the methods via which he actually believes that *p* satisfy conditions 1-4. Yet suppose our theatergoer also believes it is a theater partly because government officials, before they decided on which use they would put the building to, announced they were building a theater. Still, the theatergoer knows the building is a theater. Not all methods actually used need satisfy conditions 1-4, but we already have seen how the weak position that merely one such method is enough mishandles the case of the father.

We are helped to thread our way through these difficulties when we notice this father does not merely believe his son is innocent via the route of faith in his son; this defective route, not satisfying 1–4, also outweighs for him the method of courtroom demonstration. Even if courtroom demonstration (had it operated alone) would lead to the belief that his son is guilty, that not-p, still he would believe his son innocent, via faith in his son. Although it is the method of courtroom demonstration that gives him knowledge that p if anything does, for the father this method is outweighed by faith.[17] As a first try at delineating outweighing, we might say that method M is outweighed by others if when M would have the person believe p, the person believes not-p if the other methods would lead to the belief that not-p, or when M would have the person believe not-p, the person believes p if the other methods would lead to the belief that p.

This leads us to put forth the following position: S knows that p if there is some method via which S believes that p which satisfies conditions 1–4, and that method is not outweighed by any other method(s), via which S actually believes that p, that fail to satisfy conditions 3 and 4. According to this position, in some cases a person has knowledge even when he also actually believes via a method M_1 that does not satisfy 1–4, provided it is outweighed by one that does; namely, in the overdetermination case, and in the case when M_1 alone would suffice to fix belief but only in the absence of a verdict from the M he also uses which does satisfy 1–4.

S knows that p if and only if there is a method M such that (a) he knows that p via M, his belief via M that p satisfies conditions 1–4, and (b) all other methods M_1 via which he believes that p that do not satisfy conditions 1–4 are outweighed by M.[18]

We have stated our outweighing requirement only roughly; now we must turn to refinements. According to our rough statement, in the overdetermination case, method M_1, which satisfies 3 and 4 and which is what gives knowledge if anything does, wins out over the other method M_2 in all cases. The actual situation (Case I) is where M_1 recommends believing p as does M_2, and the person believes p. In this case we have made our answer to the question whether he knows that p depend on what happens or would happen in the two other cases where the methods recommend different beliefs. (See Table.) The first rough statement held that the person knows in Case I only if he would believe

	M_1 recommends	M_2 recommends	Does the person believe p or believe not-p?
Case I	believe p	believe p	believes p
Case II	believe p	believe not-p	?
Case III	believe not-p	believe p	?

p in Case II and not-*p* in Case III. While this is sufficient for knowledge in Case I, it seems too stringent to be necessary for such knowledge.

An alternative and more adequate view would hold constant what the other method recommends, and ask whether the belief varies with the recommendation of M_1. Since M_2 actually recommends *p* (Case I), we need look only at Case III and ask: when M_2 continues to recommend *p* and M_1 recommends not-*p*, would the person believe not-*p*? Despite his faith, would the father believe his son guilty if the courtroom procedure proved guilt? That is the relevant question — not what he would believe if the courtroom showed innocence while (somehow) his method of faith led to a conclusion of guilty.

Consider how this works out in another simple case. I see a friend today; he is now alive. However, if he were not alive, I wouldn't have seen him today or (let us suppose) heard of his death, and so still would believe he was alive. Yet condition 3 is satisfied; it includes reference to a method, and the method M_1 of seeing him satisfies 3 with respect to *p* equals he is alive at the time. But there also is another method M_2 via which I believe he is alive, namely having known he was alive yesterday and continuing to believe it. Case III asks what I would believe if I saw the friend dead (though I knew yesterday he was alive); our position holds I must believe him dead in this case if I am to know by seeing him that he is alive in Case I. However, we need not go so far as to consider what I would believe if I had "learned" yesterday that he was dead yet "saw" him alive today. Perhaps in that case I would wonder whether it really was he I was seeing. Even so, given the result in Case III, I know (in Case I) he is alive. Thus, we hold fixed the recommendation of the other method, and only ask whether then the belief varies with the recommendation of method M_1.[19]

Our test of looking at Case III cannot apply if M_1 is a one-sided method, incapable of recommending belief in not-*p*; it either recommends belief in *p* or yields no recommendation. (Perhaps M_1 detects one of a number of sufficient conditions for *p*; not detecting this, M_1 remains silent as to the truth of *p*.) What are we to say about his knowing if a person's belief is overdetermined or jointly determined by a one-sided method M_1 plus another method M_2 which fails to satisfy condition 3? Should we now look at Case II, where M_1 recommends belief in *p* and M_2 recommends belief in not-*p*, and say that believing *p* in this case is sufficient to show that M_1 outweighs M_2? That does not seem unreasonable, but we had better be careful to stipulate that this Case II situation is a sufficient condition for M_1's outweighing M_2 only when the Case III situation is impossible, for otherwise we face the possibility of divergent results. (For example, he believes *p* in Case II and in Case III, yet believes not-*p* when both methods recommend not-*p*; here the result in Case II indicates M_1 outweighs M_2 while the re-

sult in Case III indicates M_2 outweighs M_1.) It is Case III that should
predominate.

One final remark about method. Suppose a method is good for some
types of statements but not others; it satisfies 3 and 4 for the first type
but not for the second. However, S believes the method is good for all
types of statements and applies it indiscriminately. When he applies it
to a statement of the first type which he thereby comes to believe, does
he know that it is true? He does, if he satisfies conditions 3 and 4. Hesi-
tation to grant him knowledge stems, I think, from the fact that if p
were false and were of the second type, he might well still believe it.
Whether or not this undercuts condition 3 for knowledge depends
upon the disparity of the two types; the greater the gulf between the
types, the more willing we are to say he knows a statement of the type
where M works.

In explaining the nature of knowledge by reference to a method or
way of believing, we leave large questions open about how to individu-
ate methods, count them, identify which method is at work, and so on.
I do not want to underestimate these difficulties, but neither do I want
to pursue them here.[20] Still, some clarifying remarks are needed.

A person can use a method (in my sense) without proceeding me-
thodically, and without knowledge or awareness of what method he is
using. Usually, a method will have a final upshot in experience on
which the belief is based, such as visual experience, and then (a) no
method without this upshot is the same method, and (b) any method
experientially the same, the same "from the inside," will count as the
same method. Basing our beliefs on experiences, you and I and the person floating in the tank are using, for these purposes, the same
method.

Some methods are supervenient on others, for example, "believing
what seems to be true to you" or "believing what seems true given the
weighting of all other methods." The account of outweighing is not to
apply to such supervenient methods, otherwise there always will be
such a one that outweighs all the others. There are various gerryman-
dered (Goodmanesque) methods that would yield the same resulting
belief in the actual situation; which method a person actually is using
will depend on which general disposition to acquire beliefs (extending
to other situations) he actually is exercising.[21]

Although sometimes it will be necessary to be explicit about the
methods via which someone believes something, often it will cause no
confusion to leave out all mention of method. Furthermore, some
statements play a central role in our continuing activities, or in our picture of the world or framework wherein we check other statements, for
example, "I have two hands," "the world has existed for many years already;" it is misleading to think of our coming to believe them via some

delimited method or methods.[22] So nested are these statements in our other beliefs and activities, and so do they nest them, that our belief or acceptance of them is (for almost all purposes) best represented apart from any particular methods. In considering our knowledge of them we may revert to the earlier simpler subjunctives

(3) not-$p \rightarrow$ not-(S believes that p)

(4) $p \rightarrow$ S believes that p.

The very centrality of the specific p means that 4 will be satisfied without reference to a specific method or way of believing. In contrast, I know there is a pair of scissors on my desk (in front of me) now; but it is not accurate simply to say that if there were a pair of scissors there, I would believe there was. For what if I weren't looking, or hadn't looked, or were elsewhere now? Reference to the method via which I believe there are scissors on the desk is needed to exclude these possibilities. With the most central statements, however, there is no similar "what if"; their centrality ensures they will not escape notice.

Knowledge of Necessities

Otherwise plausible accounts of knowledge often stumble over mathematical or ethical truths. Though they can seek safety by restriction to "empirical" truths, it seems desirable to offer a unified account of knowledge of all types, even if the distinctions among truths bring differences in how the one account applies.

Assume, as does the literature, that statements of mathematics when true are necessarily true. Our third condition of tracking speaks of what the person would believe if p were false, but in the case of mathematical truths p, this is a necessarily false supposition, an impossible one. When p is necessarily true, the antecedent of condition 3 is necessarily false. Perhaps a theory of subjunctives can be constructed to cover such cases—none has yet been proposed that is remotely satisfactory—but we should try to avoid such a desperate expedient.

Since condition 3 does not come into play for necessary truths p, the account of tracking for these statements, when truly believed, reduces to

(4) If p were true and S were to use method M to arrive at a belief whether (or not) p, then S would believe, via M, that p.

When M is the method of coming to believe something on the basis of a mathematical proof then, since this method guarantees truth, it is p that will be believed and so 4 is satisfied.[23] However 4 is not satisfied by someone's method of dogmatically believing what his parents told him, in this case the necessary truth p, even though p will be true in all close situations or worlds. For if there are close worlds in which his parents told him not-p, the method leads to false belief in those worlds, so it is not actually true of him that he would believe the truth by that method. It is not enough for the dogmatist to firmly believe something; he must come to the belief in a way that not only does but would yield a true belief (when it yields any belief at all).

Although methods of mathematical proof may guarantee truth, through the formal relations they specify,[24] we are fallible creatures who can make mistakes in our application of such methods. Do we know mathematical truths via our application of these methods? (When correctly followed the recipe always leads to an exquisite dish, but success lies in the execution.) That depends not on whether a mistake is logically possible but whether we would or might make one under those conditions.

Many mathematical statements we believe on the basis not of proofs but of authority or hearsay: we have been told they are true. Here, the question is whether our source is tracking the truth and whether the particular channel via which we learn it preserves tracking. More generally, a channel of communication C will transmit knowledge that p if C counts as a method of knowing: if S's belief via C that p satisfies the four conditions (when applicable) for S's knowing via M that p, and if the channel outweighs any other methods actually operating which do not satisfy 3 and 4. Believing via a channel of communication is just a particular case of believing via a method or way of believing. Channels include reading books, being told something by another, and so on. It is the channel condition that describes how we can learn from others and acquire knowledge from them. Mathematical truths raise no special questions about learning from others.*

---

*There is another interesting question, though, about channels. It is natural to regard a channel as follows: someone else knows that p and does something (writes, speaks, or whatever) to transmit that knowledge to me. A theory of my acquiring knowledge becomes a theory of the conditions under which his knowledge, already there, flows to me. If he doesn't know that p, he has no knowledge that p, and so no knowledge to transmit; I cannot acquire knowledge that p *from him if he doesn't already know* p. (I am imagining that the content of p is not about his transmitting. If he says, "I am speaking boringly," or "I am speaking loudly enough for you to hear," but doesn't believe it, still, you may come to know it from his saying it.)

Consider a situation where the person believes that p, yet does not track that fact: if p were false, he still would believe that p. However, suppose that actually if p were false, he wouldn't convey his belief to me. (He is ill and says he took his special pill; but another one similar in appearance was next to it, and if he had taken that one, he still would believe he'd taken the special one. If he had not taken the special pill, though, he wouldn't have said anything to me at all, not because he is especially scrupulous about what he says but because the special pill has the effect of giving him enough energy to talk. So if he had not taken it, I wouldn't believe he had.)

Thus, we see two ways the falsity of p can stop his transmitting the statement that p to me: by getting him not to believe p, and by getting him (though believing p) not to transmit his belief. In this second case, do I come to know via his transmission? Not if the method via which I come to believe it involves inferring it from the statement that he knows it.

Cases and Complications

In the case of necessary truths, we have said, condition 4 is enough for tracking and for knowledge when there also is true belief, even though condition 3 does not apply. Now we face a puzzle. If 4 without 3 is enough in these cases, why not make 4 (along with 1 and 2) the whole account of tracking for other cases as well? Why is 3 needed even for those cases where it is able to apply, if 4 alone is sufficient where 3 cannot apply? Why not simply say that for any true statement *p* (and not merely necessary ones) a person knows that *p when: if p* were true he would believe it.

Recall that the root notion of knowledge we have uncovered is one where not only does a person truly believe that *p*, but he would truly believe that *p*, and he wouldn't falsely believe that *p*. When *p* is a necessary truth, this last part drops away—we needn't worry about his falsely believing that *p*, since *p* (necessarily) cannot be false. With contingent truths, however, it is not enough that the person would truly believe it. For when some not-*p* world could easily be (or have been) the case, if the person would believe *p* even then, he doesn't actually know that *p*; he would or might falsely believe that *p*. Thus, it is clear why we cannot merely require condition 4 in the case where *p* is contingently true: 4 alone does not show the person wouldn't or mightn't falsely believe that *p*.[25]

In the Gettier example where a person believes someone in his office owns a Ford, neither of the two conditions for tracking was satisfied, and so this did not count as knowledge according to our account. It was not true that if no one in the office owned a Ford, the person wouldn't believe that someone did. For if the friend had come in without the stranger, which might have happened, then the person still would believe that someone in the office owned a Ford. Suppose we modify the example somewhat, so that the friend would not come to the office unless the stranger did, and so wouldn't have been there alone. Still, the stranger might not have owned a Ford, and in that case the person still would believe that someone in the office did. Modify the case still further: suppose that (for whatever reason) the friend would not come into the office unless accompanied by someone with a Ford. Isn't 3 now satisfied? Still, 4 is not, for if the stranger were there alone, the person wouldn't believe that someone in the office owned a Ford. Modify the case still further: suppose also the stranger would not come to the office without the friend, neither would come without the other. It is not clear, even in these cases, that the subjunctives 3 and 4 hold true; that would depend upon the constituent subjunctives being transitive, which is not always so. Moreover, the examples thus far ignore the method via which the person comes to believe the statement.

Gettier-type examples often involve inferring a truth from a (justifiably believed) falsehood.[26] While condition 3 without mention of method excludes many of these cases, there may seem to be other cases of nonknowledge that do satisfy condition 3 because the person wouldn't have been led to have the false belief q from which he infers p, unless p were true.*

Gilbert Harman formulates a requirement that "the lemmas be true" to explicitly rule out such inferences from falsehood. Perhaps our account can yield this result, by treating "infers it from q" as the method the person uses to arrive at his belief that p. When q is false, the person using this method will not satisfy condition 3; for if p were false and the person arrived at his belief about the truth value of p by inference from q, he still would believe p. Therefore, he does not know p unless he also uses some other method M_1 satisfying 3 and 4 that outweighs this defective one.

In this case imagined, however, the person would not use the method if p were false. Nevertheless, we are holding the method fixed and asking what the person would believe, via this method, if p were false.[27] Many of the counterexample cases to simpler conditions involve situations where even though the method does not satisfy condition 3, if p were false the person would not be using that method and so would not be believing p. This may give rise to the illusion that 3 is satisfied; but according to our formulation, it is not.

Let us take a quick run through some examples presented in the literature, to illustrate and test our account.[28]

(a) As an effect of brain damage a person is led (irrationally) to believe he has brain damage, which he would not believe if he didn't have brain damage.[29] However, condition 4 is not satisfied: if the brain damage had been slightly different, though using the same route to belief he would not believe he had it.

(b) A magician in mid-routine moves a coin blatantly, but those who have been watching do not believe it, having been fooled so frequently during his performance. A person who wanders by just then, not knowing a magician is performing, sees him move the coin and believes he moved it.[30] He does not know the coin has been moved. For if it had not been moved he might well believe it had (if the magician had done a trick), so 3 is not satisfied; also, it might be that it was moved yet he

---

*Here is an example suggested to me by Eddy Zemach. A Persian child is brought to Nazi Germany in the 1930s as part of an Aryan ingathering, and grows up there thinking himself German, and learns the concept Aryan. He believes all Germans are Aryans, believes (falsely) that he is German, and so believes that he is Aryan. Condition 3 is satisfied because if he were not Aryan, he wouldn't have been gathered in by the Germans and so would not have come to believe he was Aryan. (To suppose condition 4 satisfied, we would have to suppose also that in varying circumstances he would be gathered in by the Germans.)

would not believe it (either because he had seen the act from the beginning or because the magician tricked him), so 4 is not satisfied either.

(c) A person comes to believe a vase is in a box by seeing an illuminated hologram, part of a machine that alternates between displaying the hologram and the real vase contained in the box.[31] The person does not know, even when seeing the vase (a case suggested by Shope), for if it weren't there, he would see the hologram and still believe it was. Modify the example so that the machine, in alternate time periods, displays a hologram of a vase only when a vase is pressing down on a lever (it somehow detects a vase and not another thing). Hence if there weren't a vase there, he wouldn't believe there was one; and if there were one there, he would come to believe, by looking, that there was. Thus, our account has the consequence that he knows a vase is there, even when he is seeing the hologram but thinks he is seeing the vase. This consequence is somewhat counterintuitive; however, we certainly do not want to hold that a person knows that *p* only if he has no false beliefs about the process via which he comes to believe that *p*. The Greeks had many false beliefs about the visual process.

(d) Talking to her on the telephone, a man believes his friend is wishing him a happy birthday. Unsuspected by the man, his psychiatrist was concerned that the friend would not call and so hired an actress who can perfectly imitate the friend's voice; this actress was attempting to get through on the telephone at the same time as the friend spoke, and would have performed if the friend had not called.[32] Supposing the actress could do the imitation undetected, in this case, the man does not know he is talking to his friend; if he weren't talking to her he still would believe he was.

Consider another case, of a student who, when his philosophy class is canceled, usually returns to this room and takes hallucinogenic drugs; one hallucination he has sometimes is of being in his philosophy class. When the student actually is in the philosophy class, does he know he is? I think not, for if he weren't in class he still might believe he was. (Is this made more plausible if we add that he knows he sometimes hallucinates his being in a philosophy class?) Two students in the class might be in the same actual situation, having (roughly) the same retinal and aural intake, yet the first knows he is in class while the other does not, because they are situated differently subjunctively — different subjunctives hold true of them. Suppose, in addition, that a hypnotist is going around and hypnotizing some students outside class into thinking they are in class. He has never encountered the first student, but does his prowling nearby change which subjunctives hold of this student, so that he no longer knows he is in class?

(e) Faced by one of two identical twins, Judy and Trudy, a person believes it is Judy before him, but only because he has bumped his head which (somehow) gave him the idea that Judy has a mole; coincidentally, Judy just developed a mole.[33] He doesn't know it is Judy who is before him. Condition 4 is not satisfied; if Judy were before him, but in the very close situation of not having developed the mole, he wouldn't believe it was she. (And does condition 3 also block it, since it might have occurred that Trudy had developed a mole and stood before him?)

(f) You see a man named Tom remove a book from the library, concealing it in his coat, and you believe truly that Tom took the book. Unbeknownst to you, Tom's mother is across the library room, telling someone else that Tom is out of town, and it is his identical twin John whom they are looking at in the library. Do you know that Tom took the book? Now add the fact that Tom's mother is a pathological liar, and he has no twin brother; next alter the fact that she was in the library, and place her across town saying that Tom is out of town, and his twin John is in the library. In each of those cases, do you know that Tom is taking the book?[34]

Condition 3 is satisfied; if it were not Tom then (since there is no twin), you wouldn't believe it was. But is condition 4 satisfied? Do the similar situations in which you must, by seeing him, believe it is Tom, include overhearing the mother (something you easily could have done)? Our answer here about the application of 4 may be unclear, as it should be if the epistemological status of the example also is unclear.

There are two types of philosophical accounts of a notion N. The first type classifies cases exactly as they are classified under the notion N, correctly classifying clear cases of N and clear cases of non-N, while leaving the unclear cases unclear. In terms of the conditions of the account, one can understand why the clear cases fall as they do, and why the unclear cases are unclear, either because different conditions of the account conflict, or because we can see why some of the account's conditions do not apply clearly. The second type of account sharpens up the notion; it classifies the clear cases correctly and moreover classifies the cases whose status was left unclear by the notion N itself, thereby making N more serviceable for some purposes. Accounts also can mix these features, reclassifying some previously unclear cases while leaving others to their old status. Our account of knowledge is of this last mixed sort, and the present example is, I think, an unclear case which it leaves so. For it is unclear how far afield the subjunctive condition 4 is to travel in such cases. Similar remarks probably should apply to the question whether there is knowledge in the case[35] where someone some distance away sees and hears a stationary sheep, but does not hear the farmer nearby playfully deceiving the city-person he is then speaking to, telling him that out in the field is a carefully contrived wooden replica covered with wool and containing an electronic bleater.

(g) You see a light on in a neighbor's house and conclude (on the basis of this plus other evidence) that it is lit by electricity supplied by the electric company; it is, but this homeowner has an alternate power generator that would switch on and supply electricity to the light even if there was some failure in drawing power from the electric company.[36]

Assume the case can be specified so that condition 3 is violated; if it weren't supplied by the company, you would still believe it was. So you do not know it is. The probability of a central power failure is very small; does this affect the matter? We shall consider issues about probability; such issues also enter into whether condition 4 is satisfied: if the electricity were supplied centrally (and he had told you of his own power generator) would you still believe it was centrally generated, or only that it probably was?

(h) The reference to method helps with the case where the person might not happen to use it, for example, he might not have glanced that way and so might not have seen the criminal escaping. Still, he knows when he sees. What of the cases where what is seen (rather than his looking) is a matter of happenstance,[37] for example, the bank robber's mask slips off as he is escaping and the bystander sees it is Jesse James, whose picture is on many wanted posters. (This example will not work with the Lone Ranger for, leaving aside the issue of whether he would rob a bank, we recognize him only when his mask is on.) The bystander knows that Jesse James is robbing the bank. Condition 3 is satisfied, but is condition 4, even with the method explicit? If Jesse James were to rob the bank would he know it via that method? His method is looking and concluding it is Jesse James on the basis of seeing certain things. By that method (applied in this way) he would know in other cases also. To be sure, some other situations might not allow that method to be used — these situations do not yield any belief (see the discussion above of knowledge via methods and of the importance of holding the method fixed) — but that causes no difficulty for condition 4, properly understood.

Since we have not specified a precise theory of subjunctives or specified precisely how to identify a method and tell when it is held fixed, there is some leeway in our account. It may be this leeway that enables the account to cope with these examples and other cases, by using the constituent notions loosely and intuitively. This is not an objection but a reason to think the notions can be specified more precisely to handle the cases — a condition on their specification is that they handle the cases adequately — provided the discussion of the cases did not exploit the leeway or wobble inconsistently, first leaning in one direction, then in another.

Until now we have considered only temporally local conditions for knowledge, ignoring any problems raised by wider contexts. Consider a situation where p contains the term "now" and the truth value of p keeps changing, as do the truths of the subjunctives 3 and 4. However, from the observer's own point of view, there is no apparent change. Some of these cases we would not hold to exhibit knowledge, but the intricate problems and considerations these raise are best set aside; perhaps some additional condition is needed — but whatever additional intricate contextual condition is appropriate can be plugged into our structure.

Another issue about the temporal width of application of the conditions can be discussed usefully now. Suppose at time t_1 S knows that p and also knows that at a later time t_2 others will attempt to brainwash him into believing not-p. So between times t_1 and t_2 S unalterably fixes in himself the belief (that p) he already has, perhaps through psychosurgery. At time t_2, does S know that p? We might say not, for if p were false at t_2 then S still would believe p; or we might hold that S does know that p then, for if p were false he would not have cemented that belief in. Should we view the method by which S at t_2 believes p as "cementing," which fails to satisfy condition 3, or as "cementing after knowing (that is, believing in the way he did)," which does satisfy 3?

There is reason for not insisting upon the narrowest time interval. Many of us may have become cemented into some of our beliefs; as we become older, it is said, we can less easily learn new tricks or unlearn old ones. According to the interpretation of the condition as locally focused, much of our knowledge therefore would be passing into mere belief.* Second, evolution, which doth make trackers of us all, would select for global tracking rather than especially favoring the local version. (Also, in this particular example, might cementing be the person's way of satisfying condition 4?)

Therefore, I lean toward calling such cases knowledge; yet since now if p were false S still would believe p, I am reluctant to say simply that he knows. Thus, the general issue of local versus global analysis that crosses so many philosophical problems, as seen in the first chapter, comes into play again. Perhaps it suffices here to note the sources of the contrasting pulls, which subjunctives hold and which ones do not, and to note that 3's holding as a local subjunctive is better than 3's

---

*We have focused on methods of arriving at beliefs, but not on methods (including inertia) of retaining them. If the method via which someone now has a belief is a combination of the acquiring and the retaining methods, clearly an adequate account of the conditions under which he knows now will have to incorporate details about subjunctives including these joint methods.

holding as a global subjunctive which in turn is better than 3's not holding in any version at all.

There are variations also in the ways 3 can hold globally. Consider another case: a parent, knowing that p and knowing that an attempt will be made to brainwash his child at time t_2 acts before time t_2 to cement in the child the belief that p. At time t_2, does the child know that p? Here again, we can note which subjunctives hold and which ones do not; without attempting to decide whether this is a case of knowledge, we can say that 3's holding globally in this way is better than its not holding at all, but worse than its holding due to an earlier choice to cement the belief made by the person himself. I am content here to rank order these global cases without forcing a classification as knowledge or not, especially since my interest lies in the examples of action corresponding to them which we shall encounter in the next chapter as we pursue the parallel of action to knowledge. Note, though, that the issues we mention here are the ones underlying the question of whether innate beliefs instilled by a process that tracks their truth constitute innate knowledge.[38]

A belief that p may be true in some situations because the person believes it, rather like a "self-fulfilling prophecy." For example, suppose my children (through a misunderstanding or however) believe I will get them a puppy and, discovering they believe this, I do so in order to avoid their being disappointed. If they didn't believe it, I would not get the puppy. It may be true that for all close-by situations where p is true, they believe it; for those p situations are precisely the ones where they already believe it and I get one (there is no other reason I would choose to do so) in order to make their belief come true. Yet, though it seems that conditions 3 and 4 are satisfied, the children do not know I will get them a puppy. (It would be a different situation where the children manipulate me into getting one, knowing I will make their expressed belief come true, and so expressing it and, indeed, therefore believing it.) We might reach the result that the children do not know they will get a puppy by holding that 3 is false. For there are very close situations where I don't learn of their belief, or decide not to get them the puppy; so they would believe they were going to get it even if they were not.

Consider another case, which David Armstrong discusses, of a sick person who believes he will recover and thereby does so.[39] Suppose that if it were true, he would believe it; for there is no way he could recover from this illness except via the effects of believing he will. Is it also the case that if it weren't true, he wouldn't believe it? Well, at least if it weren't to be true, he wouldn't have been believing it. (But wouldn't he also believe in his recovery, even if his condition differed slightly so as to be unimprovable via this belief?)

These seem to be cases not of a belief's tracking the truth, but of the truth's tracking a belief. Yet we do not simply want to require that believing it does not make it true; consider "I believe something now." Perhaps a sharper theory of subjunctives, a better understanding of how they function, will show clearly that 3 and 4 are not satisfied in these cases. Or perhaps the difficulty lies in the fact that if it weren't believed it wouldn't be true, where a better understanding of subjunctives might enable us to add a condition denying this, namely not-(not-believing $p \rightarrow$ not-p), without undercutting the truth of the subjunctives 3 and 4. Or perhaps it will turn out, on any theory of subjunctives, that this is cutting things too finely. In that case, one might add a further condition about why conditions 3 and 4 hold, requiring it not be the case that 3 or 4 hold solely because: not-believing $p \rightarrow$ not-p, or believing $p \rightarrow p$. These are matters I must leave open here. There is some attraction, in any case, to including within our account of knowledge some further condition on why subjunctives 3 and 4 hold true: this also may aid with previous and further problem cases.[40]

One last remark. Suppose that though the person's belief that p is tracking the fact that p, yet the person believes it is *not*. We might doubt in this case that he knows. While it would be too strong to require the belief that 3 and that 4 in order for the person to know — don't children know? — perhaps it is appropriate to require that he not believe the negations of 3 and 4.[41]

We are now ready to turn to the subject of skepticism. Even readers who find difficulties with the account of knowledge, with the precise way the subjunctive conditions are formulated, should read on.* The points made in applying the account to issues about skepticism might well still hold, invariant under whatever changes are needed to meet the difficulties.

II. SKEPTICISM

The skeptic about knowledge argues that we know very little or nothing of what we think we know, or at any rate that this position is no less reasonable than the belief in knowledge. The history of philosophy exhibits a number of different attempts to refute the skeptic: to prove him wrong or show that in arguing against knowledge he presupposes

---

*In the second part of the next chapter, we return to this chapter's opening question: whether actions can be connected to something in the same way belief is connected to the truth when there is knowledge. If the parallel between beliefs and actions is an illuminating one, we should expect illumination to be cast in both directions. Therefore, we should be especially alert to see whether any additional considerations brought forth as we apply (analogues of) the notion of tracking and conditions 1–4 to actions do not apply also in the area of knowledge. Especially gratifying would be to discover features of knowledge we would not notice at all without pursuing the parallel to action.

there is some and so refutes himself. Others attempt to show that accepting skepticism is unreasonable, since it is more likely that the skeptic's extreme conclusion is false than that all of his premises are true, or simply because reasonableness of belief just means proceeding in an anti-skeptical way. Even when these counterarguments satisfy their inventors, they fail to satisfy others, as is shown by the persistent attempts against skepticism.[42] The continuing felt need to refute skepticism, and the difficulty in doing so, attests to the power of the skeptic's position, the depth of his worries.

An account of knowledge should illuminate skeptical arguments and show wherein lies their force. If the account leads us to reject these arguments, this had better not happen too easily or too glibly. To think the skeptic overlooks something obvious, to attribute to him a simple mistake or confusion or fallacy, is to refuse to acknowledge the power of his position and the grip it can have upon us. We thereby cheat ourselves of the opportunity to reap his insights and to gain self-knowledge in understanding why his arguments lure us so. Moreover, in fact, we cannot lay the specter of skepticism to rest without first hearing what it shall unfold.

Our goal is not, however, to refute skepticism, to prove it is wrong or even to argue that it is wrong. In the Introduction we distinguished between philosophy that attempts to prove, and philosophy that attempts to explain how something is possible. Our task here is to explain how knowledge is possible, given what the skeptic says that we do accept (for example, that it is logically possible that we are dreaming or are floating in the tank). In doing this, we need not convince the skeptic, and we may introduce explanatory hypotheses that he would reject. What is important for our task of explanation and understanding is that *we* find those hypotheses acceptable or plausible, and that they show us how the existence of knowledge fits together with the logical possibilities the skeptic points to, so that these are reconciled within our own belief system. These hypotheses are to explain to ourselves how knowledge is possible, not to prove to someone else that knowledge *is* possible.*

Skeptical Possibilities

The skeptic often refers to possibilities in which a person would believe something even though it was false: really, the person is cleverly deceived by others, perhaps by an evil demon, or the person is

---

*From the perspective of explanation rather than proof, the extensive philosophical discussion, deriving from Charles S. Peirce, of whether the skeptic's doubts are real is beside the point. The problem of explaining how knowledge is possible would remain the same, even if no one ever claimed to doubt that there was knowledge.

dreaming or he is floating in a tank near Alpha Centauri with his brain being stimulated. In each case, the p he believes is false, and he believes it even though it is false.

How do these possibilities adduced by the skeptic show that someone does not know that p? Suppose that someone is you; how do these possibilities count against your knowing that p? One way might be the following. (I shall consider other ways later.) If there is a possible situation where p is false yet you believe that p, then in that situation you believe that p even though it is false. So it appears you do not satisfy condition 3 for knowledge.

(3) If p were false, S wouldn't believe that p.

For a situation has been described in which you do believe that p even though p is false. How then can it also be true that if p were false, you wouldn't believe it? If the skeptic's possible situation shows that 3 is false, and if 3 is a necessary condition for knowledge, then the skeptic's possible situation shows that there isn't knowledge.

So construed, the skeptic's argument plays on condition 3; it aims to show that condition 3 is not satisfied. The skeptic may seem to be putting forth

R: Even if p were false, S still would believe p.[43]

This conditional, with the same antecedent as 3 and the contradictory consequent, is incompatible with the truth of 3. If 3 is true, then R is not. However, R is stronger than the skeptic needs in order to show 3 is false. For 3 is false when if p were false, S might believe that p. This last conditional is weaker than R, and is merely 3's denial:

T: not-[not-p → not-(S believes that p)].

Whereas R does not simply deny 3, it asserts an opposing subjunctive of its own. Perhaps the possibility the skeptic adduces is not enough to show that R is true, but it appears at least to establish the weaker T; since this T denies 3, the skeptic's possibility appears to show that 3 is false.[44]

However, the truth of 3 is not incompatible with the existence of a possible situation where the person believes p though it is false. The subjunctive

(3) not-p → not-(S believes p)

does not talk of all possible situations in which p is false (in which not-p is true). It does not say that in all possible situations where not-p holds, S doesn't believe p. To say there is no possible situation in which not-p yet S believes p, would be to say that not-p entails not-(S believes p), or logically implies it. But subjunctive conditionals differ from entailments; the subjunctive 3 is not a statement of entailment. So the existence of a possible situation in which p is false yet S believes p does not show that 3 is false;[45] 3 can be true even though there is a possible situation where not-p and S believes that p.

What the subjunctive 3 speaks of is the situation that would hold if p were false. Not every possible situation in which p is false is the situation that would hold if p were false. To fall into possible worlds talk, the subjunctive 3 speaks of the not-p world that is closest to the actual world, or of those not-p worlds that are closest to the actual world, or more strongly (according to my suggestion) of the not-p neighborhood of the actual world. And it is of this or these not-p worlds that it says (in them) S does not believe that p. What happens in yet other more distant not-p worlds is no concern of the subjunctive 3.

The skeptic's possibilities (let us refer to them as SK), of the person's being deceived by a demon or dreaming of floating in a tank, count against the subjunctive

(3) if p were false then S wouldn't believe that p

only if (one of) these possibilities would or might obtain if p were false; only if one of these possibilities is in the not-p neighborhood of the actual world. Condition 3 says: if p were false, S still would not believe p. And this can hold even though there is some situation SK described by the skeptic in which p is false and S believes p. If p were false S still would not believe p, even though there is a situation SK in which p is false and S does believe p, provided that this situation SK wouldn't obtain if p were false. If the skeptic describes a situation SK which would not hold even if p were false then this situation SK doesn't show that 3 is false and so does not (in this way at least) undercut knowledge. Condition C acts to rule out skeptical hypotheses.

C: not-p → SK does not obtain.

Any skeptical situation SK which satisfies condition C is ruled out. For a skeptical situation SK to show that we don't know that p, it must fail to satisfy C which excludes it; instead it must be a situation that might obtain if p did not, and so satisfy C's denial:

not-(not-p → SK doesn't obtain).

Although the skeptic's imagined situations appear to show that 3 is false, they do not; they satisfy condition C and so are excluded.

The skeptic might go on to ask whether we know that his imagined situations SK are excluded by condition C, whether we know that if p were false SK would not obtain. However, typically he asks something stronger: do we know that his imagined situation SK does not actually obtain? Do we know that we are not being deceived by a demon, dreaming, or floating in a tank? And if we do not know this, how can we know that p? Thus we are led to the second way his imagined situations might show that we do not know that p.

Skeptical Results

According to our account of knowledge, S knows that the skeptic's situation SK doesn't hold if and only if

(1) SK doesn't hold

(2) S believes that SK doesn't hold

(3) If SK were to hold, S would not believe that SK doesn't hold

(4) If SK were not to hold, S would believe it does not.

Let us focus on the third of these conditions. The skeptic has carefully chosen his situations SK so that if they held we (still) would believe they did not. We would believe we weren't dreaming, weren't being deceived, and so on, even if we were. He has chosen situations SK such that if SK were to hold, S would (still) believe that SK doesn't hold — and this is incompatible with the truth of 3.[46]

Since condition 3 is a necessary condition for knowledge, it follows that we do not know that SK doesn't hold. If it were true that an evil demon was deceiving us, if we were having a particular dream, if we were floating in a tank with our brains stimulated in a specified way, we would still believe we were not. So, we do not know we're not being deceived by an evil demon, we do not know we're not in that tank, and we do not know we're not having that dream. So says the skeptic, and so says our account. And also so we say — don't we? For how could we know we are not being deceived that way, dreaming that dream? If those things *were* happening to us, everything would seem the same to us. There is no way we can know it is not happening for there is no way we could tell if it were happening; and if it were happening we would believe exactly what we do now — in particular, we still would believe that it was not. For this reason, we feel, and correctly, that we don't know — how could we? — that it is not happening to us. It is a virtue of our account that it yields, and explains, this result.

The skeptic asserts we do not know his possibilities don't obtain, and he is right. Attempts to avoid skepticism by claiming we do know these things are bound to fail. The skeptic's possibilities make us uneasy because, as we deeply realize, we do not know they don't obtain; it is not surprising that attempts to show we do know these things leave us suspicious, strike us even as bad faith.* Nor has the skeptic merely pointed out something obvious and trivial. It comes as a surprise to realize that we do not know his possibilities don't obtain. It is startling, shocking. For we would have thought, before the skeptic got us to focus on it, that we did know those things, that we did know we were not being deceived by a demon, or dreaming that dream, or stimulated that way in that tank. The skeptic has pointed out that we do not know things we would have confidently said we knew. And if we don't know these things, what can we know? So much for the supposed obviousness of what the skeptic tells us.

Let us say that a situation (or world) is doxically identical for S to the actual situation when if S were in that situation, he would have exactly the beliefs (*doxa*) he actually does have. More generally, two situations are doxically identical for S if and only if he would have exactly the same beliefs in them. It might be merely a curiosity to be told there are nonactual situations doxically identical to the actual one. The skeptic, however, describes worlds doxically identical to the actual world in which almost everything believed is false.†

Such worlds are possible because we know mediately, not directly.

---

*Descartes presumably would refute the tank hypothesis as he did the demon hypothesis, through a proof of the existence of a good God who would not allow anyone, demon or psychologist, permanently to deceive us. The philosophical literature has concentrated on the question of whether Descartes can prove this (without begging the question against the demon hypothesis). The literature has not discussed whether even a successful proof of the existence of a good God can help Descartes to conclude he is not almost always mistaken. Might not a good God have his own reasons for deceiving us; might he not deceive us temporarily — a period which includes all of our life thus far (but not an afterlife)? To the question of why God did not create us so that we never would make any errors, Descartes answers that the motives of God are inscrutable to us. Do we know that such an inscrutable God could not be motivated to allow another powerful "demon" to deceive and dominate us?

Alternatively, could not such a good God be motivated to deceive itself temporarily, even if not another? (Compare the various Indian doctrines designed to explain our ignorance of our own true nature, that is, Atman–Brahman's or, on another theory, the purusha's nature.) Whether from playfulness or whatever motive, such a good God would temporarily deceive itself, perhaps even into thinking it is a human being living in a material realm. Can we know, via Descartes' argument, that this is not our situation? And so forth.

These possibilities, and others similar, are so obvious that some other explanation, I mean the single-minded desire to refute skepticism, must be given for why they are not noticed and discussed.

Similarly, one could rescrutinize the *cogito* argument. Can "I think" only be produced by something that exists? Suppose Shakespeare had written for Hamlet the line, "I think, therefore I am," or a fiction is written in which a character named Descartes says this, or suppose a character in a dream of mine says this; does it follow that they exist? Can someone use the cogito argument to prove himself is not a fictional or dream character? Descartes asked how he could know he wasn't dreaming; he also should have asked how he could know he wasn't dreamed. See further my fable "Fiction," *Ploughshares,* Vol. 6, no. 3, Oct. 1980.

†I say almost everything, because there still could be some true beliefs such as "I exist." More limited skeptical possibilities present worlds doxically identical to the actual world in which almost every belief of a certain sort is false, for example, about the past, or about other people's mental states. See the discussion below in the section on narrower skepticisms.

This leaves room for a divergence between our beliefs and the truth. It is as though we possessed only two-dimensional plane projections of three-dimensional objects. Different three-dimensional objects, oriented appropriately, have the same two-dimensional plane projection. Similarly, different situations or worlds will lead to our having the very same beliefs. What is surprising is how very different the doxically identical world can be — different enough for almost everything believed in it to be false. Whether or not the mere fact that knowledge is mediated always makes room for such a very different doxically identical world, it does so in our case, as the skeptic's possibilities show. To be shown this is nontrivial, especially when we recall that we do not know the skeptic's possibility doesn't obtain: we do not know that we are not living in a doxically identical world wherein almost everything we believe is false.[47]

What more could the skeptic ask for or hope to show? Even readers who sympathized with my desire not to dismiss the skeptic too quickly may feel this has gone too far, that we have not merely acknowledged the force of the skeptic's position but have succumbed to it.

The skeptic maintains that we know almost none of what we think we know. He has shown, much to our initial surprise, that we do not know his (nontrivial) possibility SK doesn't obtain. Thus, he has shown of one thing we thought we knew, that we didn't and don't. To the conclusion that we know almost nothing, it appears but a short step. For if we do not know we are not dreaming or being deceived by a demon or floating in a tank, then how can I know, for example, that I am sitting before a page writing with a pen, and how can you know that you are reading a page of a book?

However, although our account of knowledge agrees with the skeptic in saying that we do not know that not-SK, it places no formidable barriers before my knowing that I am writing on a page with a pen. It is true that I am, I believe I am, if I weren't I wouldn't believe I was, and if I were, I would believe it. (I leave out the reference to method.) Also, it is true that you are reading a page (please, don't stop now!), you believe you are, if you weren't reading a page you wouldn't believe you were, and if you were reading a page you would believe you were. So according to the account, I do know that I am writing on a page with a pen, and you do know that you are reading a page. The account does not lead to any general skepticism.

Yet we must grant that it appears that if the skeptic is right that we don't know we are not dreaming or being deceived or floating in the tank, then it cannot be that I know I am writing with a pen or that you know you are reading a page. So we must scrutinize with special care the skeptic's "short step" to the conclusion that we don't know these things, for either this step cannot be taken or our account of knowledge is incoherent.

Nonclosure

In taking the "short step", the skeptic assumes that if S knows that p and he knows that 'p entails q' then he also knows that q. In the terminology of the logicians, the skeptic assumes that knowledge is closed under known logical implication; that the operation of moving from something known to something else known to be entailed by it does not take us outside of the (closed) area of knowledge. He intends, of course, to work things backwards, arguing that since the person does not know that q, assuming (at least for the purposes of argument) that he does know that p entails q, it follows that he does not know that p. For if he did know that p, he would also know that q, which he doesn't.

The details of different skeptical arguments vary in their structure, but each one will assume some variant of the principle that knowledge is closed under known logical implication. If we abbreviate "knowledge that p" by "Kp" and abbreviate "entails" by the fishhook sign " $\dashv$ ", we can write this principle of closure as the subjunctive principle

P: $K(p \dashv q) \mathbin{\&} Kp \rightarrow Kq.$

If a person were to know that p entails q and he were to know that p then he would know that q. The statement that q follows by modus ponens from the other two stated as known in the antecedent of the subjunctive principle P; this principle counts on the person to draw the inference to q.

You know that your being in a tank on Alpha Centauri entails your not being in place X where you are. (I assume here a limited readership.) And you know also the contrapositive, that your being at place X entails that you are not then in a tank on Alpha Centauri. If you knew you were at X you would know you're not in a tank (of a specified sort) at Alpha Centauri. But you do not know this last fact (the skeptic has argued and we have agreed) and so (he argues) you don't know the first. Another intuitive way of putting the skeptic's argument is as follows. If you know that two statements are incompatible and you know the first is true then you know the denial of the second. You know that your being at X and your being in a tank on Alpha Centauri are incompatible; so if you knew you were at X you would know you were not in the (specified) tank on Alpha Centauri. Since you do not know the second, you don't know the first.[48]

No doubt, it is possible to argue over the details of principle P, to point out it is incorrect as it stands. Perhaps, though Kp, the person does not know that he knows that p (that is, not-KKp) and so does not draw the inference to q. Or perhaps he doesn't draw the inference because not-KK(p —ᴣ q). Other similar principles face their own difficulties: for example, the principle that K(p → q) → (Kp → Kq) fails if Kp stops p → q from being true, that is, if Kp → not-(p → q); the principle that K(p —ᴣ q) → K(Kp → Kq) faces difficulties if Kp makes the person forget that (p —ᴣ q) and so he fails to draw the inference to q. We seem forced to pile K upon K until we reach something like KK(p —ᴣ q) & KKp → Kq; this involves strengthening considerably the antecedent of P and so is not useful for the skeptic's argument that p is not known. (From a principle altered thus, it would follow at best that it is not known that p is known.)

We would be ill-advised, however, to quibble over the details of P. Although these details are difficult to get straight, it will continue to appear that something like P is correct. If S knows that 'p entails q' and he know that p and knows that '(p and p entails q) entails q' (shades of the Lewis Carroll puzzle we discuss below!) and he does draw the inference to q from all this and believes q via the process of drawing this inference, then will he not know that q? And what is wrong with simplifying this mass of detail by writing merely principle P, provided we apply it only to cases where the mass of detail holds, as it surely does in the skeptical cases under consideration? For example, I do realize that my being in the Van Leer Foundation Building in Jerusalem entails that I am not in a tank on Alpha Centauri; I am capable of drawing inferences now; I do believe I am not in a tank on Alpha Centauri (though not solely via this inference, surely); and so forth. Won't this satisfy the correctly detailed principle, and shouldn't it follow that I know I am not (in that tank) on Alpha Centauri? The skeptic agrees it should follow; so he concludes from the fact that I don't know I am floating in the tank on Alpha Centauri that I don't know I am in Jerusalem. Uncovering difficulties in the details of particular formulations of P will not weaken the principle's intuitive appeal; such quibbling will seem at best like a wasp attacking a steamroller, at worst like an effort in bad faith to avoid being pulled along by the skeptic's argument.

Principle P is wrong, however, and not merely in detail. Knowledge is not closed under known logical implication.[49] S knows that p when S has a true belief that p, and S wouldn't have a false belief that p (condition 3) and S would have a true belief that p (condition 4). Neither of these latter two conditions is closed under known logical implication.

Let us begin with condition

(3) if p were false, S wouldn't believe that p.

When S knows that p, his belief that p is contingent on the truth of p, contingent in the way the subjunctive condition 3 describes. Now it might be that p entails q (and S knows this), that S's belief that p is subjunctively contingent on the truth of p, that S believes q, *yet his belief that q* is not subjunctively dependent on the truth of q, in that it (or he) does not satisfy:

(3′) if q were false, S wouldn't believe that q.

For 3′ talks of what S would believe if q were false, and this may be a very different situation than the one that would hold if p were false, even though p entails q. That you were born in a certain city entails that you were born on earth.* Yet contemplating what (actually) would be the situation if you were not born in that city is very different from contemplating what situation would hold if you weren't born on earth. Just as those possibilities are very different, so what is believed in them may be very different. When p entails q (and not the other way around) p will be a stronger statement than q, and so not-q (which is the antecedent of 3′) will be a stronger statement than not-p (which is the antecedent of 3). There is no reason to assume you will have the same beliefs in these two cases, under these suppositions of differing strengths.

There is no reason to assume the (closest) not-p world and the (closest) not-q world are doxically identical for you, and no reason to assume, even though p entails q, that your beliefs in one of these worlds would be a (proper) subset of your beliefs in the other.

Consider now the two statements:

p = I am awake and sitting on a chair in Jerusalem;

q = I am not floating in a tank on Alpha Centauri being stimulated by electrochemical means to believe that p.

The first one entails the second: p entails q. Also, I know that p entails q; and I know that p. If p were false, I would be standing or lying down in the same city, or perhaps sleeping there, or perhaps in a neighboring city or town. If q were false, I would be floating in a tank on Alpha Centauri. Clearly these are very different situations, leading to great differences in what I then would believe. If p were false, if I weren't awake and sitting on a chair in Jerusalem, I would not believe that p. Yet if q were false, if I was floating in a tank on Alpha Centauri, I would believe that q, that I was not in the tank, and indeed, in that case, I would still believe that p. According to our account of knowledge, I know that p yet I do not know that q, even though (I know) p entails q.

This failure of knowledge to be closed under known logical implication stems from the fact that condition 3 is not closed under known log-

---

*Here again I assume a limited readership, and ignore possibilities such as those described in James Blish, *Cities in Flight*.

ical implication; condition 3 can hold of one statement believed while not of another known to be entailed by the first.[50] It is clear that any account that includes as a necessary condition for knowledge the subjunctive condition 3, not-$p \rightarrow$ not-(S believes that p), will have the consequence that knowledge is not closed under known logical implication.[51]

When p entails q and you believe each of them, if you do not have a false belief that p (since p is true) then you do not have a false belief that q. However, if you are to know something not only don't you have a false belief about it, but also you wouldn't have a false belief about it. Yet, we have seen how it may be that p entails q and you believe each and you wouldn't have a false belief that p yet you might have a false belief that q (that is, it is not the case that you wouldn't have one). Knowledge is not closed under the known logical implication because "wouldn't have a false belief that" is not closed under known logical implication.

If knowledge were the same as (simply) true belief then it would be closed under known logical implication (provided the implied statements were believed). Knowledge is not simply true belief, however; additional conditions are needed. These further conditions will make knowledge open under known logical implication, even when the entailed statement is believed, when at least one of the further conditions itself is open. Knowledge stays closed (only) if all of the additional conditions are closed. I lack a general nontrivial characterization of those conditions that are closed under known logical implication; possessing such an illuminating characterization, one might attempt to prove that no additional conditions of that sort could provide an adequate analysis of knowledge.

Still, we can say the following. A belief that p is knowledge that p only if it somehow varies with the truth of p. The causal condition for knowledge specified that the belief was "produced by" the fact, but that condition did not provide the right sort of varying with the fact. The subjunctive conditions 3 and 4 are our attempt to specify that varying. But however an account spells this out, it will hold that whether a belief that p is knowledge partly depends on what goes on with the belief in some situations when p is false. An account that says nothing about what is believed in any situation when p is false cannot give us any mode of varying with the fact.

Because what is preserved under logical implication is truth, any condition that is preserved under known logical implication is most likely to speak only of what happens when p, and q, are true, without speaking at all of what happens when either one is false. Such a condition is incapable of providing "varies with"; so adding only such conditions to true belief cannot yield an adequate account of knowledge.[52]

A belief's somehow varying with the truth of what is believed is not closed under known logical implication. Since knowledge that *p* involves such variation, knowledge also is not closed under known logical implication. The skeptic cannot easily deny that knowledge involves such variation, for his argument that we don't know that we're not floating in that tank, for example, uses the fact that knowledge does involve variation. ("If you were floating in the tank you would still think you weren't, so you don't know that you're not.") Yet, though one part of his argument uses that fact that knowledge involves such variation, another part of his argument presupposes that knowledge does not involve any such variation. This latter is the part that depends upon knowledge being closed under known logical implication, as when the skeptic argues that since you don't know that not-SK, you don't know you are not floating in the tank, then you also don't know, for example, that you are now reading a book. That closure can hold only if the variation does not. The skeptic cannot be right both times. According to our view he is right when he holds that knowledge involves such variation and so concludes that we don't know, for example, that we are not floating in that tank; but he is wrong when he assumes knowledge is closed under known logical implication and concludes that we know hardly anything.[53]

Knowledge is a real factual relation, subjunctively specifiable, whose structure admits our standing in this relation, tracking, to *p* without standing in it to some *q* which we know *p* to entail. Any relation embodying some variation of belief with the fact, with the truth (value), will exhibit this structural feature. The skeptic is right that we don't track some particular truths — the ones stating that his skeptical possibilities SK don't hold — but wrong that we don't stand in the real knowledge-relation of tracking to many other truths, including ones that entail these first mentioned truths we believe but don't know. . . .

Skepticism and the Conditions for Knowledge

We have considered how the skeptic's argument from the skeptical possibilities SK plays off condition 3: if *p* weren't true S wouldn't believe that *p*. His argument gains its power by utilizing this condition ("but even if SK held, you still would believe it didn't, so you do not know it doesn't"); the deep intuitive force of the argument indicates that condition 3 (or something very much like it) is a necessary condition for knowledge. Similarly, are there any skeptical arguments or moves that play off condition 4: if *p* were true then S would believe that *p* (and wouldn't believe that not-*p*)? If condition 3 specifies how belief somehow should vary with the truth of what is believed, condition 4 specifies how belief shouldn't vary when the truth of what is believed does not vary. Condition 3 is a variation condition, condition 4 is an adherence condition. Both conditions together capture the notion that S (who actually truly believes p) would have a true belief that p. He wouldn't have a false belief that p if p weren't true (condition 3), and he would have a true belief that p if p were true (condition 4). Just as the skeptic argued earlier than the belief wouldn't vary when it should, he also can argue that it would vary when it shouldn't, concluding both times that we don't have knowledge.

We would expect skeptical arguments playing off condition 4 to be less powerful and compelling than ones playing off 3. Condition 3 requires that we wouldn't falsely believe p, and we can be led to worry not only whether we might but whether we do. While condition 4 requires that we would truly believe p (and wouldn't falsely believe not-p), and though we might worry whether we might violate this, we need have no fear that we are—for we know we are believing p and are not believing not-p. Skeptical arguments playing off condition 4, unlike those with 3, cannot make us wonder also whether we violate the condition's indicative version.

Condition 4 is an adherence condition, so the relevant doubts concern how securely you are tied to the truth. For many (most?) of the things p you believe, if a group of people came and deceitfully told you not-p, you would believe them and stop believing p. (Relevant experiments frequently have been done by social psychologists.) So do you really know p? If physicists told you that Newton's theory turns out to have been correct after all, wouldn't (or mightn't) you believe them? So do you really know Newtonian theory is false?

But, as before, the mere possibility of its being true while you do not believe it is not sufficient to show you don't actually know it. That possibility must be one that might arise. Call this possibility of p's being true while you don't believe it: sk. (Lowercase "sk" is p's being true and your not believing it, while capital SK is p's being false and your believing p.) Possibility sk need not concern us when: if p were true, sk wouldn't hold; $p \rightarrow$ not-sk; sk is false throughout the first part of the p neighborhood of the actual world. It is fortunate for my knowing that p that there wouldn't be people who trick me, just as it is fortunate for my knowing I am in Emerson Hall that whatever would occur if I weren't there does not include people tricking or hypnotizing me into believing I am there.

Suppose I present a certain argument to someone who believes (truly) that p, and he is convinced by it and comes to believe not-p. Look how easily he can be moved from believing p to believing not-p. Suppose it happens that I do not present the argument to him, so he does not start to believe not-p, and he continues to believe p. Does he know that *p*? Is it merely the case that his knowledge is insecure, or does such instability show it is not knowledge after all?

A skeptic might argue that for almost each *p* we (think we) know, there is an argument or happening that would get us to believe not-*p* even though *p* was true. We reply to this skeptic as before – the fact that some possible argument or happening would get us to believe not-*p* when *p* doesn't show that it is false that 4: if *p* were true then S would believe *p* and S wouldn't believe not-*p*. To show the falsity of 4, the skeptic would have to refer to something that might occur if *p* were true; if it wouldn't hold if *p* were true, what he refers to is irrelevant.

Among the arguments that get people to stop believing things are the skeptic's arguments themselves. These arguments often puzzle people, sometimes they get people to stop believing they know that *p*. They do not know that they know. Should we describe this as a case of people who first know that they know but who, after hearing the skeptic's arguments, no longer know that they know because they no longer believe that they know (and knowledge entails belief)? Our present view is that such people did not know that they knew that *p*, even before hearing the skeptic. For their previous belief that they knew that *p* would vary when it shouldn't, so it violates condition 4. Similarly, some people who never have heard the skeptic's arguments would (if they heard them) become convinced that they don't know that *p*. It is pleasant to grant the skeptic a partial victory after all, one gained by the plausibility of his arguments, not their cogency. Because of the skeptical arguments, some people would falsely believe they don't know that *p*, and these people do not know they know it. The existence of skeptical arguments makes one type of skeptical conclusion (that we don't know we know things) true of some people – those the shoe fits have been wearing it.

Meno claimed he could speak eloquently about virtue until Socrates, torpedolike, began to question him. He did not know what virtue was, for Socrates' questions uncovered Meno's previously existing confusions. Even if it had been a sophist's questions that bewildered Meno, getting him to believe the opposite, what he previously had would not have been knowledge. Knowledge should be made of sterner stuff.[54]

Thus, some skeptical arguments play off condition 3, others off condition 4. In addition to these conditions, our (full) account of knowledge formulates a condition about outweighing to cover the situation when multiple methods, not all satisfying 3 and 4, give rise to the belief. Do any skeptical arguments play off this outweighing condition? Here, presumably, would fit various attempts at unmasking the dominant sources of our belief as methods that do not track: faith, prejudice, self-interest, class-interest, deep psychological motives. The out-

weighing view involves subjunctives, but does anything here correspond to the skeptic's focusing upon a possibility that is so far out
that it wouldn't occur, even if *p* were false? Perhaps the following is
comparable. Recall that it was not necessary for the tracking method
to win out against the combined opposed weight of all other methods;
the person's belief merely had to vary with the verdict of the tracking
method when the recommendations of every other way used to arrive
at belief were held fixed. (It was only Case III in the chart that needed
to be examined.) Any actual split in the verdict of nontracking methods will be welcome support. The skeptic should not load the other
methods against what tracking recommends, any more than they actually are; to suppose more counts as too far out.

Some skeptical arguments play off condition 3, some off condition
4, some (perhaps) off the outweighing condition when multiple methods are involved. Still other skeptical arguments play off the methods
themselves, off the fact that knowledge is gained via methods or ways
of believing. In the situations when we are aware of what methods we
are using, do we know we are using those methods? To decide whether
we know this, according to condition 3 we must consider what we
would believe if we weren't using the methods. Would we then still believe we were? If so, condition 3 is violated, and so we did not actually
know we were using the methods.

Along this pathway lies trouble. For if we weren't using that method,
the very method we use to track various facts — a situation we have to
contemplate in applying condition 3 — who knows what we would believe about what methods we are using? That method M we are using to
track various facts may be the very method via which we believe that
we are using method M. This is likely if (and only if) M is described
widely and deeply enough, for example, as the sum total of our (rational or effective) methods. But then, how are we to treat the question
of what we would believe if we weren't using that method M, a question
condition 3 pushes at us in order to decide if we know we are using M?
"If I weren't using M, would I still believe I was?" What methods of
believing am I left by this question? After all, condition 3 when fully
formulated says: not-*p* and S, via M, comes to a belief about the truth
of *p* → not-(S believes that *p*). And the method M of condition 3 is the
very one said to be actually utilized, in condition 2: S believes, via M,
that *p*.

Yet now we face the situation where S believes of himself that he is
applying method M, via an application of method M itself;[55] moreover, in this situation the statement *p*, which we are trying to decide
whether S knows, is: S is using method M. The result of substituting
this *p* in the full condition 3 is: If S weren't using method M, and S, via
using M, were to decide about the truth of 'S is using method M' then S

would not believe 'S is using method M.' But the antecedent of this subjunctive is supposing both that S is not using method M (this supposition is the not-*p* of the antecedent of condition 3) and that S is using method M (he uses this method in 3 to decide whether or not *p*, since that is the method via which, in condition 2, he actually believes *p*). We have no coherent way to understand this.*

Yet if we cannot simply include the use of method M in determining what S would believe if he were not using M, neither can we simply suppose (for the purposes of condition 3) that S is using some other method to arrive at a belief about this matter. We saw earlier, in considering a range of examples, the great importance of holding the method fixed in deciding questions about knowledge. Recall the grandmother who sees her grandson visit her and so believes he is healthy and ambulatory; yet if he weren't ambulatory, other relatives would tell her he was fine to spare her anxiety and upset. She sees her grandson walking; does she know he is ambulatory? According to condition 3 we must ask what she would believe if he weren't ambulatory. If the method via which she believes is not held fixed, the answer will be wrong. True, if he weren't ambulatory, she would then believe he was (via hearing about him from other relatives). But the relevant question is: what would she believe if he weren't ambulatory and (as before) she saw him and spoke to him. Thus, to reach the correct answer about her knowledge, the method must be held fixed — that is one of the reasons why we introduced explicit reference to the method or way of believing.

How then are we to treat the question of whether the person knows he is using method M, when he believes he is via that very method M? If he knows he is, then his belief that he is tracks the fact that he is, and varies with that fact. To determine whether it so varies, we must look to the question of what he would believe if *p* were false, that is, if he weren't using method M. How are we to understand this question? It seems we must hold fixed the method M via which he believes, in order to reach the correct answer about knowledge (as is shown by the case of the grandmother), and that we cannot hold the method M fixed, for then we have the (apparently) incoherent supposition that he is applying the method to the situation where he is not using it, in order to determine whether or not he is — and this supposes that he both is and isn't using the method.

This problem does not arise when we know via another method that we are using some particular method; it arises only for our knowledge

---

*Similar questions arise about our knowledge of other statements such that if they were false, we would not be using the methods via which we know they are true, for example, "there are eyes," "I am alive," "I am sentient," perhaps "I sometimes am tracking something."

of our use of our deepest methods, though not for shallower specifications of these methods in specific instances. Still, what should we say about our knowledge of these deepest methods or of the conditions in which we apply them. Do you know you are rational, do you know you are sane? If you were irrational or insane, mightn't you think you were rational and sane? Yes, but not by applying methods under (fixed) conditions of rationality and sanity. We cannot conclude simply that condition 3 is not satisfied so you don't know you are rational or sane; for that condition is not satisfied only when the method is allowed to vary. It would be best to be able coherently to discover whether or not that method is being used. I can use M to discover whether you are using M (if you weren't, I wouldn't believe, via M, that you were), or whether I was using M in the past (if I hadn't been, I wouldn't now believe, via M, that I had been). The difficulty is to make sense of saying that M, if currently used, would detect that it was not being used (if it weren't). And while I do not think this simply is incoherent, neither is it pellucidly clear.*

Questions about knowing one is rational or sane need not depend on varying the method used. If what we have to go on as we apply methods is the appearance of rationality and sanity, then mightn't we appear sane and rational to ourselves even if we are not? So how do we know we are? We do have more to go on than how we appear to ourselves; there also is the agreement with others. Let us leave aside the possibility that all those others also might be insane and irrational, or be engaged in a plot to convince me (falsely) that I was rational and sane. Neither of these is what (actually) would or might occur if I weren't rational or sane. Might an insane and irrational person also be mistaken about whether others are agreeing with him, though, interpreting their disagreement as concord? If a person were insane or irrational in this way then others would appear (to him) to agree with him, and so he would appear sane and rational to himself. Things would appear qualitatively indistinguishable to him from the situation where he rationally and sanely judges the world. There appears to be no shift in method here, at least insofar as how using the method is experienced internally by the user. Do you know, then, that you are not in that particular skeptical situation SK? Perhaps not, but (as before) from our not knowing that particular not-SK it does not follow that we don't know other things, including that we are being sane and rational in particular situations in particular ways. For if we weren't, we wouldn't believe we were; if we weren't then sane and rational in those particular ways, what would or

---

*Should we say for these cases discussed in the text that condition 3 does not apply, so that, as in the previous case of necessary truths, the whole weight of tracking devolves upon condition 4? The issue then simply turns on whether in similar situations where the person uses method M, he also would believe he does.

might obtain is not this skeptic's possibility SK. These points emerge even more clearly if we consider positions skeptical not about (almost) all knowledge in general, but about particular kinds of knowledge.

Narrower Skepticisms

The skeptical arguments we have examined thus far apply to knowledge in general. Other skeptical arguments focus upon particular kinds of knowledge, upon a particular type of statement or one arrived at in a particular way. Thus, in addition to general skepticism there are narrower philosophical skepticisms: about other minds, about a world existing unperceived, about induction, and so on.

Our account of knowledge says of these more particular skepticisms what it said of general skepticism; though the sweeping (skeptical) conclusion is too broad, the skeptic is not to be dismissed. He is correct in saying there are some things we do not know, even though unreflectively we might have thought we did; but while it might appear that much knowledge depends on having this first knowledge (which we don't have), this appearance is misleading.

Let us begin with the problem of other minds.[56] How can we know another person is in pain, or thrilled, or overcome with emotion, or thinking about philosophy? All we have to go on is her external behavior and speech, yet such behavior does not entail the existence of the felt psychological state. It is logically possible that accompanying the behavior we have observed is a very different felt state, or even no feeling at all. So how can we know what anyone else feels, or that they feel or experience anything? Can you know you are not surrounded by unfeeling bodies in motion?

Suppose a terrorist bomb explodes nearby and I am singed by the heat. I rush forward to help and find someone on the ground, bleeding, writhing, and screaming. Others are moaning. I know the person is in pain. The situation is the sort that can cause extreme pain, and I see a victim writhing and screaming (in pain). I believe it because of what I see and other things I know, for example, that I am not in Los Angeles on a movie set. The person is in pain, and my belief that the person is tracks the fact that he is. If the person were not in pain he wouldn't be behaving like that, and so I wouldn't believe he was in pain; moreover, if he were in pain I would (in this situation, via this way) believe he was. My belief that my children are happy, as they play with the animal, tracks the fact that they are; my belief that my friend is depressed tracks the fact that he is — I know my children are happy, I know my friend is depressed. The conditions for knowledge are satisfied in these cases, so our account yields the result that I do know what these people are feeling then, and so do have this knowledge of other minds. Nothing said by the skeptic shows that I am not in fact tracking (the state of) other minds in these cases; no general skepticism about (all) knowledge of other minds is justified or true.

But could it not be that the person on the ground is an actor in a film, my friend is out to trick me, my children are pretending to enjoy playing with the animal, or even that all of them, and all others as well, are extraterrestrials without human feelings or are cleverly constructed robots without any feelings at all—humanoid automata? Do I know this is not the case?

Let p be the specific statement about another's experience, and let SK be some skeptical scenario wherein although my belief that p is based exactly as it actually is apart from the scenario (for example, upon the behavior of others and the way the setting appears), p is false nonetheless. Do I know that SK does not hold, do I know that not everyone else on earth is a feelingless robot cleverly constructed by beings from another galaxy in whose psychological experiment I am a participant? (You know this is not true of yourself but do you know it is not true of others, including me?) How could I know that SK doesn't hold? If it held, things would seem exactly the same to me as they do now. (If things wouldn't seem exactly the same, it is not the right possibility SK.) So I don't know that not-SK; condition 3 for knowledge of not-SK is not satisfied. If SK were true I (still) would believe not-SK. My belief that not-SK does not track the fact that not-SK, so I don't actually know that not-SK. Since SK is incompatible with p, and I realize this, how can it be that (not knowing not-SK, still) I know that p? My belief that p does track the fact that p, and knowledge is not closed under known logical implication.

The situation exactly parallels our earlier discussion of knowledge and a general skepticism based (for example) upon the logical possibility of being immersed in the tank near Alpha Centauri. The skeptic is correct in saying we don't know particular skeptical possibilities SK do not hold, but he is wrong in concluding from this that we don't know anything of a particular sort, about other minds, for instance. The skeptic's alternative SK is not what actually would or might obtain if p did not; so, we can track and therefore know p without tracking or knowing not-SK. The dream hypothesis is similar. I can know I am not now dreaming if: if I were dreaming I wouldn't be dreaming this. Yet I don't know I'm not dreaming *this,* for if I were things would seem exactly the same. Still, though not knowing this I now do I know I am sitting before paper and writing, and so on.

Do I really mean to say I don't know my children are not feelingless automata? (How will they feel when they read this?) I know their feelings when they are happy, sad, proud, embarrassed, frightened. I track these feelings and sometimes cause them. Furthermore, I know I don't have children who are feelingless robots. The (closest) world in which I (would) have children like that is a world in which, for example, I volunteered to adopt a robot or to participate in a genetic-engineering experiment that risked that eventuality, and I know that nothing of this sort is the case. But do I know that the skeptic's alternative SK doesn't hold, in which, among other things, I have automata children; of this SK whose obtaining would not reflect itself back into the evidence available to me, do I know it does not hold? Of course not. How could I? Do I believe it doesn't hold? Of course. (Don't worry, children.) Would I stake my life on its not holding? I have.

Consider Wittgenstein's view (in the *Philosophical Investigations*) of how stage setting and context are crucial to the application of a mental term, to the situation's fitting the term. (So he often points out what else will have to be true for something to be a case of, for example, understanding or reading or — the most difficult case for his view — pain.) The behavioral evidence does not entail the occurrence of the particular mental state, for there could be a wider context including this behavioral 'evidence' that shows the person wasn't in that specific mental state. Similarly, feelings of understanding will not constitute *understanding* unless they are embedded in an appropriate wider context. In both cases, each appropriate wider context could be undercut by a still wider context (which itself could be undercut by a yet wider one); that is why there's no entailment, why Wittgensteinian criteria are not logically sufficient conditions.[57] Wittgenstein's view structures mental predicates in the global closest relation mode, to invoke a category from Chapter I above; these terms involve a negative existential quantifier excluding a certain wider context. This seems not only to leave room for but to invite skepticism. For to know on some basis that a mental term applies to someone, won't I have to know also that there is no wider context (which includes that basis), itself not undercut, that undercuts the application of the mental term in question? And how can I know this? Is it not always possible that there is such a wider context, undetectable from where we stand and look?

Our comment follows a now familiar path. In applying a mental term to someone, I don't know that such a wider context does not obtain (for I don't track the fact that it does not). Yet I do know (for I track the fact that) the mental term applies in a particular case; if it didn't apply, I wouldn't believe it did. For if it weren't to apply, that would not actually be (because of) the undetectable wider undercutting context.

Wittgenstein's points about context and stage-setting apply not only to our application of mental terms to others, but (as he emphasizes) to ourselves as well. This might give rise, for each of us, to a problem of our own minds, parallel to the problem of other minds. Do I know a particular mental term currently applies to me, do I know the wider context will not undercut it, or that the earlier unremembered context hasn't already done so? And so on.

We can imagine even a problem of "my own mind" similar to the traditional "other minds" problem discussed earlier, which did not focus on issues of context. Do I know on a particular occasion that I am in pain? Yes. My belief that I am tracks the fact that I am. Indeed, the relation between my belief and the fact seems stronger than tracking. The two vary together across (almost?) all possible worlds, not merely the closest ones. So it is not surprising that theorists searching for a foundation for knowledge found such psychological statements especially appropriate. Freud claimed that not all occurrent psychological facts are tracked by belief, so only some would remain for foundationalist purposes. But even of this subclass one might imagine skeptical possibilities. Perhaps I am so wired up that I say and think there is a felt phenomenological quality, although there really isn't any such thing but merely a connection of physical states to my speech and thoughts and reports of "introspection."[58]

If some clever skeptical alternative SK can be specified to drop out the felt quality yet leave everything else as it is, then I will not know that not-SK. Skepticism about minds begins at home. Still, I will know that I feel pain, and that it phenomenologically feels that way. If it didn't, I wouldn't think it did; the skeptic's alternative SK (in which nothing feels that way yet I do think and say that something does) is not what would or might occur if p were false, if I weren't feeling a pain of a certain phenomenological sort.

We can proceed more quickly with the next example of a skepticism narrower than total skepticism, for our points are the same as before. (This saves time and intellectual effort, yet leads to a certain mechanical quality in the writing and — no doubt — in the reading. I apologize.) Do I know that my desk continues to exist when I am not perceiving it? Yes, you see it then and tell me it does. Do I know it continues to exist during a time when no one is perceiving it? Yes, for examination shows the rebound rate of the carpet tuft underneath the desk to be the same as the rebound speed of the carpet underneath a desk continuously observed for that length of time, and if the unperceived desk had not been there all the time, its (downtrodden) piece of carpet wouldn't have behaved like that; so I know it was there continuously. Do I know the carpet ever exists when it is not perceived or filmed? Yes, because I did see the table on it, and when I later examined the tuft, its rebound speed indicated that that part of the carpet had been under pressure for three hours, though it was observed for only one half hour. Do I know that anything ever exists when it is neither perceived nor known to be connected with other perceived things; rather (to leap to it) do I know that some skeptical possibility SK doesn't hold, under which some un-perceived things undetectably are not there temporarily? Some such skeptical possibility SK can be specified, I suppose; if so, I do not know it doesn't hold. Consider next the statement that there is a chair behind me now at the other end of this room. I know that statement is true. If it weren't there now, that would be because it wasn't there be-fore (but I saw it then) or because someone removed it since then (but I would have heard that). "But couldn't Martians have silently and invis-ibly entered to remove it, or couldn't the skeptic's possibility SK hold, with this being one of the moments the chair is not there?" Since these skeptical possibilities are not what would or might obtain if the chair weren't there now, they don't show I am not tracking the fact that it is. I can know that *p* even though I don't know these skeptical possibilities (each known to be incompatible with *p*) do not hold; knowledge is not closed under known logical implication.

Let us turn to the third of the particular skepticisms: skepticism about induction, about knowledge of the future or about any inference from sample to population or to facts outside the sample. We hold a belief *p* about the future on the basis of some current and past facts. Do we know that *p*? Only if our belief that *p* tracks the fact that *p*. Since our belief that *p* is based on current and past facts, we know that *p* only if these current and past facts track the fact that *p*. That is, only if: if *p* weren't true, this actually would have been reflected back so that some of the current and past facts wouldn't have held. Do we know that the sun will rise tomorrow, that the earth will continue to rotate on its axis during the next 24-hour period? If the sun were not going to rise tomorrow, would we have seen that coming, would that alteration in the earth's rotation have been presaged in the facts available to us to-day and before? If so, then we do know the sun will rise tomorrow; our belief that it will tracks the fact that it will, by being based on facts that would have been different otherwise.*

But isn't it logically possible that everything was as it was until now,

---

*Therefore, the relevant not-*p* world is not a world identical to the actual one until now and then diverging so as to produce not-*p*. There are delicate questions about how best to construe subjunctives that reach back in time, of the sort: if *p* weren't (to be) the case, *q* wouldn't have been the case. If determinism holds true, the (supposed) falsity of *p* might send ripples of change all the way back to the initial conditions of the universe, and with these an-tecedently changed, forward again through time, leading to (who knows what) enormous changes in the present. Perhaps the matter should be handled by saying the changes in the current evidence (the *q* that wouldn't have been the case) have to come as part of the rippling changes on the way back from the supposition that not-*p*, rather than as part of the forward movement of change from even more extensive backtracking. No doubt, a more complicated theory will be needed; my hope is that any such theory can be plugged into the text above, producing only minor modifications in it. For a recent discussion, not jibing with the tenor of this footnote, see David Lewis, "Counterfactual Dependence and Time's Arrow," *Nous,* Vol. 13, 1979, pp. 455–476.

yet the earth will not continue to rotate tomorrow? Yes, there are such skeptical logical possibilities SK: the bread no longer nourishes us, the sun stops in the sky, an event of a certain sort no longer continues to produce its usual effects. If they are elaborated suitably, so that everything we can detect up until now would have remained the same, then we don't know they do not hold. The skeptic about induction is right to say we don't know these possibilities do not hold, but he is wrong to deny we know those particular results of inductive inference whose falsity would have been reflected back and presaged in the facts upon which we based the inference.

These very general remarks are not restricted to particular modes of inductive inference. What matters for such inferential knowledge is that the evidence upon which we base our beliefs actually be subjunctively connected in a suitable way with the facts inferred. (We shall return to this point, and to induction, later when we discuss the theory of evidence.) Specific patterns of inductive inference are to be judged by their mesh with subjunctive relations. There is no reason in principle, though, why our knowledge must be limited to facts about the past and present, no reason in principle why our tracking and our knowledge must be limited to our sample.

Let h be some statement believed on the basis of evidence e. One question is whether I know h; here the answer might be "yes, on the basis of e," when e is subjunctively connected with h in a way so as to yield knowledge of h (when believed on the basis of e). A second question is whether I know it's not the case that e and not-h, or know that not-SK (where SK entails e and not-h); here the answer might be "no". From this last, however, it does not follow that I do not know that h; for my belief that h, based upon e, might still track the fact that h, since e itself might track h.

There is one question, though, that appears to fall between these two, being like the first in apparently asking whether h is known, and being like the second in depending upon whether not-(e and not-h) is being tracked. This question is: *given* that e is true, do I know that h? Given that the person is behaving in that way (writhing, screaming, complaining), do I know he is in pain? Given that I saw the chair before and hear no noise now, do I know the chair now is behind me? Given that the earth has rotated on its axis as it has previously and given all the other astronomical facts holding today and before, do I know the earth will rotate tomorrow? Given that e, do I know that h?

The "given that e" in the question holds e fixed; it holds fixed (among that which is accessible to me) what would vary if h were false. Thereby it blocks the answer, "I know h, because if h were false, e wouldn't hold true," for that answer seems directed to another question, and does not speak to whether given that e, I know that h. To the question "given that he is behaving that way, do you know he is feeling pain?" we cannot answer "yes, for if he weren't feeling pain he wouldn't be behaving that way." Holding *e* as fixed and given allows only *h* to vary, or *h* along with some other things that do not include *e*. "Given that *e*, do you know that *h*?" To answer this we must consider whether condition 3 is satisfied, and so examine what you would believe if *h* were false. But the "given that *e*" requires that in considering the situation where *h* is false, we hold *e* true; so it requires us to consider an *e* and not-*h* world. What we believe in that world cannot be determined by *e*'s not holding there because *h* does not, for *e* does hold there — that is given. To ask "given that *e*, do you know that *h*?" seems to ask merely whether we know that *h*, noticing by the by that *e* is true. However, really it asks whether we know that not-(*e* and not-*h*), a different question, and one that may merit a negative answer. Though it is an easy slide from this negative answer — "we don't know that not-(*e* and not-*h*)" — to the conclusion that therefore we don't know that *h*, this move should be resisted.

If the answer to "given that *e*, do you know that *h*?" is negative, then: given that *e*, I do not know that *h*. Since *e* is (let us suppose) true, it seems an easy step to detaching the simple conclusion: I do not know that *h*. Even if that cannot legitimately be inferred from *e*, how can it be that I do know that *h*? If I do, that must be on the basis of *e* which is all the evidence I have, and we already have seen that: given that *e*, I do not know that *h*. Although given that *e* I don't know that *h*, still, I can know (on the basis of *e*) that *h*. For I do not live in a world in which *e* is given, in which *e* is fixed and must be held constant. So I can know that *h* on the basis of *e*, on the basis of the *e* which is able to vary and so, because it hasn't, shows me that *h* is true. If *h* were false, *e* wouldn't hold either, and so I would not believe *h*. Thus, condition 3 can be satisfied and I can track *h*.

To speak of knowing *h* given that *e* forces us to look at a not-*h* world (in considering condition 3) which is not one that would or might hold if *h* were false, for it forces us to look at a not-*h* world which also is an *e* world; it forces us to look at an *e* and not-*h* world. The linguistic device "given that" holds things constant, and by preventing certain variations may force us to consider worlds farther out. Other linguistic devices, such as demonstratives, also may fix things as constant; so sentences containing these also may be like "given that" sentences in really being about a (skeptical) world farther out than the closest not-*h* world, while apparently being simply about *h*. It is not my purpose to pursue the theory of demonstratives, merely to note and illustrate the complication. Do I know I am holding in my hand the pen my children bought for me in the Harvard Coop as a Chanukah gift? Yes, if I wasn't holding it in my hand, I wouldn't think I was. (Either my hand would be empty, or I would be holding something other than a pen, or another pen but then I would notice it wasn't red.) Do I know that this red Parker $2.98 ballpoint pen is the one my children bought for me? Yes, it has a bent clip, resulting from my clumsiness soon after I got it. Do I know that this red Parker $2.98 ballpoint pen with the bent clip and these certain marks is the very pen my children bought in the Coop for me as a Chanukah gift? Perhaps not. If this were not that very pen, then I would still think it was; how, after all, would I tell the difference? All the features by which I am able to tell it is the original gift pen are held constant by the question "given that it has these stated characteristics do I know it is the pen my children bought me?" and also by the question "do I know that this red Parker with the bent clip is the very pen my children bought me?" The two questions "given that e, do I know that h?" and "do I know that this e thing is h?" each hold e fixed and thus appear to force the skeptical answer that h isn't known — when actually it is not-(e and not-h) which isn't known.

When e is all our evidence for h yet does not entail h, the skeptic asks whether given e we know that h. A negative answer to this question does not require us to conclude we don't know that h. The skeptic has more to say, however, about his particular skepticisms. He points out that our evidence e falls into one class or type of statement while the h we conclude falls into another, and that no amount of evidence taken from the first class can yield an affirmative answer to "given the evidence, do we know that h?" The evidence consists completely of statements about behavior, or about objects when they are observed, or about the past and present, or about the sample; and each time we go to an h beyond, we run risks. We acknowledge the risk due to the fact that h is not entailed by e but stands in subjunctive relations to it. (The skeptic also will ask whether and how we know these subjunctive evidence relations hold, a topic we leave for a later section.) Some skeptical partitionings of the statements into two classes are more illuminating than others, marking a natural distinction among types of statements with stable membership. Such is the distinction between statements about behavior in a setting and statements about felt psychological states. The skeptic's division is less illuminating when it simply reduces to the general point about whether given e we can know h, or gerrymanders the contours of the statement-classes solely to make the skeptical point, or when a statement can shift from one class to another with ease, for example from being about the future to being about the past, from being about something unobserved to being about it when observed, from being about the front of a surface to being about an undistinguished area.[59] Even the general point, though, is worth making; but correctly understood it is a point about our lack of knowledge (when e is all the evidence we have for h) that not-(e and not-*h*), not a point about our lack of knowledge that *h*. Furthermore, when *e* is just part of the evidence we have for *h*, even holding *e* fixed we may well know that *h* (given that *e*) and also know that not-(*e* not-*h*), *provided the rest of the evidence for h* would vary with the truth of *h*, thereby indicating *h*'s truth-value.

Details of Nonclosure

Knowledge is not closed under known logical implication; therefore some specific rules of inference also must exhibit nonclosure. Let us investigate a few details.

Knowledge is not closed (in general) under a known application of the principle of universal instantiation, which licenses the inference from 'For all x, Px' (written as "(x)Px") to '*a* is P', for arbitrary *a* (written as "Pa"). For if knowledge were closed under the known application of this more limited rule, it also would be closed under known logical implication in general.[60]

This result appears surprising, that someone may know that for all x, Px, without knowing that Pa for some particular *a* (he knows to exist). If a person knows that something is true of everything, won't he also know it is true of each particular thing?[61]

We can gain an intuitive understanding of how a person can know that everything is P without knowing of some particular specified thing that it is P, by recalling that knowledge involves a belief that somehow varies with the truth of what is believed. It might be that a person's belief that everything is P somehow varies with the truth of that, yet his belief that *a* is P, does not vary with the truth of *that*. If "everything is P" were false, then in that situation which would obtain, he wouldn't believe that everything is P. Suppose or assume that the situation that would obtain if "everything is P" were false is not the situation where *a* isn't P — rather it is one where something else *b* isn't P — and suppose that the person would realize then that *b* is not P, and so not believe that everything is P. Thus, he satisfies condition 3 for knowing that everything is P. Yet even so, he might fail to satisfy condition 3 for knowing that *a* is P; for it might be that if *a* weren't P, the person would still believe it was, and so he does not know *a* is P. The truth of the universal generalization that everything is P can vary without the truth of *a* being P varying, precisely in the case when if something weren't P, it would be something other than *a*. (If something weren't P, then that something, which was not P and which made (x)Px false, would be something other than *a*.) Thus, we have an intuitive argument for the result that not only is knowledge not closed in general under known logical implication, it is not (always) closed under known application of the rule of universal instantiation (even when this is known to be a valid rule). A person may know that everything is P without knowing that a is P, even though he realizes that Pa follows logically from (x)Px. There is a difference between knowing that everything is P, and knowing of each and every thing that it is P.[62]

Similarly, a person may know a conjunction without knowing each of the conjuncts. The knowledge of q, Kq, does not follow from K(p&q) and K(p&q $\dashv$ q). It may seem that this is an especially clear and close logical consequence and that knowledge should follow along with it when this entailment is known. But if we grant this, and maintain that knowledge is closed under known logical equivalence, then we will have the (undesired) result that knowledge is closed under known logical implication generally.[63]

S's belief that p & q tracks the fact that p & q; if it were true he would believe it, and if it were false he wouldn't believe it. It may be that if the conjunction p & q were false, it is the first conjunct p that would be false, and in that situation the person wouldn't believe p and so wouldn't believe p & q. However, it does not follow that his belief in q tracks the fact that q; for if q were false (which is not what would or might be the case if the conjunction were false − p would then be the culprit) he might still believe q. We can satisfy condition 3 for a conjunction by satisfying it for its most vulnerable conjunct, the one that would be false if the conjunction were false; it does not follow that we satisfy condition 3 for the other conjuncts as well.

So, we must adjust to the fact that sometimes we will know conjunctions without knowing each of the conjuncts. Indeed, we already have adjusted. Let p be the statement that I am in Emerson Hall, not-SK be the one that I am not on Alpha Centauri floating in that tank; since p entails not-SK, p is (necessarily) equivalent to p & not-SK. I know that p, yet I do not know that not-SK.

Also, it is possible for me to know p yet not know the denial of a conjunction, one of whose conjuncts is not-p. I can know p yet not know (for I may not be tracking) not-(not-p & SK). I know I am in Emerson Hall now, yet I do not know that: it is not the case that (I am in the tank on Alpha Centauri now and not in Emerson Hall).

However, we have seen no reason to think knowledge does not extend across known logical equivalence. When p entails not-SK and hence is known to be equivalent to p & not-SK, the person who knows p will know p & not-SK. I know I am in Emerson Hall now and not floating in that tank on Alpha Centauri; I believe it, and my belief tracks that conjunctive fact. If the conjunction weren't true, it is p that would be false (rather than SK's being true) and in that situation I would not believe I was in Emerson Hall. But, though I believe the second conjunct, not-SK, my belief in that (alone) doesn't track the fact; if SK were true, I would still believe not-SK. So I don't know not-SK.

Some people are convinced that the skeptic is wrong even in saying we don't know not-SK. Perhaps their conviction stems from the fact that we do know (and track) conjunctions that included not-SK. (It is perfectly true to say "I do know I am in Emerson Hall in Massachusetts and not in that tank on Alpha Centauri.") However, we cannot detach that conjunct; knowledge is not closed under inference of a conjunct. The feeling that the skeptic is wrong about our not not knowing not-SK may stem from our focusing on wider conjunctions we do know which include not-SK. Earlier, we said the skeptic could maintain his belief that we know practically nothing only when he attends to the possibility SK; when he focuses upon other statements *p* (other than not-SK) which do track, he too falls into thinking he knows it, until he attends again to his skeptical arguments and shifts his focus of attention to SK and to the specific belief that not-SK. Similarly, I think, the person who denies everything the skeptic says maintains his belief only by a shift of attention. He maintains his belief that he knows even not-SK only by shifting his attention to some other *p* (incompatible with SK) that is tracked, or to some tracked statement that includes not-SK as a conjunct. It is easier for the nonskeptic to shift his attention supportively than for the skeptic to shift attention to SK. There are so many different things the nonskeptic can focus on other than the isolated not-SK, thereby maintaining his position; while the skeptic has to stay with attention fixed on SK (or on the belief that not-SK) to maintain his position. Still, the position of each involves a shift of attention, an averting of gaze; only this slide into misfocus enables each to maintain his uniform position, be it that knowledge extends everywhere or nowhere.

Proof and the Transmission of Knowledge

We have seen that knowledge is not (in general) closed under the inference of a conjunct (called in the literature "simplification") or under the rule of universal instantiation, inferring an instance from a universal generalization, itself a kind of simplification. Is knowledge closed under the inference of existential generalization, inferring from 'Pa' the statement 'there is an x such that Px'? It seems that a person can track 'Pa' without tracking 'there is an x such that Px'. Condition 3 can be satisfied for one yet not for the other. If *a* weren't P, the person wouldn't believe it was; yet if there were not any x such that Px, perhaps he still would believe something was P (though he wouldn't believe this of *a*). But this apparent nonclosure result surely carries things too far.[64] I am now writing with a blue pen. I know the pen is blue. I realize this entails that something now is blue, and I know that something now is blue, even solely on the basis of this inference.

These last points about nonclosure under existential generalization (or under addition, inference of a disjunction that includes a premiss) cut things too finely. Surely our knowledge that p does not stand in such splendid isolation from knowledge of other things so closely connected to p. There is a further difficulty. The general view of knowledge as not closed under known logical implication appears incompatible with the fact that sometimes we come to know something via a deduction or proof. What a proof shows us is that the premisses logically imply the conclusion; but if knowledge is not closed under known logical implication then how could we ever come to know something via a proof? However, we have not said knowledge is never closed under known logical implication, that knowledge never flows down from known premisses to the conclusion known to be implied, merely that knowledge is not always so closed, it does not always flow down. This leaves room for sometimes coming to know something via a proof, for situations where because the premisses are known and known to logically imply the conclusion, the conclusion also is known. We need to identify and delineate which situations these are.

Under what conditions is knowledge transmitted from the premisses of a proof to its conclusion? (Of course, truth is transmitted always if the proof is valid.) It is not fruitful to look for a subset of the formal rules of proof that always preserves knowledge; whether knowledge is preserved will depend on what subjunctives are true of each step. It would be inadequate, though, merely to say that knowledge is preserved in cases where the proof is valid and the statement to be proven also is known in that it too satisfies the four conditions for knowledge. This would fail to explain how sometimes we can come to know something via a proof.

Let us adapt the four conditions for knowledge to our current concern of inferring q from p. S knows via inference (from p) that q if and only if

(1) S knows that p

(2) q is true, and S infers q from p (thereby, we assume, being led to believe that q).

If S is to know q via this inference, the third condition for knowledge will have to be satisfied, namely: if q were false then S wouldn't infer q from p. Most notably for our purposes, this will hold when and because: if q were false S wouldn't believe p (from which to infer q). Alternatively, it might be that if q were false S, though believing p, wouldn't make the inference of q from p. The following condition (call it "I" for *inference*) specifies when the inference of q from p (which is known) yields knowledge that q.

I: if q were false, S wouldn't believe p (or S wouldn't infer q from p).

When, for some skeptical hypothesis SK, an inference is made to not-SK from another statement *p* which is tracked and known, his condition I is not satisfied, and so one does not come to know that not-SK through that inference. Let *q* be the statement (not-SK) that S is not in the (relevant) tank on Alpha Centauri, and let *p* be the statement that S is sitting and reading in Massachusetts. S knows that *p* entails *q*, and infers *q* from *p* (and from many other things as well, but we may leave these aside, or imagine them included in the premiss *p* which becomes a very large conjunction). If *q* were false and he were floating in that tank, he still would believe *p* (and infer *q* from *p*). Thus, to show the inference to a conclusion *q* from a known premiss *p* yields knowledge that *q*, the condition I (for transmission of knowledge via inference) will have to be satisfied. In this case, in particular, we will need: if *q* were false S wouldn't believe *p*.* If the conclusion of the inference were false, he wouldn't believe the premisses.

This additional condition will be needed if the method of inferring *q* from *p* is to yield knowledge that *q*. But can't we view the method of arriving at belief that *q* as: inferring *q* from *p* which is tracked, that is, known to be true? When *p* entails *q*, if *q* were false the person would not be using *that* method to arrive at a belief that *q*, and so would not believe *q* via that method. So doesn't he thereby satisfy the third condition for knowledge that *q*: if *q* were false he wouldn't believe *q* via that method? The problem is that the method of inferring *q* from known *p* is indistinguishable by the person from the method of inferring *q* from (believed) *p*. We have said that knowledge is a real connection of belief to the world, tracking, and though this view is external to the viewpoint of the knower, as compared to traditional treatments, it does treat the method he uses as identified from the inside, to the extent it is guided by internal cues and appearances. Is he, basing his belief in the way he does (from the inside), actually in a subjective connection with the truth? But if we are willing to look at the actual factual connection externally, why don't we similarly view his method of arriving at belief on

---

*There are additional imaginable routes whereby if *q were false the person would not infer* *q* from *p*, thereby satisfying condition I and also the third condition for knowledge. One is that the inferential relation from *p* to *q* itself depends upon the truth of *l*, and so if *q* were false the inference could not be made. Since deductive relations are not dependent in this way, this consideration is irrelevant to our present concerns. Under the second additional route, if *q* were false the inference from *p* to *q* would not actually be made; if *q* were false the person wouldn't apply his inferential power to *p* or to the question of *q*'s truth, and so on. Here, however, the method is not held fixed. More relevant is the case where the person would apply his deductive powers but, if *q* were false, would not perceive the deductive connection between *p* (which he believes) and *q*. However, these additional considerations are so messy that, while a completely adequate theory would have to include them, the specification of condition I as

not-*q* → not-(S believes *p*)

is good enough for all our present purposes.

a particular occasion not from his viewpoint (from the inside), but as it really is externally? The notion of knowledge holds the method fixed (recall the grandmother case) but not that fixed — fixed enough only to exclude differences the person would detect, believing it to constitute a difference. The method used must be specified as having a certain generality if it is to play the appropriate role in subjunctives. This generality is set by the differences the person would notice; the methods are individuated from the inside. Otherwise, you needn't reach to inference to establish your knowledge that you are not floating in the tank on Alpha Centauri. You see you are not on Alpha Centauri, and via this method, externally specified, you track the fact that you are not — even though if you were it would seem perceptually the same as it does to you now. That perceptual seeming, though indistinguishable internally from your actual current seeing, is distinguishable externally as a distinct method, if such external individuation of methods is allowed to count. Would even Dr. Johnson have said, "How do I know I am not dreaming? By seeing what is in front of me"?

A person uses method M_1 to track the fact that p and used M_2 to deduce from p the conclusion that not-SK. He comes to believe not-SK via the method $M_1 + M_2$. But this (combined) method doesn't yield his tracking not-SK; for if SK were true, he still would believe, via $M_1 + M_2$, that not-SK.

Thus, if S is to know that q when he infers it from p, if the third condition for knowledge that q is to be satisfied (namely, not-$q \rightarrow$ not-S believes, via M, that q), then so must the following further condition: not-$q \rightarrow$ not-S believes p. A similar treatment is needed for the fourth condition on knowledge that q: $q \rightarrow$ S believes, via M, that q. If knowledge that q is to be gained by the inference of q from p, these additional conditions must be satisfied: $q \rightarrow$ S believes, via M, that p (or at least, not that if q were true S wouldn't believe via M that p); and also $q \rightarrow$ S, inferring q or inferring not-q from p, infers q from p. Previously, we said the person wouldn't believe the premiss if the conclusion were false; now we add: the person would believe the premiss (or at least: wouldn't stop believing it) if the conclusion were true.[65]

We do sometimes come to know something via a proof from known premisses, namely, when we wouldn't believe the premisses if the conclusion were false and we would (continue to) believe them if the conclusion were true. (I assume this case is one where we come to believe the conclusion via inferring it from the premisses.) These two conditions for knowledge being transmitted in the inference of q from p

not-$q \rightarrow$ not-(S believes that p)

$q \rightarrow$ S believes that p

are tracking conditions, like conditions 3 and 4 for knowledge, except that they state that S's belief that p tracks the fact that q. An inference yields knowledge of the conclusion, we now see, when the belief in the premisses tracks the truth of the conclusion.[66]

When the belief in the conclusion is based upon (because inferred from) the belief in the premisses, if this belief in the premisses does not track the truth of the conclusion, then the belief in the conclusion will not track its truth either. The belief in the conclusion will not be knowledge, will not track the fact, unless the belief in the premisses (from which it is inferred) tracks that very (conclusory) fact. It is not enough for the belief in the premisses to track some other fact, even if that other fact is the very fact stated in the premiss — that gives us knowledge just of the premiss, not of the conclusion.

The skeptic specifies possibilities SK so that, even when we deduce not-SK from some p, we violate the condition that SK → not-(S believes that p). In fact, they have been carefully designed so that SK → S believes that p; if SK were true, S still would believe p (and also believe not-SK). The inference from p to the nonskeptical conclusion not-SK does not yield knowledge, for the belief in the premiss (upon which the belief in the conclusion is based) does not track the truth of the conclusion.

We have said that when a person knows p and infers not-SK from p, where SK is the skeptic's possibility incompatible with p, then he does not know not-SK. His belief that not-SK does not track the fact that not-SK, nor does his belief that p. A person can know that p without knowing of "far out" possibilities incompatible with p, that they do not hold. It is otherwise with possibilities incompatible with p that are closer, for example, a possibility q_1 which would or might hold if p were not to hold. Call such a q_1, a first subjunctive alternative to p; p entails not-q_1, and if p weren't the case q_1 would be the case or at least might be; not-p → q_1, or at least not-(not-p → not-q_1). A second subjunctive alternative to p is a q_2 incompatible with p which would or might obtain if both p and q_1 did not. If a person knows that p is true, mustn't he also know that the first subjunctive alternative q_1 to p doesn't hold; mustn't he at least know of that alternative incompatible with p (as he doesn't know of SK) that it does not hold? We would not want to require or suppose that in order to know that p a person must know independently, apart from inferring this from p, that its first subjunctive alternative q_1 doesn't hold. That requirement would threaten to move us all the way up the line; to know that not-q_1 is also to know that its first subjunctive alternative doesn't hold, and so on. Or is this regress stopped by the simple knowledge that not-q_1?

Although the person who knows p need not know that not-q_1 independently of p, he will know it if (realizing that p entails not-q_1) he infers it from p. That inference puts him into a position of tracking not-q_1.[67] However, we cannot move up the line to more remote subjunctive alternatives q_m to p, to knowing that not-q_m by inferring it from p. For the inference to not-q_m from p will not preserve knowledge unless $q_m \rightarrow$ not-(S believes p). This last condition earlier set a limit to the transmission of knowledge via deductive inference; here it limits how remote are the subjunctive alternatives a person will know don't hold, via the deductive inference from p. However, our theory does have the consequence that when S knows that p, he can know, by inferring this from p, that p's first subjunctive alternative q_1 does not hold. Knowledge is not closed under known logical implication, yet the knowledge that p is not cut so finely that a person does not know, when he infers it, that the first subjunctive alternative to p doesn't hold. Under that inference (to the denial of what is a first subjunctive alternative — the person needn't identify it as such) knowledge is preserved.*

Return now to the inference of existential generalization. Earlier, the view of knowledge as tracking apparently led to the consequence that someone might know a is P, infer from this that something or other is P, yet not know (because he doesn't track) that. It was this unsatisfactory consequence that led us to worry that nonclosure involved too fine a delineation of our knowledge, and led us to investigate how (and under what conditions) it was possible to acquire knowledge via a deductive proof or inference, given that knowledge is not always closed under known logical implication. The crucial condition, we saw, is that the belief in the premises track the truth of the conclusion of the inference. Let us apply this now to the inference of existential generalization. Suppose that S knows (and tracks) Pa, by some method M_1, and let M_2 be his method of coming to believe 'there is something that is P' by (realizing it follows and so) inferring it from Pa. S knows 'there is something that is P' by the combination of the methods $M_1 + M_2$. If there weren't anything that was P, this combined method wouldn't yield his believing there was, or that Pa, for in that case of there being no P's, 'Pa' would be false, and since (by hypothesis) his belief that Pa tracks the fact that Pa, he wouldn't then believe that Pa — I leave aside a complication here — and so wouldn't then use it as a premiss from which to infer "there is something that is P." His belief in the premiss Pa tracks the truth of the conclusion "something is P," and so when he infers this conclusion, he thereby comes to know it.

---

*One might feel that tracking p does not give us knowledge when we don't know that all alternatives incompatible with p don't hold. For in that case, how can we find out that p holds? But "finding out" that p, is a notion like tracking; where q is some alternative incompatible with p which wouldn't hold even if p did not, we can find out that p without finding out that not-q.

Knowledge, almost always, will be closed under existential generalization.[68] Similar remarks apply to inferring a disjunction from a disjunct. In contrast, we can believe a conjunction without our belief tracking the truth of one particular conjunct; we can believe a universal generalization without our belief tracking the truth of one particular instance. (Here, I use "tracking" to refer to condition 3.) With these latter inferences, of course, sometimes the belief in the premisses will track the truth of the conclusion; in those cases the person will come to know the conclusion is true via the inference from the known premisses.

Knowledge also seems to be (always) closed under (known application of) adjudication: the inference from the two premisses p, q to the conjunctive conclusion p & q. Contrast evidential theories of knowledge which set a limit to how low the probability of a statement may be if it is to be known; it is known that under these theories adjudication can fail, since a conjunction (each of whose conjuncts has a probability less than unity) will have a lower probability than either of the conjuncts, and this lessening of probability may send it below the lower cutoff limit.

The fact of the nonclosure of knowledge under various known implications and entailments, at first surprising, has the side effect of helping to solve a little puzzle about evidence. I take this to support a theory of knowledge incorporating such nonclosure; it is difficult to see how else to solve the puzzle (while maintaining knowledge exhibits closure) without conceding too much to the skeptic.

This conundrum is due, I believe, to Saul Kripke.[69] Why should one look at or listen to arguments or evidence against what one knows? If p is true then all evidence showing (or tending to show) that p is false will be misleading. Someone who knows this and who knows that p is true will therefore know that all evidence against p is misleading. So wouldn't it be perfectly all right for him to ignore any evidence against p, to refuse to consider any evidence against p, for doesn't he already know that such evidence will be misleading? Why is it not all right for him to ignore such evidence? An adequate view of knowledge should illuminate and dispel this conundrum.

Rather than rest our discussion upon some particular theory of the evidence relation, let us suppose instead that all evidence relations are deductive. This simplification certainly does not make it easier to deal with the conundrum. For if such relations were all deductive, the case appears even stronger that a person may ignore such evidence, may ignore propositions entailing (and not merely otherwise supporting) the negation of what he knows. On the deductive view of evidence, adopted here only temporarily, we interpret evidence against p as statements that entail not-p. On this view, to say all evidence against p is

misleading is to say (r)(r —∃ not-p ⊃ *not-r), which is logically equivalent to p.* A person who knows one will know the other, and so we can
assume that K(r)(r —∃ not-p ⊃ not-r).

It will be legitimate for the person to ignore evidence *e* (against *p*)
only if he knows that (considering) evidence *e* will be misleading. A
person may know that *p* is equivalent to: all evidence against *p* will be
(to the extent that it is against *p*) misleading, in that it tends to get him
to believe something false (not-*p*) or not believe something true (*p*).
Since we are assuming knowledge is closed under known mutual entailment, he will know this latter general statement that all evidence
against *p* is misleading. However, he may not know of some particular
evidence *e* that it will be misleading (even though he thinks of it and
sees it conflicts with *p*); he can infer this instance from the general
statement by the rule of universal instantiation, but knowledge is not
always closed under known applications of this rule. So he does not
know that *e* is misleading merely by virtue of inferring this from the
general statement (by universal instantiation); it does not follow
merely from his knowing the general statement that he has this particular knowledge.

Does he know of the evidence that it would or will be misleading?
Does he know of *e* that ignoring it would not or will not be misleading?
If he does not know these things, it is not legitimate for him to ignore
the evidence *e*. Therefore, the nonclosure of knowledge under known
logical implication leaves room for a solution to the conundrum,
showing how the person may know *p* yet may not legitimately ignore
evidence *e* against *p*. Simply pointing to this room, however, does not
constitute a solution to the conundrum. For though knowledge is not
always closed under known logical implication, perhaps this is one of
the cases where knowledge is transmitted down to the inferred
conclusion.

Whether he knows of this evidence *e* that it would or will be misleading depends on whether his belief that *p* tracks the truth of this conclusion, tracks the fact that the evidence is misleading. This is the crucial
factor in determining whether, in inferring the conclusion from the
premiss, he knows the conclusion is true. Here, we have to investigate
what he would or might believe if the evidence weren't misleading:
would or might he continue to believe *p*, would or might he continue to
believe the evidence was misleading? Only then can we see whether
condition 3 is satisfied, whether he knows the evidence is misleading.
The details showing he does not know this consequence are messy, and
left as an exercise for excessively masochistic readers.

Not knowing of *e* that it is misleading, he may not legitimately simply ignore it, refusing to consider it as evidence against *p*. Various

statements about counterevidence to *p* do follow from the truth of *p*, but since knowledge is not closed under known logical implication, these are pruned away; what he knows is simply *p*, and this knowledge does not make it legitimate for him to ignore counterevidence.

Our view that knowledge is not closed under known logical implication has yielded, as a side effect a way of handling the conundrum. Other views of knowledge must show that they too can avoid its snares, without saying that we don't really know that *p*, or that we can ignore evidence only if we know we know that *p* but we never do, or any other similar skeptical move.

We should not conclude, however, that we can never ignore (purported) evidence against what we know. For example: we (or one of us) must examine evidence presented by the critics of the Warren Commission Report who hold that John Kennedy was killed by a conspiracy, but surely we can refuse to examine someone's presented evidence that Kennedy was killed by a conspiracy from Sirius. We need not examine every conspiracy or paranoid or crackpot batch of evidence; to delineate which (type) we may ignore is the job of a general theory of evidence.

We have said that whether knowledge is transmitted from premises down to an inferred conclusion depends not only on whether the conclusion follows, but also on whether the belief in the premises tracks the truth of the conclusion. Whether or not this (further) condition is satisfied is not settled by the formal character of the rule of inference. If a proof is something that always transmits knowledge (in contradistinction to truth, which is transmitted by valid deduction — of which there is a formal theory) then there is no formal theory of proof.[70]

Let us look more closely at this notion of proof. A proof, we have said, transmits knowledge. If there is to be a proof to S of *q* from *p* it must be that

(1) S knows that *p*.

Otherwise, there is no knowledge to transmit. Second, it must be that

(2) not-*q* → not-(S believes that *p*).

Otherwise, we have seen, knowledge will not be transmitted by the sequence of deductive or inferential steps, though truth may be, even when

(3) *p* entails (or logically implies) *q*.

However, an argument for *q* may satisfy all these conditions, yet still not be a proof that *q*, because it begs the question. An argument begs the question (as a proof) when, if S didn't know the conclusion, he wouldn't know (one of) the premises. We need to add the further condition

(4) not-(S doesn't know that $q \rightarrow$ S doesn't know that p).

A proof must pick its premises carefully; it must have premises which wouldn't be believed if the conclusion were false (point 2), but which might be known even if the conclusion weren't known (point 4).[71]

The subjunctive 4 talks of a particular person's knowledge; let us say that a proof begs the question for S when: if S weren't to know that q, he wouldn't know that p. And let us say that a proof is circular when it would beg the question for everyone, when it is and would be true for every person S that if he weren't to know that q then he wouldn't know that p.

Since the aim of a proof is to bring knowledge, the conditions for a proof's being circular or begging the question are stated in terms of knowledge. However, the goal might be to bring or transmit some thing other than knowledge; an argument, for example, aims at producing and transmitting belief or perhaps conviction. We may say that an argument from p to q begs the question for S when: if he weren't to believe q, he wouldn't believe p—and that an argument is circular if it would beg the question for everyone. Justification, on most views aims at producing something else: rational or justified be-lief.[72] A similar account can be offered of when a justification of q from p begs the question for a person, or is circular. These elucidations leave open the possibility that the very same movement from p to q may beg the question for one person but not for another, or may beg the question for someone as one of these things but not as another, as a proof but not as an argument, for instance.[73]

Skepticism Revisited

Knowledge is not closed under known logical implication. There are two ways to extend our notion of knowledge, as specified by condi-tions 1–4, in order to insure closure: the way of the skeptic and that of the anti-skeptic. Retaining "know" for our ordinary notion, the skeptic introduces a notion 'know*' that satisfies the following conditions:

(1) if S doesn't know that p, he doesn't know* that p

(2) if S knows that p entails q and S doesn't know that q, then S doesn't know* that p.

---

*But do I know: no doxically identical world of that sort obtains? No, but this is just one isolated thing I do not know, another not-SK.

His notion 'know*' is closed under known logical implication; under it we know* almost nothing. The skeptic might obtain his notion by requiring that

not-p → not-(S believes that p)

is true only if S wouldn't believe p both in the not-p situation or world that would obtain if p did not, and also in all not-p worlds doxically identical to the actual world. After all (he might say) we don't know we are not in one of those worlds.

On the other hand, the anti-skeptic introduces a notion 'know^' that satisfies these conditions:

(1) if S knows that p then S knows^ that p

(2) if S knows that p and S knows that p entails q then S knows^ that q.

His notion 'know^' is closed under known logical implication; under it we know^ quite a lot, including that we are not floating in that tank, and so forth.

Neither of these deductively closed notions is our own. Still, we can raise the question: if knowledge *were* deductively closed under known logical implication, would it be more like know* or like know^ ? If there were a notion N such that S N's that p if and only if

(a) p is true

(b) S believes p

(c) not-p → not-(S believes that p)

(d) p → S believes that p & not-(S believes that not-p)

and N were closed under N-ed implication (that is, if S N's that p and S N's that p entails q then S N's that q), then would we N quite a lot or almost nothing?

Perhaps we suspect the skeptic to be right subjunctively; perhaps we are troubled by the suspicion that if there were a notion worthy of being called KNOWLEDGE — I am tempted to write, in Hyman Kaplan fashion, K*N*O*W*L*E*D*G*E — the skeptic would be right about that notion. Do we think (why?) that for knowledge to be all it should be, it would have to be closed under known logical implication? For condition 3 to be so closed, whenever p entails q, the not-q situation or world that would obtain (if q did not) would have to be no farther from the actual world than the world that would obtain if p did not (the closest not-p world). But when this entailed statement q is not-SK, the statement that the skeptic's doxically identical world doesn't obtain, this would mean that SK is no farther from the actual world than any other not-p world is. In that SK world, we would continue to have the beliefs we do (almost all of them then being false); this has the consequence that almost all subjunctives of the form of 3, not-p → not-(S believes p), are false, thereby eliminating almost all cases of knowledge. Knowledge would be deductively closed only if the skeptic's imagined worlds SK would or might obtain if p weren't true; but then we would or might believe p even if it were false, and so we do not know that p.[74] Thus, if our notion of knowledge was as strong as we naturally tend to think (namely, closed under known logical implication) then the skeptic would be right. (But why do we naturally think this? Further exploration and explanation is needed of the intuitive roots of the natural assumption that knowledge is closed under known logical implication.)

The skeptic might ask whether we know he is not right. If he says

s: we know practically nothing

then I do know that not-s. I correctly believe s is false; and if s weren't false if it were true, I wouldn't then believe not-s. For if s were true, it wouldn't be because some doxically identical world existed; in the not-s world that would obtain if s were false (which is not the skeptic's imagined world SK) I wouldn't continue to believe not-s.* However, suppose I am wrong about this; suppose that if s were true (not-s were false) it would be a skeptic's doxically identical world SK that obtained wherein I would continue to believe not-s. So I don't know not-s; I don't know it is false that we know practically nothing. Yet it does not follow from this that I don't know that I am now sitting while writing on paper, for instance — call this p. Perhaps if not-s were false I still would believe not-s. Be that as it may, still, if p were false, I wouldn't believe p. (Even if the skeptic's doxically identical world SK would obtain if not-s were false, that does not mean it, SK, would obtain if p were false.)

The skeptic need not merely put forth s, of course. He may also put forward a full-blown skeptical theory SK which includes s and which is doxically identical to the actual world (as s alone is not) — and we will not know this skeptic's theory SK is wrong. However, it will not follow from this that you don't know you are now reading a book, for example, any more than that followed from your not knowing other not-SK's, such as that you are not floating in that tank.

One skeptic says we don't know we are not floating in the tank and therefore we don't know that p. That skeptic's "therefore" is wrong. Another skeptic may actually put forward as true the hypothesis that I am in a doxically identical world SK in which almost everything I believe is false. I do not know his hypothesis is false — but still I know that *p.* This skeptic may say: "if you don't know my hypothesis is false, then perhaps you know that *p*; but you certainly don't know that you know. How can you know you know that *p*, unless you know that my skeptical hypothesis SK does not hold? Perhaps skeptical arguments don't show you know practically nothing, but they do show you don't know you know much of anything."

This skeptical argument trades on some purported closure property of knowledge; our suspicions should be aroused, therefore. I interpret this skeptic's argument (where SK is his skeptical possibility about person S) as beginning with

(a) SK → not-(S knows that *p).*

If S is floating in the tank, he does not know that *p* (whether or not *p* is true); if S is dreaming, he does not know that *p*, even if *p* happens also to be true. (G. E. Moore refers to the story of someone who dreamed he was speaking in the House of Lords only to wake up and discover that he was speaking in the House of Lords.)[75]

Moreover, the skeptic assumes the person S knows proposition a, and also that he knows the contrapositive of it. So we have the skeptic's second assumption:

(b) S knows (S knows that *p* → *not-SK).*

His third assumption is the (correct) hypothesis:

(c) not-(S knows that not-SK).

From these, the skeptic could derive the conclusion that

(d) not-(S knows that S knows that *p*)

if he had use of the closure principle:

S knows that (S knows that *p* → r) & S knows that S knows that *p* → S knows that *r*.

This principle may have more appeal than the simple closure principle (of which it is a special instance): S knows that '*p* entails *q*' and S knows that *p* → S knows that *q*. However, it fails because (and when) the skeptic's possibility SK is not the first subjunctive alternative to S's knowing that *p*. It is possible for a person's belief that he knows, his belief that Kp, to vary subjunctively with the truth of Kp, while his belief that not-SK does not vary subjunctively with the truth of not-SK.

It is worth noting that, and why, the skeptic tries to prove something stronger than is necessary for the truth of his thesis. We will not know *p* if there is a *q* incompatible with *p* such that we don't know that not-*q*, while yet if *p* were false *q* might be true. Whether or not we could know not-*q*, if we actually don't know not-*q*, we do not know *p*.

We will know almost nothing if this situation holds true of almost everything we believe, that is, if

I. For almost all p, there exists a q such that q entails not-p and q might be true if p were false, and we do not know that not-q.

This says that for each p, there is some q or other which . . . ; it need not be the very same q for every p. The skeptic however attempts to prove I by introducing his skeptical possibility SK — this one possibility is to do the job for almost every p. That is, the skeptic argues for

II. There is a q such that for almost every p, q entails not-p and q might be true if p were false, and we do not know that not-q.

He suggests SK is such a possibility q, serving for all p. Statements II and I are very similar, but with the order of the quantifiers reversed. Statement II is stronger than I, and implies it; if the skeptic's argument did establish II, he also would have shown that I holds. The problem, as we have seen, is that in specifying one possibility SK to do the job for almost every p, he has specified one so remote that it would not hold even if p did not; he has specified an SK such that not-$p \rightarrow$ not-SK. Thus, his possibility SK does not satisfy the middle clause of II (that the possibility might hold if p were false), and so does not show that II is true. The economical way to establish I is by producing one q that makes it true, that is, to show the truth of II. It is not surprising that no example serves to show II is true; any q that is incompatible with almost every p and is not known to be false will be so remote that the middle clause will not be satisfied. There is no one q incompatible with most of what we know such that for each piece of our knowledge, that q also would or might obtain if the thing known did not obtain.

The skeptic needs, yet cannot find, an SK incompatible with almost every (supposedly known) p, that also is a first subjunctive alternative to each and every one of these p's. No wonder he cannot find a possibility that establishes his point in one fell swoop.

Since the argument for I via II is bound to fail, the skeptic must seek an argument for I that does not go through II. It is not clear what such a general argument would be like — one almost would have to believe there was an actual demon who strewed the world with different pitfalls q_i, one for each p_i we believe. The prospects are not bright for less bizarre skeptical arguments, in view of our earlier observation that if S knows (and tracks the fact) that p, and S infers not-q_i from p, where q_i is the first subjunctive alternative to p, then S knows that not-q_i.

Knowing That One Knows

The topic of knowing that one knows is interesting in its own right, apart from the skeptical arguments purporting to show this knowledge almost never occurs. According to our account of knowledge as tracking, to know that one knows that p is to truly believe that one knows that p, and to have this belief track the fact that one knows. Spelling it out further, this belief that one knows tracks the fact of tracking that p; that is, the belief that one knows tracks the fact that one's belief that p tracks the fact that p. Thus, with knowledge that one knows that p, there is tracking embedded in tracking—a particular tracking is tracked.

Some writers have put forth the view that whenever one knows, one knows that one knows. There is an immediate stumbling block to this, however. One may know yet not believe one knows; with no existing belief that one knows to do the tracking of the fact that one knows, one certainly does not know that one knows.* Even the weaker thesis that S knows he knows that p whenever he believes truly that he knows that p fails. Nor is this surprising. We have held that knowledge is a certain factual relationship of the belief that p to the fact or truth believed, a relationship specified by the subjunctive conditions 3 and 4. To know that p is to actually be related to the world in a certain way, namely, to track it. But the nature of the tracking relation is such that you can track the fact that p without also tracking the fact that you are tracking p. Your belief that p may somehow vary with the truth of p even though your belief that you are tracking does not vary with truth of "you are tracking p." If knowledge is a real relationship in the world, such as tracking, then it will be a fact that you stand in that relationship to p; so room will be left for failing to stand in that very (tracking) relationship to the fact that you stand in it to p. If the knowledge relationship is a stringent one, not easily satisfied, there will be many cases of knowing without knowing that one knows.

Is there some argument of the skeptic which, while failing to show lack of knowledge that p, at least shows lack of knowing one knows that p? We might imagine two skeptics: the first claims that for almost all the p you think you know, you do not, while the second claims that for almost all the p you think you know, you do not know you know it. The first skeptic's problem was that since knowledge is a real relationship in the world, that of tracking, his imagined possibility doesn't show that relationship does not hold. The second skeptic faces a similar problem. How can his imagined possibility show a real relationship (of tracking) does not hold to another fact: that tracking holds to p? The skeptic's doxically identical possibility SK, for example, of an evil

---

*A person who knows that p might not believe he does because he doesn't believe he satisfies conditions 3 and 4, even though he does actually satisfy these conditions. We might say that someone S is a stickler about his beliefs if for all p, S believes that $p \rightarrow$ S believes that he knows that p, or at least, for all p, S believes he doesn't know that $p \rightarrow$ S does not believe that p. A stickler about his beliefs would not believe something he didn't think he knew, or at least, that he thought he didn't know.

demon or of floating in a tank, did not show the falsity of condition 3, not-p → not-(S believes that p). For even if p were false his possibility SK wouldn't hold, anyway. Similarly, his possibility will not show the falsity of

not-3 → not-(S believes that 3)

when even if 3 were false his possibility SK also wouldn't hold; that is, when

not-3 → SK does not hold.

The skeptic's possibility SK can show that a certain (purportedly real) subjunctive relationship does not hold in the world, only when SK is the first subjunctive alternative to the antecedent of that subjunctive relation, that is, only if SK would (or might) hold if the antecedent didn't. To show the factual (subjunctive) relationship does not hold, he would have to show that SK is the relevant first subjunctive alternative. Even if it is not, his possibility SK might show that the person doesn't know he knows . . . he knows, that is, that there is some limit to the iteration of the knowledge operator K.[76]

Some remarks are in order about the n-fold iteration of K, K^n. People who know that p will differ in the n up to which they K^n that p. Perhaps some differences between people in their depth of understanding p are reflected in differences in the n up to which they K^n that p. And some channels that can transmit knowledge (K^1) from one person to another need not be able to transmit a person's full knowledge, his full K^n. People sometimes speak not merely of knowing that p, but of knowing for certain that p. Perhaps this should be interpreted as claiming an even stronger relation of tracking than 3 and 4 put forth. But there is another possibility, that of interpreting "knowing for certain that p" as meaning KKp. On this view, even to know for certain that p would not exclude all (distant) possibility of mistake.

It may seem strange that on our view a person can know up to a certain level, without knowing exactly up to which level he knows. Suppose $K^3p (= KKKp)$, yet not-K^4p. Suppose also that the person knew that he was at exactly this third level, KK^3p & K not-K^4p. but KK^3p just is K^4p, which we already supposed was false. If we knew precisely where we were, we would not be there but up one more level instead. Therefore, we should expect that if we are at some finite level K^np, we will not know exactly at which level we are. The width of the interval in which one can know one falls must be greater than one, greater than an exact position; we shall not undertake to investigate various conditions that might limit the width this interval can take.

III. EVIDENCE

In treating knowledge as a real subjunctive relation between belief and fact, holding in the world, we have said nothing thus far about evidence or justification, topics other views take to be central to the subject of epistemology, if not to constitute it. These other views sometimes view knowledge simply as justified true belief or true belief on the basis of (adequate) evidence. The tradition cannot have been wholly mistaken. These notions surely have something to do with knowledge, and an adequate theory of knowledge as tracking should delineate, at least roughly, what this linkage is, and show why it was plausible to take evidence and justification as definitive of knowledge. What follows is only a sketch of the domain, as it connects with the tracking view of knowledge; we ignore much of the relevant technical details, hoping these will not require a significant alteration in the following overview. Although an adequate view of knowledge as tracking will say something about evidence, it need not, we should emphasize, say what follows. This part of the chapter is one way of elaborating the first two parts — it does not underlie them.

The Evidential Connection

What is evidence, what is the connection between evidence e and a statement or hypothesis h for which it is evidence? The evidential connection is a subjunctive one. Let us begin with the simplest model, then work our way to slightly more complicated cases.

Evidence for a hypothesis is something that would hold if the hypothesis were true. If e is evidence for h, then

(a) $h \rightarrow e$; if h were the case e would be the case.

However, this is not sufficient for an evidential connection between e and h; for perhaps e would hold anyway, even if h were not true. In that case, e's holding is no evidence for the truth of h. Let us add, then

(b) if h weren't true, e wouldn't hold; not-$h \rightarrow$ not-e.

In this situation, where e would hold if h did and would not hold if h did not, let us say that e is strong evidence for h.

From conditions a and b, along with the statement that the evidence does hold,

(c) e,

we can deduce the hypothesis h. From the holding of the evidence, plus the fact that that evidence is strong evidence for the hypothesis, the truth of the hypothesis (logically) follows.

The subjunctive conditions a and b are tracking conditions; they specify that evidence *e* stands in the same relationship to the hypothesis as belief does to the truth when belief tracks the truth. Conditions a and b correspond to conditions 4 and 3, respectively, in our account of knowledge. Strong evidence tracks the truth of what it is evidence for; let us say it strongly tracks the truth of that for which it is evidence.

Consider someone who believes *h* on the basis of his belief in (what is) strong evidence *e*; his belief that *h* depends upon (and varies with) his belief that *e*. And let us suppose he knows the evidence is true, his belief that *e* tracks the fact that *e*. In this case, his belief that *h* tracks his belief that *e* (because it depends on it) which in turn tracks the fact that *e* (because he knows that *e*) which in turn tracks the fact that *h* (because, by hypothesis, *e* is strong evidence of *h*). Thus, there is a tracking chain. Although tracking sometimes can fail to be transitive, with the relevant qualifications and details filled in, transitivity will obtain. The person's belief that *h*, because it tracks *e* which tracks *h*, will track the fact that *h*. Since his belief tracks the fact, the person knows that *h*. To believe something *h* on the basis of (what is) strong evidence *e*, where *e* is known, is to know *h*.

Consider the (nondeductive) inference from *e* to *h*. Under what conditions will a person know *h* which he infers from known *e*? We have seen that knowledge is not always closed under known logical implication; the critical condition for the transmission of knowledge down to the conclusion, in a deductive inference, was that the belief in the premisses tracked the truth of the conclusion. Although deductive implication preserves truth its crucial feature in transmitting knowledge is this tracking condition. Knowledge also can be transmitted by a nondeductive inference (treated as the employment of a method M) provided that belief in the premisses tracks the truth of the conclusion. In evaluating nondeductive inferences, we consider how (well, frequently, and so on) the belief in the premisses tracks the truth of the conclusion; the standard for evaluating particular nondeductive inferences, and general modes of nondeductive inference, is a complicated one which makes reference to tracking. When *e* is known and *e* is strong evidence for *h*, the inference of *h* (from *e*) yields knowledge that *h;* the belief in the premisses (the evidence) strongly tracks the truth of the inferred conclusion (the supported hypothesis). The subjunctive conditions written as plausible for the relation of strong evidence to hypothesis turn out to be the very conditions crucial for the (knowledge-preserving validity of the inference from evidence to hypothesis.

Unfortunately, the evidence we have for hypotheses is not usually strong evidence; too often although the evidence would hold if *h* were true, it also might hold if *h* were false. Earlier, we said that if *e* would hold also if *h* were false, if not-*h* → *e*, then *e* is not evidence for *h* at all. The denial that *e* would hold (also) if *h* were false, is:

(b') not-(not-*h* → *e*); if *h* were false, *e* might be false.

This b' is weaker than the earlier b which said that if *h* were false, *e* *would* be false; under b' *e* only *might* be false (if *h* were false). When b' holds but the stronger b does not, if *h* were false then *e* might be true and might be false. When conditions a and b' both hold, the evidence *e* would obtain if *h* were true and might not obtain if *h* were false. Let us say in this situation that *e* is weak evidence for *h*, and that this evidence *e* weakly tracks *h*.[77]

Consider the notion of a test of a hypothesis. To test a hypothesis *h* is to look for data that would not hold if *h* were true. Finding that data, call it not-*e*, counts against the truth of *h* — *h* fails the test. To say data not-*e* would not hold if *h* were true is to say

(a) *h* → *e*; if *h* were true *e* would hold.

It would not be a real test of *h* to look for particular data not-*e* that wouldn't hold even if *h* were false — failure to find that (held) would not signify that *h* had passed any test. Someone who looks only for those not-*e*'s that are so outlandish that even if *h* were false they wouldn't hold runs little risk of discovering *h* is false. To test *h* is to look for data not-*e* that might actually hold if *h* were false, that is, to look for data not-*e* such that

(b') not-(not-*h* → *e*); if *h* were false, *e* might be false, not-*e* might hold.

A severe test will look not only for data not-*e* that might hold if *h* were false; it will look for data not-*e* that would hold if *h* were false. A severe test satisfies a condition stronger that (b'), namely,

(b) not-*h* → not-*e*; if *h* were false, not-*e* would hold, and *e* would not.

To test *h* severely is to look in just the place where *h* would (turn out to) be false if it were false. And *h* fails the test if data not-*e* is discovered to hold true; it passes the test if *e* is discovered to be true.

These conditions for a test, and for a severe test, are the very same conditions as the ones for evidence, weak and strong. A test of *h*, however, seeks the opposite of evidence; it seeks data not-*e* while the evidence (for *h*) would be *e*. A test of *h* looks for the falsity of what, if true, would be weak evidence for *h*; a severe test looks for the falsity of what, if true, would be strong evidence for *h*.* Experimental science is a testing of hypotheses, manipulating conditions (and controlling other variables) so that the subjunctives (or their probabilistic variants) hold true; artificial conditions are created so as to connect a particular hypothesis *h* with observable data by the subjunctive evidential relations.[78]

Evidence Based on Probability

We have seen that the inference of *h* from (known) evidence *e* that is weak does not yield knowledge that *h*; in this case, the belief in the premisses (the evidence) does not (strongly) track the truth of the conclusion (the hypothesis *h*). When evidence *e* weakly supports *h*, how weak is the support it provides? To answer intuitively, that depends on whether the 'might or might not' applying to *e* when *h* is false is closer to a 'would' or to a 'would not.' Just as *e* is not evidence for *h* when *e* would hold even if *h* were false, so too *e* is not very significant evidence for *h* when, if *h* were false, although *e* *might* not hold it almost certainly or most probably would. Leaving the notion unexplained for now, let us write "prob (e, h)" for the probability that *e* would hold (occur, be true) given that *h* is true.[79]

Our first condition (a), $h \rightarrow e$, can be represented as

prob (e, h) = 1;

while the second condition (b) for strong evidence, not-*h* → not-*e*, can be represented as

prob (e, not-h) = 0.*

Tentatively, let us specify a measure of support as follows:

support (e, h) = prob (e, h) − prob (e, not-h).

The support of *e* for *h* is the difference between the probability of *e* given *h* and the probability of *e* given not-*h*. This degree of support has

---

*Evidence need not be obtained in the course of a test, of a procedure intending to test (although how it is obtained will affect the probabilities to be mentioned below). What is crucial about evidence, and the inferences based upon it, is which subjunctives hold. We seek facts for which such subjunctives hold, that is, we test and sometimes severely; but its being evidence does not depend on our seeking it — we can just stumble across evidence. If the evidential effects of tests could be had only by searching, then we could not ever have evidence for a hypothesis about a phenomenon that includes (postulated) interaction effects with an observer so that the phenomenon does not occur when the hypothesis is tested. We can come across such evidence unsought, though.

*In treating a probability of 1 or 0 as identical to its being the case than an event would or would not occur, I ignore sets of measure zero. Though I am writing as if numerical probability values can be assigned, much of what I say below can be reformulated using only the qualitative terms "almost certain," "almost impossible."

an upper value of 1, when the first probability is 1 and the second zero. It is equal to zero when the two probabilities are equal, in which case *e* gives *h* zero support. However, when the probability of *e* given not-*h* is greater than the probability of *e* given *h*, then the support (*e, h*) takes on a negative value, and can reach as low as -1.[80]

The answer to our question of how much support weak evidence gives to its hypothesis, when condition b' holds, depends on the probability of *e* given not-*h*, prob (*e,* not-*h*). The smaller this is, the greater the support that *e* gives to *h*.

Just as we have weakened condition b to consider b', where *e* might or might not occur if not-*h* were true, so also we can consider a relationship weaker than '*h* → *e*' as the relationship between the hypothesis and evidence for it. We can, that is, consider situations where it is not guaranteed that if *h* were true, *e* would hold; however, although *e* might not hold, it almost certainly would. In these situations, the prob (*e, h*) is less than 1 but very close to it. Such cases are common in statistical practice; for example, *h* may be a hypothesis about a proportion of something or other in a population, or about a chance mechanism having a certain outcome (a coin coming up heads), while *e* is evidence about the proportion of something or other in a sample drawn (in a specified way) from the population, or about the results of a certain number of operations of the chance mechanism (the proportion of heads in a certain number of tosses of that coin). These are not situations where if the hypothesis *h* were true then the evidence would (definitely) have a specified character; rather, there are various probabilities of obtaining various outcomes or data if the hypothesis were true. If the coin were "fair," having an equal probability of giving heads or tails on each toss, then it would be very likely that 100 heads would not be tossed in a row on the first hundred tosses — it would be very unlikely that tosses of that character would be made. Such tosses would be evidence against the coin's being fair.

Thus, we are set adrift on the perilous more general case where neither *h* → *e* nor not-*h* → not-*e* holds, yet these are approximated by the probabilities, prob (*e, h*) and prob (*e,* not-*h*), so the degree of support of *e* for *h* is very high.[81]

Let us pause to say a word about how 'not-*h*' is to be treated here. Since it appears in subjunctives (or subjunctively related statements), it is to be understood as what would or might be the case if *h* were false; 'not-*h*' includes all those h_i which might hold if *h* were false, all the h_i such that not-(not-h → not-h_i). How are we to understand the probability of *e* given not-*h*? Suppose that *e* would occur if one of the h_i held, say h_1, but would not occur if any of the other h_i (which are first subjunctive alternatives to *h*) held. The probability of *e* given not-*h* then depends on (and is equal to) the probability of h_1 given not-*h*. And though prob (e, h_1) is (we are supposing) equal to 1, the prob $(e, \text{not-}h)$ is very small, because prob $(h_1, \text{not-}h)$ also is very small. In assessing by how much evidence e supports hypothesis h, we shall have to take account of such a possibility h_1, even though it is buried in not-h.[82] But let us leave that matter aside for now.

Inference Based on Probability

We have formulated a measure of the degree of evidential support of e for h, but what are we to do with this measure, what use are we to make of it? We wish to see how a person might base his belief that h upon the evidence for it, the evidential support. For other purposes, one might need only a procedure for assigning degrees of belief to various hypotheses or for acting in situations of uncertainty or risk; however, for our purpose here, the upshot is to be belief that h.

It has seemed reasonable to many that we should believe h when its support is very high, close to 1. When evidence e is obtained (and we have no other evidence) that is very likely if h were true, and very unlikely if h were false, then it has seemed plausible to propose that we should believe (on the basis of e) that h is true. Taking a probability of .05 to demarcate 'almost impossible,' and .95 to demarcate 'almost certain,' the following is the inference proposed:

From prob $(e, h) \geq .95$
   prob $(e, \text{not-}h) \leq .05$
   e

infer h.

Evidence e has been obtained, but if not-h held it would be very unlikely ($\leq .05$) that e would obtain; on the other hand, e's obtaining is very likely ($\geq .95$) if h were true — we therefore conclude, on the basis of e, that h is true. If not-h were true, then e's holding would be the holding of a very improbable thing. It seems reasonable to conclude that nothing so improbable has occurred in this situation, and therefore that not-h is false, h is true. Note that it is not enough merely that e be very improbable given not-h, that prob $(e, \text{not-}h) \leq .05$. For perhaps e is very improbable no matter what, including given h. In that case, clearly, we should not conclude that not-h is false, merely because e (which occurred) was very improbable given not-h. The premiss that prob $(e, h) \geq .95$ also is needed in the inference.

Although this specified inference looks quite plausible, we must scrutinize it more carefully. Merely from the facts we have been given

e
prob $(e, h) \geq .95$
prob $(e, \text{not-}h) \leq .05$

can we reasonably conclude, does it follow, that *e* most probably arose from *h* (rather than not-*h*)? We cannot. How it is most likely that *e* arose depends also on how probable *h* was, and how probable not-*h* was, apart from *e*. Even if it is very improbable that *e* given that not-*h*, if it is much more improbable that *h* holds at all, then it may well be that *e* arose from not-*h* after all. Letting $prob_0$ (*h*) represent the initial or otherwise determined probability of *h*, and $prob_0$ (not-*h*) that of not-*h* (where these sum to one), then the probability of *e* occurring is the sum of its conditional probabilities of occurring, as weighted by the probabilities of that upon which it is conditional. Thus prob (e) = prob (e, h) $\times$ $prob_0$ (h) + prob (e, not-h) $\times$ $prob_0$ (not-h). Which way it is most probable that *e* arose depends on which of the two weighted conditional probabilities is greater, prob (e, h) $\times$ $prob_0$ (h) or prob (e, not-h) $\times$ $prob_0$ (not-h). So it is rash to make the previously proposed inference without taking any account of information about the probabilities of *h* and of not-*h* themselves — (as they are called in the literature) the prior or a priori probabilities of *h, and of not-h.*

There is a developed body of theory, Bayesian statistics and decision theory, which takes such prior probabilities heavily into account. From the point of view of a methodology to arrive at belief (rather than merely degrees of belief, or optimal actions under risk or uncertainty), belief that is to be closely connected with knowledge (tracking), this Bayesian emphasis on prior probabilities is too heavy.*

---

*Some philosophers have based theories of the acceptance of hypotheses upon Bayesian or more general decision-theoretic considerations in another way. Taking the rule of maximizing expected utility from decision theory, these theorists delineate epistemic or cognitive utilities whose expected value is then to be maximized by a decision about acceptance of a hypothesis. (The most elaborate development and exposition of such a view is found in Isaac Levi, *Gambling with Truth,* Knopf, New York, 1967; that project is continued in Levi's *The Enterprise of Knowledge,* MIT Press, Cambridge, 1980, to which also the strictures of this note apply; see especially his chapters, 2, 4–8.) However, one cannot simply assume that it is the expected value of epistemic utilities that is to be maximized. Within writings on decision, it was a matter of some controversy whether (higher moments of) variance also should be taken account of in a decision rule.

It was the accomplishment of John von Neumann (in the appendix to the second edition of his work with O. Morgenstern, *Theory of Games and Economic Behavior,* Princeton University Press, Princeton, 1947) to show that the (interval scale) measurability of utility followed from a set of plausible normative conditions on preference among probability mixtures, and that preference went along with the expected value of this defined function, utility. Essentially, utility was *defined* as that function whose expected value was to be maximized. To take the simplest case, where *a* is the most preferred alternative and *z* is the least, it follows from the conditions, when *m* is an intermediate alternative, that there is a unique probability *p*, between zero and 1, such that the person is indifferent between the option of *m* (for sure) and the probability mixture of *a* with probability *p* and *z* with probability (1-p), written pa, (1-p)z. Utility numbers are assigned to *a* and *z* arbitrarily, subject only to the constraint that u(a) > u(z), and the utility of *m*, u(m), is defined as $p \times$ u(a) + (1-p) $\times$ u(z). Similarly for the utility of any other intermediate alternative. The rest of the von Neumann conditions function to guarantee that everything works out, multiplies through all right, and so on. It might seem to trivialize the rule of maximizing expected utility to define utility as that function whose expected value is to be maximized. What was not trivial was to formulate conditions which

Rather than incorporate Bayesian considerations into (the previous conditions in) the principle of inference, we can impose them as a constraint upon the principle. The intuitive rationale behind the previously formulated principle was that we should conclude something very unlikely was not happening; since e was very unlikely given not-h, and was likely given h, we should, the principle said, conclude not-h was not true. However, if the guiding (rough) intuition is that the very unlikely is not happening, then we shouldn't conclude that not-h is false and therefore that h is true without first checking to see whether h also isn't very unlikely (in that it has a very low prior probability).

The revised principle of inference, then, is the following.

From prob $(e, h) \geq .95$
      prob $(e, \text{not-}h) \leq .05$
      e
      $\text{prob}_0(h) > \text{prob}(e, \text{not-}h)$

infer h

If $\text{prob}_0(h)$ is low, yet e has occurred, then something unlikely holds true, either e or h. It seems reasonable to conclude that h is true in this situation only when it is the lesser improbability, when it is more probable that h than that e given not-h.

This revised principle of inference gives some role to judgments of

---

guaranteed the existence of a function that behaved appropriately so that the (trivial) definition then could be offered.

Von Neumann's theory essentially ended the controversy over whether it was expected utility that should be maximized — although some bit continued in discussions of whether the underlying conditions on preference among probability mixtures should be satisfied, in discussions of the utility of gambling, and so on. Other writers were not in a position to say there is (a coherent notion of) utility, but that its expected value should not be maximized. The only coherent notion in the field was that defined and specified so as to fit the rule of maximizing expected utility, which rule thus flourished and won theoretical adherents. Other axiom systems for measurable utility were proposed which involved direct ordering judgments of differences (see Chapter 5 below, note 87); these left open the question whether it was the expected value of utility, thus measured, that was to be maximized in situations or risk.

When some other things are specified as goals on the basis of cognitive criteria, such as informativeness, and these somehow are measured so that numbers are assigned, it cannot be assumed that (in probabilistic situations) it is the expected value of these things that is to be maximized. Calling these other desirable things (cognitive or epistemic) utilities does not help. Since these "utilities" are specified independently of the von Neumann conditions and hence independently of the rule of maximizing expected utility, there is no reason to think this rule should be applied to these things. Since the question of the appropriate decision rule for these things is left completely open, the old controversies will return (along with some new ones).

The moral of this story is that though technical results can provide suggestive analogies elsewhere, when they are moved out of their home area they do not carry with them their support or authority, perhaps not even their meaning.

prior probability, as a constraint on when we can conclude that something with a low probability or plausibility is true. However, though the revised principle allows prior probabilities sometimes to block beliefs, it does not allow them a central role in giving rise to beliefs. It is a defect of Bayesian procedures that very high but uninformed prior probabilities will lead (when the evidence is not heavily against them) to high posterior degrees of belief. Our principle does allow prior probabilities to thwart believing what the evidence supports, but not to require believing what the evidence is neutral toward or opposes. The principle we have formulated, a sufficient condition for belief, makes evidence the central factor in producing belief.[83] It is some such principle, mirroring subjunctive tracking relations, that is an appropriate principle of inference.

However, I would not want to rest much on precisely what is sketched here. My departmental colleagues are meticulous intellects who instill in students the importance of mastering all the details whereof they speak; while I think it important for students also to learn how (and when) to *fake* things, to glide over topics with a plausible patina, trusting (fallible) intuitions that something like what they say, something of that sort, can be worked out — preferably by someone else. I agree, of course, that sometimes gliding over the details shields one from seeing that one's general conception just cannot be worked out, and a very different one is needed. (I learned this lesson as a graduate student from C. G. Hempel, who did not glide over details). On the other hand, often the details merely reinforce a picture, adding nothing of real philosophical interest. What then can one do but follow one's hunches? I mention this now, because of a special worry: while I think the general subjunctive picture of evidence is correct, and that some principle of inference embodying it is appropriate, I also believe that serious flaws may be uncovered in the particulars of the proposals here. It is many years since I have thought carefully about probabilistic inference, then along different lines than now, so I feel on very shaky ground in this section, suspecting that even points and details I previously knew might overturn things I say here.

We now need, I think, to introduce explicitly the alternative hypotheses h_1, h_2 . . . which fall under not-h, which might hold if h were false. One way would be to use the previous principle only when: there is no h_1 that might be true if h were false that also satisfies the conditions of the principle, so that

prob $(e, h_1 \geq .95$
prob $(e, \text{not-}h_1) \leq .05$
$\text{prob}_0 (h_1) > \text{prob} (e, \text{not-}h_1)$.

More to the point is to add: and there is no h_1 that might be true if h were false, that also is unexcluded by previous applications of the principle (that is, not-h_1 hasn't already been concluded via the principle), such that prob (e, h_1) < .05. This is a stringent addendum: no other unexcluded h_1 that might hold gives e a probability greater than .05. (But the path of weakening it ends at a Bayesian assignment of degrees of belief.)

In specifying the principle of inference, we have required that prob (e, h) be ≥ .95, and that prob (e, not-h) be ≤ .05. This guarantees that the support of e for h, defined as the difference between the two conditional probabilities, is at least .9. Perhaps it is sufficient to require simply this, that support (e, h) ≥ .9; this would allow prob (e, h) to dip below .95 toward .9 provided the prob (e, not-h) dipped correspondingly.

When support (e, h) ≥ .9, we have a situation which approximates (strong) tracking. So the method of inference (when the premisses all are made explicit, and hold true) gets us close to (strong) tracking. That prob (e, h) ≥ .95 is almost like 'h → e' (especially since we are imagining that some account of the probability of e given h is given that builds on the nature of subjunctive conditionals and is designed to approximate them); that prob (e, not-h) ≤ .05 is almost 'not-h → not-e'. Should we say that a person who infers h from e in such a situation knows that h is true (when h is true)? It seems to me more accurate to say — and why should we not? — that the person almost-knows. On the basis of the information about the tosses of the coin, or the properties of the sample, we do not know the coin or population has a certain specified other feature, as connected in the inference, but we almost-know it. In almost-knowing, our belief stands in a real, probabilistic connection to the fact, a connection that barely falls short of tracking. In failing only by a little to know, we succeed in something almost as good. Some problem cases the tracking account excluded, with discomfort, from knowledge now can get classified as almost-knowledge.

Let me say a brief word about how these very general considerations connect with current approaches to statistical theory. Our concept of evidence is a likelihood concept, based on the probabilities of the evidence on various hypotheses.[84] The principle of inference we formulate, a sufficient condition for believing h, uses this likelihood notion. We constrain the operation of this principle (as a sufficient condition) by the requirement that the prior probability of h be greater than the probability of e on not-h. Although this Bayesian consideration constrains our principle, we have not put forward a program of determining degrees of belief by application of Bayes Theorem, a process heavily dependent on the choice of prior probabilities; high prior probabilities cannot fix belief by themselves in the absence of sufficient empirical evidence.

The principle of inference takes as premisses prob (e, h) $\geq$ .95; prob (e, not-h) $\leq$ .05. These probability values within the principle are meant to approximate the nonprobabilistic subjunctives $h \rightarrow e$ and not-$h \rightarrow$ not-e. How closely to zero and one these values are set is to some degree arbitrary; how close is a "good enough" approximation to the subjunctives? However, this degree of approximation is not part of a decision problem, to be fixed by various practical losses or gains. Though these numbers resemble the Neyman-Pearson values for errors and nonerrors,[85] their rationale as an approximation of the nonprobabilistic evidential subjunctives is different. Still, external to the formulated principle of inference, we can ask what the probabilities are that it will be utilized to accept h when h is false (a type II error) or to fail to accept h when it is true (a type I error). Since our principle is a sufficient condition for belief, into which different evidence can be fed, the issue is more cloudy than it appears at first. With h fixed, what is the probability that some evidence or other e' will be found such that prob (e', h) $\geq$ .95, and so forth, while yet h is false? When a particular e is specified in advance, discussions of the likelihood relations need to distinguish e holds true, from e is found or known to be true but not as part of a test procedure wherein the character of e is fixed in advance, and from e is found to be true within such a specified test procedure. Each of these can have a different probability given h (or given not-h), and so the evidential likelihoods will depend on precisely which evidence it is.

Even if things about the type of evidence e are dovetailed correctly, we cannot conclude simply from the premiss within the inference (to h) that prob (e, not-h) $\leq$ .05, to the conclusion about this inference that it will have a probability of type II error (accepting h when it is false) of less than .05. The relevant question is not one about the probability given not-h, that this principle will lead to the acceptance of h. Rather, since e already has been found and h already has been accepted, the question is: given that e and that h has been accepted according to the principle, what is the probability that h is false, that not-h is true? The probability of type II error cannot be simply computed from the application of the principle of inference, without more precise knowledge of the prior probabilities (via Bayes Theorem).[86] Here the Neyman-Pearson theorist enters, saying we should not use a principle of inference unless its probabilities of type I and type II errors can be fixed at certain magnitudes.[87] And so on into the controversies of current statistics. My purpose is not to solve these controversies and issues, merely to show the relation of our notion of evidence to them — strong evidence avoids them altogether while being sufficient for tracking and knowledge, weak evidence (unfortunately) encounters them.* Probability numbers enter into the discussion in two places, within the premisses as likelihoods, and in evaluations of the principle of inference as (estimates of) the probabilities of type I and type II errors. These numbers are not unconnected, but they have different rationales and play different roles.[88]

The Contingency of the Evidential Tie

The evidential connection is a subjunctive one, a real factual relationship which holds in the world. Whether or not e is evidence for h depends on what factual empirical connection holds between e and h. The dominant view on the evidential relation in the philosophical tradition, however, has held it is a logical connection, one which holds necessarily if it holds at all. Hilary Putnam has pointed out that such views (unrealistically) assume evidence is assessed relative to the best possible formulatable theory.[89]

Whether we hold e is evidence for h depends on what other theories we accept connecting e and h; we assess (whether something is) evidence for h against a background of theory, other beliefs, and so on. If relative to these other theories and beliefs that we accept, the relevant subjunctives (or probabilistic connections) hold between e and h, then we will hold that e is evidence for h. If later we discover that one of our background assumptions is false, so that the relevant subjunctive connections did not actually hold, we will say that e was not evidence for h after all, though we thought it was; just as when we later discover some p is false, we will say we didn't know that p, but only thought we knew it. This is not to say that there can never be evidence for something false. Perhaps e did arise from not-h, even though prob (e, h) is very much greater than prob (e, not-h), even though e is evidence for h. The fact upon which e's being evidence depends is not h's being true, but e's standing in a factual probabilistic relation to h (were it to hold), and also in one to not-h, of lesser magnitude. If we discover that (by our best later accepted theory) actually prob (e, h) $\leq$ prob (e, not-h), we will, in looking back, say that e was not evidence for h after all.

Granting that these factual probabilistic and subjunctive connections between e and h are crucial to the evidential status of e, cannot we

---

*The tracking account of knowledge was formulated without having statistical errors in mind, but conditions 3 and 4 can be (roughly) put as: the person wouldn't commit a type II error about p, and he wouldn't commit a type I error about p. In contrast to Neyman-Pearson testing, our discussion of knowledge (though not the mere statement of the conditions, each of which was given equal weight as necessary conditions) seemed to make avoiding type II errors more crucial than avoiding type I errors, so that in their terminology, the power of a test should be fixed as high, and the level of significance minimized subject to that.

still treat 'evidence for' as a formal logical relation simply by making explicit the background beliefs and theories, by including them in? First, it is unclear whether those background theories will entail the subjunctives or probabilistic connections, but second, into where are they to be built? If into the evidence, added to e to form a new conjunction e', then this plays havoc with foundationalist hopes in epistemology, a major motive for the construction of formal inductive logics; while if the theory and other beliefs are to be added to the hypothesis, forming a new conjunctive hypothesis, it is difficult to see how such hypotheses will get supported by such meager evidence e. Still, perhaps these points can be handled by ingenious technical devices. The major objection to the program of formulating an inductive logic within which evidential relations are formal or logical or necessary still stands. The evidential relations really are factual and contingent; the point of making the background context and theories explicit would be to guarantee these factual connections hold. But this strategy will not work, for even if these connections do hold in the wider context, this context can be embedded in a still wider one that undercuts the subjunctive's holding, a context relative to which there are different factual probabilistic connections between h and e.[90] This kind of contingency of the relevant evidential subjunctives is not adequately handled by the (at least) two relativities already present within inductive logics: that probability is relative to evidence, and that some principle of total evidence is to be utilized in applications of probability statements.

Other formalist attempts have been made, apart from inductive logic, to specify evidential relations, for example, that data e is evidence for what would explain e.[91] When the appropriate explanatory connection holds, the subjunctive ones also will, and it is on the latter that the evidential connection rests. There are many instances of an evidential connection without that explanatory one: seeing lightning is evidence that a sound of thunder will follow, though it is the former that explains the latter; seeing one of a disease's unique symptoms is evidence for the presence of another one, although neither explains the other — each is explained by a third thing. I do not deny that explanatory connections somehow weave through the fabric of the subjunctive and probabilistic connections; although if there is some fundamental correlational law, irreducibly probabilistic, between the two features connected thereby there will be no explanatory link — yet each is evidence for the other. (Don't say the correlational law makes each the explanation of the other.)

Only if the factual subjunctive or probabilistic relations actually hold between e and h is e evidence for h; whether these do will not depend on formal features of e and h, but on what other truths hold, what specific deeper explanatory theories, and so on. But might there not be some very general contingent truths whose holding is sufficient to establish the requisite factual subjunctive or probabilistic connections between statements as specified on the basis of their formal features and relations; mightn't the general statement show (given it) that certain formally related statements also are factually related? It is as attempts at this that we should see Keynes' principle of limited variety, principles of the uniformity of nature, and other postulational or presuppositional approaches to induction.[92]

Is There Evidence for Skepticism?

Let us pause to note the relevance of this notion of evidence to skeptical hypotheses SK. The skeptic produces a hypothesis SK relative to which everything still would seem the same to us, including all of the evidential data e we have, our observations and so on. Is the sum total of this evidential data evidence for the skeptical hypothesis SK? It fits the skeptical hypothesis, for the skeptical hypothesis was designed to fit it. If the skeptical hypothesis were true, this data e (still) would hold:

(a) SK → e.

However, this does not settle the question of whether e is evidence for SK, for perhaps e would or might hold even if SK did not. We need, that is, to consider whether

(b) not-SK → not-e;

only if b holds will e be strong evidence that SK. Clearly, b does not hold, however; for one other thing that might hold if SK did not is the usual situation, the situation as we nonskeptics usually view it, and in this case e also would hold. There is no strong evidence for the skeptical hypothesis SK. Is there any weak evidence? Here, we have to consider whether

(b') if SK were false, e might not hold; not-(not-SK → e);

and if b' does hold, we must consider whether

prob (e, SK) − prob (e, not-SK) > 0.

The skeptic's alternative SK is specified so that prob (e, SK) = 1; but there is a similar nonskeptical alternative h specifiable (though not specifiable simply as not-SK) which might hold if SK did not, such that the probability of e given it also is 1. There is an asymmetry, however, for this alternative h might (indeed perhaps would) hold if SK did not, while SK *wouldn't* hold even if h did not.

Thus, assuming the subjunctives are as we think, there is not evidence for the skeptic's hypothesis SK, even though this hypothesis is in conformity with all the data and would yield it. But although there is no evidence for the skeptic's hypothesis SK, and there is evidence for *h* (since SK is not, we assume, something that might hold if *h* did not), still, we do not know not-SK. Our belief that not-SK does not track that fact, and we have no evidence that not-SK. (Such evidence would have to be something that wouldn't also hold if SK did; but SK leaves all our observations the same.) The subjunctively constituted notion of evidence, too, exhibits nonclosure under logical implication.[93]

Knowledge, Evidence, and Justification

In contrast to more traditional treatments of justification, some recent writing has held that a person's belief is justified if the method via which the person arrives at the belief is reliable, is likely to produce mostly true beliefs.[94] It is a delicate task to state adequately this probabilistic fact about the method M via which the belief is arrived at, to specify the propensity interpretation of probability or the appropriate narrow reference class.* However, our purpose is not to linger over the details, but to notice that this view of justification externalizes it, just as we already (in comparison to traditional epistemological writings) have externalized knowledge and evidence.

On this account, when a belief is arrived at by a method that usually (more than half the time) is right, or at least is likely to be right, the belief is probably true and the person is justified in holding it. More generally, one might say the person is justified to degree *n* in his belief if the method is reliable to degree *n*, having that probability of yielding the truth.

We shall follow the externalized treatment of justification as reliability, but without holding that some particular degree of reliability is either sufficient or necessary for the belief's being justified. Even if a method M_1 has a reliability with regard to *p* of greater than ½, if it is not the most reliable method available to the person (with regard to the salient type of belief which *p* is) then the person is not justified in believing *p*. (I here omit considerations of cost; perhaps the other more reliable method takes much time and energy to apply.) To be justified

---

*Which is the reference class of belief acquisitions within which the method is reliable and has a high proportion of successes? Not the class of actual belief acquisitions thus far, for an unreliable method may be accidentally lucky until now, or a reliable one unlucky so far; not the class of all possible belief acquisitions, for a method's reliability is unaffected by the fact that it would frequently fail in situations that would not arise. Is the appropriate reference class those situations that might arise in the actual world, and how is this to be spelled out? Thus, there are problems in specifying the reference class, even apart from the difficult ones about delineating appropriate narrowness.

It might also be worth investigating a stronger notion of reliability, one wherein the application of a method reliably yields knowledge (tracking) rather than simply truth.

in his belief, the person must reach it by the most reliable appropriate method. Second, if this method has a degree of reliability less than ½, but still is more reliable than yet other methods, a person will be justified in believing on its basis. Scientific methods need not yield true theories more than half the time for us to be justified in believing their results — they just have to be better methods than anything else available to us.* (Notice that we have structured the notion of justification in the best instantiated realization mode.)

There was evolutionary selection for believing via particular methods when that was the best available, even if the reliability was less than ½; also, against believing by methods with reliability greater than ½ when even better are available. None of the rest of our discussion, though, will depend on this point that arising via the most reliable method is necessary and sufficient for a belief's being justified.

The reliability of a method is its probability of yielding true beliefs. A statement about reliability looks at the body of beliefs yielded and says something about the percentage which is true, rather, about the probability that each is true. Reliability is a connection between belief (by the method) and truth, in the direction from belief to truth: if belief (by the method) then probably true. This direction is opposite to the direction of tracking, of subjunctive conditions 3 and 4 which have truths in the antecedents and belief or lack of it (by the method) in the consequents. When tracking holds, if it is true (false) you would (not) believe it — when reliability holds, if it is believed (by the method) then it (probably) would be true. It is important to keep these directions distinct, as it is to be clear about the direction in assessing type I and type II errors. There is a distinction between the probability that a specified method gets you to believe p given that it is false, and the probability that p is false, given that a specified method has persuaded you to believe it. The first concerns whether the method approximates tracking, the second concerns its reliability. (Recall now the principle of inference we formulated, and consider the directions of the likelihood probabilities within the premisses, and of the type II error evaluations about the mode of inference.)

Let us briefly consider some questions about the relationships among knowledge, evidence, and justification. Can one know without evidence? A person can believe without having inferred it from any-

---

*Better for reaching narrowly specific beliefs; otherwise a more reliable method might be to believe not-p when scientific methods yield particular p's.

Consider also the case of newspaper stories. Every story about which I have had firsthand knowledge I have known to contain errors of fact. I believe therefore that almost every newspaper story does. Still, when I read a story, I believe each statement (and also the conjunction); I do not know which the falsehoods are, or in which direction the story is false, so, for lack of a better alternative for arriving at such beliefs, I believe the story as written.

thing else; a person might wake up each morning with a belief about which horse will win a horse race that day.[95] If the subjunctives do hold, although we may not understand the mechanism whereby they do, he knows — and not by (even let us suppose unconscious) inference from evidence. Still, when a person knows that p there is a fact available to him that is evidence that p. For when he knows that p, his belief that p tracks the fact that p. Thus, the fact that he believes that p (a fact I assume is accessible to him) is strong evidence that p. Conditions 3 and 4 for tracking in our account of knowledge

not-$p \rightarrow$ S does not believe p
$p \rightarrow$ S believes p

are also the conditions for S's believing p being strong evidence that p. Hence, whenever someone knows that p, he "has" strong evidence that p, namely, the fact that he believes that p; but this will not be evidence *from* which he arrives at his belief. In the horse race example, knowing of his past history of successes, the person might use the fact that he has a belief as an indicator, as evidence on which he bases very strong confidence — which he did not have before — about which horse will win the race.

A person may believe that p on (weak) evidence that p without knowing that p. However, perhaps there is this connection between evidence and knowledge: though truly believing on (perhaps weak) evidence does not entail knowledge, it is evidence for knowledge. For it seems plausible that truly believing p on the basis of e which is evidence for p, itself stands in the subjunctive evidential relation to conditions 3 and 4 for tracking.

Justified true belief is not sufficient for knowledge (recall the Gettier examples); a true belief may be arrived at by a reliable method without the belief tracking the truth. What about the other direction — whenever someone knows that p will he also have a justified true belief that p? Not if a person can believe via a method that is highly unreliable (and less reliable than others available to him) yet which not only yields the truth that time but also tracks that one time. However, since tracking involves some generality to other (subjunctive) situations, it seems plausible that whenever a person knows, there will be some reliable submethod via which he knows. So it seems plausible that justified true belief is a necessary condition for knowledge; but I prefer to leave this question unsettled. A further relation is worth mentioning: although justified true belief is not sufficient for knowledge, it does seem to be evidence for knowledge, to stand in the evidential relation to the holding of the tracking conditions 3 and 4.

What of the relationship of evidence and justification — is believing something on the basis of evidence a reliable method, a method that yields justified belief? When the inferential method based upon evidence is the principle we put forth earlier, with prob (e, h) ≥ .95 and prob (e, not-h) ≤ .05, then when the prior probability of *h* is greater than .05, the posterior probability of *h* (on *e*) will be greater than ½. But we cannot say that principle is reliable (to degree greater than ½) when it accepts an *h* whose prior probability is greater than .05, for factual probabilities and subjective priors cannot be combined in this way.[96] However, according to our earlier view of justified belief as one based on the most reliable relevant method, the question is whether believing on evidence is the method most reliable.

Knowing Inside Out

The account we have offered treats knowledge as a real subjunctive relation to the world, tracking, and it treats evidence as a real factual (subjunctive or probabilistic) relation in the world. Moreover, we have referred to an account of justification as the factual (dispositional) reliability of the method via which something is believed. These accounts are all external; what has become of epistemology, the subject which treats how, as things appear from the inside, a person builds up his body of knowledge?[105] About each such external fact, concerning the tracking or reliability or evidential connection of our belief, it is logically possible that we could be mistaken; we could think the fact holds when it does not really, and it could hold when we don't think so. So we seem as distant from these facts of tracking, reliability, and evidential connection, as we were from the fact that *p*. Knowledge was supposed to connect us closely with the fact that *p*, yet apparently it turns out that the connections of knowledge (tracking, reliability, evidence) are no clearer to us than *p* was. What we want is some connection with the fact that *p* that links it all the way to us, all the way to us on the inside. Given the skeptical arguments, it seems that nothing else could show us that we know. (Did he not show me his new baseball glove, because the glove was *out there*?)

These notions of 'inside' and 'external' are unclear but evocative. We might describe an internalist, more precisely, as someone who believes that if *q* is (known to be) entailed by S's knowing that *p*, and if S does know that *p*, then S knows that *q* also. If the internalist is right, we know each and every precondition of our knowing—whenever we know we also know that we know, and so on. Notice that so delineated, internalism goes beyond the condition of deductive-closure extensively discussed earlier; under internalism not only does the person who knows that *p* know every consequence (known to be one) of *p*, he also knows every consequence (known to be one) of knowing *p*.

Let us not, however, overemphasize the externality of our accounts.

It is your belief that is connected by the tracking relation to the facts; moreover, when a method shows an inner face, tracking via the method depends on what would happen in other situations identical in inner cues. And the notion of justification (in contrast to that of tracking) starts from the belief end and works toward the facts.

Still, although the (external) fact that p is linked to us, even to something internal (such as belief might be), the connecting link itself is external to us. So this linkage is out of our (let us say) ken; even if we have a belief about this linkage which tracks it, *that* tracking linkage is out of our ken.

How could things be otherwise? If there is an external fact to which we are linked, then eventually the linkage must turn external. (Or else there must be an external gap between the end of the connecting link and the fact — but then are we linked to *it*?) You can't get there from here, by staying here. And it is certainly there that we want to get; when various philosophical reductionisms (such as Berkeley's and phenomenalism) make there a version of here, we say they have not gotten us to where we want to be, to an external reality that exists independently of us. Neither do we want the gap closed by the externalization of ourselves, omitting relfexive self-consciousness, so that we were there all the time.

Any theory of knowledge that succeeds in connecting us with some external fact (we know) will make some part of the linkage external. Different theories may draw the boundary in different places, but each will countenance some externality — this in virtue of not flaws in us as connectors but the character of that to which we are to be connected. The transition to externality may be camouflaged, there may be internal glimmerings of the closest external portion, but (at least part of) the linkage between these internal glimmerings and the external portion itself will be external. Even if some internal item said of itself that it was connected with something external, there would be the question (marking a gap) of whether it was — unless the saying made it so. (A performative account of externality seems unpromising, but could one be offered of the epistemological connection itself?) The solipsist who is happy in his solipsism will face an opposte predicament, worrying that perhaps it happens that he *is* linked externally. Can anything internal show him he is not?

Perhaps it is the narrowness of the tracking relation that makes externality seem so salient. If belief varied with the fact across a wider range of possible situations than the tracking subjunctives specify, would our connection to the fact seem closer? If it varied with the fact in all possible worlds, would it be close enough? Or would we need also to believe in this wider or complete variation, and also to have that belief widely or completely vary with its truth, and so forth?

Yet if we had that complete linkage, would it be with something external? When something is external, isn't there a gap between us and it, and so room for something (else) to intervene and prevent complete covariation across all possible situations between it and, say, our belief? And is this lack of complete and universal covariation a consequence of externality, involving (as it does) a gap, or is it a defining feature of externality? Is something external in virtue of its lack of universal covariation?[106] Still, though we want some failure of covariation, we might prefer that our beliefs covaried far more widely with the facts than is specified by the tracking subjunctives.[107] Yet this would not check or satisfy the internalist desire of the epistemologist, who insists on having his external reality and eating it too. . . .

NOTES

6. Despite some demurrals in the literature, there is general agreement that conditions 1 and 2 are necessary for knowledge. (For some recent discussions, see D. M. Armstrong, *Belief, Truth and Knowledge,* Cambridge University Press, 1973, ch. 10; Keith Lehrer, *Knowledge,* Oxford University Press, 1974, chs. 2, 3.) I shall take for granted that this is so, without wishing to place very much weight on its being belief that is the precise cognitive attitude (as opposed to thinking it so, accepting the statement, and so on) or on the need to introduce truth as opposed to formulating the first condition simply as: p.

I should note that our procedure here does not stem from thinking that every illuminating discussion of an important philosophical notion must present (individually) necessary and (jointly) sufficient conditions.

7. Below, we discuss further the case where though the fact that p causes the person's belief that p, he would believe it anyway, even if it were not true. I should note here that I assume bivalence throughout this chapter, and consider only statements that are true if and only if their negations are false.

8. See Robert Stalnaker, "A Theory of Conditionals," in N. Rescher, ed., *Studies in Logical Theory* (Basil Blackwell, Oxford, 1968); David Lewis, *Counterfactuals* (Harvard University Press, Cambridge, 1973); and Jonathan Bennett's critical review of Lewis, "Counterfactuals and Possible Worlds," *Canadian Journal of Philosophy,* Vol. IV, no. 2, Dec. 1974, pp. 381–402.

Our purposes require, for the most part, no more than an intuitive understanding of subjunctives. However, it is most convenient to examine here some further issues, which will be used once or twice later. Lewis' account has the consequence that $p \rightarrow q$ whenever p and q are both true; for the possible world where p is true that is closest to the actual world is the actual world itself, and in that world q is true. We might try to remedy this by saying that when p is true, $p \rightarrow q$ is true if and only if q is true in all p worlds closer (by the metric) to the actual world than is any not-p world. When p is false, the usual accounts hold that $p \rightarrow q$ is true when q holds merely in the closest p worlds to the actual world. This is too weak, but how far out must one go among the p worlds? A suggestion parallel to the previous one is: out until one reaches another not-p world (still further out). So if q holds in the closest p world w_1 but not in the p world w_2, even though no not-p world lies between w_1 and w_2, then (under the suggestion we are considering) the subjunctive is false. A unified account can be offered for subjunctives, whatever the truth value of their antecedents. The p neighborhood of the actual world A is the closest p band to it; that is w is in the p neighborhood of the actual world if and only if p is true in w and there are no worlds $w^{\bar{p}}$ and w^p such that not-p is true in $w^{\bar{p}}$ and p is true in w^p, and $w^{\bar{p}}$ is closer to A than w is to A, and w^p is at least as close to A as $w^{\bar{p}}$ is to A. A subjunctive $p \rightarrow q$ is true if and only if q is true throughout the p neighborhood of the actual world.

If it is truly a random matter which slit a photon goes through, then its going through (say) the right slit does not establish the subjunctive: if a photon were fired at that time from that source it would go through the right-hand slit. For when p equals A photon is fired at that time from that source, and q equals the photon goes through the right-hand slit, q is not true everywhere in the p neighborhood of the actual world.

This view of subjunctives within a possible-worlds framework is inadequate if there is no discrete p band of the actual world, as when for each positive distance from the actual world A, there are both p worlds and not-p worlds so distant. Even if this last is not generally so, many p worlds that interest us may have their distances from A matched by not-p worlds. Therefore, let us redefine the relevant p band as the closest spread of p worlds such that there is no not-p world intermediate in distance from A to two p worlds in the spread unless there is also another p world in the spread the very same distance from A. By definition, it is only p worlds in the p band, but some not-p worlds may be equidistant from A.

Though this emendation allows us to speak of the closest spread of p worlds, it no longer is so clear which worlds in this p band subjunctives (are to) encompass. We have said it is not sufficient for the truth of $p \rightarrow q$ that q hold in that one world in the p band closest to the actual world. Is it necessary, as our first suggestion has it, that q hold in all the p worlds in the closest p band to the actual world? Going up until the first "pure" stretch of not-p worlds is no longer as natural a line to draw as when we imagined "pure" p neighborhoods. Since there already are some not-p worlds the same distance from A as some members of the p band, what is the special significance of the first unsullied not-p stretch? There seems to be no natural line, though, coming before this stretch yet past the first p world. Perhaps nothing stronger can be said than this: $p \rightarrow q$ when q holds for some distance out in the closest p band to the actual world, that is, when all the worlds in this first part of that closest p band are q. The distance need not be fixed as the same for all subjunctives, although various general formulas might be imagined, for example, that the distance is a fixed percentage of the width of the p band.

I put forth this semantics for subjunctives in a possible-worlds framework with some diffidence, having little inclination to pursue the details. Let me emphasize, though, that this semantics does not presuppose any realist view that all possible worlds obtain. (Such a view was discussed in the previous chapter.) I would hope that into this chapter's subjunctively formulated theoretical structure can be plugged (without too many modifications) whatever theory of subjunctives turns out to be adequate, so that the theory of knowledge we formulate is not sensitive to variations in the analysis of subjunctives. In addition to Lewis and Stalnaker cited above, see Ernest W. Adams, *The Logic of Conditionals* (Reidel, Dodrecht, 1975); John Pollock, *Subjunctive Reasoning* (Reidel, Dodrecht, 1976); J. H. Sobel, "Probability, Chance and Choice" (unpublished book manuscript); and a forthcoming book by Yigal Kvart.

9. G. C. Stine, "Skepticism, Relevant Alternatives and Deductive Closure," *Philosophical Studies,* Vol. 29, 1976, p. 252, who attributes the example to Carl Ginet.

10. This last remark is a bit too brisk, for that account might use a subjunctive criterion for when an alternative q to p is relevant (namely, when if p were not to hold, q would or might), and utilize some further notion of what it is to rule out relevant alternatives (for example, have evidence against them), so that it did not turn out to be equivalent to the account we offer.

11. More accurately, since the truth of antecedent and consequent is not necessary for the truth of the subjunctive either, 4 says something different from 1 and 2.

12. I experimented with some other conditions which adequately handled this as well as some other problem cases, but they succumbed to further difficulties. Though much can be learned from applying those conditions, presenting all the details would engage only the most masochistic readers. So I simply will list them, each at one time a candidate to stand alone in place of condition 4.

(a) S believes that not-$p \rightarrow$ not-p.

(b) S believes that not-$p \rightarrow$ not-p or it is through some other method that S believes not-p. (Methods are discussed in the next section.)

(c) (S believes p or S believes not-p) $\rightarrow$ not-(S believes p, and not-p holds) and not-(S believes not-p, and p holds).

(d) not-(S believes that p) $\rightarrow$ not-(p and S believes that not-p).

(e) not-(p and S believes that p) → not-(not-p and S believes that p or p and S believes that not-p).

13. Gilbert Harman, *Thought* (Princeton University Press, Princeton, 1973), ch. 9, pp. 142–154.

14. What if the situation or world where he too hears the later false denials is not so close, so easily occurring? Should we say that everything that prevents his hearing the denial easily could have not happened, and does not in some close world?

15. This reformulation introduces an apparent asymmetry between the consequents of conditions 3 and 4.

Since we have rewritten 4 as

p → S believes that p and not-(S believes that not-p),

why is 3 not similarly rewritten as

not-p → not-(S believes that p) and S believes that not-p?

It is knowledge that p we are analyzing, rather than knowledge that not-p. Knowledge that p involves a stronger relation to p than to not-p. Thus, we did not first write the third condition for knowledge of p as: not-p → S believes that not-p; also the following is not true: S knows that p → (not-p → S knows that not-p).

Imagine that someone S knows whether or not p, but it is not yet clear to us which he knows, whether he knows that p or knows that not-p. Still, merely given that S knows that _____, we can say:

not-p → not-(S believes that p)
p → not-(S believes that not-p).

Now when the blank is filled in, either with p or with not-p, we have to add S's believing it to the consequent of the subjunctive that begins with it. That indicates which one he knows. Thus, when it is p that he knows, we have to add to the consequent of the second subjunctive (the subjunctive that begins with p): S believes that p. We thereby transform the second subjunctive into:

p → not-(S believes that not-p) and S believes that p.

Except for a rearrangement of which is written first in the consequent, this is condition 4. Knowledge that p especially tracks p, and this special focus on p (rather than not-p) gets expressed in the subjunctive, not merely in the second condition.

There is another apparent asymmetry between the antecedents of the two subjunctives 3 and 4, not due to the reformulation. When actually p is true and S believes that p, condition 4 looks some distance out in the p neighborhood of the actual world, while condition 3 looks some distance out in the not-p neighborhood, which itself is farther away from the actual world than the p neighborhood. Why not have both conditions look equally far, revising condition 3 to require merely that the closest world in which p is false yet S believes that p be some distance from the actual world. It then would parallel condition 4, which says that the closest world in which p yet p is not believed is some distance away from the actual world. Why should condition 3 look farther from the actual world than condition 4 does?

However, despite appearances, both conditions look at distance symmetrically. The asymmetry is caused by the fact that the actual world, being a p world, is not symmetrical between p and not-p. Condition 3 says that in the closest not-p world, not-(S believes that p), and that this 'not-(S believes that p)' goes out through the first part of the not-p neighborhood of the actual world. Condition 4 says that in the closest p world, S believes that p, and that this 'S believes that p' goes out through the first part of the p neighborhood of the actual world. Thus these two conditions are symmetrical; the different distances to which they extend stems not from an asymmetry in the conditions but from one in the actual world — it being (asymmetrically) p.

16. D. M. Armstrong, *Belief, Truth and Knowledge* (Cambridge University Press, 1973), p. 209; he attributes the case to Gregory O'Hair.

17. Some may hold the father is made more sure in his belief by courtroom proof; and hold that the father knows because his degree of assurance (though not his belief) varies subjunctively with the truth.

18. If there is no other such method M_1 via which S believes that p, the second clause is vacuously true.

Should we say that no other method used outweighs M, or that M outweighs all others? Delicate questions arise about situations where the methods tie, so that no subjunctive holds about one always winning over the other. It might seem that we should require that M outweigh (and not merely tie) the other methods; but certain ways of resolving the ties, such as not randomly deciding but keeping judgment suspended, might admit knowledge when a true belief is arrived at via a tracking method M which is not outweighed yet also doesn't (always) outweigh the others present. There is no special need to pursue the details here; the outweighing condition should be read here and below as a vague one, residing somewhere in the (closed) interval between "outweighs" and "not outweighed," but not yet precisely located. This vagueness stands independently of the refinements pursued in the text immediately below.

19. When a belief is overdetermined or jointly produced by three methods, where only the first satisfies conditions 3 and 4, the question becomes: what does the person believe when M_1 recommends believing not-p while the two others each recommend believing p? Notice also that in speaking of what would happen in Case III we are imposing a subjunctive condition; if there is no "would" about it, if in each instance of a Case III situation it is determined at random which method outweighs which, then that will not be sufficient for knowledge, even though sometimes M_1 wins out.

It is worrisome that in weakening our initial description of outweighing by looking to Case III but not to Case II, we seem to give more weight to condition 3 for tracking than to condition 4. So we should be ready to reconsider this weakening.

20. For example, in the case of the father who believes on faith that his son is innocent and sees the courtroom demonstration of innocence, does the father use two methods, faith and courtroom demonstration, the second of which does satisfy conditions 3-4 while the first (which outweighs it) does not satisfy 3-4; or does the father use only one method which doesn't satisfy 3-4, namely: believe about one's son whatever the method of faith tells one and only if it yields no answer, believe the result of courtroom demonstration? With either mode of individuation, knowledge requires the negative existentially quantified statement (that there is no method . . .) somewhere, whether in specifying the method itself or in specifying that it is not outweighed.

21. One suspects there will be some gimmick whereby whenever p is truly believed a trivial method M can be specified which satisfies conditions 3 and 4. If so, then further conditions will have to be imposed upon M, in addition to the dispositional condition. Compare the difficulties encountered in the literature on specifying the relevant reference class in probabilistic inference and explanation; see Henry Kyburg, *Probability and the Logic of Rational Belief* (Wesleyan University Press, Middletown, 1961), ch. 9; C. G. Hempel, *Aspects of Scientific Explanation* (Free Press, New York, 1965), pp. 394-405; also his "Maximal Specificity and Lawlikeness in Probabilistic Explanation," *Philosophy of Science*, Vol. 35, 1968, pp. 116-133.

22. See Ludwig Wittgenstein, *On Certainty* (Basil Blackwell, Oxford, 1969), §§ 83, 94, 102-110, 140-144, 151-152, 162-163, 166, 411, 419, 472-475.

23. This statement is not affected by Church's Theorem on the absence of a decision procedure for theoremhood, the absence of an algorithm for discovering a proof in a fixed finite number of steps. In some nearby worlds the method of seeking a proof, because failing to find one, will not yield any belief and so not the belief that p; but a belief that p will result via the method of believing p on the basis of a found proof that p. More generally, even with contingent statements, if M is a method that always would give the right answer when it gives an answer, but only rarely gives an answer, a person who believes on the basis of M's answer does have knowledge. His method is not 'applying M' but 'believing M's answer'.

Similar points apply to our knowledge of mathematical axioms, where it is only condition 4 that comes into play. The topic of how condition 4 comes to be satisfied for our beliefs about mathematical axioms, the topic of how we know necessary truths, is an interesting one, but is not our topic here. Neither is it our current task to formulate a theory of the nature and basis of necessary truths.

24. Michael Rabin has proposed methods of mathematical proof which do not guarantee truth, though the probability of error can be reduced to, for example, one in one billion. (Reported in *Science,* June 4, 1976, pp. 989-990.) We discuss below the complications that prob-

ability adds. (See also Hilary Putnam's discussion of "quasi-empirical methods" in mathematics in his "What Is Mathematical Truth?", *Philosophical Papers,* Cambridge University Press, 1976, Vol. I, pp. 60–78.)

25. A more difficult issue is whether a weaker 'would not' isn't enough. Granted that in all worlds close to the actual world the person would truly believe that p (when it is true) and would not falsely believe that p (when p is false), this last is satisfied if no situation or world close to the actual one is a not p world. Why require in addition that in the closest not-p worlds, even when these are very far away, the person not believe that p? We take up these questions below, in Part II on skepticism.

26. But not always. George Pappas and Marshall Swain (*Essays on Knowledge and Justification,* Cornell University Press, Ithaca, 1978, p. 16) report the point by Fred Feldman that the person might infer the truth that someone in the office owns a Ford directly from the true evidence for the statement that the friend does, without going through this intermediate falsehood.

27. The simplicity of the antecedents of 3 and 4, not-p and p respectively, enables us to avoid the type of objections raised in Robert Shope, "The Conditional Fallacy in Contemporary Philosophy," *Journal of Philosophy,* Vol. 75, 1978, pp. 397–413. With the above holding of the method fixed, however, things become more complex and the issues Shope raises may become relevant.

28. I have obtained most of my knowledge of this literature, belatedly, from George Pappas and Marshall Swain, eds., *Essays on Knowledge and Justification* (Cornell University Press, Ithaca, 1978), and from an unpublished survey article by Robert Shope, "Recent Work on the Analysis of Knowledge," an expanded version of which will appear as a book. One of Shope's own cases also involves not holding the method fixed.

29. Ernest Sosa, "Propositional Knowledge," *Philosophical Studies,* Vol. 20, 1969, p. 39, cited in Shope.

30. L. S. Carrier, "An Analysis of Empirical Knowledge," *Southern Journal of Philosophy,* Vol. 9, 1971, p. 7, cited in Shope.

31. Keith Lehrer and Thomas Paxson, Jr., "Knowledge: Undefeated Justified True Belief," *Journal of Philosophy,* Vol. 66, 1969, p. 236, cited in Shope.

32. Carrier, *Southern Journal of Philosophy,* Vol. 9, 1971, p. 9, cited in Shope.

33. Alvin Goldman, "Discrimination and Perceptual Knowledge," *Journal of Philosophy,* Vol. 73, 1976, p. 789, cited in Shope.

34. Lehrer and Paxson, *Journal of Philosophy,* Vol. 66, 1969, pp. 225–237, reprinted in George Pappas and Marshall Swain, eds., *Essays on Knowledge and Justification* (Cornell University Press, Ithaca, 1978).

35. Thomas Paxson, Jr., "Professor Swain's Account of Knowledge," in Pappas and Swain, *Essays on Knowledge and Justification,* pp. 100–105.

36. George Pappas and Marshall Swain, "Some Conclusive Reasons against 'Conclusive Reasons,' " in Pappas and Swain, *Essays on Knowledge and Justification,* pp. 63–64.

37. I owe this question to Lawrence Powers.

38. See Alvin Goldman, "Innate Knowledge," in Stephen Stich, *Innate Ideas* (University of California Press, Berkeley, 1975), pp. 111–120.

39. Armstrong, *Belief, Truth and Knowledge,* pp. 180–182.

40. Here, I can only make the vague and obscure suggestion, not pursued below, that believing something (partly) in virtue of its truth may be distinct from believing p (partly) because p. There may be a difference between explaining why someone believes something which is true (and explaining why it is true), and (on the other hand) explaining why he believes the truth. Perhaps we want the explanation of someone's belief, why it is knowledge, to bring in the notion of 'truth qua truth', rather than merely the fact p (which is believed and is true); and perhaps it is in explaining why conditions 3 and 4 hold that the notion of 'truth qua truth' must enter. Compare Quine's discussion of the necessary role of the "truth" predicate *pace* the redundancy theory of truth, in *Philosophy of Logic* (Prentice-Hall, Englewood Cliffs, 1970), pp. 10–13.

41. It is along these lines that we should treat the examples in Laurence Bonjour, "Externalist Theories of Empirical Knowledge," *Midwest Studies in Philosophy,* Vol. V (University of Minnesota Press, Minneapolis, 1980), pp. 53–73. Should we also add, when we come to the later account of justification, a further condition that it not be the case that

the person is justified in believing he does not know that p? (Or, that he not be justified in believing he's not justified in believing p?) It is not clear whether this is necessary.

42. There is an immense amount of literature concerning skepticism. See, for example, Sextus Empiricus, *Writings* (4 vols., Loeb Classical Library, Harvard University Press, Cambridge); Richard Popkin, *History of Skepticism from Erasmus to Descartes* (rev. ed., Humanities Press, New York, 1964); Arne Naess, *Skepticism* (Humanities Press, New York,1968); René Descartes, *Meditations on First Philosophy* (Liberal Arts Press, New York, 1960); G. E. Moore, "Proof of an External World," "A Defense of Common Sense," "Certainty," and "Four Forms of Skepticism" in his *Philosophical Papers* (Allen and Unwin, London, 1959); J. L. Austin, "Other Minds" in his *Philosophical Papers* (Oxford University Press, 1961); Ludwig Wittgenstein, *On Certainty* (Basil Blackwell, Oxford, 1969); Keith Lehrer, "Why Not Skepticism?" (in Swain and Pappas, eds., *Essays on Knowledge and Justification*, pp. 346–363); Peter Unger, *Ignorance* (Oxford University Press, 1975), pp. 7–24; Michael Slote, *Reason and Skepticism* (Allen and Unwin, London, 1970); Roderick Firth, "The Anatomy of Certainty," *Philosophical Review*, Vol. 76, 1967, pp. 3–27; Thompson Clarke, "The Legacy of Skepticism," *Journal of Philosophy*, Vol. 69, 1972, pp. 754–769; Stanley Cavell, *The Claim of Reason* (Oxford University Press, 1979).

43. Subjunctives with actually false antecedents and actually true consequents have been termed by Goodman *semi-factuals*. R is the semi-factual: not-$p \rightarrow$ S believes p.

44. Should one weaken condition 3, so that the account of knowledge merely denies the opposed subjunctive R? That would give us: not-(not-$p \rightarrow$ S believes p). This holds when 3 does not, in situations where if p were false, S might believe p, and also might not believe it. The extra strength of 3 is needed to exclude these as situations of knowledge.

45. Though it does show the falsity of the corresponding entailment, "not-p entails not-(S believes that p)."

46. If a person is to know that SK doesn't hold, then condition 3 for knowledge must be satisfied (with "SK doesn't hold" substituted for p). Thus, we get

(3) not-(SK doesn't hold) $\rightarrow$ not-(S believes that SK doesn't hold).

Simplifying the antecedent, we have

(3) SK holds $\rightarrow$ not-(S believes that SK doesn't hold).

The skeptic has chosen a situation SK such that the following is true of it:

SK holds $\rightarrow$ S believes that SK doesn't hold.

Having the same antecedent as 3 and a contradictory consequent, this is incompatible with 3. Thus, condition 3 is not satisfied by the person's belief that SK does not hold.

47. Let $w_1, \ldots, w_n$ be worlds doxically identical to the actual world for S. He doesn't know he is not in w_1, he doesn't know he is not in $w_2, \ldots$; does it follow that he doesn't know he is in the actual world W_A or in are very much like it (in its truths)? Not if the situation he would be in if the actual world W_A did not obtain wasn't one of the doxically identical worlds: if the world that then would obtain would show its difference from the actual one W_A, he then would not believe he was in W_A.

However, probably there are some worlds not very different from the actual world (in that they have mostly the same truths) and even doxically identical to it, which might obtain if w_A did not. In that case, S would not know he was in w_A specified in all its glory. But if we take the disjunction of these harmless worlds (insofar as drastic skeptical conclusions go) doxically identical with w_A then S will know that the disjunction holds. For if it didn't, he would notice that.

48. This argument proceeds from the fact that floating in the tank is incompatible with being at X. Another form of the skeptic's argument, one we shall consider later, proceeds from the fact that floating in the tank is incompatible with knowing you are at X (or almost anything else).

49. Note that I am not denying that $Kp \,\&\, K(p \dashv q) \rightarrow$ Believes q.

50. Thus, the following is not a deductively valid form of inference.

$p \dashv q$ (and S knows this)
not-$p \rightarrow$ not-(S believes that p)
Therefore, not-$q \rightarrow$ not-(S believes that q).

Furthermore, the example in the text shows that even the following is not a deductively valid form of inference.

$p \dashv q$ (and S knows this)
not-$p \rightarrow$ not-(S believes that p)
Therefore, not-$q \rightarrow$ not-(S believes that p).

Nor is this one deductively valid:

$p \dashv q$
not-$q \rightarrow r$
Therefore, not-$p \rightarrow r$.

51. Does this same consequence of nonclosure under known logical implication follow as well from condition 4: $p \rightarrow$ S believes that p? When p is not actually true, condition 4 can hold of p yet not of a q known to be entailed by p. For example, let p be the (false) statement that I am in Antarctica, and let q be the disjunction of p with some other appropriate statement; for example, let q be the statement that I am in Antarctica or I lost some object yesterday though I have not yet realized it. If p were true I would know it, p entails q, yet if q were true I wouldn't know it, for the way it would be true would be by my losing some object without yet realizing it, and if that happened I would not know it.

This example to show that condition 4 is not closed under known logical implication depends on the (actual) falsity of p. I do not think there is any suitable example to show this in the case where p is true, leaving aside the trivial situation when the person simply does not infer the entailed statement q.

52. Suppose some component of the condition, call it C', also speaks of some cases when p is false, and when q is false; might it then provide "varies with," even though C' is preserved under known logical implication, and is transmitted from p to q when p entails q and is known to entail q? If this condition C' speaks of some cases where not-p and of some cases where not-q, *then C' will be preserved under known logical implication if, when those cases of not-p satisfy it, and p entails q, then also those cases of not-q satisfy it.* Thus, C' seems to speak of something as preserved from some cases of not-p some cases of not-q, which is preservation in the reverse direction to the entailment involving these, from not-q to not-p. Thus, a condition that is preserved under known logical implication and that also provides some measure of "varies with" must contain a component action saying that something interesting (other than falsity) is preserved in the direction opposite to the logical implication (for some cases); and moreover, that component itself must be preserved in the direction of the logical implication because the condition including it is. It would be interesting to see such a condition set out.

53. Reading an earlier draft of this chapter, friends pointed out to me that Fred Dretske already had defended the view that knowledge (as one among many epistemic concepts) is not closed under known logical implication. (See his "Epistemic Operators," *Journal of Philosophy,* Vol. 67, 1970, pp. 1007–1023.) Furthermore, Dretske presented a subjunctive condition for knowledge (in his "Conclusive Reason," *Australasian Journal of Philosophy,* Vol. 49, 1971, pp. 1–22), holding that S knows that p on the basis of reasons R only if: R would not be the case unless p were the case. Here Dretske ties the evidence subjunctively to the fact, and the belief based on the evidence subjunctively to the fact through the evidence. (Our account of knowledge has not yet introduced or discussed evidence or reasons at all. While this condition corresponds to our condition 3, he has nothing corresponding to 4.) So Dretske has hold of both pieces of our account, subjunctive and nonclosure, and he even connects them in a passing footnote (*Journal of Philosophy,* Vol. 67, p. 1019, n.4), noticing that any account of knowledge that relies on a subjunctive conditional will not be closed under known logical implication. Dretske also has the notion of a relevant alternative as "one that might have been realized in the existing circumstances if the actual state of affairs had not materialized" (p. 1021), and he briefly applies all this to the topic of skepticism (pp. 1015–1016), holding that the skeptic is right about some things but not about others.

It grieves me somewhat to discover that Dretske also had all this, and was there first. It raises the question, also, of why these views have not yet had the proper impact. Dretske makes his points in the midst of much other material, some of it less insightful. The independent statement and delineation of the position here, without the background noise, I hope will make clear its many merits.

After Goldman's paper on a causal theory of knowledge (in *Journal of Philosophy*, Vol. 64, 1967), an idea then already "in the air," it required no great leap to consider subjunctive conditions. Some two months after the first version of this chapter was written, Goldman himself published a paper on knowledge utilizing counterfactuals ("Discrimination and Perceptual Knowledge," *Journal of Philosophy*, Vol. 78, 1976, pp. 771–791), also talking of relevant possibilities (without using the counterfactuals to identify which possibilities are relevant); and Shope's survey article has called my attention to a paper of L. S. Carrier ("An Analysis of Empirical Knowledge," *Southern Journal of Philosophy*, Vol. 9, 1971, pp. 3–11) that also used subjunctive conditions including our condition 3. Armstrong's reliability view of knowledge (*Belief, Truth and Knowledge*, pp. 166, 169) involved a lawlike connection between the belief that *p* and the state of affairs that makes it true. Clearly, the idea is one whose time has come.

54. Is it a consequence of our view that of two people who know *p*, each believing he knows *p* and satisfying condition 3 for knowing he knows *p*, one may know he knows and the other not, because (although identical in all other respects) the second might encounter skeptical arguments while the first somehow lives hermetically sealed from the merest brush with them?

55. Our task now is not to wonder whether it is legitimate to use M to reach a belief that M is being used. What, after all, is the alternative? Presumably, an infinite regress of methods, or a circle, or reaching a method which is used but either is not believed to be used, or is believed to be though not via any method or way of believing.

56. See H. H. Price, "Our Evidence for the Existence of Other Minds," *Philosophy*, Vol. 13, 1938, pp. 425–456; John Wisdom, *Other Minds* (Basil Blackwell, Oxford, 1952), chs. I–V, VII; Bertrand Russell, *Human Knowledge* (Simon and Schuster, New York, 1948), Part III, ch. 2; A. J. Ayer, *The Problem of Knowledge* (Penguin Books, London, 1956), ch. 5; Norman Malcolm, "Knowledge of Other Minds," *Journal of Philosophy*, Vol. 55, 1958, pp. 969–978; P. F. Strawson, *Individuals*, ch. 3; Robert Nozick, "Testament — a Story," *Mosaic*, Vol. 12, Spring 1971, pp. 24–27, and "R.S.V.P. — a Story," *Commentary*, Vol. 53, March 1972, pp. 66–68; Stanley Cavell, "Knowing and Acknowledging" in his *Must We Mean What We Say?* (Scribners, New York, 1969), pp. 238–266, and *The Claim of Reason* (Oxford University Press, 1979), Part IV.

57. See also Cavell, *The Claim of Reason*, Part I.

58. See Daniel Dennett, "On the Absence of Phenomenology," in D. F. Gustafson and B. L. Tapscott, eds., *Body, Mind, and Method* (Reidel, Dodrecht, 1979), where this possibility is discussed but not as a skeptical hypothesis.

59. See Frederick Will, "Will the Future Resemble the Past?," *Mind*, Vol. 56, 1947, pp. 332–347; Thompson Clarke, "Seeing Surfaces and Physical Objects," in Max Black, ed., *Philosophy in America* (Cornell University Press, Ithaca, 1965), pp. 98–114.

60. First, note that our reasons for holding that knowledge is not closed under known logical implication do not extend to thinking it is not closed under known logical (or known necessary) equivalence. So let us assume K(p $\equiv$ q) and Kp $\rightarrow$ Kq. Assume Kp, and that the person knows that *p* is logically equivalent to T: (r) (r $\rightarrow$ not-p $\supset$ not-r). Briefly, let us show this equivalence. We can see that *p* follows from T, by substituting not-*p* for *r* in T (applying universal instantiation to T), which yields: (not-p $\rightarrow$ not-p) $\supset$ not-(not-p), that is, (not-p $\rightarrow$ not-p) $\supset$ p. Since the antecedent is logically true, that logical truth and the preceding statement, by modus ponens, gives us *p*. In the other direction, to see T follows from *p*, assume *p* is true. Then not-*p* is false, and since anything that entails a falsehood is false, so must anything be which entails not-*p*; that is, (r) (r $\rightarrow$ not-p $\supset$ not-r). Now that the equivalence is shown, let us continue with the derivation. Since knowledge is (assumed to be) closed under known logical equivalence and since p is equivalent to T, from Kp we have

(1) K(r)(r $\rightarrow$ not-p $\supset$ not-r).

He knows: everything that entails not-*p* is false. If knowledge were closed under known application of the rule of universal instantiation, it would follow from this that for any statement *q* which the person knows is a logical consequence of *p*, that is, such that K(p $\rightarrow$ q), and such that he also knows the contrapositive, not-q $\rightarrow$ not-p, knowing that not-q entails not-p, the person also knows that not-q $\rightarrow$ not-p $\supset$ not-not-q, that is, it would follow that

(2) K(not-q $\rightarrow$ not-p $\supset$ q).

But when not-q does entail not-p, (not-q ⊣ not-p) ⊃ q is necessarily equivalent to *q*. Since knowledge is closed under known necessary equivalence it follows that Kq. We have derived Kq, the conclusion that *q* is known, from the assumptions that *p* is known, *p* entails *q* (and this is known), and that knowledge is closed under known application of the rule of universal instantiation. That is, on these assumptions, we have derived the conclusion that he knows the known logical consequences of what he knows.

61. In the previous note, 2 does not follow by universal instantiation from 1. We cannot apply universal instantiation within the scope of "K" for that is to assume that knowledge is closed under known application of the rule of universal instantiation. Statement 2 can follow via this rule only from a statement whose quantifier is outside the scope of the "K," that is, from

(1') (r)K(r ⊣ not-p ⊃ not-r).

Statement 1' says that of each *r*, the person knows that if it entails not-*p, then not-r* (that is, then *r* is false). Whereas 1 says that the person knows that everything that entails *r* is false. These may appear to be equivalent but they are not.

(a) Statement 1' does not entail 1. Of each *r* a person might know something P without knowing that these are all the *r*'s there are. So he need not know (r)Pr.

(b) Statement 1 does not entail 1'. If it did, since statement 2 follows from 1', 2 would follow from 1 as well. But since Kq follows from 2 when 'not-q ⊣ not-p' is known and when '(not-q ⊣ not-p ⊃ q)' is known to be necessarily equivalent to '*q*', Kq would follow from 1 as well. This is just to say that knowledge is closed under known logical implication, which is false. That knowledge is not closed under known logical implication shows us that the universal quantifier cannot be exported ouside the scope of the "K", that (x)KPx does not validly follow from K(x)Px.

Though these external considerations demonstrate the point, they may not give an intuitive understanding of how it can be that a person can know (x)Px without, for a given particular *a*, also knowing Pa.

62. This result has been obtained by applying the account of knowledge directly to the proposition (x)Px. However, one might think that when a universal statement is known, not only must belief in it somehow vary with its truth, but also belief in each instance must somehow vary with the truth of that instance. To make this a necessary condition for knowing that (x)Px would mar a uniform account of knowledge; it is an appropriate condition, however, for knowing of each thing that it is P.

63. Let r ⊣ s. Then r Ɛ s&(s ⊃ r). We may assume this is known: at least I know this further fact and so for me when I know r ⊣ s then I know r Ɛ s&(s ⊃ r). Suppose Kr. Then Ks&(s ⊃ r). Now if K is closed under known entailment of a conjunct, then Ks. But *s* is anything known to be a logical consequence of *r* so knowledge would thereby be closed under known logical implication. Thus, if knowledge is not closed generally under known logical implication, it is not closed generally under known entailment of a conjunct.

64. As would the apparent result of nonclosure under the propositional calculus rule of inferring '*p* or *q*' from '*p*', which stands to existential generalization as simplification stands to universal instantiation.

65. I have more confidence in the analogue of condition 3, that if the conclusion weren't true the person wouldn't believe the premises, as a component of the condition for the transmission of knowledge via proof, than I do in the other part of the condition, the analogue of condition 4, that if the conclusion were true then the person would believe the premises. Whatever results are based upon this second component of tracking must be taken provisionally, with the hope that these results are robust and relatively insensitive to changes in this particular condition.

66. With mathematical proof of necessary truths, the condition

not-*q* → not-(S believes *p*)

falls away (as condition 3 did earlier in our discussion of necessary truths), and so the transmission of mathematical knowledge via deductive proof from known premises depends upon whether the (fallible) person creating or reading the proof and making the inference would believe the premises if the conclusion held and (similarly considering the matter) would make the inference.

67. We can see this as follows. The person knows p and so, inferring the entailed not-q_1, truly believes not-q_1. Condition 3 for knowledge that not-q_1 also is satisfied, namely

(3) $q_1 \rightarrow$ not-(S believes not-q_1).

For, by condition 3 for knowledge that p, if p weren't to hold, he wouldn't believe p. Since q_1 is a first subjunctive alternative to p, it is one of the ways p *wouldn't or mightn't hold, and so:* $q_1 \rightarrow$ not-(S believes p). Since he has actually inferred not-q_1 from p, we see that he wouldn't believe the premiss p unless the conclusion not-q_1 were true. (This is the condition for knowledge to be closed under an inference.) And so he would not believe the not-q_1 he infers from p unless not-q_1 were true, which is the condition 3 written above for knowledge that not-q_1.

The fourth condition for knowledge that not-q_1

(4) not-$q_1 \rightarrow$ S believes that not-q_1

is satisfied, since the fourth condition for knowledge that p holds, $p \rightarrow$ S believes that p, and the method of inferring not-q_1 from p would give S the belief that not-q_1 for some distance out in the p neighborhood and so in the not-q_1 neighborhood of the actual world.

68. I include the qualification to take account of the situation where although the person's belief that Pa does track the fact that Pa, under the situation of there being no P — one so far out it wouldn't hold even if not-Pa — the person still would believe Pa, even when the method of belief is held fixed. In that case, the belief in the premiss would not track the truth of the conclusion, and the person would not know, via the inference, that the conclusion was true.

69. See Gilbert Harman's presentation, *Thought* (Princeton University Press, Princeton, 1973), p. 148. The puzzle arises quite naturally out of Hintikka's extendability thesis, *Knowledge and Belief*(Cornell University Press, Ithaca, 1962), pp 20–21.

70. Can we attach all failure of closure to the failure of conjunction to distribute, and see this, when p $\sqsupset$ q, as stemming from the closest not-p world and the closest not-q world being different distances from the actual world? Even if this is a necessary condition for nonclosure, it will not be sufficient. For sometimes, even when the (closest) not-q world is further out, the belief that p will track the truth of q, and the person will not believe p in that further not-q world. The satisfaction of the relevant condition, that the belief in the premisses tracks the truth of the conclusion, does not depend solely on formal features.

71. Do we also need a condition to represent the fact that the knowledge gets transmitted from p to q, such as Kp $\rightarrow$ Kq? Simply writing this would not represent the fact that knowledge gets transmitted via the proof (and so it would conflict with point 4). For it says, if S knew that p, whether or not he knew the proof of q from p, he would know that q. In this case, the proof is superfluous. To write a condition representing the fact that the proof transmits knowledge would require more apparatus than we have available here.

72. We suppose for the moment that a justification is meant to transmit this property from premises that have it. On another view, "justifiedness" emerges in a process yielding q from other statements which are believed or have initial credibility, but which themselves need not be justified. See Israel Scheffler, "On Justification and Commitment," *Journal of Philosophy*, Vol. 51, 1954, pp. 180–190.

73. There also is the possibility of defects more serious than begging the question, as when in a purported proof of q from p, if the person weren't to know q he wouldn't (even) believe p.

74. Strictly, then, to reach our earlier conclusion that knowledge is not closed under known logical implication, we would have to add the explicit premiss that not all possible situations equally might occur (if actuality were changed or different). Within the framework of a "possible worlds" account of subjunctives, the premiss would be added that not all nonactual possible worlds have the same distance from the actual world, and in particular that there are statements p and q such that p entails q and the distances of the closest not-p world and the closest not-q world from the actual world differ.

75. Note that if

he would not have had this dream if he were not speaking in the House of Lords,

and

if he were speaking in the House of Lords, he would believe it, whether because awake or because if he had a dream it would be this one, then our account of knowledge holds that he does know that he is speaking in the House of Lords (supposing it true to say he believes what he dreams).

76. Though the skeptic's argument does not show S doesn't know he knows that p, perhaps it does show something. Let

$$p^1 = \text{not-}p \to \text{not-(S believes } p)$$
$$p^2 = \text{not-}(p^1) \to \text{not-(S believes } p^1)$$
$$\cdots$$
$$p^i = \text{not-}(p^{i-1}) \to \text{not-(S believes } p^{i-1}).$$

The person knows that p only if p_1 is true. He knows he knows that p (KKp) only if he knows p_1 is true, and so only if p^2 is true. He KKKp only if p^3 is true, and so forth. Let us abbreviate p preceded by i K's as $K^i p$. A person will $K^i p$ only if p^i is true.

The skeptic's doxically identical possibility SK doesn't show that p^1 is not true, or that p^2 is not true. But for some $n + 1$, it will show that p^{n+1} is not true, if eventually there will be reached a p^n such that if p^n were false then SK would or might happen—a p^n, that is, such that not-$p^n \to$ SK, or at any rate not-(not-$p^n \to$ not-SK). In that case, p^{n+1} isn't true, and the person doesn't know p^n. Therefore, the person does not $K^{n+1} p$ (although $K^n p$). Perhaps one of the p^i is false before we reach p^n with SK as a first subjunctive alternative to its antecedent; but if not, the skeptic's possibility may show that there will be a finite $n + 1$ such that the person doesn't $K^{n+1} p$.

I assume that the skeptic's alternative, although farfetched, is reachable in a finite number of steps; further, that for some i, it is an ith subjunctive alternative to p. The crucial question is whether for some finite n, the skeptic's alternative SK is what would hold if not-p^n. If the skeptic can show that each time we get farther away from the actual world, the closest world where p^n doesn't hold is farther away than the closest world where p^{m-1} does not (for all m) then he will be able to show that for some n, not-$(K^{n+1} p)$.

Thus perhaps the skeptic's example of a doxically identical world does show that for some finite $n + 1$, not-(K^{n+1}). Perhaps the skeptic's example does show that somewhere up the line of K's, we do reach a not-K, that is, that the following finite disjuncton is true: not-Kp or not-KKp or not-KKKp or . . . But even if the skeptic does show this, what he shows may be remote. I trust that the reader will not now think it legitimate to swoop down the line, to argue that if not-$K^{n+1} p$ then not-$K^n p$. Still, we should reiterate that the skeptic is correct in saying that we do not know that his doxically identical possibility SK doesn't hold; and also perhaps that for the most of the p we think we know, for some finite $n + 1$, we do not $K^{n+1} p$.

77. When first formulating the account of knowledge, we considered a third condition for knowledge paralleling condition b': not-(not-$p \to$ S believes that p); if p were false he might not believe p. We held this was too weak a requirement to replace condition 3; it allowed knowledge that p when if p were false it would be a random matter whether the person believed p or not.

78. A randomized experiment simplifies the calculation of the probabilities, the likelihoods discussed below. I do not mean to exclude Duhemian considerations about testing hypotheses in isolation. The manipulation of conditions to yield the (hoped for) holding of subjunctives proceeds against a background of assumed theory. I comment below on the relevance of this assumed factual background to "logical" theories of confirmation and evidence.

Experimental manipulation of conditions to make h true also makes more secure the inference that any correlated events are effects of h. Generally, when correlations between two variables are observed we must ascertain that the correlation is not spurious, the effect of some third variable that causes each. However, when one of the variables is purposefully manipulated, we forgo such ascertaining because we assume that our manipulative act itself is not causally determined, or at least that its causes do not also cause the correlated events.

79. We do not want this probability to be simply the probability of the subjunctive conditional '$h \to$ e', for (given the semantics of this conditional) it might have a high probability of being true even though (speaking loosely) if h were true, e would very probably be true. (See David Lewis, "Probabilities of Conditionals and Conditional Probabilities," *Philosophical Review*, 1976, Vol. 85, pp. 297–315.) We might want this probability prob (e,h) to be simply the conditional probability of e given h, prob (e/h), defined as prob (e and h) ÷ prob (h). Perhaps not; perhaps we want an explanation closer to the spirit of the account of subjunctives. (For some suggestions, see Jordan Howard Sobel, "Probability, Chance and Choice," unpublished manuscript.) For now though, so as not to introduce too many issues at once, we

may proceed as if it is a conditional probability. Since 'prob (e,h) is very high' is meant to be related to, and approximate 'h → e', we presuppose there will be some suitable interpretation of probability as a real empirical (perhaps dispositional) fact in the world. Theories of logical probability or personal probability are unsuitable for our purposes; those of statistical probability (as a limit of frequencies) at least are empirical; best, however, I think, would be some refinement of the propensity view of probability. See Karl Popper, "the Propensity Interpretation of Probability," *British Journal for the Philosophy of Science,* Vol. 10, 1959, pp. 25–42; and the criticisms in Lawrence Sklar, "Is Probability a Dispositional Property?," *Journal of Philosophy,* Vol. 67, 1970, pp. 355–366; see also D. H. Mellor, *The Matter of Chance* (Cambridge University Press, 1971); D. A. Gilles, *An Objective Theory of Probability* (Methuen, London, 1973). It is not my purpose to formulate such a theory here.

80. In my treatment of evidence, I leave aside issues about conflicting evidence; these are suggestively discussed in Glenn Shafer, *A Mathematical Theory of Evidence* (Princeton University Press, Princeton, 1976).

81. These probabilistic considerations also should be applied to our earlier remarks about a test of a hypothesis.

82. It would sow confusion throughout the theory, however, to calculate the prob (e, not-h) differently, as the maximum probability of e given any h_i that might hold if not-h did. It is best, when the times, to add additional clauses referring to, or excluding, such h_i.

83. Another way to see how centrally the evidence functions is to notice that, even though the rough intuition was not to believe that an improbability obtains, the additional condition we formulated was

$$\text{prob}_0 \text{ (h)} > \text{prob (e, not-h)},$$

rather than

$$\text{prob (e,h)} \times \text{prob}_0(\text{h}) > \text{prob (e,not-h)} \times \text{prob}_0 \text{ (not-h)}.$$

In "Detachment, Probability, and Maximum Likelihood" (*Nous,* Vol. 1, 1967, pp. 401–411), Gilbert Harman formulates another principle combining maximum likelihood with Bayesian considerations, and investigates whether it gives rise to the lottery paradox. I have not investigated whether the principle of inference we propose, all epicycles included, is open to any version of the lottery paradox. For a treatment of various approaches to this latter problem, due to Henry Kyburg (*Probability and the Logic of Rational Belief,* Wesleyan University Press, Middletown, 1961, p. 197), see Risto Hilpinnen, "Rules of Acceptance and Inductive Logic," *Acta Philosophica Fennica,* Vol. 22, 1968, pp. 1–134.

84. See R. A. Fisher, *Statistical Method and Scientific Inference,* 3rd ed. (Hafner, New York, 1973); A. W. Edwards, *Likelihood* (Cambridge University Press, 1972); Ian Hacking, *The Logic of Statistical Inference* (Cambridge University Prress, 1965); Allen Birnbaum, "Concepts of Statistical Evidence," in *Philosophy, Science, and Method,* S. Morgenbesser, P. Suppes, and M. White, eds. (St. Martins Press, New York, 1969), pp. 112–143; Barry Loewer, Robert Laddaga, and Roger Rosenkrantz, "On the Likelihood Principle and a Supposed Antinomy," in Peter Asquith and Ian Hacking, eds., *Philosophy of Science Association Proceedings* (East Lansing, Michigan, 1978), Vol. 1, no. 1, pp. 279–286.

85. For a standard and extensive exposition of this theory, commonly called the "classic" theory, see E. L. Lehman, *Testing Statistical Hypotheses* (John Wiley, New York, 1959). For difficulties relevant to some points later, see also D. P. Cox, "Some Problems Connected with Statistical Inference," *Annals of Mathematical Statistics,* Vol. 29, 1958, pp. 357–363; John Pratt, "Review of Lehman," *Journal of American Statistical Association,* Vol. 56, 1961, p. 166; Birnbaum, in *Philosophy, Science and Method;* Hacking, *Logic of Statistical Inference, ch. 7.*

86. We are given that e holds and that the principle has been applied, so that prob (e,h) > .95 and prob (e, not-h) < .95; and we want to know the probability of not-h given all this. By Bayes Theorem, the prob (not-h/e) as a function of this is equal to:

$$\frac{\text{prob}_0 \text{ (not-h)} \times \text{prob (e, not-h)}}{\text{prob}_0 \text{ (not-h)} \times \text{prob (e, not-h)} + \text{prob}_0 \text{ (h)} \times \text{prob (e,h)}} .$$

When prob_0 (h) = .06, prob_0 (not-h) = .94, prob (e,h) = .95, prob (e, not-h) = .05, all compatible with the premises of our inference, then prob (not-h/e) is about .45, and so the probability of a type II error is greater than .05, greater than prob (e, not-h). However, it will be less than ½; this depends not only on keeping prob (e, not-h) very low, but also keeping prob (e,h) very high.

87. The Neyman-Pearson theorist computes this on the basis of likelihoods (before the evidence is gathered) rather than computing it given that e has been found to hold and that the principle of inference has led to accepting h. So his computation is unsuitable for our purposes.

88. Might the differences leave space for finding a role for the notion of weight of evidence; there is greater weight of evidence for the probability judgment that a coin has a ½ probability of yielding heads on the basis of many tosses where this ratio if approximated, than there is when this judgment is based on fewer (or no) tosses plus symmetry considerations, yet the probability of heads may be the same in the two cases, namely, ½. Intuitively, the weight of evidence should play some role, yet it is difficult to see how to utilize it appropriately. (See Keynes, *Treatise on Probability,* pp. 71-78.) When evidence is more weighty, it can be partitioned into parts $e_1, \ldots, e_n$ where each e_1 is sufficient to bring the principle of inference into play. Weightier evidence yields multiple applications of the principle of inference to the same conclusion. Looking externally, can the probability that all those are in (type II) error be different from (and less than) the probability of $e_1\&e_2\& \ldots \&e_n$ given not-h?

89. For the dominant view see John Maynard Keynes, *A Treatise on Probability* (Macmillan, London, 1921); Harold Jeffreys, *Theory of Probability* (Oxford, 1939); Rudolf Carnap, *The Logical Foundations of Probability* (Chicago, 1950); various recent articles by J. Hintikka and his students. Hilary Putnam's criticism can be found in " 'Degree of Confirmation' and Inductive Logic," in P. A. Schilpp, ed., *The Philosophy of Rudolf Carnap* (Open Court, LaSalle, 1963), pp. 761-784.

90. Compare our earlier discussion of Wittgenstein on criteria, stage setting, and context. The criteria are not logically sufficient conditions for the application of a mental predicate because there is a (logically) possible wider context where (it is shown) the criteria hold but the mental predicate does not. See also the discussion of whether explanation is deductive, how boundary conditions enter into explanation, in John Canfield and Keith Lehrer, "A Note on Prediction and Deduction," *Philosophy of Science,* Vol. 28, 1961, pp. 204-208.

91. See Norwood Russell Hanson, *Patterns of Discovery* (Cambridge University Press, 1958), p. 86; Gilbert Harman, "The Inference to the Best Explanation," *Philosophical Review,* Vol. 70, 1965, pp. 88-95.

92. See Keynes, *Treatise on Probability,* pp. 253-264; Bertrand Russell, *Human Knowledge; Its Scope and Limits* (Simon and Schuster, New York, 1948), Part VI.

93. This kind of nonclosure occurs also under some other theories of evidence, for example, Carnap's, wherein e confirms h if $c(h,e) > c_0(h)$. On this account, e may confirm h yet disconfirm a logical consequence of h, for example, the consequence 'h or not-e', which may have a degree of confirmation on e lower than its a priori degree of confirmation.

94. See William Talbott, "The Reliability of the Cognitive Mechanism: A Mechanist Account of Empirical Justification," unpublished doctoral dissertation, Harvard University, 1976; Alvin Goldman, "What Is Justified Belief?," in George Pappas, ed., *Justification and Knowledge* (Reidel, Dodrecht, 1979), and "The Internalist Conception of Justification," *Midwest Studies in Philosophy,* Vol. V (University of Minnesota Press, Minneapolis, 1980), pp. 27-52.

95. See A. J. Ayer, *The Problem of Knowledge* (Penguin Books, London, 1956), pp. 31-34.

96. One currently influential view of justification views it as a process of overall adjustment among initially credible general principles and specific instances. (See Nelson Goodman, *Fact, Fiction and Forecast,* Harvard University Press, Cambridge, 1955, pp. 65-68; Israel Scheffler, "On Justification and Commitment," *Journal of Philosophy,* Vol. 51, pp. 180-190; John Rawls, *A Theory of Justice,* Harvard University Press, Cambridge, 1971, pp. 19-22, 577-582; Nicholas Rescher, *The Coherence Theory of Truth,* Oxford University Press, 1973.) These initial credibilities presumably are like Bayesian prior probabilities or plausibilities. Such a process of mutual adjustment so as to maximize some (usually unstated) function, is not (logically) guaranteed to be empirically reliable, to have a propensity to yield true beliefs, and so it is not guaranteed to yield justified beliefs. Still, in particular types of situations it might do so; we need investigation of when and under what conditions.

97. See Alvin Goldman, "The Internalist Conception of Justification," *Midwest Studies in Philosophy,* Vol. V (University of Minnesota Press, Minneapolis, 1980), pp.27–52.

98. Covariation with what? With something internal to us. So there must be some theory of how the inner starting point is fixed, such as that in Chapter 1, Part II, above.

99. Unless (beyond the minimal amount of covariation needed for there to be a connection) the more the covariation with it, the less external it is. Such a monotonic relation, though, is implausible. Our belief covaries with the fact that there is an external universe in a wide range of situations.

105. See Alvin Goldman, "The Internalist Conception of Justification," *Midwest Studies in Philosophy,* Vol. V (University of Minnesota Press, Minneapolis, 1980), pp.27–52.

106. Covariation with what? With something internal to us. So there must be some theory of how the inner starting point is fixed, such as that in Chapter 1, Part II, above.

107. Unless (beyond the minimal amount of covariation needed for there to be a connection) the more the covariation with it, the less external it is. Such a monotonic relation, though, is implausible. Our belief covaries with the fact that there is an external universe in a wide range of situations.

part two

CRITICAL RESPONSES
*Knowledge, Justification,
and Evidence*

one

EVIDENCE AS A TRACKING RELATION

Richard Foley

What is evidence? According to Robert Nozick,[1] it is a tracking relation. One claim, proposition, or hypothesis constitutes evidence for another claim, proposition, or hypothesis, just if the first tracks the second in close counterfactual situations. The more intimate this tracking relation is, the stronger the evidence. So, one proposition constitutes strong evidence for another proposition just if in all close counterfactual situations where the second is true the first is true and in all close counterfactual situations where the second is false the first is false. If we let A $>>$ B stand for if A were the case then B would be the case and if we assume that A $>>$ B is true just in case B is true in all close counterfactual situations in which A is true, then Nozick's idea can be expressed as follows: p is strong evidence for q just in case (i)q $>>$ p and (ii) not-q $>>$ not-p.

This account of evidence has obvious affinities with Nozick's account of knowledge. According to Nozick, both knowledge and evidence are best understood in terms of a tracking relation, in the case of knowledge one's belief tracks that which one believes in close counterfactual situations, and in the case of evidence one's evidence tracks that for which it is evidence in close counterfactual situations. The close parallel between these two notions allow Nozick to exlain in a straightforward way how it is that evidence can generate knowledge. If an individual S knows that p and believes that q on the basis of p, where p is strong evidence for q, then at least ordinarily S also knows that q. This is so because S's belief that q tracks his belief that p (since it is based on his belief that p) which in turn tracks p (since he knows that p) which in turn tracks q (since p is strong evidence for q) and because ordinarily such tracking chains are transitive (249).

Nozick claims that there are a number of other ways in which his account of evidence meshes well with his account of knowledge. For example, he claims (197–204) that just as his account of knowledge implies that one cannot know that standard skeptical hypotheses are false (hypotheses, for example, concerning the possibility of our being deceived by an evil demon or our being brains in a vat), so too his account of evidence implies that one cannot have strong evidence that these skepticial hypotheses are false (264). For, our beliefs, experiences, and so on do not track the proposition that these skeptical hypotheses are false. Suppose, for instance, we let not-SK be the claim that I am not now in the clutches of a deceiving evil demon. Given Nozick's account of evidence, my beliefs, experiences, and so on do not constitute evidence for not-SK, since were SK to be true I would have the same beliefs, experiences, et cetera that I now have.

So, says Nozick, we do not know and we do not have strong evidence for not-SK. However, this precludes neither our knowing nor our having strong evidence for the everyday claims we believe, claims that we believe as a result of ordinary perception, memory, and the like. Thus, there is this additional parallel between knowledge and evidence. Just as I can know that there is a table in front of me even though I do not know that not-SK, so too I can have evidence for the claim that there is a table in front of me even if I lack evidence for not-SK. For example, my having a visual experience of a table in front of me may very well track the fact that there is a table in front of me. Of course, were SK true, I would have this table-like visual experience even though there is not a table in front of me. The demon would see to this. But this does not rule out the possibility that my having a table-like visual experience tracks there being a table in front of me in *close* counterfactual situations. What we have to ask, says Nozick, is whether the closest counterfactual non-table situations are SK-situations or whether they are not-SK-situations in which my vision is working pretty much as I now take it to be working but in which there in fact is no table in front of me. If the latter, then my having a visual experience of a table in front of me presumably tracks there being a table in front of me both in close table-situations and in close non-table-situations. But then, my having a visual experience of a table constitutes evidence for there being a table in front of me.

Thus, many of the claims that we know are claims for which we have strong evidence. Indeed, a stronger result follows. Namely, it is *necessary* the case that we have evidence for anything we know. This follows because an individual knows that *p* only if his belief tracks the truth of *p*. But then, whenever an individual knows that *p*, his belief that *p* itself constitutes good evidence for *p*. In this way, Nozick's account of evidence preserves the traditional connection between evidence and knowledge.[2]

So Nozick thinks that his account of evidence and his account of knowledge mesh well with one another,[3] and Nozick takes this to be an advantage for each account. Be this as it may, the two accounts, as Nozick recognizes (248), are not in any robust sense dependent upon one another. One might well accept Nozick's account of evidence without accepting his account of knowledge, or vice versa.

Accordingly, for purposes of evaluating Nozick's account of evidence, I propose to set to one side Nozick's account of knowledge. My concern is to inquire whether Nozick's elegantly stated account of evidence is a plausible account of evidence, regardless of whether it fits well with his account of knowledge and regardless of the plausibility of his account of knowledge. In effect, the strategy will be to pretend that Nozick does not have an account of knowledge. Or alternatively, it will be to assume without argument that what he has said about knowledge is implausible. In this way, Nozick's account of evidence is forced to stand or to fall on its own merits.

So, the main concern here is to inquire whether the evidential relation is best understood in terms of Nozick's proposed tracking relation, a relation whereby evidence tracks the truth and the falsity of that for which it is evidence. Consider this relation in more detail. Nozick, as I have said, explicates a notion of strong evidence in terms of two subjunctives. p is strong evidence for q just in case (i) $q >> p$ and (ii) not-q $>>$ not-p. But frequently, Nozick admits, we have only weak evidence at our disposal. As an explication of weak evidence, Nozick proposes the following: p is weak evidence for q just in case (i) $q >> p$ and (iii) not(not-$q >> p$). (250) Condition (iii) here is weaker than condition (ii). Condition (ii) says that if not-q were the case, not-p *would* be the case; condition (iii) says that if not-q were the case, not-p *might be the case. So, intuitively the idea is that p* is weak evidence for q just if p tracks the truth of q strongly but tracks the falsity of q only weakly. In other words, in all close counterfactual situations in which q is true p also is true, whereas in some but not necessarily all close counterfactual situations in which q is false p is false.

Nozick never explicitly amends this explication of weak evidence, but it is best to regard it only as his initial attempt at explicating weak evidence. For, shortly after introducing the above notion of weak evidence, he introduces a notion of evidential support that allows p to provide positive evidential support for q even though (i) and (iii) are not satisfied. According to Nozick, the degree of evidential support that p provides for q is equal to the probability that p would be true were q to be true minus the probability that p would be true were q to be false (252). Expressed more formally, the idea is that the degree of evidential support that p gives $q = \text{pr}(p/q) - \text{pr}(p/\text{not-}q)$. This measure of evidential support works well enough for strong evidence. Nozick assumes that when $q >> p$ is true, $\text{pr}(p/q)$ is 1. So, when p is strong evidence for q—that is, when the above conditions (i) and (ii) are satisfied—$\text{pr}(p/q)$ is 1 and $\text{pr}(\text{not-}p/\text{not-}q)$ also is 1. Accordingly, $\text{pr}(p/\text{not-}q)$ is 0. Thus, when p is strong evidence for q, the degree of evidential support that p gives q is equal to $\text{pr}(p/q) - \text{pr}(p/\text{not-}q)$, and this in turn is equal to 1.

However, when we turn to weak evidence, this measure of evidential support does not work as well. Whenever p constitutes weak evidence for q,p will provide positive evidential support for q. This is as it should be. The problem, however, is that p can provide positive evidential support for q without it being even weak evidence for q. Indeed, p can provide powerful evidential support for q, support approaching that given by strong evidence, without it being even weak evidence for q. This is possible because p might give q powerful positive evidential support even if the above condition (i)—a condition of weak evidence as well as strong evidence—is not met. For, even if $q >> p$ is not true, $\text{pr}(p/q)$ might still be significantly greater than $\text{pr}(p/\text{not-}q)$. Indeed, the difference between the former probability and the latter probability might be close to 1. But if so, it will be possible for p to provide a degree of evidential support for q that approaches that provided by strong evidence even though it is not even weak evidence for q. Likewise, it will be possible for some other proposition r to be weak evidence for q (since it satisfies (i) and (iii)) and for p not to be weak evidence for q (since is does not satisfy (i) and (iii)) even though p provides more evidential support for q than does r.

To avoid such consequences, let us agree that Nozick's explication of evidential support supercedes his earlier remarks about weak evidence. More exactly, let us say that p constitutes weak evidence for q just in case p provides positive evidential support for q—that is, just in case $\text{pr}(p/q) - \text{pr}(p/\text{not-}q)$ is greater than zero. Nozick's notion of strong evidence is unaffected by this recommendation. p is strong evidence for q just in case (i) $q >> p$ and (ii) not-$q >>$ not$p$. When these conditions are met, $\text{pr}(p/q) - \text{pr}(p/\text{not-}q)$ is 1, and thus the degree of evidential support that p gives q is maximal. Expressed in terms of tracking conditions, the idea is that p is strong evidence for q just in case p strongly tracks q in close counterfactual situations. And, p is weak evidence for q just in case p weakly tracks q in close counterfactual situations—that is, just in case p is more likely to be true in close counterfactual situations in which q is true than it is in close counterfactual situations in which q is false. So, the higher the percentage of close q-situations that are also p-situations and the lower the percentage of close not-q-situations that are p-situations, the stronger the evidential support that p provides for q. In the limiting case, *all,* close q-situations are p-situations and *no* close not-q-situations are p-situations. Accordingly, in this limiting case the degree of evidential support that p provides for q equals 1, and p is strong evidence for q.

In terms of this notion of evidential support, Nozick introduces other evidential notions[4] and also defends a principle of rational inference.[5] But for our purposes here, I propose not to worry about these. The above notion of evidential support and the related notions of strong evidence and weak evidence constitute the core of Nozick's account of evidence. As such, they are enough to provide a basic understanding of how Nozick thinks about the evidential relation and a basic understanding as well of his motivations for thinking about evidence in the way that he does. One such motivation, of course, is that in terms of this notion of evidence, he can explain (given his account of knowledge) why having knowledge is frequently a matter of having belief that is based on evidence. But even if (as I have proposed) we set aside this motivation, another equally important motivation remains. Namely, his account is one that allows the evidential relation to be naturalized. The evidential relation, says Nozick, is "a real factual relation which holds in the world," a subjunctive relation. What constitutes evidence for what is a contingent fact about our world. It may be true in our world that p is evidence for q, but this need not be the case in all other possible worlds (261–63).

What are we to say about this naturalized account of evidence? Is it at all plausible? To help answer this question, let us see how Nozick's account works in a simple case. Consider what kind of evidence lie detectors provide in favor of the guilt or in favor of the innocence of an individual who is accused of a crime. Those who defend the efficacy of lie detectors claim that their readings, when interpreted by experts, rarely generate 'false positives.' That is, they rarely give indications of guilt when the individual being tested is in fact not guilty. On the other hand, it is admitted even by some of their defenders that lie detectors do generate "false negatives." It is admitted by some, in other words, that lie detectors sometimes (and perhaps even frequently) fail to generate indications of guilt when the individual being tested is in fact guilty. But, it is pointed out, this is a relatively acceptable flaw in the machine, since it is better to err in this way than in the first way. It is better for the machine to fail to give 'guilty' readings when there is guilt than it is for the machine to generate 'guilty' readings when there is no guilt.

There is, of course, much that can be questioned about this 'official theory' of lie detectors. However, suppose we grant for purposes here that it is essentially right. In particular, let us assume that lie detectors never give 'guilty' readings when the individual being tested is in fact not guilty. However, let us alter the official theory with respect to false negatives. Suppose that lie detectors only very rarely give indications of guilt; they only rarely give readings of 'guilty' even when there is guilt. The lie detectors *never* give 'guilty' readings for the non-guilty, but they likewise *almost never* give 'guilty' readings for the guilty. No doubt lie detectors with characteristics of this sort would be of little practical use, but they are of use for evaluating Nozick's account of evidence.

For, consider what Nozick's account of evidence implies with respect to the readings of such lie detectors. Consider, for example, those rare occasions on which we do get a 'guilty' reading from the machine. On Nozick's account, is this strong evidence for the individual's guilt? No. The 'guilty' reading does provide positive evidential support for the claim that the individual is guilty, but it is only very weak evidential support. Specifically, the evidential support will be equal to the probability of getting a 'guilty' reading given that there is guilt, minus the probability of getting a 'guilty' reading given that there is innocence. In other words, the degree of evidential support is equal to pr('guilty'/ guilt) − pr('guilty'/innocence). By hypothesis, this latter probability is 0 and the former probability is very low. Indeed, we can make the former probability as close to 0 as we like. Suppose, for example, that we stipulate that pr('guilty') is .0001. Since the pr('guilty'/innocence) is 0, this makes pr('guilty'/guilt) = .0001. But then, on Nozick's account of evidence, the degree of evidential support that a 'guilty' reading provides for guilt is only .0001. In other words, a 'guilty' reading provides virtually no positive evidential support whatsoever in favor of guilt. And this is so despite the fact that by hypothesis 'guilty' readings always indicate guilt.

By way of contrast, suppose that we somehow know on independent grounds that an individual S is guilty and that we now want to know what kind of evidential support this information provides for the claim that the lie detector will generate a 'guilty' reading for him. According to Nozick's account, does the information that S is guilty provide positive evidential support for the claim that we will get a 'guilty' reading on the machine? Yes. In fact, it provides relatively strong support for the claim that we will get a 'guilty' reading on the machine. The degree of evidential support that S's being guilty provides for our getting a 'guilty' reading on the machine is equal to the probability of his being guilty given when we get a 'guilty' reading minus the probability of his being guilty given that we do not get a 'guilty' reading. That is, it is equal to pr(guilty/'guilty') − pr(guilty/'innocent'). The former probability in our case is 1. Readings of 'guilt' always indicate guilt. The latter probability is .4999. Readings of 'innocent' provide only slightly better indications of innocence than of guilt (assuming that the prior probability of testing a guilty person is the same as the prior probability of testing an innocent person).[6] So, the degree of evidential support that the information that S is guilty provides for the claim that we will get a 'guilty' reading from the lie detector is equal to .5001.

Accordingly, given Nozick's account of evidence, the information that an individual is guilty would provide stronger evidential support for our getting a 'guilty' reading on the machine than getting a 'guilty' reading on the machine would provide for guilt. And this is so despite the fact that by hypothesis a 'guilty' reading is always an indication of guilt whereas a guilty person almost never receives a 'guilty' reading.

Something has gone wrong here. What is it? The answer, I think, is relatively simple. What has gone wrong is the direction of the tracking in Nozick's account of evidence. His account of evidence requires that evidence track that for which it is evidence rather than vice versa. In order for p to be good evidence for q, q need not be true in most close counterfactual situations where p is true. Rather, p needs to be true in most counterfactual situations in which q is true. In effect, q must be a reliable indicator or mark of p's truth but p need not be a reliable indicator or mark of q's truth. Thus, in the lie detector case, a 'guilty' reading on the machine generates only the weakest of evidential support that the individual is guilty even though by hypothesis 'guilty' readings always indicate guilt. For, although a 'guilty' reading is a reliable indicator of guilt, guilt is not a reliable indicator that we will get such a reading.

Consider some additional examples of what Nozick's tracking relation would do to our notion of evidence. Consider, for example, the various relations of evidential support between a disjunction (p or q) and its disjuncts. Intuitively, we think the information that p is true always would constitute good evidence for (p or q). Moreover, we think also the information that q is true always would constitute as good evidence for (p or q) as would the information that p is true. On Nozick's account, however, it will not be unusual for the information that p is true to be such that it would provide only weak evidential support for (p or q). Likewise, it will not be unusual for the information that q is true to be such that it would provide a different degree of evidential support for (p or q) than would p. Worse still, it will not be unusual for the information that the disjunction (p or q) is true to be such that is would provide stronger evidential support for p than p would for (p or q).

There are a variety of cases that could be used to illustrate these consequences of Nozick's account with respect to disjunctions, but here is a particularly straightforward one. Suppose we have a standard deck of cards from which we have randomly drawn a card. Let p be the claim that the drawn card is a club, and let q be the claim that the drawn card is a jack. Support we are told that p is true. What kind of evidence does this provide for (p or q)? According to Nozick, the degree of evidential support that p provides for (p or q) is equal to pr[p/(p or q)] − pr[p/not(p or q)]. So, in the case here the degree of evidential support that p provides for (p or q) is equal to .8125. Suppose we had been told q, that the drawn card is a jack. What kind of evidential support would this have provided for (p or q)? According to Nozick, the degree of evidential support that q would provide for (p or q) is equal to pr[q/(p or q)] − pr[q/not(p or q)], which in the case here equals .25. Suppose we had been told that (p or q), that the card drawn is either a jack or a club. What kind of evidential support would this provide for the claim the card drawn is a club? According to Nozick, the degree of evidential support that (p or q) would provide for p equals pr[(p or q)/p] − pr[(p or q)/not$p$], which here equals .9231. So, given Nozick's account of evidence, our being told that the card drawn is a jack would provide significantly less evidential support for the claim that the card drawn is either a club or a jack than would our being told that the card drawn is a club. Moreover, our being told that the card drawn is either a club or a jack would provide stronger evidential support for the claim that the card drawn is a club than vice-versa.

Analogous problems arise with respect to conjunction. What kind of support would the information that the conjunction (p and q) is true provide for its conjuncts? Given Nozick's account, it depends on which conjunct you have in mind. Let p and q be the same as in the above case. Suppose you have been told that the card drawn is the jack of clubs. What kind of evidential support does this provide for the claim that the card drawn is a club? On Nozick's account, the degree of evidential support that (p and q) provides for p is equal to pr[(p and q)/p] − pr[(p and q)/not$p$], which in the case here is only .0769. What kind of evidential support does the information that the card drawn is the jack of clubs provide for the claim that the card drawn is a jack? The degree of evidential support that the former gives the latter, given Nozick's account, is equal to pr[(p and q)/q] − pr[(p and q)/not$q$], which here is .25. However, suppose that we had been told only that the card drawn is a jack. According to Nozick's account, the degree of evidential support that this would provide for the claim that the card drawn is the jack of clubs equals pr[q/(p and q)] − pr[q/not(p and q)], which is equal to .9412. So, on Nozick's account of evidence, the information that the card drawn is the jack of clubs provides different evidential support for the claim that the card drawn is a jack than it does for the claim that the card drawn is a club. Specifically, it provides more support for the former claim than it does for the latter claim. But even for the former claim, it provides only relatively weak support. By contrast, the information that the card drawn is a jack would provide powerful evidential support for the claim that the card drawn is the jack of clubs.

Moreover, as one might expect given the above consequences of Nozick's account, *p* can constitute better evidence for a conjunction (*q* and *r*) than it does for one of the conjuncts. Indeed, *p* can be better evidence for the conjunction than it is for either conjunct taken individually. It even can be better evidence for the conjunction (*q* and *r*) than it is for the disjunction (*q* or *r*). Suppose once again that a card has been randomly drawn from an ordinary deck of cards. Suppose we are told that the card drawn is either the king of clubs or the queen of clubs. Let this information be *p*. Let *q* be the claim that the card drawn is a face card, and let *r* be the claim that the card drawn is a club. Nozick's account of evidence implies that *p* is fairly good evidence for (*q* and *r*), although not as good evidence as we intuitively would think. The degree of evidential support that *p* gives to (*q* and *r*) equals $\mathrm{pr}[p/(q$ and $r)] - \mathrm{pr}[p/\mathrm{not}(q$ and $r)]$, which here is .667. But, *p* provides only very weak evidential support for *r*. And, likewise it provides only very weak evidential support for *q*. The degree of evidential support that *p* provides for *r* equals $\mathrm{pr}(p/r) - \mathrm{pr}(p/\mathrm{not}\text{-}r)$, which here equals .1538. The degree of evidential support that *p* provides for *q* equals $\mathrm{pr}(p/q) - \mathrm{pr}(p/\mathrm{not}\text{-}q)$, which is equal to .1667. And, the degree of evidential support that *p* provides for the disjunction (*q* or *r*) is weaker still; it is equal to $\mathrm{pr}(p/q$ or $r) - \mathrm{pr}([p/\mathrm{not}(q$ or $r)]$, which in turn is equal to .0909. So, not only does *p* here constitute significantly better evidence for the conjunction (*p* and *q*) than it does for either conjunct, it also constitutes better evidence for the conjunction of *q* and *r* than it does for their disjunction.

It would be easy enough to go on, to show yet other strongly counterintuitive consequences of Nozick's account of evidence, but there is little point in doing so. Any *one* of the above examples is enough to indicate that there is something seriously wrong with Nozick's account of evidence. Moreover, *all* of the above examples suggest the same diagnosis of what it is that has gone wrong. It is the problem mentioned above. Namely, although Nozick may be right in proposing that evidence plausibly can be thought of as a tracking relation, he has the tracking going in the wrong direction. On his view, *p* is evidence for *q* to the extent that *q* is an indication of *p* and not-*q* is an indication of not-*p*. But intuitively, the evidence relation goes in the reverse direction, such that *p* is evidence for *q* to the extent that *p* is an indication that *q* is true.

So, although Nozick's account of evidence is attractively simple as well as powerfully suggestive, it also is fundamentally wrong-headed. However, the way in which it is wrong-headed is revealing; it reveals how it might be possible to generate an equally simple and equally suggestive characterization of evidence that is fundamentally rightheaded. Namely, perhaps we can do so by turning Nozick's account almost directly on its head. In other words, perhaps we can get a plausible characterization of the evidential relation by understanding it as a subjunctive tracking relation, but not as a tracking relation that has evidence tracking truth (as Nozick would have it) but rather as a tracking relation that has truth tracking the evidence. Suppose we say that p is evidence for q to the extent that in close counterfactual situations in which p is true, q also is true. In particular, let us say that p is evidence for q—that is, p provides positive evidential support for q—just in case q is more likely to be true than is not-q in close counterfactual situations in which p is true. Intuitively then, the greater the percentage of close p-situations that are q-situations, the greater the degree of evidential support that p provides for q. If q generally would be true in these close p-situations, then p is good evidence for q. And if q is true in all these close p-situations—that is, if $p >> q$ is true—then p provides maximal evidential support for q.

This characterization of evidence is the mirror image of *half* of Nozick's account. One half of Nozick's account requires that the truth of p track the truth of q if p is to be evidence for q; the other half requires that the falsity of p track the falsity of q. The above suggestion reverses the first part of Nozick's account, requiring that the truth of q track the truth of p if p is to be evidence for q. However, it simply drops the second part of Nozick's account. But, why not try to understand evidence as the perfect mirror image of what Nozick takes it to be? That is, why not say that the degree of evidential support that p gives q is a function of how likely q would be were p true *and* how unlikely not-q would be were not-p true? Specifically, why not say that p provides q with positive evidential support just in case the likelihood of q, were p to be true, is greater than the likelihood of q, were not-p to be true—that is, just in case $\mathrm{pr}(q/p)$ is greater than the $\mathrm{pr}(q/\text{not-}p)$? Given such a notion of evidential support, the degree of evidential support would reach its upper limit 1 only if $p >> q$ *and* not-$p >>$ not-q are both true. Would this be a plausible notion of evidential support?

No; it would not be much more plausible than Nozick's notion, and for a related reason. Namely, like Nozick's notion, this notion would represent a departure from the intuitively attractive idea that p is evidence for q to the degree that p is an indication of q's truth. It would have us think that p is evidence for q to the degree that p is an indication of q's truth *and* not-p is an indication of not-q's truth. This suggestion, however, makes the mistake of running together two questions about evidence; it runs together the question of whether p is evidence for q with the question of whether not-p is good evidence for not-q. If we are to have a plausible account of evidence, we must separate these questions, allowing p to be good evidence for q even if not-p is not particularly good evidence for not-q.

For, suppose that we do not. Suppose, following the above suggestion, we grant that the degree of evidential support that p gives q is a function of both how likely q would be if p were true *and* how unlikely q would be if not-p were true. That is, suppose we say that the degree of evidential support that p gives q equals $\mathrm{pr}(q/p) - \mathrm{pr}(q/\text{not-}p)$. Then many of the problems that plague Nozick's account reappear. For example, a conjunction need not provide the same degree of evidential support for each of its conjuncts, and the support that it provides for one of its conjuncts can be very weak. Indeed, the information that a conjunction is true can provide weaker evidential support for one of its conjuncts than the information that the conjunct is true would provide for it.[7] Likewise, the information that a proposition p is true might provide only very weak evidence for the disjunction (p or q); it might even provide weaker evidential support for this disjunction than the information that the disjunction is true would provide for it.[8] And so on.

All these difficulties are eliminated by insisting that p is evidence for q just to the extent that q tracks p in close counterfactual situations in which p is true. This notion of evidence, like Nozick's, has the advantage of being one that characterizes the evidential relation in terms of a subjunctive tracking relation. However, unlike Nozick's notion of evidence, it preserves the intuitively attractive idea that p is evidence for q just to the extent that p is an indication or mark of q's truth.

Consider in a little more detail how the above characterization preserves this idea. Consider implication, for example. If p implies q, then q is true in all situations in which p is true. A fortiori, q is true in all close counterfactual situations in which p is true. So, whenever p implies q, p will be good evidence for q. Moreover, given the above characterization, evidence is closed under implication. If p is good evidence for q and q implies r, p is at least as good evidence for r. For, if q is true in most close counterfactual situations in which p is true (making p good evidence for q) and if q implies r, then r will be true in at least as many close p-situations as is q (making p good evidence for r as well).[9]

So, if p implies q and if the evidential relation is characterized as a relation in which truth tracks evidence, p will be evidence for q. However, suppose that p makes q highly probable without implying q. Does the above characterization of evidence insure that p will be evidence for q? It does if we can assume that whenever q is highly probable given p, q would at least weakly track p in close p-situations. This seems like a plausible assumption to make (and it is an assumption that Nozick does make in explicating his account of evidence). However, it is not easy to say what a close counterfactual situation is, and until we decide exactly what makes a counterfactual situation a close counterfactual situation it seems prudent not to simply assume that whenever p makes q probable, q will at least weakly track p in close p-situations. Even so, this does not pose a serious difficulty for the suggestion that evidence may be characterized in terms of a subjunctive tracking relation whereby evidence is tracked by that for which it is evidence. For, whatever we decide about how best to understand the notion of a close counterfactual situation, we can *stipulate* that for the purpose of characterizing evidence, the appropriate notion of closeness *must* be one that guarantees that q generally tracks p in relevant close p-situations if p makes q highly probable. Thus, to take a simple example, suppose we have vigorously spun a fair roulette wheel and randomly have placed the ball on the wheel. Given this information, it is probable that the ball will not stop on zero. However, suppose that unbeknownst to us the improbable will happen and the ball will stop on zero. Then it presumably is the case that in counterfactual situations that are *very* close to the actual situation, the ball also would have stopped on zero. For, it presumably is the case that had the wheel been spun with the *smallest difference in velocity, zero still would have come up. Likewise, it presumably is the case that had the ball been the smallest* bit heavier, zero still would have come up. And so on. However, the above stipulation insures that for the purpose of characterizing evidence these *very close* counterfactual situations are not the only *relevant close* counterfactual situations. Let p be the information that the ball randomly has been placed on a fair wheel that is vigorously spinning, and let q be the claim that a zero will not come up. What the above stipulation insures is that however we decide to identify those close situations in which q must track p if p is to be evidence for q, it must turn out that the relevant close situations are not simply those that are so close to the actual situation that the outcome in the actual situation is the outcome in them as well. On the contrary, it must turn out that in the relevant close situations, zero generally does not come up.[10]

Of course, this leaves open the question of exactly how this result is to be generated; it leaves open exactly what notion of a relevant close counterfactual situation it is best to use in order to generate this result. It is for this reason that I call the above suggestion only a 'characterization' of evidence, rather than an account or a theory of evidence. It provides us only with a rough way of thinking about evidence. It in effect constitutes only the barest outline of an account of evidence. It tells us that p is evidence for q just to the extent that q tracks p in relevant close counterfactual situations in which p is true. It also tells us that the notion of a relevant close counterfactual situation must be understood in such a way that if p makes q probable, q generally tracks p in relevant close p-situations. However, it does not tell us how to fill in this outline. In particular, it does not tell us in a general way what it is that makes a p-situation belong to the set of those p-situations in which q must generally be true if p is to be evidence for q.

I do not propose to remedy this here, since I do not propose to bring forward anything like a fully detailed account of evidence. For present purposes, I will be content with the claim that the above characterization of evidence provides a simple and attractive way of thinking about evidence. It is a way of thinking about evidence that insures that p is evidence for q just in case p is an indication or mark of q's truth. It insures as well that the degrees of evidential support that p provides for q and related propositions (such as propositions that q implies) will conform to the probability calculus. Moreover, it insures these results while conceiving of the evidential relation as a real factual relation, a subjunctive tracking relation.

A couple of additional details about this characterization of evidence are worth mentioning. Notice, first, that whatever notion of a relevant close situation we decide is best for understanding what is involved in p providing positive evidential support for q, it need not imply that there are infinitely many p-situations that are relevant close p-situations. On the contrary, there may be relatively few relevant close p-situations. As I am using the notion of a situation, a possible situation is not the same as a possible world. A possible world can be thought of as a special kind of possible situation, one that is demarcated by a maximally consistent set of propositions. A world in effect is a maximally specific situation. So, a less than maximally specific situation — a situation that is demarcated by a less than maximally consistent set of propositions — is a possible situation that can occur in many worlds (even in infinitely many worlds).

Accordingly, the notion of a relevant close situation that we decide is best for understanding evidence need not be a notion that picks out maximally specific situations. Indeed, it need not even pick out highly specific situations. Thus, in our roulette case where p is the proposition that the ball randomly has been placed on a vigorously spinning fair roulette wheel and q is the proposition that the ball will not land on zero, perhaps the criterion of a relevant close situation will identify only 37 relevant close spin-of-the-wheel situations, each of which is very general. One of these 37 situations, for example, might be demarcated by the following consistent set of propositions (the wheel is vigorously spun, the ball is placed at random on the wheel, and number 1 comes up); another such situation might be demarcated by the set of propositions (the wheel is vigorously spun, the ball is placed at random on the wheel, and number 2 comes up); and so on for each of the 35 other numbers. Indeed, it would be desirable for the criterion to imply that something like these are the only relevant close p-situations, since this would guarantee that the proposition p provides what we intuitively regard as exactly the right degree of evidential support for q.

This roulette example also can be used to illustrate a related feature of relevant close situations. Namely, it can be used to illustrate that one p-situation might be closer *simpliciter* to the actual situation than another p-situation even though the second belongs to the set of *relevant close p-situations* and the first does not. Thus, in our roulette case we have supposed that the wheel is fair, it has been vigorously spun, and the ball has been placed at random on the wheel. We have further supposed that unbeknownst to us the ball will stop on zero. Then presumably all (or at least most) of those highly specific situations that are *very* similar to the actual situation are situations in which the ball also would stop on zero. In addition, presumably all such situations are closer *simpliciter* to the actual situation than any situation (of whatever degree of specificity) in which zero does not come up. And yet, some of these latter situations will be relevant close p-situations while most of the former (perhaps all but one) will not be relevant close p-situations.

In a more general vein, notice also that this notion of evidence, according to which p is evidence for q just in case q generally tracks p in relevant close p-situations, is a notion that allows one to have evidence even in the face of skeptical possibilities. Thus, for example, my having a visual experience of a table in front of me (perhaps along with other appropriate experiences) can be good evidence for there actually being a table in front of me despite the fact that were I a brain-in-a-vat or were I under the control of an evil demon or were some other such skeptical hypothesis true, I would have just these experiences without there being a table in front of me. For even though there are countless such skeptical possibilities, none (much less all) of these situations need be relevantly close situations. And so, the mere possibility that some such skeptical hypothesis is true in no way implies that our perceptual experiences cannot provide us with good evidence about the world.

Finally, notice that the above notion of evidence is an objective notion of evidence. Given this notion of evidence, there is no guarantee that what we take to be good evidence is in fact good evidence. For example, there is no guarantee that I or that most members of my community or that those recognized as experts are right in regarding something p to be evidence for q. Likewise, there is no guarantee that a proposition p might in fact constitute good evidence for another proposition q even though neither I nor most humans nor the experts recognize this to be the case.

The lack of such guarantees creates a problem for the epistemologist. The problem is that it is natural to want an account of evidence to be of use in generating an acceptable account of epistemically rational belief. In particular, we want to be able to say that it is epistemically rational for an individual to believe *p* just in case he has adequate evidence for *p*. However, it is difficult for any objective notion of evidence, a notion that makes evidence independent of what an individual or the members of his community or the experts believe and independent even of what they would believe were they to be extremely careful in their investigations, to satisfy this desideratum. The problem, most generally stated, is that what it is epistemically rational for us to believe seems to be in some way a function of current human abilities, either our own abilities or the abilities of most people in our communities or the abilities of experts. But, this idea does not fit well with the idea that evidence objectively construed is closely connected with what it is epistemically rational for us to believe. For, it seems possible for *p* to be good evidence for *q* even though no one in fact sees that this is so and perhaps even though no one would see that this is so even if they were to spend a huge amount of time thinking about the relationship between *p* and *q*. Indeed, it even is possible, it seems, for *p* to be good evidence for *q* even though almost everyone (even the experts) now takes *p* to be good evidence for not-*q* and even though they would continue to think this even if they were to be as careful as they could be in their deliberations about *p* and *q*.[11] Under these conditions, would it be epistemically rational for an individual S to believe that *q* if he knew that *p*? It is hard to convince oneself that the answer to this question is "yes." After all, by hypothesis the fact that *p* constitutes good evidence for *q* lies beyond the pale of not only S himself but also his community and those recognized by his community as experts. And so, a "yes" answer here would seem to have the effect of imposing an overly demanding standard of epistemic rationality upon S, a standard that is not sufficiently sensitive to current human resources and abilities.

What then are our options? There are at least three basic options, I think. First, one can simply deny that it is epistemically rational for an individual to believe *p* just in case he has adequate evidence for *p*. Second, one can insist that although the evidential relation is an objective relation, it is a relation to which normal adults (or at least the experts) have access, a relation about whose presence they cannot be mistaken if the reflect carefully enough.[12] In this way, it is assured that evidential relations are not beyond our pale (or the pale of experts). Third, one can deny that we have anything like an infallible access to what constitutes good objective evidence for what we believe and yet also insist that having epistemically rational beliefs is *in some sense* a matter of having adequate evidence for what we believe. One can do this by introducing a nonobjective notion of evidence. In introducing this notion, one need not reject the idea that there also is an objective notion of evidence. On the contrary, an attractive idea is to introduce the relevant nonobjective notion of evidence, the notion that (unlike the objective notion) *is* intimately related to epistemic rationality, in terms of the objective notion. Thus, for example, one *might* say that if an individual S knows a proposition $p,$ then p constitutes for him good evidence for q in this nonobjective (or epistemic) sense just in case S would regard p as good objective evidence for q were he to be carefully reflective. Or if one is inclined toward a social conception of epistemic rationality, one *might* instead say that for an individual S a proposition p constitutes good evidence for $q,$ given that he knows that $p,$ just in the case most members of S's community think that p is good objective evidence for q or just in case those recognized by S's community as experts think this.

In any event, whatever the details of this last option, it has a number of advantages over the other options. Unlike the first option, it has the advantage of allowing us to preserve the intuitively plausible idea that there is some notion of evidence that is closely connected with epistemically rational belief. And unlike the second option, it allows us to preserve this idea without insisting that evidential relations are some sort of special logical relations to which we or the experts have something like an infallible access (at least if we reflect carefully enough). Finally, it preserves this idea without rejecting the equally plausible idea that there is an important objective notion of evidence—perhaps, for example, a tracking notion. On the contrary, this last option requires there to be an objective notion, since the epistemic notion of evidence is introduced in terms of it—in terms, for example, of what the individual or the members of his community or the experts believe, or in terms of what they would believe on careful reflection, about what constitutes good objective evidence for what.

The general idea here, then, is that in our investigations we seek good objective evidence. In investigating the truth of $q,$ for example, we seek truths that are good indications or marks of q's truth. But although this is what we seek, it is not a prerequisite of our having an epistemically rational belief in $q.$ It can be epistemically rational for us to believe q even if what we or most members of our community or the experts take to be good objective evidence for q is in fact not good objective evidence. And on the other hand, q might not be epistemically rational for us to believe even if we know a proposition p that is good objective evidence for $q,$ since it might be the case that neither we nor most members of our community nor the experts realize (or even would realize on more careful reflection) that p is a mark of q's truth.

NOTES

1. Robert Nozick, *Philosophical Explanations* (Cambridge: Harvard University Press, 1981). Further references to this book will be included in the text.

2. However, it is preserved in an unusual way. Namely, it is preserved by guaranteeing that *whenever* one knows that p, one's belief that p is self-evident — i.e., the mere fact that one believes that p constitutes good evidence for the truth of p.

3. However, they do not mesh quite as well as Nozick seems to think. Consider, for example, his claim that just as we cannot know the falsity of a skeptical hypothesis SK, so too we cannot have strong evidence for the falsity of SK. Nozick seems not to realize that this conclusion follows from his account of evidence only if we make an assumption that he generally seems reluctant to make. Namely, it follows only if we assume that our evidence consists solely of internal states (beliefs, experiences, thoughts, etc.). For, suppose we were to say that part of S's evidence consists of noninternal states — e.g., the state of S's seeing a table in front of him. Then S might very well have strong evidence for not-SK, since both (not-SK $>>$ S sees a table) and [SK $>>$ not(S sees a table)] might very well be true. Indeed, if S's vision is relatively normal and conditions are relatively normal, they presumably both are true. (I owe this point to Richard Fumerton.)

4. For example, he introduces the notion of a strong test of a hypothesis and the notion of a weak test of a hypothesis. A strong test of a hypothesis H, says Nozick, seeks the opposite of evidence; it looks for the falsity of what if true would be strong evidence for H. A weak test of H looks for the falsity of what if true would be weak evidence for H. Nozick, op. cit., 251.

5. The principle is roughly as follows: If (1) p is true and if (2) the evidential support that p provides for q is greater than or equal to .90 and if (3) pr(q) is greater than pr(p/not-q) and if (4) there is no q^1 such that q^1 is inconsistent with q and such that q^1 might be true if q were false and such that q^1 that satisfies the above conditions (2) and (3), then infer p. These conditions, as Nozick emphasizes, are very stringent. But this should not be a cause for concern. On the contrary, it should be reassuring, since the conditions are intended only to be sufficient for rational inference. No doubt there are many other principles of rational inference, but the above principle, says Nozick, is at least one such principle.

6. The pr $\left(\dfrac{\text{guilty}}{\text{'innocent'}} \right) = 1 - \text{pr}\left(\dfrac{\text{innocence}}{\text{'innocent'}} \right) =$

$$\dfrac{1 - \text{pr}\left(\dfrac{\text{'innocent'}}{\text{innocence}} \right) \times \text{pr(innocence)}}{\text{pr('innocent')}} = 1 - \dfrac{1 \times .5}{.9999} = 1 - .5001 = .4999.$$

7. For example, suppose a card has been drawn at random from a normal deck of cards. Let p be the claim that the card drawn is not a jack. Let q be the claim that the card drawn is not a club. Suppose we are told that (p and q) is true. According to the above suggestion, what degree of evidential support does this information provide for the individual conjuncts? It depends on which conjunct one considers. The degree of support that (p and q) gives $q =$ pr(q/p and q) $-$ pr[q/not(p and q)] $= .8125$. However, the degree of support that (p and q) gives $p =$ pr(p/p and q) $-$ pr[p/not(p and q)], which here is equal only to .25. Worse still, the information that p here is true would provide stronger evidential support for (p and q) than (p and q) provides for p, since the degree of support that p would give (p and q) $=$ pr(p and q/p) $-$ pr(p and q/not$p$) $= .75$.

8. Let p and q be the same as in note 7. Then the degree of evidential support that p would provide for (p and q) $=$ pr(p or q/p) $-$ pr(p or q/not-p), which here is .25. This is much less than the degree of evidential support that (p or q) would provide for p, which here equals .9412.

9. I am not assuming here that it is desirable for *all* evidence-related notions to be closed under implication. On the contrary, I agree that it may be useful to introduce evidence-related notions that are not closed under implication — for example, the notion of confirmation. As this notion is often used, p confirms q just if p increases q's prior probability. Accordingly, p might very well confirm q even though it disconfirms (i.e., even though it confirms the negation of) some proposition r that q implies. For, it might very well raise the prior probability of q and lower the prior probability of r. (Suppose, e.g., that r here is the

disjunction q or not-p.) So, I am not insisting that all evidence-related notions be closed under implication. However, I am insisting that any evidence-related notion that is not closed under implication is not intimately related to our standard notion of evidence, a notion that requires p to be a mark or an indication of q's truth if p is to be evidence for q. Thus, e.g., I am insisting that from the fact that an individual S knows p and knows as well that p confirms q, it does not follow that S has even weak evidence for q. For, although p may well raise the prior probability of q, it still may be the case that not-q is more likely than q given p.

10. There obviously is a close parallel here with theories of probability. Consider frequency theories, for example. According to such theories, the probability of zero coming up (as by hypothesis it will) equals the limit of the relative frequency of zeros in an infinite series of similar spin-of-the-roulette-wheel-events. But, if the events in this series are *very* similar to the actual event, zero almost always will come up. So, frequentists need to introduce some notion of a relevantly similar event, and a constraint on this notion is that it insure that in the above case (and in like cases) the relevantly similar events not be so similar to the actual event that the limit of the relative frequency of zeros in an infinite series of such events is anywhere close to 1. On the contrary, the notion they introduce must insure that the relative frequency is at least close to $^1 \in _{37}$ (or $^1 \in _{38}$ if the wheel is an 'American-style' wheel, one with a double-zero as well as a zero). For, we intuitively think that any account of probability that does not make the probability of a zero coming up on a fair roulette wheel equal to (or at least close to) $^1 \in _{37}$ is an account that for this very reason is implausible.

11. In raising this possibility, I am not raising issues that are in any straightforward manner related to recent disputes about realism. For, even ardent anti-realists do not tie the meaningfulness of a claim to our *current* abilities to ascertain its truth or its falsity.

12. One who is inclined toward this view will be inclined also to claim that the evidential relation is best understood as a logical relation (rather than as anything like a tracking relation).

two

EVIDENCE AND THE CASE OF PROFESSOR ROBERT NOZICK*

Thomas D. Paxson, Jr.

Professor Robert Nozick is well recognized for insightfully addressing broad and important philosophical concerns. He sketches the philosophical landscape with clear, bold strokes, like a Renaissance master frequently leaving to others the task of filling in the details. His artistry is such that those strokes are often highly creative — some suggesting subtle refinements of themes others have explored and others suggesting interesting new lines of inquiry. Professor Nozick's approach invites us to probe the lacunae. The core of this essay is an assessment of Professor Robert Nozick's account of evidence. This core is enveloped by some reflections on more traditional epistemology, especially that tradition which derives from the pioneering work of Descartes. The gap between the two — a gap which Professor Nozick would readily acknowledge — is a subsidiary theme.

In a widely influential paper Professor Roderick Firth distinguished truth-evaluating, warrant-evaluating, and testability-evaluating senses of certainty.[1] This threefold distinction illuminates Descartes's project. Descartes seems to have sought a certainty that contained all three senses. If something's being the case was certain for S, it was true, it was as warranted for S as S's own existence, and it was testable via the methods of doubt and reconstruction. Its truth was either manifest or guaranteed by God. It was warranted by the clearness and distinctness with which it was apprehended, and it was tested by the method of doubt, and if dubitable, by the reconstruction which displayed the inferential relations by which it was connected with other certain beliefs.

*An earlier version of this essay was read to the St. Louis Philosophical Society. I am especially grateful for discussions with my colleagues Professors John Barker and Robert Pendergrass. Thanks also are due to the editor for his helpful suggestions.

It is well recognized that Descartes did not accomplish the unassailable reconstruction he sought. Almost immediately philosophers sought to revise the conception of the epistemic task that Descartes had set. Now epistemologists seem to have abandoned the goal of a certainty that is at once truth-, warrant-, and testability-evaluating.

Although the conception of the epistemologist's task has been revised continually since Descartes, the demand for warrant may be seen as an enduring legacy. In a series of lectures given in Amherst, Massachusetts in 1972, Professor Firth focused on the question, "If a person, A, believes some proposition, p, then . . . what are the . . . conditions in virtue of which A's belief that p would be warranted?" The only way to answer this question, he maintained, is to reconstruct knowledge — that is, to "order propositions in a way that exhibits the inferential relations among them." Epistemic warrant, he stressed repeatedly, does not entail truth. Indeed, his very cautious neo-Cartesian program stipulated that all empirical propositions that are self-warranted for one are such because, first, one believes them (or would do so if one considered them) and, second, because they are about and only about the intrinsic character of one's immediate experience. Their warrant does not stem from their truth.

Professor Firth contrasted his approach with Professor Roderick Chisholm's. Chisholm's procedure (for example, in "A Version of Foundationalism"[2]) is to define a self-presenting *property* and then introduce as his first epistemic principle that if one has a self-presenting property and considers whether one has it, then it is certain that one has the property. Thus whereas Professor Firth's account of self-warranted propositions begins with belief, Professor Chisholm's account begins with properties of persons. But Chisholm's account leaves open the possibility that one may *believe* that one has the property and nonetheless fail to have it. His epistemic principles, if I understand them correctly, do entail that if I believe that I have a self-presenting property, directly attributing it to myself, then it is certain for me that I have that property if the attribution "is beyond reasonable doubt" for me and if "it is at least as reasonable" for me "as is the direct attribution of any other property."[3] I take it that even in cases of false direct attribution these conditions can be, though they are not always, met. Professor Chisholm's "certain" does not have the truth-evaluating sense, though it is warrant-evaluating. It is not as different from Professor Firth's, in this respect anyway, as might have been expected.

With respect to empirical knowledge both Professors Firth and Chisholm hold that it is grounded in beliefs or attributions regarding the immediate content of one's experience. The foundation of one's knowledge is open to immediate access. This notion of access is clearly stated in the following desideratum that Professor Chisholm gives for an adequate theory of evidence.[4]

> Some of the things I am justified in believing are such that by reflection I can *know* that I am justified in believing them; and I can find out just *what,* if anything, justifies me in believing them.

Professor Chisholm's notion of access to the grounds of one's warrant seems to be presupposed by Professor Firth and others working in that tradition. The Neo-Cartesian reconstruction of knowledge seems to presuppose, concerning at least most[5] of my warranted beliefs, that I can find out what, if anything, justifies them for me — and by reflection! As we have seen, this will not guarantee their truth. Nonetheless it is this aspect of the Cartesian legacy that links *evidence* and justification to knowledge. So natural is it to those like myself steeped in this tradition, that it is rather surprising to read in Baldwin's *Dictionary of Philosophy and Psychology* that knowledge is[6]

> a cognition fulfilling three conditions: first, that it holds for true a proposition that really is true; second, that it is perfectly self-satisfied and free from the uneasiness of doubt; third, that some character of this satisfaction is such that it would be logically impossible that this character should ever belong to satisfaction in a proposition not true. . . .

The certainty involved in this definition is truth-evaluating and not either warrant- or testability-evaluating. There is no hint of a requirement of access through reflection to whatever character it is of one's "satisfaction" that would make it "impossible that this satisfaction should ever belong to satisfaction in a proposition not true."

The position taken by Baldwin's *Dictionary* may be construed as retaining Descartes's truth-evaluating certainty at the expense of warrant. Professor Nozick's view is closer to this position than it is to that of either Professors Firth or Chisholm. If the "satisfaction" is interpreted as belief, and if we change the logical modality to the more plausible *de re* modality, the following analysis is suggested:

S knows that *p* if and only if
    (a) *p* is true,
    (b) S believes without reservation that *p,* and
    (c) S's believing that *p* is necessarily such that if S believes without reservation that *p* then *p.*

Compare this with Professor Nozick's analysis of knowledge in *Philosophical Explanations* (172–78)[7]

S knows that *p* if and only if
    (a) *p* is true,
    (b) S believes that *p,*

(c) if p were false, S wouldn't believe that p, and

(d) if p were true, S would believe that p and not believe that not-p.

The *Dictionary's* account as reformulated with *de re* modality is strikingly similar to Professor Nozick's account less condition (d).

What happened to the notions of evidence and justification, notions that traditionally have been given considerable weight in analyses of knowledge? Professor Nozick, at least, specifically denies that evidence and justification are part of his analysis of knowledge — even implicitly. He does discuss evidence in a section separate from his analysis of knowledge.

I. EVIDENCE, AND PROFESSOR NOZICK ON EVIDENCE

Professor Nozick's treatment of evidence has not received the attention that it deserves. It is, admittedly, a puzzling discussion. In the beginning he sets himself the task of providing an account of why evidence and justification have been regarded as so importantly connected with knowledge (248), yet he gives an account of evidence that is far removed from the usual understanding of it. Professor Nozick's view departs from the traditional in several respects. First, there is no stipulation that evidence be available to an inquirer or believer. Second, he gives only what he regards as necessary conditions for something's being evidence and a set of necessary conditions for something's being strong evidence. I shall focus on the conditions proposed as necessary for being evidence at all, rather than strong evidence. His first condition is too strong and his second too weak to capture our intuitions. Furthermore, Professor Nozick gives no indication as to what he might want to add to the necessary conditions he specifies in order to construct a set of jointly sufficient conditions for something's being evidence. I shall propose modifications of Nozick's account which may help to meet some of these problems, but the results do not advance the program significantly. There remains the difficulty intrinsic to externalist epistemologies that they are not able to address many of the epistemic questions that have most interested philosophers historically.

A brief summary of Professor Nozick's account of evidence will facilitate discussion of the problems which I find in his treatment of evidence and will make it easier for others to identify any misinterpretations that shape my discussion. To oversimplify Nozick's view, evidence "tracks" the truth of the hypothesis for which it is evidence: (248–51):

If *e* is strong evidence for *h,* then
(a) if *h* were the case, *e* would be the case, and
(b) if *h* were false, *e* would be false.

If *e* is evidence for *h,* then
(a) if *h* were the case, *e* would be the case, and
(b') if *h* were false, *e* might be false.

Now prima facie (a) appears to be too strong. Indeed, I think that it is. In many cases of reasoning in ordinary, nonscientific contexts we take a piece of evidence to be sufficient to warrant a belief, but not necessary for its truth. Professor Nozick's account requires that anything that counts as evidence, whether strong evidence or weak evidence, will be such that its occurrence would be necessary for the truth of the hypothesis.

Imagine that Jack and James Thomas are twins and that they are talking with one another at the door of my classroom. One would expect that the conjunctive state of affairs *e,* Jack's being in my classroom and Jack's being a twin, would not only be evidence but would be strong evidence for the hypothesis that there is a twin in my classroom. On the other hand, it does not seem to be correct intuitively to suppose that if there were a twin in my classroom then it would be the case that Jack is in my classroom and is a twin. It could just as easily be James who was in my classroom — whether or not in actuality James is in my room or is just outside the door. Thus (a) is not satisfied and *e* is not evidence at all, on Professor Nozick's view, let alone strong evidence. He often uses possible worlds to give some intuitive content to his subjunctive conditionals. But the world in which James is in my classroom and not Jack could be ever so close to the actual world in which Jack is in the room. Let us turn to an example in which *e* does not logically imply that *h.*

Let us take the familiar example of a match.[8] Consider the two propositions,

p. The match ignites.

q. Oxygen is present.

Suppose that we ask ourselves which of the two seems better evidence for the other. My intuitions are that we would regard *p,* the match's ignition, as very strong evidence for *q,* oxygen's presence, but regard oxygen's presence as at best very weak evidence for the match's ignition unless it is supplemented by other evidence regarding the presence of heat, absence of moisture, and so on. But consider the consequences of Professor Nozick's account. A necessary condition of *e*'s being evidence for *h* is that if *h* were true *e* would hold. Compare the following two propositions:

If oxygen were present, the match would ignite.

If the match were to ignite, oxygen would be present.

It is far more clear, I submit, that the second would hold than the first. Thus on Professor Nozick's account *q* is a more likely candidate to be evidence for *p* than the other way around. Indeed, in ordinary circumstances it may be that the match's ignition cannot be evidence of the presence of oxygen at all. This is just the reverse of our pre-analytic intuitions. Something has gone askew.

The foregoing objections might be dismissed as overlooking the requirements of the subjunctive conditional. It is not any and every time that *e* is evidence of *h* but this time, in this actual world and in those closest to it. We must be careful, nonetheless, not to turn the subjunctive conditional into an indicative conditional. In this world my wife takes a match and tries to ignite it in order to light a candle on the window sill. It is in just this sort of circumstance that it may be plausible to hold that if oxygen were present, the match would ignite — since she has selected a dry match and struck it in her customarily successful manner. But it is even more evident that if the match were to ignite, oxygen would be present. And it is in just such a concrete case that the match's ignition seems to be better evidence of oxygen's presence (though its failure to light would not be good evidence of oxygen's absence) than oxygen's presence would be evidence of the match's ignition. The worlds closest to the actual world, we would suppose, are far more likely to include wet or defective matches or worn striking pads than to include our livingroom devoid of oxygen. Thus in the actual world in which my wife tries to ignite the match, its ignition is not evidence of oxygen's presence on Professor Nozick's analysis. Condition (a) is not met. To limit the relevant possible worlds in such a way that all factors pertaining to the match's ignition in this world remain constant and unvarying in the "closest worlds" allowed for comparison, except for the presence of oxygen, does not seem to be an option that Nozick does, or should, allow himself. Condition (a) is too strong.

It is a commonplace that a very good way to test a hypothesis is to seek to show that a consequence of it is false. Assuming the conditional to be true that if a hypothesis *h* were to be true, then consequence *c* would obtain, then the failure of *c* to obtain would be good evidence that *h* did not obtain. The failure of diligent attempts to show that not-*c* helps confirm *h*. It is not so much that *c* is good evidence of *h* as that not-*c* is good evidence that not-*h*. But not all evidence is of this character, as our earlier examples have shown. The Popperian strategy, which is appropriate to experimental science, rests on the two facts that ordinarily it is easier to disprove a general proposition than to prove it (the easier to disprove it is, the more content it has), and that more information is gained from a single instance if it disconfirms a general hypothesis than if it accords with it. The effort to turn this important strategy into a general theory of evidence seems to lead Professor Nozick to the peculiar view that *c* is evidence for *h,* because not-*c* would prove that not-*h* (250–51), while a *p* that is causally sufficient for *h,* but not necessary, wholly fails to be evidence of *h* at all.

"Evidence" is frequently used in a nonconclusive sense, as when detectives gather evidence for the solution of a crime or when people look for evidence that might help confirm or disconfirm a rumor. Many pieces of evidence may be quite weakly connected to the hypothesis, it being a matter of chance to some extent that there be a connection at all. More to the point, such pieces of evidence would not seem to be necessitated by the hypothesis in the sense required and therefore evidence of this sort would not satisfy Professor Nozick's condition (a). Suppose that a supervisor, Smith, abruptly fires Robinson as a result of *accidentally* surprising Robinson in the act of dealing drugs. The other employees are only told that Robinson has been fired, but there have been some suspicions among the rank and file that Robinson has been engaged in selling drugs. In such circumstances it would seem that

(e) Smith abruptly fired Robinson

is some evidence, though perhaps not strong evidence, that

(h) Robinson was dealing drugs.

But this case does not fit Professor Nozick's account of evidence. In order for (e) to be evidence of (h), whether strong or weak, it would have to be the case that if *h* were the case, then *e* would be the case. This condition is not satisfied. The drug dealing had gone on undetected (until the accidental encounter) and could have continued undetected. It was a mere chance encounter that led to Smith's discovery and consequent dismissal of Robinson. Furthermore, this counterexample has a form similar to that of an example which Professor Nozick himself gives to a subjunctive conditional employed in one of his preliminary analyses of knowledge (179). Both examples turn on someone's happening upon some evidence, although in the drug dealing example the happenstance bears on the causal relation between the drug dealing and the dismissal, the latter being the evidence that is not at all accidentally known by the rank and file. Again (a) has turned out to be too strong.

So far we have focused entirely on (a). It is presented as a necessary condition of something's being evidence at all. Now let us look at (b') which is also to be a necessary condition of something's being evidence:

(b') If *h* were false, *e* might be false.

Although (a) and (b') are presented as individually necessary conditions only, it is useful to see that they cannot constitute jointly a sufficient condition of something's being evidence; they are too weak for this purpose. Reflect briefly once more on the match example. Let *e* be 'oxygen is present' and *h*, 'the match ignites.' Then (a) is satisfied, since if *h* were the case, *e* would be the case, and (b') is satisfied since if *h* were not the case then *e* might not be the case. The oxygen *might* be displaced by a heavier gas which could have leaked into the house as a result of some extraordinary accident. To see whether (b') is satisfied we may look at worlds far removed from the actual world, not just the closest ones. Thus the conditions are satisfied. But under the circumstances, I submit, the presence of oxygen is no evidence at all of the match's ignition because in all worlds reasonably close to this one oxygen will be present. It is a stable, ever-present background condition present whether or not the match ignites.

Perhaps (b') was intended to block such cases, but it does not. It is extraordinarily weak. As my colleague Professor John Barker has pointed out in a conversation, it is so weak that it is hard to see how this condition could fail to be satisfied whenever condition (a) is satisfied, that is whenever if *h* were true, *e* would be true, using the Lewis modal system employed in (b') by Professor Nozick. I am assuming here that *e* is contingent, that we are concerned with a theory of empirical evidence. That it might be weak is recognized by Nozick, who connects the likelihood of *e*'s being false with the strength of the evidential connection. Consider the following Marshall Swain type of example: Mr. Dunnit murdered Mr. Killedgore on a deserted pier at 11:05 P.M. March 15th. The blood from Mr. Killedgore's fatal wound soaked into the deck of the wooden pier staining it. Let *h* be "Dunnit murdered Killedgore," and let *e* be "the pier was stained with Killedgore's blood." Does *e* meet Professor Nozick's necessary condition (b')? To answer this question we have to determine whether if *h* were false, *e* might be false. The answer is clearly that it might; thus (b') is satisfied by *e*. Suppose we let *e'* be that the pier remained standing on March 16th. If *h* were false, *e'* might be false as well. There are no restrictions on what alteration would have rendered *h* false, and so it could quite well be the case that what intervened to make *h* false would make *e'* false as well. Perhaps *h* would have been false because Dunnit, while lying in wait for Killedgore, carelessly disposed of a cigarette thus causing an explosion — destroying both the pier and himself. In short, (b') is too permissive. It would seem that anything that met (a) would meet (b').

II. PROBABILITY

If (a) is too strong and (b') too weak, we might be able to improve both by giving probabilified versions of each. Nozick obliges us by giving us these in his discussion of the measure of support weak evidence gives to a hypothesis. The probabilified versions of his two conditions of strong evidence, (a) and (b) respectively are (252)

$$\text{prob}(e, h) = 1$$
$$\text{prob}(e, \text{not-}h) = 0.$$

Given that these are to be interpreted as representing some kind of propensity[9] that derives from, or is reflected in, the subjective conditionals, the first says neither more nor less than (a). It is therefore too strong. In the section, "Inference Based on Probability," Professor Nozick proposes the following principle (257):

From $\text{prob}(e, h) \geq .95$
$\quad \text{prob}(e, \text{not-}h) \leq .05$
$\quad e$
$\text{prob}_o(h) > \text{prob}(e, \text{not-}h)$

infer h.

Nozick explains that "$\text{prob}_o(h)$ refers to "the initial or otherwise determined probability of h" (255)[10] such that $\text{prob}_o(h)$ plus $\text{prob}_o(\text{not-}h)$ equals one. For the purposes of this discussion $\text{prob}_o(h)$ will be treated as (arithmetically) equivalent to the absolute probability of h and thus to the probability of h on e or $not\text{-}e$.

The first thing to note is that the numerical limits given in the principle are specified arbitrarily. Professor Nozick admits not checking to see whether this specification of numerical limits will make his account vulnerable to some version of the lottery paradox. Nor does he revise his definition of evidence in light of this inference principle. This latter has the peculiar and unacceptable consequence that circumstances that are countenanced as adequate bases for inference do not count as evidence.

My interest in the proposed inference principle is that it provides suggestions as to how to modify Professor Nozick's theory of evidence to meet the objections I have raised. In particular, it would be desirable to weaken (a) and (b) while strengthening (b'). It does not seem to be at all promising, however, to assign numerical limits to these in the manner of the first two conditions of Nozick's inference principle. Consider, instead, the following analysis:

e is evidence for h if and only if
$\text{prob}(e, h) > \text{prob}(e, \text{not-}h).$

Where e is strong evidence for h, on Professor Nozick's account, $prob(e,h) = 1$ and $prob(e, not\text{-}h) = 0$. This analysis of evidence, therefore, includes Nozick's notion of strong evidence but (in effect) weakens (a) and (b) while strengthening (b'). Further, it would seem to be in the spirit of Nozick's analysis in that it analyzes evidence in terms of the probabilities of e given h and e given not-h rather than in terms of the probabilities of h given e and h given not-e.

It is just this feature of Professor Nozick's analysis that I found initially so counterintuitive. I even tried to find an example in which the proposed definition was satisfied yet in which the initial probability of h was greater than that of h given e. This would represent a compelling counterexample to the analysis of evidence since the probability of h on the evidence e should exceed the initial probability of h. But no counterexample of this kind is possible since it can be proved that

$$prob(e,h) > prob(e, not\text{-}h) \text{ if and only if } prob(h,e) > prob_o(h).$$

A proof is given in the appendix. It follows that the proposed analysis is equivalent (at least truth-functionally equivalent) to

e is evidence for h *if and only if* $prob_o(h) < prob(h,e)$.

This seems to be intuitively correct but quite trivial. Pragmatic considerations lead me to suggest the following amended analysis:[11]

> e is evidence for h if and only if
> $prob(e,h) > prob(e, not\text{-}h)$ or
> $prob(h,e) > prob_o(h)$.

It seems advisable to include both disjuncts because, although they are truth-functionally equivalent, it may be easier in some circumstances to ascertain directly one of the disjuncts than the other. For example it might be easier to calculate the relative probabilities of e on h and e on not-h than the probability of h on e and the initial probability of h. This is but a pragmatic matter affected by the circumstances and the nature of the hypothesis and evidential statement involved. One advantage of this modest proposal is that e's being evidence of h would be entailed by any e and h satisfying Nozick's principle of inference based on probability. Thus he could escape the aforementioned paradox that an e from which one could appropriately infer h not be evidence at all.

I have argued that Professor Nozick's analysis of evidence is too strong, because the first condition is too strong. The second condition, (b'), is much too weak. Replacing the two conditions by a single probabilified condition, we arrived at something truth-functionally equivalent to the intuitive, but still very weak, condition that e is evidence for h only if the probability of h on e is greater than the initial probability of *h*. It may be appropriate that it is weak, since evidence can be ever so weak; unfortunately, it is trivial as well.

III. LIMITATIONS OF THE EXTERNALIST APPROACH

Earlier it was noted that Professor Nozick nowhere stipulates that evidence be available to an inquirer or believer. There is no reference in the analysis to the person for whom something is evidence nor to any *awareness* of that which is to serve as evidence. He is concerned with evidence in an absolute sense rather than as relativized to a person at a time. This is, perhaps, the major reason why his discussion of evidence diverges so much from an account that would link evidence with knowledge. Yet, if I understand him correctly, he thinks that he has done just that:

> Consider someone who believes *h* on the basis of his belief in (what is) strong evidence *e;* his belief that *h* depends upon (and varies with) his belief that *e*. And let us suppose he knows the evidence is true, his belief that *e* tracks the fact that *e*. In this case, his belief that *h* tracks his belief that *e* (because it depends on it) which in turn tracks the fact that *e* (because he knows that *e*) which in turn tracks the fact that *h* (because, by hypothesis, *e* is strong evidence of *h*). . . . To believe something *h* on the basis of (what is) strong evidence *e,* where *e* is known, is to know *h*. (249)

This is an account of a special case. Knowledge does not require such an *e* since one's belief that *h* might track *h* without there being such an *e*. Furthermore, even if there is an *e* of this sort the dependence of S's belief that *h* on S's belief that *e* might be nonrational. It might be the product of the system of magic which S has been taught by the prevailing culture, or worse, by associations rooted in that magic which suggest to S (and perhaps no one else) when coming to believe *e* that *h*. The situation in which a person believing some *e* validly infers and comes thereby to know that *h* is, on Professor Nozick's view simply a special case of reliably believing that *h*. As such it accounts for the traditional view that evidence and justification are importantly connected with knowledge — but only because undue attention has been paid to this special case. His account, then, does not accord with the traditional view that "evidence is equivalent to the reasons, not the causes, of a judgment, and thus has always an objective and universal significance," as Baldwin puts it.[12]

That the evidence would be part of whatever it is that would make our beliefs "track" the truth is not enough. Perhaps, like Professor Dretske, Professor Nozick regards our intentional states to be little more than the state of a thermometer that "tells" the temperature — or why not a clock that "tells" the time?[13] Consciousness or awareness, on this model, are not essential properties of cognitive states. This is a far different enterprise than that of Descartes. Warrant-evaluating certainty is provided no grounds at all since, as Professor Firth explains the operative sense of warrant, warrant is "a property that statements possess in relation to what I have called the 'warrant-conferring' characteristics of a particular person at a particular time."[14] To be sure, Firth meant his expression to be neutral with respect to competing coherence and foundationalist theories of justification, but all of them regard the warrant-conferring characteristics as rationally, not just causally or subjunctively, supportive of the hypothesis they warrant. But no reasoning or perceptual skills are called for by Professor Nozick's account, though they are not excluded. There is no doubt that there are such states of things that are the products of tracking mechanisms, in the sense that Nozick specifies. Indeed such things and such states, like the strand of horsehair in the homemade hygrometer, might be very useful. But, I submit, they would be epistemically useful only to a deliberative consciousness for which (or should I say for whom?) they would serve as indicators.

Professor Nozick presents his epistemological reflections solidly in the context of wider philosophical issues and concerns. This has the merit of reminding us that epistemology cannot be done in a vacuum and informs us explicitly of the context in which Nozick is working. Whether we acknowledge it or not, our wider philosophical concerns will affect and be affected by our epistemology. It seems to be evident, however, that the issues and concerns which shape Nozick's thought are different in important respects than those which have shaped modern epistemology for the most part.

In the beginning of this chapter reference was made to Descartes. The relevance of this historical note is that it provides a context in which to place Professor Nozick's contributions to epistemology. Modern epistemology was born in revolution against scholasticism. This revolution called for deliberate efforts to root out the presuppositions which the tree of scholasticism had sent deep into the soil that was the European world view. Scholasticism was to be rooted out and the ground prepared for a more fruitful tree of knowledge, the validity of whose roots could be ascertained directly by the new epistemologists. To change the metaphor, the first revolutionaries failed to complete the revolution; Descartes, for example, was unsuccessful in freeing himself of all scholastic presuppositions. Their theories may have fallen victim to the destructive forces they loosed on their adversaries. But out of this revolution grew modern empiricism, nourished by the myth that the validity of its foundations could be ascertained directly through the individual inquirer's own experience.

Descartes had sought a presuppositionless philosophy, according to the standard interpretation. This is a theoretically impossible ideal. Nonetheless, the insistence that knowledge presupposes that one's belief be warranted in such a way that one has access to that which warrants it, that one can in principle epistemically justify one's belief, remains an important, normative element in the concept of knowledge. It includes the notion of one's having an epistemic "right to be sure,"[15] the notion that one's warrant meets certain epistemic norms. It presupposes that we are responsible for believing what we do believe, whether or not believing is a volitional act (which is doubtful). That our beliefs track the truth is irrelevant, on this understanding, if we have no awareness that they do and no reason to believe that they do.

APPENDIX

Thesis to be proven: $P(E/H) > P(E,not-H)$ if and only if $P(H/E) > P(H)$.

Assume H and E pick out numbers within a universe, U, such that
$$U = \{H \cap E\} \cup \{H \cap \overline{E}\} \cup \{\overline{H} \cap E\} \cup \{\overline{H} \cap E\}.$$

Name the sets as follows:
$$\{H \cap E\} = F$$
$$\{\underline{H} \cap \overline{E}\} = G$$
$$\{H \cap \overline{E}\} = J$$
$$\{\overline{H} \cap E\} = K.$$

Then
$$P(E/H) = \frac{P(F)}{P(F \cup G)} = \frac{P(F)}{P(F) + P(G) - P(F \cap G)}$$
$$= \frac{P(F)}{P(F) + P(G) - 0} = \frac{P(F)}{P(F) + P(G)}$$

$$P(E/\overline{H}) = \frac{P(K)}{P(J \cup K)} = \frac{P(K)}{P(J) + P(K) - P(J \cap K)}$$
$$= \frac{P(K)}{P(J) + P(K) - 0} = \frac{P(K)}{P(J) + P(K)}$$

$$P(H/E) = \frac{P(F)}{P(F \cup K)} = \frac{P(F)}{P(F) + P(K) - P(F \cap K)}$$
$$= \frac{P(F)}{P(F) + P(K) - 0} = \frac{P(F)}{P(F) + P(K)}$$

$$P(H) = \frac{P(F \cup G)}{P[(F \cup G) \cup (J \cup K)]}$$

$$= \frac{P(F) + P(G) - P(F \cap G)}{P[(F \cup G) \cup (J \cup K)]}$$

$$= \frac{P(F) + P(G)}{P(F) + P(G) + P(J) + P(K)} \, .$$

By substitution we get

$$P(E/H) > P(E/\overline{H}) = \frac{P(F)}{P(F) + P(G)} > \frac{P(K)}{P(J) + P(K)}$$

$$= [P(F) \times P(J)] + [P(F) \times P(K)] >$$
$$[P(F) \times P(K)] + [P(G) \times P(K)]$$
$$= [P(F) \times P(J)] > [P(G) \times P(K)]$$

$$P(H/E) > P(H) = \frac{P(F)}{P(K) + P(F)} > \frac{P(F) + P(G)}{P(F) + P(G) + P(J) + P(K)}$$

$$= [P(F) \times P(F)] + [P(F) \times P(G)] + [P(F)$$
$$\times P(J)] + [P(F) \times P(K)] > P(F) \times P(F)$$
$$+ [P(F) \times P(G)] + [P(F) \times P(K)] + [P(G)$$
$$\times P(K)]$$

$$= P(F) \times P(J) > P(G) \times P(K).$$

Thus, since both are retraceable, $P(E/H) > P(E/\overline{H})$ if and only if $P(H/E) > P(H)$.

NOTES

1. Roderick Firth, "The Anatomy of Certainty," *The Philosophical Review* 76 (1967): 3-27, especially 7-14.

2. Roderick Chisholm, "A Version of Foundationalism," *Midwest Studies in Philosophy,* 5 (1980): 543-64.

3. Ibid., 548.

4. Ibid., 546.

5. Professor Chisholm does not explain in the article quoted above why he uses "some" rather than all, but he does refer in a footnote to Prof. James Van Cleve's article, "Foundationalism, Epistemic Principles, and the Cartesian Circle" (*The Philosophical Review* 88 (1979): 55-91). Van Cleve argues there that it is possible to be justified in believing that one is justified in believing that *p* by being justified in believing that *p* has some property (one

happens not to be able to identify) such that for whatever has this property one is justified in believing it. Perhaps Professor Chisholm had cases of this sort in mind. I have used the language of "at least most" because an externalist epistemology of the kind proposed by Professor Nozick will countenance far more cases in which I am unable to discover the warrant for my belief than will traditional internalist epistemologists like Professor Chisholm.

6. James Baldwin, ed., *Dictionary of Philosophy and Psychology,* vol. 1 (New York: Macmillan, 1918). The entry is attributed to C. S. Pierce and Mrs. C. Ladd-Franklin.

7. Robert Nozick, *Philosophical Explanations* (Cambridge, Massachusetts: Harvard University Press, 1981). All references to Nozick's book will be included in this text.

8. There is a long history of match cases, the most famous of which seems to be Brian Skyrms' "Sure-Fire Matches" in "The Explication of 'X Knows That p'," *The Journal of Philosophy* 64 (1967): 373–89.

9. See Paul Humphreys, "Why Propensities Cannot be Probabilities" (*The Philosophical Review* 94 (1985): 557–70) for an argument that undercuts the effort to use probability to represent the propensities thought to underlie uncertainty.

10. It is not altogether clear what Professor Nozick means here. Two possibilities suggest themselves. One is that $prob_0(h)$ is equivalent to the probability of h on any tautology. This, I take it, would be the case if $prob_0(h)$ were the absolute probability of h. The other possibility is that $prob_0(h)$ is equivalent to $prob(h, E)$ where E includes *all* evidence bearing on h *except* e, the evidence to be used in the inference. This latter interpretation is suggested by the language "otherwise determined probability of h." Although something like this might have been intended, I do not know how it could be employed usefully in a way that would distinguish it from the first interpretation, especially given that we are not concerned here with anything relativized to a subject at a time.

11. In an effort to escape this trivial condition, I explored the possibility of incorporating something from the fourth condition of Professor Nozick's inference principle based on probability, the condition that requires the initial probability of h to be greater than the probability of e given not-h. Unfortunately, the motivation for including that condition in the inference principle does not apply to including it as a condition of something's being evidence.

12. James Baldwin, "Evidence" in Baldwin, op. cit.

13. Fred Dretske, "The Intentionality of Cognitive States," *Midwest Studies in Philosophy* V (1980): 281–94, especially 282.

14. Roderick Firth, op. cit., 10–11.

15. Alfred J. Ayer, *The Problem of Knowledge* (London: Macmillan & Co., 1956), 34.

three

SUDDENLY HE KNOWS

George S. Pappas

What has come to be called 'internalism' within recent epistemology, both with respect to the analysis of factual knowledge and theories of epistemic justification, is a network of doctrines that many now believe to be seriously problematic. Part of the reason for this growing consensus is the general development of competing analyses and theories of an externalist sort — analyses and theories which seem to fare nicely in many areas or contexts that cause trouble for internalist theories. Nozick's recent work in epistemology is squarely within this externalist approach. His tracking accounts of knowledge and evidence are both externalist, as is his reliable process account of justification, despite the fact that the latter differs from the former two in important ways.

In this essay I will be concerned with just the reliable process theory of justified belief. I will discuss a number of cases involving memory which seem to cause problems for the reliable process theory. Specifically, I will examine several cases of what Ulrich Neisser has called 'flashbulb memory'[1] with an eye towards seeing what implications they may have for the reliable process theory. My general conclusion is that there are no resources within that theory as Nozick has presented it for plausibly dealing with flashbulb memory phenomena. I think it is likely that flashbulb memory examples cause problems for other epistemological theories as well; however, in this paper I will not explore that possibility.

I. THE PIANO PLAYER

It is a familiar fact that people often forget things. Let us mean by 'things' in this context facts or propositions, rather than objects or events or skills. So the familiar fact is that people often suffer from factual forgetting. Smith may forget *that* his neighbor, Jones, is a skilled pianist, or forget *that* Ronald Reagan is the President of the United States.

One sort of factual forgetting is *momentary*. While doing his schoolwork, Smith may suddenly "go blank" on the addition of 9 and 14. For a short time he is unable to recall that the sum is 23, and during this period he may engage in various activities in the attempt to recall. Suddenly, his mind clears and he sees that the sum is 23. He proceeds with his work.

In this situation, I think we should say that Smith knows all along that 9 + 14 is 23. He knows this even during the short period when, as we say, his mind has gone blank, and he cannot remember that the sum is 23. Moreover, he certainly had this knowledge prior to the blank period; and it seems quite clear that he knows that 9 plus 14 is 23 upon the moment of recall.

Protracted factual forgetting is a different matter. Imagine that Smith has known for quite a while that Jones, his neighbor, is a pianist. Suppose, further, that he has often had reconfirmation of the relevant fact: he has gone to concerts at which Jones has performed, attended rehearsals at Jones' home, strolled past Jones' house and seen and heard Jones practicing the piano. A time comes, however, when Smith utterly forgets that Jones is a pianist. He may think: "There is something that Jones is quite good at — I know that, certainly. But what *is* it? I just don't know; I cannot remember." Smith may try various activities to aid recall. He may ask other people, or try to remember the first letter of the word that describes Jones' skill, or try to picture Jones in his mind and the like, all to no avail. He has completely forgotten that Jones is a pianist.

His plight may be a source of constant irritation to Smith. The question, "What is it that Jones does so well?" may recur often; it and related thoughts may haunt his waking moments and interfere with other thoughts and perhaps with activities in which Smith is to engage. But, try as he might, he simply cannot remember, for a long period of time just what it is about Jones that he formerly knew and now has lost.

One day while Smith is engaged in some unrelated activity, and while he is not thinking about Jones at all, it suddenly comes back to him: Jones is a pianist. "Of course," he exclaims to himself, "a pianist. Lord, how could I have forgotten *that*?" He feels greatly relieved that now he knows just what it is about Jones that had eluded him for such a long time. He knows now that Jones plays the piano.

Examples such as this, the Jones case, are common and familiar enough in everyday life. Sometimes recall of the lost fact is aided by coaxing from other people, or by seeing something with which, in one's own past experience, piano playing has been associated. Just as often, however, aids such as these fail even after much trial or exposure. That is, in some cases what occurs is suddenly remembering — an event that is apparently triggered by nothing in particular that has any connection to the forgotten fact, any more than it is occasioned by some coaxing or prodding from another person. The memory simply "comes back," quite as though that very occurrence is an isolated event, unrelated to events which immediately precede it.

Not all cases of protracted memory loss are like the Jones case. For example, in some cases where one has long forgotten some fact, one can "retrieve" that fact by simply trying to do so. It is this feature of one's memory ability, it seems to me, that explains why we are willing to say that in such cases, one still knows the relevant fact. The same thing explains what I earlier claimed about momentary factual forgetting: one retains knowledge of the fact in question because one can retrieve that fact. And it is the lack of this ability, on the other hand, that explains why one fails to know, loses one's knowledge, in the Jones case. One is unable to retrieve the fact at issue, however one tries.

The Jones case is thus an example of flashbulb memory. In such cases, a long-forgotten and formerly known fact is suddenly recalled. There are a number of different kinds of cases here. Some are like the Jones case in that recall is triggered by no discernibly associated item and when the individual is not in any way trying to retrieve the lost item. We might think of these as *pure* flashbulb memory phenomena. A closely related example is one in which the triggering item is manifest, as is its status as causally operative in retrieval of the lost item. Thus, to modify the Jones case, imagine that Smith notices a sign advertising a concert by Andre Watts, and this event induces recall of the fact that Jones is a concert pianist. What makes this different from a pure flashbulb example is that Smith is also aware that it is this perception of the concert advertisement that yields recall. A third sort of example would be one in which the lost fact itself is presented to Smith and this event causes more or less instant recall. Imagine that a friend, Brown, who knows that Smith has been unsuccessfully trying to remember something about Jones, learns in some independent way that Jones is a concert pianist. The next time he sees Smith, he goes directly up to him and says, "A concert pianist!" "Of course, that's it, now I remember," Jones remarks, doubtless with some feeling of relief.[2]

A great deal more can usefully be said about flashbulb memory, as well as about closely related memory phenomena. However, except for the second case to be discussed below, we need not enter into that discussion. We need to consider, instead, how this sort of case relates to some important epistemological concerns.

I said earlier that in the Jones case our individual Smith does not know that Jones is a concert pianist during the long period when he has forgotten this fact. On the other hand, it seems clear that at the moment of recall, Smith *does* know that Jones is a concert pianist (let this known proposition be *h*). Moreover, it is reasonable to hold that at the moment of recall Smith believes that *h*, consciously and occurrently. For, at that moment he does in some sense affirm that *h*; he outright exclaims, "A concert pianist — of course," in the Jones case, and something similar often occurs even if the person does not actually give voice to the affirmation of the now-recalled fact. If we also accept the widely assumed and quite plausible KJ thesis — the thesis that knowledge implies justification[3] — we are then naturally led to ask, what *is* Smith's justification for his belief that *h* at the moment of recall?

One general answer to this question would be in terms of reliability: a belief is justified for a person just in case, roughly, the method by which he arrives at that belief is a generally reliable method. Two sorts of important concerns for such a theory are the degree of reliability a method or process has to have in order for the resultant belief to be justified, and the issue of just how the belief-forming method is to be described or individuated. Let us consider the latter issue in connection with the Jones case.

We might want to identify the process or method by which Smith comes to believe that Jones is a pianist, upon recalling that Jones is one, with Smith's memory. After all, it is true that Smith remembers that Jones is a pianist, even though this is something that occurs suddenly and after a long period during which Smith could not remember that very fact about Jones. However, there are reasons for not taking Smith's memory, construed in general terms, to be the relevant belief-forming method. His memory may not typically be very reliable in the sense that he often misremembers various things, but even if this were so, he would still know that Jones was a pianist when he suddenly recalled this fact. So, given the KJ thesis, he would be justified in believing that Jones is a pianist as well. This causes problems for the usual way of describing the reliable process theory of justification, for on that construal the likelihood that a belief-forming process will produce true beliefs must be greater than the likelihood that it will produce false beliefs in order for the process to count as reliable. Smith's memory generally may not qualify as reliable by this condition, despite the fact that on suddenly recalling he knows, and (we are assuming) is justified in believing, that Jones is a pianist. The latter belief, given the reliable process account of justified belief, is formed by a reliable process.

A more important reason for not identifying Smith's memory as the reliable process at issue is that memory in general is not a belief-*forming* process or method. Rather, it is a belief-sustaining method. Thus, even if Smith's memory were reliable qua belief sustainer, this fact would not in any obvious and automatic way carry over to belief formation.

The same points apply if we specify memory more finely: perhaps as Smith's memory with respect to music, or to friends, or to Jones, or to people who live in his neighborhood, or the like. No one of those methods need be especially reliable for Smith, yet that fact will not affect the example of his suddenly remembering that Jones is a pianist; and, such methods are themselves belief sustainers rather than belief-forming methods.

Should we say, then, that the reliable method used by Smith is simply the event of suddenly recalling that h, that Jones is a pianist? Here we have two cases to consider: first, a situation in which Smith has had episodes of flashbulb memory in the past, though not necessarily or even probably on matters pertaining to Jones; and, secondly, the situation in which his suddenly recalling that h is Smith's first episode of flashbulb memory. In the first case, I think we would at least have the beginnings of the sort of reliable process or method that is needed. We simply consider a case in which on most or even all past occasions of flashbulb memory for Smith, the resulting beliefs were indeed true. Hence, his suddenly recalling various facts constitutes a reliable process of belief formation, and thus his presently suddenly recalling that h can be said to be justified because it results from that reliable belief-forming method. I think we can agree that in such a case, the reliable process account of justification handles the case of Smith suddenly recalling that h. It can even trivially specify the belief-forming method: it is just the method of forming beliefs via flashbulb memory episodes. However, a problem arises when we consider the second sort of case, one in which Smith experiences an episode of flashbulb memory for the first time. In that situation, I think, it is still true of Smith that he knows that h, and so, given the KJ thesis, is also justified in the belief that h. In this first occurrence of flashbulb memory, the reliable process is just a one-event story: the single event of Smith's suddenly recalling that h.

Of course, we could say that *this* method is perfectly reliable, since it consists of just this one event of Smith gaining the relevant belief and, since that belief is true, the reliability of the method is 100 percent. However, such a line would leave it open to identify any lucky guess as productive of a justified belief—hardly something that would be welcomed by a defender of a reliable process account of justification.

Perhaps we should say that the relevant method is that of retrieving something from long-term memory storage. Here, too, some care is needed in describing the relevant process. In the normal case of long-term storage of a fact, it is correct to say that the person knows this fact all along, during all of those moments when the person is not at all attending to that fact. Yet, in the flashbulb memory example, the person does not know the relevant fact in the period after forgetting it and before recalling it. The capacity for (unaided) retrieval seems again to be the operative criterion. In typical cases of long-term memory storage, the person can retrieve the stored item, just by trying to "bring it back." It is just this feature which is generally lacking in flashbulb memory cases, however. So, we would thereby have some reason not to classify the present method of belief formation, in Smith's situation, as retrieval from long-term memory.

The problem in the case of Smith suddenly recalling that *h* is not that the process by which he comes to believe that *h* is *un*reliable, nor that it's reliability falls below a certain minimum (points which would not affect Nozick's account in any case). Rather, it is that if we take the belief-formation process to be just the event of suddenly recalling that *h*, then the notion of reliability does not nontrivially apply at all.

The problems raised for reliable process theories of justification by flashbulb memory cases may be thought of as falling within the scope of the generality problem.[4] If we describe the process too broadly — say as memory in general, or Smith's memory with respect to some things or sorts of things — the result is a process that need not be particularly reliable nor a belief-forming process, despite the fact that Smith does gain knowledge and justified belief that *h* at the moment of recall. On the other hand, if we specify the reliable process too finely, say as consisting of just those instances of flashbulb memory experienced by Smith, we run the risk of ending with a single-event process which will perforce be reliable but in such a way that no aid is provided for the reliable process theory.

Perhaps, however, there is a plausible reply that can be made in behalf of the reliable process theory. In the discussion thus far we have assumed that not only does Smith not know that *h* across the relevant time span when he has forgotten it, but also that he does not *believe* that *h* across that span. Only with this assumption was it pertinent to note that memory functions as belief sustainer rather than a belief-forming mechanism. Yet, one might urge, here is a mistake. Smith does not have to come to believe that *h* at the moment of recall that *h*; he has believed that *h* all along, ever since the moment he forgot that *h*. Hence, we can simply specify the relevant reliable process or method as memory with respect to certain sorts of facts. This method is reliable provided that it sustains an appropriate number of proportion of true beliefs across time. Being sustained by that method is what justifies Smith's belief that *h*.

On one reading of this line of thought, we would be forced to say that Smith's belief that *h* was justified across the relevant time span, a result that seems at least counterintuitive. But let us agree to waive this consideration, and concentrate instead on whether it is true that Smith believed that h all along.

Certainly Smith does not occurrently believe that h across the time span when he has forgotten that h, either continuously or from time to time. Not continuously, surely, for occurrent believing does not function in that way generally, no matter what the belief may be. And not on occasion either, for it seems reasonable to say that had Smith ever occurrently believed that h during the forgetting time span, then that occurrent belief would have been the event of, or have been the triggering event for, his suddenly remembering that h. The time during which he had so utterly forgotten that h would thus have been shorter in duration than it actually is. Does Smith have a dispositional belief that h across the time span in question? Here the answer might seem to be *yes*, particularly if we think of a dispositional belief as picked out by what a person would assent to if queried in a certain manner (for example, "Do you believe that h?"). Certainly, if anyone had happened to query Smith in the right way about Jones, he would have assented, for the question put to him would have been something such as "Do you believe that Jones is a pianist?"

I am not sure that this would be the right conclusion to draw, however. An alternative description of what is happening would have it that the question thus put to Smith functions not to elicit a belief he has had all along, to bring it up to an occurrent level, but rather actually to cause Smith to take on that belief. The question would thus function as the triggering event, one that induces knowledge and belief acquisition simultaneously.

I am not sure about how to settle this matter, nor even about whether it can be settled without a full theory of belief and belief formation. However, it does seem that treating the question put to Smith, hypothetically, as causing him to take on the belief afresh is at least as plausible as claiming that he has dispositionally believed that h across the time span. If so, we are entitled to make use of it in setting out the case, and in drawing the conclusion that the case causes genuine trouble for the reliable process theory of justified belief.[5]

It might be thought that the foregoing considerations are of no concern to Nozick's account of justification since he does not quite endorse the KJ thesis, and also because he speaks not of a reliable belief-forming process *simpliciter,* but rather of the most reliable method of belief formation available to the person. With regard to the former, Nozick says only that ". . . it seems plausible that justified true belief is a necessary condition for knowledge, but I prefer to leave this question unsettled." (267)[6] And concerning the latter, he says: "Even if a method M_1 has a reliability with regard to p of greater than $1/2$, if it is not the most reliable method available to the person (with regard to the salient type of belief which *p* is) then the person is not justified in believing *p*." (265) I take up the issue concerning the KJ thesis in the next section. With regard to the availability of the method of belief formation, we may concede that in some cases of flashbulb memory, that very event may not be the most reliable method available to the person. For example, in some cases it may well be open to the person simply to ask someone some pertinent questions, in the above example questions pertaining to Jones. But such options need not be available in all cases when flashbulb memory episodes occur; it is easy to think of scenarios in which that would be so. In that eventuality, the most "reliable" available method is just the occurrence of the flashbulb event itself, and in that case the appropriate notion of reliability does not nontrivially apply.

II. THE RUSSIAN NOVELIST

In Neisser's *Memory Observed*, there is a description of a fascinating case of multiple episodes of flashbulb memory which occurred to a woman in old age. The woman had spent her childhood in rural Russia, living with her family on a farm. She had all sorts of flashbulb memories of events, persons, and places from the period of her life when she was about seven or eight years old (the flashbulb episodes occurred when she was in her sixties), and in all particulars save one she was completely accurate. That is, when she actually described the layout of the house, the placement of pieces of furniture, the relative position of things outside the house, and the like, she was completely correct except for the description she gave of the kitchen window. Moreover, this woman had not thought about these details in many decades; they were, we may assume, things that this woman had not known or believed for all those years, though she had formerly known and believed many things concerning the house and its environs.

Consider a slight modification of this woman's actual case, namely a situation in which she has a flashbulb memory episode, all at one time, in which she suddenly recalls a number of facts concerning the house and, in the same episode, "recalls that" the window stood in a certain place relative to the door. Here I think we should describe the case by saying that the woman came to have several bits of knowledge concerning her childhood home, and one justified belief (that the window was in a certain place or part of the kitchen). If this is right, we have a case in which she suddenly came to have a justified belief, via flashbulb memory, but in such a way that there is no dependence whatever on the KJ thesis. We need to ask, again, what is the justification for her belief concerning the position of the window?

In the case as presently described, one might argue that there is an appropriate reliable process which produces this belief about the window. That is, the process is just the event which produced the several bits of knowledge along with the belief about the window. It is reliable, one might argue, in virtue of the fact that it produces several true beliefs and just one false belief. So, the belief about the window is justified in virtue of having been produced by a reliable process, namely the very event of suddenly recalling and gaining some knowledge about her childhood home.

Notice that it is not being said that the woman had several or many past episodes of flashbulb memory, all of them knowledge-producing, and that the past string of successes constitutes the reliable process by virtue of which she is justified now in believing that the window was located in a certain place. In that sort of context, it was conceded earlier, it would be reasonable to hold that the reliable process theory dealt with the example in a satisfactory manner. Here the example is different; the woman has no past string, as yet, of flashbulb memory successes, but she has the complex flashbulb memory event of all at once acquiring several bits of knowledge and a justified belief. The metaphysical notion of a complex event taking simple, or at least simpler, events as constituents is being invoked to fabricate a kind of single-event reliable process, but one that does not share the defects of the single-event context discussed in the preceding section.

It is true that, as originally developed by Goldman,[7] the reliable process theory was taken to apply to processes that operate across a stretch of time. Nevertheless, one might say, this is not an essential feature of the theory, for we can identify such a process all within one momentary complex event.

It can be granted that there is some plausibility initially attaching to this proposal, but I think further reflection will indicate that it reduces to, or is at least strongly analogous to, the sort of single-event case described earlier. Consider some other case, having nothing to do with flashbulb memory, in which the person acquires several beliefs all at the same time. Perhaps he acquires five beliefs, four of which are true, the fifth not. To make the example similar to the flashbulb one, imagine that the process by which this person acquires these five beliefs is that of rocking on his toy wooden rocking horse. That is, we here adapt the well-known D. H. Lawrence story in such a way that these five beliefs result from the very first episode of the person's having rocked on the horse. In such a context, I think we would want to say that none of these newly acquired beliefs is justified for the person, though in the sense under review, the process by which he has acquired them is reliable. In general, if the justifiedness of the Russian woman's belief consists in the fact that a reliable process is an ingredient in the one complex event which yields that belief along with some others, then in any case of a process operative for the first time and which produces several new beliefs at once, those beliefs are justified just in case a sufficient proportion of them turns out to be true. Yet to see that this is an unwelcome consequence, we need only note that it would apply equally to those processes that never recur.

It is true that there are some disanalogies present here. In the Russian woman case, she simultaneously gets several bits of knowledge as well as a justified belief, while this is not so in the adapted rocking horse. But it is not clear that this point matters. For, the feature which supposedly makes this complex event into a reliable process is that some proportion of the beliefs acquired therein are true, and not that, as it happens, some of them qualify as knowledge. So, it seems to be reasonable to conclude that the strategy of extracting a reliable process out of a single complex belief-forming event does not succeed. It leads to an analog of the single-event problem in which any newly operative process which happens to produce true beliefs thereby produces justified beliefs. The latter, I take it, is contrary to fact.

If this is right concerning the modified Russian woman case, then we may mobilize considerations adduced in the preceding section to yield a more general conclusion. That is, we note that in this example, too, the woman does not know the relevant facts across the time span, and neither does she dispositionally believe these facts during that time. Moreover, the appropriate description of the process by which she acquires knowledge and justified belief in the flashbulb event will not be in terms of her memory considered generally. Yet it seems quite clear that the woman does acquire knowledge of her past home and a justified belief concerning the window via the flashbulb event, although this fact about the example has no dependence on the KJ thesis. Thus, the more general conclusion would best be put by saying that there are genuine cases of justified belief, namely those having to do with flashbulb memory episodes, which Nozick's reliable process theory of justification can deal with only at the expense of running into some version of the single-event problem.

III. CONCLUSION

One might, of course, deny the intuitions underlying the argument of this essay (though I have no reason to think that Nozick would do so). That is, one might deny that flashbulb memory phenomena constitute actual cases of knowledge and justified belief acquisition. And it is true that I have presented no *argument* which shows that flashbulb memory cases do yield knowledge and justified belief; on the contrary, I have assumed the point. Still it does seem very plausible to make this assumption; indeed, I would claim that it reflects the way we ordinarily think and talk about familiar cases of flashbulb memory phenomena such as the piano player example presents, and that is some reason in favor of the assumption. So I am inclined to think that flashbulb memory cases serve to show that Nozick's version of the reliable process theory of justification does not fully succeed.[8]

NOTES

1. Ulric Neisser, *Memory Observed: Remembering in Natural Contexts* (San Francisco: Freeman), 1982.

2. A similar example happened to me several years ago when I could not remember (try as I might) the name of a basketball player for the Philadelphia 76ers. My then colleague Bruce Freed came up to me in the hallway and said "His name is Andrew Toney." "Of course," I said out loud, "how could I ever have forgotten that?"

3. With respect to the KJ thesis, we need to think of justification in a suitably 'nontoxic" way. It is thus *not* being claimed that knowledge implies justification in some internalist sense of 'justified' (nor, for that matter, in some externalist sense of the term). The KJ thesis is supposed to be independent of whichever theory of justified belief is correct.

4. For very insightful discussion of this problem, see Richard Feldman, "Reliability and Justification," *The Monist* 68 (April 1985).

5. Aren't there cases, completely independent of flashbulb memory contexts, where the event of a person's being asked whether he believes that *p* is part of the cause of his first coming to believe that *p*? It seems clear that there are many, though doubtless the full causal story involved in complex.

6. Parenthetical references are to *Philosophical Explanations* (Cambridge: Harvard University Press, 1981).

7. Alvin Goldman, "What is Justified Belief?" in *Justification and Knowledge,* ed. G. S. Pappas. (Dordrecht: Reidel, 1979).

8. I have benefitted from discussions, several years ago, with several people: Bruce Freed, William Alston, Ausonio Marras, John Davis, Douglas Odegard. More recently, I have received useful advice on points touched on in the essay from Brad Armendt and Dan Farrell. I doubt if any of these people would fully agree with the central arguments presented, however.

four

NOZICK'S EPISTEMOLOGY

Richard A. Fumerton

Many of us, inspired in large part by Descartes, have spent our epistemological careers taking seriously the egocentric predicament of trying
to escape the confines of our own thoughts and sensations. Lately,
however, we are in danger of being displaced by a new generation of
epistemologists who study the mind and its relation to nature the way a
computer scientist studies the input/output mechanisms of his ma-
chines. I suspect that this dramatic shift began with Quine's influential
recommendation to "naturalize" epistemology,[1] but in recent years
the recommendation seems to be stated in terms of "externalizing"
the fundamental epistemic concepts of knowledge, evidence, and
justification.

The externalist/internalist debate in epistemology is not, as we shall
see, all that easy to define, but in the epistemology of Robert Nozick
we may well have a paradigm of a philosopher who wants to naturalize
and externalize epistemic concepts. By examining his views I hope to
make more precise the nature of this dramatic division between
externalists and internalists in epistemology, and in so doing try to indicate why the 'epistemic' concepts defined by externalists are so philosophically impoverished.

In what follows I shall begin by briefly summarizing the main aspects of Nozick's epistemology in which I am particularly interested.
Many of my objections are directed at the specifics of Nozick's analysis, but I am more concerned with the extent to which at least some of
these objections can be broadened to attack the *kind* of approach
taken by Nozick, Dretske,[2] Goldman,[3] and other naturalists and
externalists, to epistemologic issues. I shall take little comfort in presenting counterexamples that lead only to the kind of endless tinkering
with analyses of knowledge that so dominated the philosophical jour-
nals following the publication of Gettier's famous counterexamples.

I

Nozick's primary concern is with the concept of propositional knowledge, although he also analyzes concepts of evidence and justification and explores their connection with knowledge. This preoccupation with knowledge may itself be a philosophical mistake as it seems to me that all the really interesting questions in epistemology can be asked employing only the concept of justification. But if it is a mistake, it is a mistake with a tradition going back over two thousand years.

According to Nozick, one knows that a given proposition p is true when one has a true belief that p and when one's belief that p *tracks* the fact that p. The all-important tracking relation is defined using subjunctive conditionals. The rough first statement is as follows (pp. 172–178)[4]: S's belief that p tracks the fact that p if and only if

(1) If not-p were true when S would not believe that p

and

(2) If p were true then S would believe that p.

This rough characterization of tracking is made more sophisticated to take into account the relevance of the method used in coming to believe that p. Nozick thinks that the mother who sees her son and on that basis concludes that he is alive and well, knows that he is alive and well even if, had he died, her friends would have conspired to keep the news from her by falsely reporting his good health. In this hypothetical situation it might appear that condition (1) is not satisfied, so Nozick needs to tinker with his analysis. To accommodate his intuitions about this sort of case Nozick revises his account of knowledge as follows (179): S knows that p is true if and only if

(1) p is true.

(2) S believes via some method M that p.

(3) If p weren't true and S were to use M to arrive at a belief about p, then S wouldn't believe, via M, that p.

and

(4) If p were true and S were to use M to arrive at a belief about p, then S would believe, via M, that p.

Yet a further complication involving the causal overdetermination of a belief arrived at via different methods leads Nozick to revise his account of knowledge again. He imagines a case in which a father believes that his son is innocent as a result of good evidence presented at a trial, when the belief arrived at by this method satisfies the requirements for knowledge, but when it is also true that the father would have believed his son innocent even *if* the evidence had showed that he was guilty. Nozick wants to say that if the belief, qua act of faith, fails to satisfy his conditions for knowledge, the father in this situation would not know that his son was innocent. To get the conclusion he wants, Nozick introduces the concept of one method of belief outweighing another in cases of overdetermination:

> M is outweighed by others if when M would have the person believe p, the person believes not-p if the other methods would lead to the belief that not-p, or when M would have the person believe not-p, the person believes p if the other methods would lead to the belief that p. (p. 000)

Refinements of this concept are discussed, but they need not concern us here. The idea of one method outweighing another is used in the account of knowledge as follows: S knows that p is true if and only if

(1) p is true.

(2) There is some method M by which S believes that p such that

(3) If not-p and S were to use M to arrive at a belief about p, then S would not believe that p.

(4) If p were true and S were to use M to arrive at a belief about p, then S would believe that p.

and

(5) There is no other method which outweighs M such that conditions (3) and (4) are not satisfied by that method.

Having noted these complications in Nozick's account of knowledge, I shall, for simplicity, refer to it as the view that knowledge is true belief in a proposition where the belief "tracks" via some method the fact that p.

Before concluding our summary of Nozick's views about knowledge, we must note one further qualification he introduces to accommodate knowledge of necessary truths. Because he doesn't know how to evaluate subjunctive conditionals whose antecedents are necessarily false, Nozick doesn't want to say that one knows a necessary truth only if one would not believe it, were it false. Rather, he suggests, for necessary truths, we should employ only the one subjunctive as a necessary condition for knowledge. Thus S knows a necessary truth p when S comes to believe it via some method M provided that in all of the close possible worlds in which p is true and S employs M, S believes that p (which is equivalent to saying, simply, that in all close possible worlds in which S employs M, S believes that p) (p. 000). Nozick takes it to be a virtue of his externalist account that he can analyze knowledge of necessary truth. As we shall see, however, his account as it stands will hardly do.

Let us now turn to Nozick's views on *evidence*. As with knowledge, Nozick also enlists subjunctive conditionals to define the epistemic concepts of evidence:

> e is *strong* evidence for p if and only if if p were true e would be true and if p were not true e would not be true. (p. 248)

and

> e is *weak* evidence for p if and only if if p were true e would probably be true and if p were not true e would probably not be true. (pp. 252–53)

If e is strong evidence for p and one knows e, one can know p by inferring it from e.

Belief in p based on weak evidence for p may not be justified, according to Nozick, for one must also take into account the "prior" probability of p. It might be true that even if e is unlikely to be true were p false, the prior probability of not-p is so high that it would still be more reasonable to conclude that e came about in some extremely unlikely way. Nozick leaves this discussion of weak evidence hanging without giving us much of a clue as to how prior probabilities are to be defined or how we are to gain access to them (257). I have no interest in attempting to help work this out since I don't think one can define epistemic probability in terms of frequency probability (as I assume is Nozick's intent in using the subjunctive conditionals).

The last fundamental epistemic concept analyzed by Nozick is justification. Here, strangely enough, he drops his tracking requirement and buys into the — still externalist — reliability account of justification. I think we may assume that he has something like Goldman's account[5] in mind. A belief that p is justified if it was arrived at via some method M such that that method is "likely to produce mostly true beliefs" (264). I don't know what the expression "likely" is doing in this externalist definition of justification, for the reliabilist's aim is to purge his analysis of justification of primitive epistemic concepts. "Likely" is either redundant (its meaning exhausted by the subsequent reference to the frequency of true beliefs) or is a primitive epistemic concept, the one in terms of which one *should* be trying to understand justification. I shall assume, however, that this was just a slip and that Nozick, like Goldman, is committed to analyzing justified belief in terms of the purely statistical concept of methods producing true beliefs more often than not. I shall also assume that Nozick would accept Goldman's distinctions, and probably his definitions, of belief-dependent conditionally reliable processes and belief-independent unconditionally reliable processes.[6] Nozick also allows that when a number of reliable methods are available to an individual vis-à-vis reaching a conclusion about p, the belief will be justified only if the most reliable method is used (though nothing is said about the critical question of what makes a method "available" to a person). The absence of the tracking relation in his account of justification has some rather odd consequences for Nozick, which I shall note later in discussing his views about the nonclosure of knowledge.

This completes my very brief summary of Nozick's analyses of epistemic concepts. Let us now turn to evaluation.

II

Many philosophers, no doubt, will be taken aback by the pervasive use of subjunctive conditionals in Nozick's analyses of knowledge and evidence. It is at least tempting, if not entirely fair, to ridicule an account of problematic epistemic concepts that relies on an understanding of the relation asserted by contingent subjunctive conditionals. Philosophical attempts to analyze the relation asserted by subjunctive conditionals have met with a singular lack of success. One might be able to solve the problem easily enough if one had already analyzed the concept of a law of nature, or perhaps, the concept of causation, but to analyze these concepts without relying on subjunctive conditionals is a Gordian knot to challenge the strongest of philosophical hearts. To be sure, some have tried to cut that knot with the sword of possible worlds semantics. Indeed, to the extent to which Nozick has anything interesting to say by way of "representing" what makes contingent subjunctive conditionals true, it is in the metaphorical language of possible words. The proposition that if not-p then S wouldn't believe that p is understood in terms of the "close" not-p worlds being worlds in which S doesn't believe that p. On some possible worlds accounts of subjunctive conditionals, the subjunctive, if p were true then S would believe that p, is automatically true if S has a true belief that p (thus making one of Nozick's conditions for knowledge redundant). Nozick argues (correctly, I think) that the truth of p and q is not sufficient for the truth of the subjunctive, if p were true then q would be true; and in his possible worlds talk he identifies such a conditional as true when all the close (not just *the* closest) "p worlds" contain S's belief that p. God (or Kripke?) only knows how "far away" from the actual world a possible world must be in order to be irrelevant to the truth of a subjunctive conditional, but the matter isn't worth much thought since the attempt to 'explicate' subjunctive conditionals using the possible worlds metaphor is at best disingenuous.

Unlike some philosophers who are just hopeless when it comes to understanding the futility of using possible worlds semantics to analyze subjunctive conditionals, Nozick (in a footnote on page 174) makes clear that he knows it's a joke to try to *define* subjunctive conditionals using the concept of possible worlds. As he himself puts the crucial point, the only measure of closeness of similarity that the not-*p* worlds must have to the actual *p* world in order to be relevant in assessing the truth of subjunctive conditionals with not-*p* as an antecedent, is that the not-*p* worlds be just like the actual world except with respect to changes that would have occurred in the actual world had not-*p* been the case. The circle is so tight that we can't help but get dizzy trying to move around it. Still Nozick thinks that possible worlds can be usefully employed to "represent" the truth of a subjunctive conditional. Personally, I do not understand what this "representation" is supposed to be or do, and I rather fear that the familiar use of the possible worlds metaphor in these (and other) contexts is just a way of avoiding the responsibility of providing informative philosopical analyses of problematic concepts.

Unfortunately, I am not in much of a position to criticize the use of subjunctive conditionals per se in the analysis of epistemic concepts, since I myself think that *every* proposition about the physical world implicitly involves the assertion of subjunctive conditionals.[7] Furthermore, if one can develop a successful analysis of lawful regularity, one might hope to analyze partially subjunctive conditionals of the sort Nozick needs for his analysis. A first approximation might be this: *p* subjunctively implies *q* if and only if

There is some law L such that (*p* and L) entails *q* where neither *p* nor L alone entails *q*; *or* there obtains some state of affairs *x* and some law L such that (*p* and *x* and L) entails *q*, where (*x* and L) alone does not entail *q* and where *x* does not contain *p* as a part.

y is a part of *x* if *x* contains *y*, or *x* contains some state of affairs that contains *y*, or *x* contains some state of affairs that contains some state of affairs which contains *y*, or . . . (where *x* is said to contain *y* if *x* is identical with the state of affairs that is *y* being related to one or more states of affairs via truth-functional connectives). The difficulty with the above 'analysis' is that, in asserting subjunctive conditionals, we often want our audience to imagine changes in addition to the specific change mentioned in the antecedent in evaluating the conditional. At the same time it's not clear that there are any hard and fast 'rules' governing what changes we are to take into account. If I ask you what would have happened at the 1985 Geneva Summit had Bella Abzug been secretary of state, are you to imagine Abzug being secretary of state while Reagan and Weinberger retain their positions as President and secretary of defense? Or, in answering my question, are you to add to the proposition that Abzug was secretary of state other propositions made *likely* by the truth of that proposition against a background of other truths about the political makeup of the American public, the nature of presidential appointments, and so on? If this latter is true, Nozick faces real difficulty trying to analyze epistemic terms using subjunctive conditionals, for evaluating the truth of conditionals will *presuppose* an understanding of the notion of one proposition making likely the truth of another.

One of the most useful discussions of the problem of interpreting subjunctive conditionals is still Chisholm's "Law Statements and Counterfactual Inference."[8] There he argues, quite plausibly, that in asserting subjunctive conditionals people can hold constant a number of different true propositions when adding to them the proposition constituting the antecedent of the subjunctive conditional, by way of trying to figure out what follows from the conjunction. In many contexts the only way to assess the truth of a subjunctive conditional is to ask the person who asserts it what he would like you to imagine as being different along with the state of affairs referred to in the antecedent (Just as the only way to assess the truth of some singular probability statements is to insist that the person making the statement make clear his reference class).

If anything like the above view of subjunctive conditionals is correct, the moral to draw is that they are extremely messy when it comes to clear, unequivocal expression of propositions. And if one *wants* philosophically interesting epistemic claims to be clear and precise, one shouldn't use subjunctive conditionals to analyze them. A clever dialectician like Nozick, on the other hand, may well try to turn all this to his advantage by arguing that the vagueness inherent in subjunctive conditionals fits nicely the "open textured" character of knowledge claims. Back in the heyday of Byzantine analyses of knowledge and the equally Byzantine counterexamples offered to those analyses, how many of us simply threw up our hands without the slightest idea of "what we would say" about certain hypothetical situations?

One advantage of analyzing contingent subjunctive conditionals without the possible worlds metaphor is that one can see more clearly the affinity between Nozick's account of knowledge and the more usual causal accounts of knowledge. If I am right, Nozick's "tracking" subjunctive conditionals will hold for my belief that p when p is a nonredundant part of a nomologically necessary and sufficient condition of S's believing that p. And this is, of course, one way of approaching the analysis of causal connection.

Let us suppose for the subsequent discussion that we do have an understanding of contingent subjunctive conditionals. Nozick does invite us to understand these conditionals any way we like, and surely we all recognize the need for some philosophical account of subjunctive conditionals. Assuming that we can make them unproblematic, what other concerns might we have with Nozick's epistemology?

Let us begin by returning very briefly to Nozick's views on knowledge of necessary truths. You will recall that according to Nozick, you know a necessary truth p via some method M if in all of the close possible worlds in which you employ M you believe that p. Given this view, it would unfortunately seem to follow that if I resolve to believe every mathematical proposition I entertain (this is my "method" of belief), I will know all of the necessarily true propositions (no matter how complex) I entertain provided that I happen to be so constituted that I would entertain these propositions in all "close" possible worlds! I won't dwell on this objection further, however, since I think that Nozick, when faced with the problem, would probably simply retreat to a reliability conception of knowledge for knowledge of *necessary* truths. As we shall see later, reliability views of knowledge have their own problems, but for now let us resolve to focus on Nozick's epistemology as an account of empirical knowledge. Here *both* subjunctive conditionals are available to distinguish knowledge from mere belief.

In his discussion of empirical knowledge, probably the most startling, original, and dialectically ingenious move that Nozick makes is to take the most devastating objection to his view and embrace it as one of its advantages.

It follows, on Nozick's account of knowledge, that I can know that e and *know* that e entails p, believe that p as a result of believing that e and that e entails p, and yet not know that p. Knowledge, for Nozick, is not closed under known implication. It also follows on his account that e can be strong evidence for p when p entails q even though e is not strong evidence for q. Nozick draws this consequence of his view when discussing some of the classical arguments for skepticism. His strategy is to leave the skeptic with his mouth agape by granting such skeptical claims as that we don't know that there is no evil demon deceiving us with respect to the external world, or that we don't know that we are not always dreaming, while at the same time claiming that we do know that we are seeing a real table before us now. How can this be? Well, it is true of me now, Nozick says, that if the table weren't there, I wouldn't believe that the table is there; and it is true that the close possible worlds containing the table are worlds in which I believe that it is there. It is *not* true that if it were false that there is no evil demon deceiving me with respect to all propositions about the physical world (there is such a demon) then I would not believe that there was no evil demon deceiving me. Intuitively, the demon's presence of absence won't affect my belief that the demon does not exist. For similar reasons it also follows on Nozick's account (and this sound really strange) that I can know the conjunction, that there is a table before me and that I am not being deceived with respect to its existence by an evil demon, even though I cannot know the conjunct, that I'm not being deceived by an evil demon. Intuitively, the close possible worlds in which the conjunction is false are the worlds in which it is false that the table is there, and these, by assumption, are worlds in which I would not believe that the conjunction holds. The close possible worlds in which the demon hypothesis is true are very far removed from the actual world, and in these worlds we would continue to believe that the demon hypothesis is false.

Nozick is right in claiming that given his account of knowledge, knowledge is not closed under known implication. I think it is also true (and not surprising given what I have said above) that on a crude causal account of knowledge, knowledge will not be closed under known implication. The table might be the cause of my belief in its existence. I might know that the table's existence entails that I am not being deceived by an evil demon, even though it is not true that my not being deceived by an evil demon is the cause of my believe that I'm not being thus deceived.

The big question, of course, is why we don't take the nonclosure of knowledge under known implication, given such accounts of knowledge, to be a decisive refutation of them. One is sorely tempted to sort through one's most caustic 'ad hominems' and in the most sarcastic voice possible inquire: You don't *really* mean that I could know that *e*, know that *e* entails *p*, and yet not know that *p*? Nozick will reply, however, that he does mean just that. What is more, he will argue that he has given us a way of reconciling what for many are genuinely conflicting intuitions. We do want to be able to say that we know the world around us. But at the same time we can't help but see the force of the claim that we can't rule out the skeptic's ingenious hypotheses. With Nozick's account of knowledge, your problems disappear. You can continue to know what you always thought you knew and at the same time give the skeptic his due.

Nozick realizes, of course, that he is going to lose everyone if he doesn't explain how we can *sometimes* know as a result of deductive inference. It would be more than just a little embarrassing, for example, if one couldn't know that someone murdered Smith by inferring it from the known proposition that Jones murdered Smith. Nozick distinguishes deductions that yield knowledge from those that do not by arguing that in order to know that *q* by deducing it from another proposition that you know, *p*, it must be true that you wouldn't believe that *p* if *q* were false (239). (Further complications, which I shall not discuss, are introduced to distinguish question-begging and non-question-begging proofs — only the latter yield knowledge from known premises) (pp. 239–40).

Now with Nozick prepared to bite the bullet on the nonclosure of knowledge under known implication, it probably won't be possible to goad him into giving up his view. The best we can do is make him as uncomfortable as possible. Nozick wants it to be the case that one can "almost" always know that there exists an f by inferring it from one's knowledge that a is f (p. 236). In a discussion relegated to a footnote (note 68, p. 693) he acknowledges that in exceptional cases even this sort of proof might fail to yield knowledge. Let us describe such a case.

Suppose that I know, in Nozick's sense of the term, that Jones murdered Smith. I know it as a result of reading it in a paper that accurately recorded the event. Suppose, further, that Jones was part of an extremely sophisticated conspiracy and that the plan to assassinate Smith involved a complicated series of backup plans. If Jones had failed, there was another assassin down the hall who would have murdered Smith. And if this assassin had failed there was a third who would have murdered Smith, and so on down a line of ten ready and able assassins. Had one of these other assassins murdered Smith, the newspaper would have accurately reported the fact that Jones was not the killer. However, in the *extremely unlikely* event that all of the assassins failed, someone trusted by the local papers would call in the false report that Jones had assassinated Smith so as to spread the sort of confusion that might help them make their getaway. As I understand Nozick's analysis of knowledge, I would know that Jones murdered Smith, if it were true, because my belief that Jones murdered Smith would track the fact that he did. In all of the close possible worlds in which Smith wasn't murdered by Jones (that is, the worlds in which one of the other assassins murdered Smith) I wouldn't believe on the basis of a newspaper story that Jones murdered Smith. I wouldn't know, however, that someone murdered Smith, because if that proposition were false I would still believe that it was true by reading the false story that would have appeared in the paper.

Now does anyone really want to allow that I could *know* (and this *is* my best sarcasm) that Jones murdered Smith without knowing that someone murdered Smith or without knowing that Smith was murdered? I realize that many philosophers have an absolute phobia about letting skeptical hypotheses interfere with the ability to make knowledge claims, but surely one's desire to avoid skepticism ought to be measured against an equally strong desire not to commit oneself to outrageously implausible claims about nonclosure.

Before we leave Nozick's discussion of skepticism, it is interesting to note that on page 265 he claims that we have no evidence that a skeptical hypothesis (for example, the demon hypothesis) is false, for if it were true it would "leave all our observations the same." This, it seems to me, is false given his analysis of evidence. The proposition that I veridically see a table is strong evidence, on Nozick's theory, for the proposition that a demon isn't deceiving me with respect to the existence of the table. It is true that an internalist might insist that the "real" evidence always consists in the sensations to which we have direct access and that they would remain unaltered by the truth of the demon hypotheses, but it is not clear what relevance this observation would have for a good externalist like Nozick. Nozick also claims (p. 249) that "To believe something h on the basis of (what is) strong evidence e, where e is known, is to know h." If the claim I made above is correct, I could infer the falsity of the skeptical hypothesis from the strong evidence for its falsity, that I veridically see the table. But Nozick has already told us that we cannot know that the skeptical hypothesis is false. I won't belabor this point, for I suspect Nozick simply overlooks the distinctions he earlier drew between proofs that yield knowledge and proofs that do not, distinctions which eliminate the need for him to deny that there is strong evidence against the skeptical hypotheses.

In the context of Nozick's discussion of skepticism, it is also interesting to note that he nowhere discusses his views about the possibility of *justifiably* believing that the skeptical hypotheses are false. Given his reliabilist concept of justification, it seems to me that Nozick is committed to the view that we might well have very strong justification for believing that there is no evil demon deceiving us with respect to the existence of the table. After all, Nozick thinks that we do know that we verdically see the table, and he is inclined to think that knowledge presupposes the existence of a reliably-formed belief (p. 267). I assume, therefore, that he thinks we have a justified belief that we veridically see a table. I further assume that if there are any belief-dependent conditionally reliable processes, deductive inference is one of them and that if I deduce that I am not being deceived by an evil demon now from the proposition that I am veridically seeing the table, the reliability of the latter belief will be transferred to the former. Indeed, it seems to me that on Nozick's account it may well be the case that I have an extraordinarily well justified belief that the skeptical hypothesis is false. The only explanation I can think of for why Nozick doesn't make this claim is that he is so very anxious to give the skeptic his due, and he implicitly realizes that it is hard to do that while insisting that the hyhpothesis you can't know to be false is one which you could have extraordinarily strong justification for rejecting.

If Nozick's account of knowledge makes it too difficult to know some propositions, it makes it far too easy to know others. We might profitably begin exploring this criticism by focusing on a rather trivial, but ultimately illuminating, aspect of Nozick's views. Nozick points out that on his account of knowledge, if one knows that p and knows that q then one will know that p and q (p. 236). And while it seems right to me that this should be the case, it presents difficulties given Nozick's account of knowledge.

It is a well-known policy of airlines to overbook flights. If they don't *know* that at least some of the passengers booked won't show up, they certainly have good reason to believe it. Suppose now that there is a naive and not very bright new employee of the airline who after looking at the reservations concludes of each passenger *p1* through *P200* that he has arrived at the airport ready to board his plane. The employee is panicked at the thought of the confusion that he assumes has ensued. Let us further assume that by a remarkable coincidence his beliefs with respect to each booked passenger that he has arrived are true and that, furthermore, each belief tracks the fact that makes it true. He just happened to have beliefs about two hundred people none of whom would fail to arrive without prior notification in any but the remotest of possible worlds. I take it that on Nozick's account of knowledge, the naive employee would know of each booked passenger that he had arrived, and would consequently know that they had all arrived. But surely this is wrong. The naive airline employee had an irrational true belief that all of the passengers showed up and for that reason didn't know that they would all show up. There was available to the employee all kinds of very good evidence from which he *should* have inferred that his belief was likely to be false.

The above points to a more general problem with tracking, causal, or reliability analyses of knowledge and justification. To allow that someone knows or has a justified belief is to bestow epistemic *praise*. In Ayer's terminology it is to grant that person the right to be sure.[9] But we can easily imagine individuals whose beliefs track facts, whose beliefs are caused in quite reliable ways, but those beliefs nevertheless fly in the face of available evidence.[10]

One might object that I am not being fair to more sophisticated reliability theories of justification. Goldman, for example, specifically allows that whether one has a justified belief depends, in part, on other reliable methods available.[11] Such a qualification, however, doesn't really help. Consider an example I have discussed elsewhere.[12]

Suppose that a Freudian explanation of belief in an afterlife is true and that it is usually the case that belief in an afterlife is caused by fear of death. I *know* this *and* that beliefs in an afterlife caused by fear of death are always false. Suppose also that the following are true: that unbeknown to me, and unbelieved by me, there is a God who once every thousand years whispers in the ear of one sleeping man that he will have an afterlife and arranges for this to be true; that God chose me and I was caused to believe in an afterlife by what is, by hypothesis, this unconditionally reliable process. Despite my firm conviction that my belief in an afterlife is caused by fear of dying, I cannot seem to rid myself of what I realize is an irrational belief. Surely we would all say of me (I would say of me) that my belief in an afterlife is irrational, and that I don't know that I will have an afterlife, despite the fact that my belief was caused by a reliable process. Does Goldman's (or Nozick's) requirement that justified beliefs must result from the most reliable process available help? It might seem to, for there was (one might argue) available to me a reliable process that could have worked on the input beliefs relevant to establishing the Freudian explanation, that, had I used it, would have prevented me from believing in an afterlife. But the revision is beside the point, for I need only suppose that I am so constituted that no process of that sort would have resulted in my believing there is no afterlife. That same God who whispered in my ear might have created me and everyone else with epistemically "defective" wiring when it comes to belief in an afterlife. Even so, surely we *should* be wired in such a way that consideration of the relevant psychological evidence would result in the belief that there is no afterlife. This is perhaps true, but to use 'should' in what is clearly an epistemic sense is to violate the whole spirit of the reliabilist enterprise (it is certainly to violate the restrictions that Goldman himself imposes on an acceptable analysis of epistemic terms).

III

The above objections to Nozick's and others' externalist accounts of epistemic concepts are legitimate, but I have the nagging suspicion that we have yet to articulate the underlying problem with Nozick's epistemological views and externalist views, in general. Crudely put, externalist analyses of epistemic concepts seem to make these concepts irrelevant to the traditional philosophical pursuit of knowledge and justified belief. We must try to indicate why externalist analyses of epistemic concepts are of no philosophic interest. In doing so, we must also try to define more precisely the essential character of an externalist epistemology. When searching for such a definition, our concern should not merely be to find some common denominator to those epistemologies commonly called externalist, that distinguishes them from epistemologies commonly called internalist. The terms 'externalism' and 'internalism' are inventions of philosophers, and we should try to understand them in a way which makes the externalist/ internalist debate a fundamental and interesting philosophical controversy.

Perhaps the most striking characteristic of epistemic concepts as defined by such philosophers as Nozick and Goldman is that given their analyses the fact that one knows, or has evidence, or has a justified belief is a fact of which one might be completely ignorant. Indeed when Nozick makes claims about what he does and does not know, one can't help but wonder *why* he makes these claims, what justification he has for making these claims. In addressing the skeptic, Nozick *sometimes* seems only concerned with arguing that it is *possible* for one to know, for example, that there is a table before one even if one can't know the falsity of certain skeptical hypotheses. And this seems a sensible position for him to take given his analysis of knowledge, since it's hard to see what would justify him in believing the subjunctives that on his view are necessary conditions for his knowing that the table exists. At the same time, however, he repeatedly claims to know ordinary propositions about the physical world, to know, for example, that his children are not cleverly constructed robots (p. 219); and the making of such assertions surely contextually implies that Nozick takes himself to be *justified* in making these knowledge claims. But nowhere does he tell us what this justification is. His speculation that evolution has insured that beliefs often track facts is surely not a justification, for to be justified in believing evolutionary theory one would have to be already justified in believing less problematic assertions about the physical world. Of course, given *his analysis* of justification, Nozick wouldn't have to be able to tell us how his belief that he knows is justified in order for this belief to be justified, and he doesn't have to be able to tell us *how* he knows that he knows in order to know that he knows. Our conviction that Nozick isn't justified in believing that he knows ordinary propositions about the physical world begs the question, the externalist might argue, by presupposing that to have justification is to have something which one can articulate or hold before the mind.

Because an externalist can obviously provide externalist definitions of having evidence that one knows and knowing evidential connections, we internalists must be careful not to *define* externalists in terms of their views about the connection between knowing and having evidence that one knows, or in terms of their views about what one needs to know in order to know that *p* on the basis of *e*. It is tempting, but mistaken, for example to suggest that an externalist is someone who holds that one can know that *p* on the basis of *e* without knowing that *e* makes *p* likely, without knowing that *e* is evidence for *p*. In fact, both Nozick and Goldman, paradigmatic externalists, would agree that one can have inferential knowledge without knowing that one's evidence is evidence. But this is surely not the defining characteristic of externalism. Suppose, for example, that Nozick gets tired of hearing us complain about the fact that on his view one could know that *p* by inferring it from *e* even though one has no knowledge of an evidential connection between *e* and *p*. Suppose that just to quiet us he adds to his analysis of inferential knowledge the claim that one doesn't know that *p* by inferring it from *e* unless one knows not only that *e* is true but that *e* is evidence for *p*. As long as he continues to understand *this* knowledge in terms of *nomological* connections between the contingent fact that *e* is evidence for *p* and the belief that *e* is evidence for *p*, surely his account remains as externalist as before. In the same way, an externalist could (typically he won't) allow that one doesn't know that *p* unless one has evidence that one knows that *p*. But as long as he offers the same externalist account of having evidence, the internalist who wants knowing to entail having evidence that one knows will be no more satisfied by the account than he was before.[13]

We might dramatize this point, and at the same time try to embarass Nozick, by focusing on his admission (p. 267) that if one knows that *p*, one's belief that *p* will be, given his analysis, strong evidence for *p*. When he makes this admission, Nozick hastens to add the observation that one will not typically infer *p* from the fact that one believes that *p*. But suppose that there is some particularly arrogant and not too bright individual who *does* go around inferring the truth of what he believes from the mere fact that he has the belief. And suppose further that his belief that *p* does track the fact that *p*. Our arrogant individual's belief that *p*, inferred from the mere fact that he had the belief, would actually be a belief based on strong evidence. Consequently, Nozick could, *given his views,* correctly respond to our insistence that he provide evidence for thinking that he sees the table by identifying the fact that he believes that he sees the table as his evidence. And in response to our request that he provide evidence for his belief that his belief that he sees the table *is* evidence, he might be able to respond *correctly* by identifying his belief that his other belief is strong evidence as his evidence. If he begins to enjoy our annoyance enough, Nozick might even consider modifying his epistemological views by allowing that one can never know without being able correctly to identify evidence for the proposition that one knows. But this lip service to what some internalists want is obviously not going to alleviate their concern that there is something seriously wrong with the way the above epistemological discussion has proceeded.

Should we say that an externalist is one who maintains that two individuals could be in identical 'internal' states of mind while one knows, or has evidence, or has a justified belief, and the other does not? This is tempting, but everything hinges on how we understand *identical* states of mind. If we include among the properties defining 'same state of mind' *relational* properties, then obviously an externalist can embrace the thesis that if my state of mind is identical to yours then I'll know what you know, I'll be justified in believing what you are justified in believing. If one restricts the relevant properties determining sameness of mental states to nonrelational properties, certain paradigmatic internalists will (and should) refuse to accept the principle: same state of mind; same epistemic status. I, for example, hold that the mind has one sort of knowledge when it stands in a certain (epistemic) *relation* of acquaintance to certain nonlinguistic aspects of the world.

But what then makes an analysis of epistemic concepts externalist?

The answer lies, I think, in returning to the roots of externalism, naturalistic epistemology. The mistake of naturalism in epistemology may be analogous to the alleged naturalistic fallacy in ethics.[14] The naturalist in epistemology (like his counterpart in ethics) is trying to define away the concepts fundamental to his discipline; he is trying to define fundamental epistemic concepts in terms of other nonepistemic concepts. Nozick wants to define epistemic concepts in terms of nomological connections between facts and beliefs. Goldman used to want to explicate (he'd probably prefer that to "define") epistemic concepts in terms of causal connections, and now he wants to explicate them in terms of the frequency (nonepistemic) concept of probability. I suggest that it is a defining characteristic of an internalist epistemology that it takes fundamental epistemic concepts to be sui generis. No matter how much lip service the externalist is willing to pay to our internalist epistemic principles, he won't satisfy us as long as he continues to define the epistemic terms with which he pays us lip service in a naturalistic way. It is the naturalistic analyses of epistemic concepts that lead us to keep moving up a level, and asking the externalist how he knows that he knows, or knows that he knows that he knows. The externalist might be able to give correct answers within the framework of his view, but we'll keep asking the question until his answer invokes a concept of knowledge or justification not captured in terms of nomological connection.

It is this that explains what is surely at the heart of our dissatisfaction with externalist accounts of epistemology. Knowing, or having a justified belief, in the externalist's sense doesn't satisfy our philosophical curiosity, doesn't answer our philosophical questions, simply because, qua philosophers trying to be rational, we want more than to be automata responding to stimuli with beliefs. As internalists, we want *facts,* including facts about which propositions make probable others, before our consciousness. But this notion of being before our consciousness is itself simply a disguised sui generis epistemic concept. The 'internalized' knowledge that the internalist wants in the case of noninferential knowledge is direct acquaintance (a sui generis epistemic relation) with the fact that makes his belief true.[15] And in the case of inferential knowledge, the internalist at least wants direct acquaintance with the fact that the propositions constituting his evidence make probable (another sui generis epistemic relation) the proposition that he infers from that evidence. Acquaintance with evidential connections would clearly be impossible if evidential connections are complex contingent facts of the sort suggested by the externalists.

I should note that an analysis of knowledge can be more or less externalist in character — externalism admits of degrees. If, for example, one defines knowledge in such a way as to allow inferential knowledge when one's evidence does not entail what one claims to know on the basis of that evidence, such an account will inevitably introduce an "external" component.[16] The truth of what one believes, as a necessary condition for knowledge, will involve an element that goes beyond any aspect of the world with which we are acquainted. It is for precisely this reason that I suggested earlier that epistemologists might be mistakenly preoccupied with knowledge. When an account of knowledge simply 'tacks on' the truth of what one justifiably believes as a *nonredundant* necessary condition for knowledge, that concept of knowledge becomes philosophically uninteresting to the philosopher trying to satisfy his curiosity on epistemological issues.[17] *Externalists* (like Nozick and Goldman) who view *externally* defined justification as necessary for knowledge make their concept of knowledge doubly irrelevant by introducing not only truth, but justification, as external elements in their analyses of knowledge.

Of course none of the above is really intended to convince externalists to abandon their accounts of knowledge and justification. In fact, I suspect that they would be delighted if they could reduce the ranks of their critics to out-of-date epistemologists ranting about the need to confront reality directly. As some philosophers see it, externalism is perhaps the one epistemological view that could unite those longtime antagonists, foundationalists and coherentists, by giving them a common foe, the externalist. But if I am right, the coherentist's views are really much more like paradigmatic externalist views. Like the externalist, the coherentist is really trying to define 'away' fundamental epistemic concepts, this time replacing them with the concept of logical connection. And like externalism, a coherence theory of justification (without a coherence theory of truth) allows one to know a proposition without in any way confronting the fact that makes that proposition true.

IV

Throughout this essay I have been unrelentingly critical of Nozick's epistemology and externalism in general. In conclusion, however, I want to temper these criticisms by admitting that there is a sense in which I may well agree with much of what I suspect motivates Nozick's externalism. Naturalistic and externalist epistemologies are tailor-made to avoid skepticism. The naturalist and the externalist are convinced that it is just not possible to be directly acquainted with facts. And even if one could be directly acquainted with facts, the noninferential knowledge that such acquaintance yields constitutes a tiny fraction of what we would like to know. Furthermore, these philosophers are convinced that one cannot be directly acquainted with a sui generis relation of making probable holding between propositions. But such awareness of a confirmation relation is the only way in which the internalist can hope to get beyond the foundations of knowledge. In some of these claims, the externalist may well be right. In fact I rather suspect (though I do not claim to be justified in believing this) that nature *has* 'arranged' for our beliefs to "track" facts in much the way that Nozick suggests. As Hume stated so eloquently in discussing the question of whether Man should believe in the existence of physical objects:

> Nature has not left this to his choice, and has doubtless esteem'd it an affair of too great importance to be trusted to our uncertain reasonings and speculations.[18]

The externalist, believing this hypothesis to be true, wants to redefine epistemology in order to ensure that nature doesn't cheat us out of knowledge and justified belief. But in the context of a *philosophical* inquiry, this is the move one must reject. Evolution may have no great need for the conscious beings that inhabit the world to have justified beliefs or genuine knowledge of the sort that would satisfy our philosophical curiosity, but if nature has been so unkind as to preclude the possibility of our knowing what we want to know, we must simply acknowledge that philosophical skepticism is true. The internalist may be unable to answer some of the fundamental epistemologic questions the way he would have liked, but at least he doesn't change the meaning of those questions before trying to answer them.

NOTES

1. W. V. Quine, "Epistemology Naturalized," in *Ontological Relativity and Other Essays* (New York: Columbia University Press, 1969), 69–90.

2. In, for example, "Conclusive Reasons," in *Essays on Knowledge and Justification,* ed. M. Swain and G. S. Pappas (Ithaca: Cornell University Press, 1978), 41–60.

3. In "A Causal Theory of Knowing" in Swain and Pappas, op. cit.; and in "What is Justified Belief?" in *Justification and Knowledge,* ed. G. S. Pappas and M. Swain (Dordrecht: Reidel, 1979), 1–23).

4. All parenthetical page references are to Nozick's *Philosophical Explanations* (Cambridge: Belknap Press of Harvard University Press, 1981).

5. in "What is Justified Belief?" op. cit.

6. Belief-dependent conditionally reliable processes take as their input beliefs and produce other beliefs which are usually true when the input beliefs are true. Belief-independent unconditionally reliable processes take as their input stimuli that are not beliefs and produce beliefs which are usually true.

7. See my *Metaphysical and Epistemological Problems of Persception* (Lincoln and London: University of Nebraska Press, 1985).

8. In *Analysis* 15 (1955): 97–105.

9. A. J. Ayer, *The Problem of Knowledge* (Edinburgh: Penguin, 1956), 31.

10. Richard Foley effectively presents this criticism against reliability conceptions of justification in "What's Wrong with Reliabilism," *The Monist,* April, 1985.

11. *Op. cit.,* 20.

12. *Metaphysical and Epistemological Problems of Perception,* 69.

13. I do not mean to suggest that all internalists would want knowing to entail having evidence that one knows. I suspect that such a claim would be implausible on *any* account of knowledge.

14. I should be somewhat embarrassed to use this analogy for rhetorical purposes, as I do not in fact think that naturalism is a mistake in ethics even though it surely is in epistemology.

15. The nature of the acquaintance that yields knowledge is actually more complicated than this suggests. To know *p* through acqaintance, one must be acquainted with the fact that *p*, the thought that *p*, and the fact that the thought that *p* corresponds to the fact that *p*. I develop this view and the account of truth and thought it presupposes in *Metaphysical and Epistemological Problems of Perception,* chap. 2.

16. Steven Luper-Foy argues that knowledge, unlike justification, always involves an external element, and I think it is true that even many analyses of knowledge usually associated with internalism have at least one "external" component. See his "The Reliabilist Theory of Rational Belief," *The Monist,* April 1985, 203-25.

17. The importance of developing a philosophically interesting account of knowledge that does not make truth a kind of "dangling" necessary condition is stressed by Panayot Butchvarov in *The Concept of Knowledge* (Evanston: Northwestern Press, 1970), chap. 3.

18. David Hume, *A Treatise of Human Nature* (London: Oxford University Press, 1888), 187.

five

NOZICK ON KNOWLEDGE: FINDING THE RIGHT CONNECTION

Alan H. Goldman

When Gettier attacked the equation of justified true belief with knowledge by appealing to true beliefs inferred from justified but false premises,[1] three types of response emerged in the subsequent literature. First, epistemologists attempted to specify a connection between the truth of the proposition believed (or the fact to which the belief referred) and the belief itself, so as to prevent the belief from being only accidentally true.[2] A second alternative was to beef up the justification condition so as to rule out misleading evidence. This alternative in turn divided into two main tactics. The first sought to specify and rule out defeaters of justification, true propositions not known to the subject that would remove his warrant for believing.[3] The second sought to guarantee justification by requiring reliability in the source or method of acquiring the belief.[4] (Advocates of this type of analysis think of reliability as justification. Whether this fits the usual notion of justification will be considered briefly below.)

I

Nozick's analysis of knowledge represented one culmination (at the time) of the first type of response to Gettier examples.[5] He requires that a belief be counterfactually related to the fact to which it refers in the following sense. S's belief that p counts as knowledge only when:

(1) if p were not true, then S would not believe it;

(2) if p were true (in nonactual close worlds), then S would believe it.

When these conditions hold, S is said to track the fact that *p*. This relation need not obtain over all possible worlds, only over the closest worlds in which the antecedents are true.

Nozick amends these conditions to accommodate examples such as that of the grandmother who sees her grandson and therefore knows he is well, but would be deceived by other relatives as to the grandson's health were he sick. Here she knows that her grandson is well even though the first condition above is violated: she would not believe him to be sick if he were. Nozick's amendment is to require that the source or method of knowing be held constant in the relevant counterfactual situations: if the grandmother were to *see* her sick grandson, then she would not believe him to be well. As so amended, the analysis assures that a knower's belief be nonaccidentally connected with the fact that makes it true (in a certain sense of 'nonaccidental'). Thus it rules out the standard Gettier counterexamples to the more traditional analysis of knowledge, in which a believer is only accidentally correct in his belief, having inferred it from a false premise.

Both tracking conditions turn out, however, to be both too strong and too weak. We may begin with the charge that the first condition is too strong, that it rules out genuine cases of knowledge. Nozick admits this when it comes to knowing that I am using a particular method for generating belief by using that very method (216).[6] I can sense that I am sensing, but cannot hold the method constant while considering the situation in which I am not sensing. Hence I cannot apply his criterion to determine that I know I am sensing by sensing that I am.

Consider next the following case, illustrative of a more general difficulty. I am playing tennis with my twelve-year-old son when I hear from a nearby radio broadcast that an assassination has occurred at a distant location. I know from seeing my son (while I hear the broadcast) that he is not the assassin. Let us suppose that in that very distant possible world in which I witness my son assassinate the political leader in question, I am so driven to distraction that I do not come to believe him guilty. That (counterfactual) fact is irrelevant to my present knowledge in the real world. What seems to make it irrelevant is the fact that the possible world in question is so very distant from this one, in which my son is young, generally well-behaved, politically unmotivated, and playing tennis with me at the time of the murder. In the absence of any preconceived analysis of knowledge, we certainly would not question my claim to know my son's innocence in the situation described. Indeed this knowledge would be almost too obvious and trivial to assert in conceivable circumstances.

An example of similar structure was suggested to me by Risto Hilpinen. I am looking at a thermometer that is accurate within the range of 0 degrees to 100 degrees F. At all temperatures below 0 the

thermometer registers 0 degrees. By observing its reading of 70 degrees
I come to have the belief that it is not − 50 degrees. I thereby know that
it is not − 50 degrees, even though if it were, I would not believe it to
be. Once again we see that a measuring instrument which links an observer to facts within its range can produce knowledge when it generates true beliefs from observations in that range. (Think of the visual
system as such an instrument in the previous example.) If the closest
world in which such a fact fails to obtain is distant, then the lack of
tracking in that world appears to be irrelevant to the knowledge claim.
(On the other hand, if the thermometer is registering close to its
threshhold of accuracy and is not always accurate around that threshhold, then my beliefs based on it regarding values just outside its range
will not qualify as knowledge. Here the possible world in which the link
between fact and belief is broken is close.)

Thus Nozick's first tracking condition is too strong. In other cases it
proves to be too weak, failing to disallow bogus claims to knowledge.
Such is the case when the truth of a proposition is counterfactually
linked to a belief, but only via a (causal or evidential) chain intuitively
considered abnormal and defective. Consider a standard Gettier case
intentionally set up to deceive its subject. I have been tricked into
believing that someone in my office owns a Ford by Haveit's having
given me evidence that Nogot owns one, when Haveit is the owner. If
my belief were not true, then Haveit would not have led me to hold it.
Yet I do not know that someone in the office owns a Ford, since the
usual Gettier conditions obtain. I have inferred my belief from a false
premise, although I would not have come to hold it if it had been false.

While the previous examples show that the first counterfactual condition in itself is too strong, this one shows that, when it links a believer
to a fact via a chain of evidence, some stronger constraint on such
chains is required. Nozick himself in another section of his chapter on
knowledge proposes a constraint on inference that transmits knowledge. Such inference must satisfy the following counterfactual condition: if the conclusion were not true, then the premises would not be
believed. Belief in the premises must track the truth of the conclusion.
But this constraint too seems to be met in the intentional Gettier case,
since Haveit would not have provided me with evidence for a false conclusion in the example. Hence we need a different constraint on such
chains.

It might be thought that this example could be avoided by appealing
to the second of Nozick's tracking conditions, since there might be a
close world in which Haveit owns a Ford but does not present the misleading evidence to me. But, for one thing, considering such a world
fails to hold constant the method by which I arrive at belief in the example. That method consists in inference from the evidence with which
I am presented.

Problems about holding the method constant in fact lead us to charges against the second tracking condition similar to those raised against the first. Nozick himself wishes to rule out as knowledge the case of a brain in a vat that is programmed to have the belief that it is a brain in a vat (175–76). He appeals to his second tracking condition, arguing that there is a close world in which the belief is true but the programmer does not enter it into the brain. Here the brain does not itself use a method for obtaining the belief, and so there is no method to hold constant in the counterfactual condition. This claim enables Nozick to contrast this case with another in which I happen to see an object and gain knowledge of its location by looking in a certain direction, when there is a close world in which I do not look in that direction or see the object. The latter possibility is irrelevant, since my method that must be held constant includes looking in a particular direction.

One problem here, however, is that this contrast breaks down given a slight modification in the first example. Suppose that the brain's programmer gives it sensations of being surrounded by a vat. Then it will have a method of arriving at the belief that there is a vat around it, namely trusting in its visual experience. This makes the case analogous to that of my seeing an object; yet, as in the original brain-in-the-vat case, the brain lacks knowledge of its surroundings. (While it can have knowledge of general propositions, it cannot, I take it, acquire knowledge of its surroundings by this method.) Nozick's second tracking condition fails to disallow the knowledge claim, since, in the close worlds in which the method is held constant, in which the brain continues to believe on the basis of its present visual experience, it continues to believe that there is a vat around it.[7] (We may also imagine that the first tracking condition is satisfied in this example, in that the programmer would not have caused this belief if it were not true.)

Thus the second condition is too weak. Like the first, it is also too strong, as the following example shows. Imagine an old logician with failing mental capacities. At this point he is still capable of deriving the correct conclusion in a particular proof, but there is a close world in which he can no longer do so. Since he is still capable at this time of deriving the correct conclusion, he knows it when he does so. Yet the second tracking condition is violated, even when the method, inferring from the premises in question, is held constant. The moral is similar to that in the previous cases in which the first condition was found to be too strong: a method that links a subject to facts within its range need not always do so outside that range. In this case relating to the second tracking condition the connection is broken in a close world, and yet the subject still appears to have knowledge. It seems that an entirely different sort of connection is required here, one that need not connect belief to fact in all close worlds.

II

That counterexamples to a given analysis of knowledge can be found is not sufficient reason in itself to give it up. We must allow tradeoffs between the simplicity of an account, its ability to guide the epistemologist on the normative level, and its ability to capture our convictions in exotic cases. It may turn out that the addition of conditions sufficient to capture all our intuitions (if indeed these are consistent) will render an analysis ad hoc, unmanageable, and of no use in the inquiry into the sources and extent of our knowledge and into methods for the improvement of those sources. Nozick's account certainly has the virtue of simplicity and elegance. It remains to be seen how well it fares with more traditional epistemological concerns.

Unfortunately, his discussion of skepticism, while unquestionably ingenious in tracing the implications of the analysis for the attempt to meet skeptical challenges, leaves us less than fully satisfied as well. According to his account we cannot know that either pervasive or more local skeptical alternatives to our beliefs do not in fact obtain. Consider the theses that our everyday perceptual beliefs systematically err because we are deceived by Descartes' demon, or that we are all those brains in vats being programmed to have the experiences we do. If these skeptical possibilities were real, we would not believe they were. Hence we do not track the fact that they are not real. Hence we do not know that we are not brains in vats or dupes of Descartes' demon.

While Nozick's analysis forces this sweeping concession to the skeptic, it also saves our everyday knowledge from skeptical refutation, saves at least the possibility of such knowledge, by implying a lack of logical closure, even in cases of obvious implications known to hold. Because subjunctive counterfactuals in general are not closed under implication, neither is tracking. According to this analysis I can know that p, know that p implies q, draw the inference, and not know that q (205-6). I can know various propositions to be true without knowing the skeptic's alternatives to be false, even though the truth of the former implies the falsity of the latter, because I track the former but not the latter. I can track the truth of everyday perceptual beliefs without tracking the denial of the skeptical theses because the skeptic's worlds are not the closest ones in which the everyday propositions I believe are false. If they were false, I would not believe them, although in the skeptic's worlds they are false and I do believe them. If my pipe were not on my desk before me now, I would not believe it to be, even though if I were now a brain in a vat, I would falsely believe there to be a pipe on a desk before me.

Despite the plausible ring of examples such as that just cited, other more local concessions to the skeptic are far less plausible. When tracking is required and closure denied, I cannot know, for example, that my son is not a robot brilliantly constructed by aliens, although I can know that I do not have a brilliantly constructed robot son. Although these propositions are not equivalent, intuitively there seems to be no distinction in my ability to know them to be true. According to Nozick's account the distinction between them is epistemically crucial, since in the closest world in which my son is a robot, I do not believe he is, while in the closest world in which I have a robot son, I know that I have one (219–20). We should prefer an analysis of knowledge that allows us to know that we are not brains in vats, that our children are not robots (or assassins), and so on.

We perhaps require here an additional qualification and reminder about the place of intuitions in epistemological analysis. Intuitions about what and when we know are not sacrosanct. Given a realist view of the world and our relation to it, a view that Nozick shares, such initial epistemic evaluations are especially vulnerable, since knowledge requires a relation between facts and beliefs about which we can be mistaken. On the other hand, we attempt in analysis to capture our shared concept of knowledge. We must therefore begin from our settled convictions as data, adjusting in the end to preserve consistency and to preserve what is important in guiding inquiry. By so doing we will capture a real relation if our theory of knowledge is a good theory and if most of our intuitions about when we know are indeed correct. (Showing their correctness is a matter of answering the skeptic.)

We must not beg questions by beginning from those intuitions that match our initially favored analysis and then dismiss others inconsistent with it. An analogous procedure is legitimate only when it becomes otherwise clear that our convictions fail to cohere internally (or with any analysis derived partially from them), or that any analysis capable of capturing them must contain too many ad hoc epicycles to express our concept or to capture the real relation we conceive as knowledge. Neither claim precedes Nozick's willingness to dismiss such convictions as that I know that I am not a brain in a vat, that my son is not an assassin, that he is not a cleverly constructed robot, and so on. Such intuitions (especially the more local ones) do not seem particularly vulnerable. Indeed they seem as certain as any convictions regarding particular claims to empirical knowledge from which I might begin to reconstruct my concept. Thus they reflect badly on an account that must dismiss them.

Perhaps more serious epistemologically than particular counterintuitive implications of the analysis regarding more local skeptical alternatives to our everyday beliefs is the incompleteness of the more general debate with the skeptic. Any analysis that avoids Gettier examples by specifying a nonaccidental connection between the knower's belief and the fact to which it refers can provide a partial answer to the skeptic. Its advocate need only stipulate that the connection in question can hold in some circumstances but not in others that are indistinguishable from the former "from the inside," from the perspective of the knower's experiential states.[8] If the connection alone is what counts, and not how things appear to the knowing subject, then knowledge is not threatened by skeptical alternatives that appear indistinguishable from the internal perspective. Nozick's claim that knowledge obtains under tracking — since the skeptic's worlds (of brains in vats and so forth) are not the closest in which our beliefs are counterfactually false — is but a special case of this more general ploy open to an advocate of this kind of analysis.

But if the possibility of knowledge is saved in this way, there is nevertheless no *demonstration* of knowledge in the face of skeptical challenge here. The epistemologist's response to the skeptic is seriously incomplete. We are left pretty much with a draw, in which, *for all we know,* the skeptic's worlds are as possible as the real world in which we believe. Nozick simply states or assumes that the skeptical alternatives are not the closest worlds in which our everyday beliefs are false. If they are indeed very distant from the actual world, then of course they are not as possible as the real world in which we believe. But his assumption is entirely unsupported and indeed must remain so according to his analysis. If we cannot know that the skeptic's worlds are not actual (as on his account we cannot), then we surely cannot know that they are distant from the actual world.

It might be thought that the draw can be avoided by moving from claims about knowledge to considerations of rational belief and evidence.[9] Nozick in fact points out that there are asymmetries between the evidence for the existence of the real world and the evidence for the existence of the skeptic's worlds (264). There is evidence for the real world, since, if there were no such world, our experience would not be as it is; while there is no evidence for the skeptic's worlds, since, if they did not exist, our experience would be exactly as it is. Our experience as evidence tracks the hypothesis that there is a material world, but it does not track the skeptical alternatives. Thus, if rational belief is to be based on the evidence, it might appear more rational to believe in the real world than in the skeptical alternatives. This outcome might suffice to grant the victory to the nonskeptical epistemologist in his debate with the skeptic.

Winning this particular round (if indeed we have) is at the same time losing the fight, however. The problem is that the evidential relation is defined by Nozick in counterfactual terms similar to those in the analysis of knowledge. *e* is (strong) evidence for *h* if it tracks *h*. According to Nozick, our experience tracks the real world but not the skeptic's worlds. But since the evidential relation is an external to our point of view as the knowledge relation itself, we again have no way of knowing this. We have access to the supposed evidence, but not to the evidential relation. In the end the latter must simply be stipulated or assumed to obtain. Thus we are left again with only the possibility of knowledge, not with anything approximating to its demonstration.

Nozick may respond that refutation of the skeptic is not among his purposes, or that it is indeed impossible. For him the lure of the skeptic's arguments seems to lie in this very impossibility of refutation. But there is an alternative explanation, and one that will satisfy the true believer more. This explanation points to the link between skepticism and the tendency to make the conditions for knowledge too strong, a link with a long tradition in epistemology. The stronger the analysis of knowledge (and of evidence), the easier the skeptic's task. We saw above that Nozick's analysis appears too strong to capture our concept of knowledge as reflected in convictions regarding particular cases. It therefore may well fit the tradition that renders skepticism more plausible and immune to refutation than it need be.

III

The problems here specified for the counterfactual analysis should motivate us to seek an alternative, despite the extent of the literature on this subject in recent years. (Measured against other areas of philosophical inquiry, progress in meta-epistemology has been actually rapid.) In so doing we may either retain Nozick's approach or opt for one of the other strategies for accommodating the now extensive file of examples and variations. In my view Nozick's approach, seeking the right connection between beliefs and facts, is entirely correct. Defeasibility and reliability accounts (that are truly distinct) face more insuperable difficulties.

The difficulties for accounts that require nondefeasible justification — justification that cannot be overturned by evidence not in the subject's possession — are of two kinds. First, nondefeasible justification implies justification, and in my view this is already too strong, at least for ordinary (internal) notions of justification. Examples that show this share a common form. They involve believers whose beliefs connect to facts in required ways but who do not know that their beliefs are so connected and who are not justified (from their points of view) in thinking so. A medium who suddenly acquired the power to truly predict the future and whose predictions begin to turn out always right would have to be said to know the future. She would know it from the time that her predictions began to be right, even though at that time she was not justified in her beliefs. Space prevents a complete defense here of the controversial import of such examples.

Less controversial is the demand that such accounts be able to separate misleading evidence that defeats justification from that which may be safely ignored. Not all misleading evidence defeats justification. If I know that Haveit owns a Ford by having the usual kinds of evidence, then the fact that Haveit has an enemy in some other city who might convince me in that distant possible world in which I meet him that Haveit stole the car he always drives is irrelevant to my present knowledge. The usual strategy for defeasibility analyses is to consider whether justification survives the correction of a subject's false beliefs. Omniscience cannot be granted in the counterfactual situation, however, since that would entail that my knowledge can never be defeated by evidence I do not possess. But suppose in our example that Haveit's enemy is in my own office, and I just happen not to have heard the false rumors that have convinced everyone else in the office.[10] The usual ploy for the defeasibility advocate is to correct only my actual false beliefs.[11] But this may not work here either, since my knowledge can then be saved simply because I have not formed certain beliefs that I should have.

Consider finally the following example here. Suppose that I have (misleading) evidence that Nogot owns the Ford he drove to work this morning, but I am very cautious. I therefore believe the disjunction: either Nogot owns a Ford or he does not own the blue Ford he drove to work this morning. The real situation is that Nogot rented the Ford he was driving but that, unknown to him (or me), he has won that very car in the rental company's annual lucky giveaway lottery.[12] Here I do not know the disjunction to be true, since I know neither disjunct (and there is a close world in which he has won a different Ford). Yet it seems that any available defeater for my belief in the first disjunct would justify me in believing the second, and conversely. Thus I would continue to believe truly and be justified in believing when seeming defeaters are added. The true propositions of which I am unaware would not prevent me from being justified in believing (truly) the disjunction, and yet I do not know it. I do not know how to handle such examples within the defeasibility framework, and I suspect that any condition that could handle them would be so complex as to render the resulting analysis unusable as a guide for normative epistemology.

As for reliability accounts, these differ according to how the concept of reliability is unpacked. If sources for beliefs are required to be only generally reliable, then the account is too weak. This becomes clear in lottery examples. We can make the reliability of the inductive source of my belief that my ticket will not win a lottery as close to 1 as we like by increasing the number of tickets. Yet no matter how high the number, I still do not know in advance that my ticket will not win. (If I knew this in advance, then it would be irrational for me to buy a ticket. But it may not be irrational to enter the lottery — it depends on the odds.) Nor can we demand perfect reliability from a source in its general operation, for that demand would disallow all knowledge gained from perception or inductive inference. We must therefore think of the sources for belief only as they operate in particular contexts. A source of belief is reliable in context if and only if it produces true beliefs all or most of the time in such contexts. Given the source of a belief in a particular situation, facts of the same type as that to which the belief refers must tend to obtain.

Properly elaborated, this requirement singles out a particular kind of (indirect) connection between fact and belief that turns out to be an instance of a more general relation that I shall later endorse as a genuine constraint on knowledge. It should be clear at this point, however, that we have returned to the Nozickian approach of seeking the proper connection of belief to fact. Reliability in this sense has little to do with justification traditionally construed (as a relation between a subject or his belief and his accessible evidence). We may then turn again directly to the quest for the right connection. Recall that we require a relation weaker in itself than Nozick's, but with an additional constraint on connecting chains that renders it also stronger than his in some contexts.

Nozick actually guides us further toward our goal in his discussion of evidential support for a belief or hypothesis. The support lent by a body of evidence to a hypothesis is measured by the probability of the evidence given the hypothesis less the probability of the evidence given the falsity of the hypothesis: $\mathrm{pr}(e/h) - \mathrm{pr}(e/\text{not-}h)$. If we seek a connection of belief to fact weaker than the counterfactual tracking relation, we might try requiring a relation similar to this notion of support. We could say that the probability of a belief given the fact to which it refers, given its truth, must be greater than the probability of the belief given its falsity: $\mathrm{pr}(\text{belief}/p) - \mathrm{pr}(\text{belief}/\text{not-}p) > 0$. We can be more stringent by raising the degree to which these probabilities must differ.

Nozick calls the relation just described (when it involves inference from evidence) "almost-knowledge." Can we simply accept it as the knowledge relation? Not quite. We saw above that when a proposition believed is false only in a very distant possible world, it is irrelevant to a knowledge claim whether it would be believed in that world. Likewise, the probability of belief in that world is irrelevant. I know that my son is neither an assassin nor a cleverly constructed robot, however probable or improbable are my beliefs to the contrary in those distant (but closest) worlds in which my present beliefs are false. Thus we do not need to subtract the second probability from the first in the formula proposed above as expressing the knowledge relation.

In my earlier paper on the analysis of knowledge I spoke rather of the relevant fact's significantly raising the antecedent probability of the belief's being held: pr(belief/p) > pr(belief). When this relation holds across close possible worlds (when the probability relations are lawlike), then the truth of the belief, or the fact to which it refers, prominently helps to explain why the belief is held. This explanatory relation is the connection necessary for knowledge.[13] While it does not require us to consider distant possible worlds, and is therefore weaker than tracking, it must be combined with an additional constraint on explanatory chains. Each (probabilistic) link in such a chain must itself make the next link more probable. This idea involves second order probabilities of probability relations (and therefore galaxies of possible worlds under that interpretation). It is therefore somewhat complex to conceive and apply, yet intuitive as a constraint on explanatory chains. It determines when prior explanations in such chains are relevant to later ones. These conditions together handle the counterexamples proposed above both to Nozick's analysis and to the other major types of account.

IV

We may briefly review those examples to see how this alternative connection holds up in them. In the assassination example, there exists an explanatory chain that accounts for my knowledge of my son's innocence. Facts that explain his innocence—that someone else commits the murder, that my son is playing tennis with me at the time, and so on—also explain my belief in his innocence. Someone else's committing the murder explains the radio broadcast, which explains my having any beliefs about the matter at all. Thus a fact that explains my son's innocence can help to explain my belief about it, even though I would not believe him guilty if he were. A similar chain exists in the thermometer example. The fact that it is 70 degrees explains the thermometer's reading, which explains my belief that it is not − 50 degrees. That fact that it is 70 degrees, or facts that explain why it is 70 degrees, also explain why it is not − 50 degrees.

Consider next the intentionally set up Gettier case in which Haveit deceives me into truly believing that someone in my office owns a Ford. Here there is an explanatory chain in which the fact that someone does own a Ford (namely Haveit), together with Haveit's intention to deceive me, explains his presenting me with the deceptive evidence, which in turn explains my true belief. But the constraint on explanatory chains is violated. My believing on the basis of the evidence presented is not made more probable (explained) by the evidence's being connected with the fact that makes my belief true. A similar violation occurs in the case of the brain in the vat programmed to believe that it is a brain in a vat. The truth of the belief helps to explain why the programmer programs it, but that connection does not help to explain why the brain believes on the basis of being programmed. Contrast these cases with ordinary perceptual beliefs, where our believing on the basis of sensory evidence is itself made more probable (given natural selection of this type of belief) by the usual connections between perceived facts and sensory evidence.

Next came the example of the logician with failing capacities, who still knew a particular conclusion by having inferred it from true premises. Here the explanatory analysis differs from Nozick's in being again weaker. The connection between fact and belief need not hold in all close possible worlds, as in the counterfactual account. It suffices for the truth of the belief to raise the probability of its being held that there are more close worlds in which the two are connected than worlds in which they are not. In this example, the fact that there is one close world in which the logician's inferential capacities have failed and he no longer believes the conclusion does not defeat his claim to knowledge in the actual world, so long as there are other close worlds in which other factors change yet he continues to infer correctly.

Epistemically more important examples pertain to both local and general skeptical alternatives to our everyday beliefs. We saw that Nozick's analysis precludes knowledge that such alternatives fail to obtain, and that this in turn precludes any satisfactory answer to the skeptic's challenge, any way to show that we have everyday knowledge in the face of that challenge. Knowledge remains possible but nondemonstrable according to Nozick's analysis. Using the explanatory account, the epistemologist can do better. He can show that we have knowledge by showing that explanations for our beliefs in common sense or scientific terms are better than the skeptic's alternative explanations. According to the ordinary inductive criteria for good explanations, the former certainly are better (simpler, more plausible, deeper, less ad hoc, generating fewer unanswerable additional questions, and so on). The difficult part of this task is showing that our ordinary and scientific inductive criteria tend to be truth preserving, that they lead us or connect us to real explanatory connections among phenomena or objects in the world. I have attempted to provide this difficult argument elsewhere and cannot begin to repeat it here. However plausible my version of it is, it is clear that our prospect for answering the skeptic is better given the explanatory analysis than under Nozick's, which in itself blocks any satisfactory answer.

The counterexamples to defeasibility and certain kinds of reliability analyses can be disposed of briefly. Consider again the two variants of the case in which I claim to know that Haveit owns a Ford. In the first Haveit has an enemy in some distant city who convinces people to believe nothing that Haveit says, while in the second that enemy is in my

office and has (falsely) convinced everyone else in the office that
Haveit stole the care he is driving. In the first case what explains my belief is the evidence I have received, which in turn is linked to the fact
that Haveit does own the Ford. The distant false rumors are irrelevant
to my knowledge claim, since the possible world in which I learn of
them is also distant, and we are interested in probability relations only
across close worlds. But in the second case, if there are many close
worlds in which I hear the false rumors, then my belief is explained not
simply by the evidence I possess, but by my happening not to have
heard the rumors, since the evidence raises the probability of my belief
only in the context of my not having heard them. Thus our intuitions
are supported by the analysis in both cases.

The disjunction case that is so problematic for defeasibility accounts
presents no problem here either. My lack of knowledge (despite remaining justified in my true belief when supposed defeaters are added)
is explained by the lack of any explanatory or probabilistic connection
between the fact that Nogot has just won the car and my belief in the
disjunction.

Finally, the explanatory analysis correctly evaluates the lottery example that defeats straightforward fallibilistic reliability accounts.
The best explanation for my not winning involves the drawing of another ticket (which in turn is explained by the configuration of tickets
in the barrel, the position of the person drawing the winner from the
barrel, and so on—not simply by the number of tickets). But these
facts are unconnected with my belief prior to the drawing that I will not
win. Nor are they (sufficiently) explained by what explains my belief—
that is, the large number of tickets. (Remember that in most contexts
we require that the fact significantly or prominently raise the probability of the belief's being held. Contexts vary in this respect, however,
and perhaps if we wanted to be extremely lax here, we might grant
knowledge prior to the drawing. The point is that the reliability account must grant it, whereas ordinarily we wold not.) The more promising way of spelling out the notion of reliability turns out to instantiate
one type of permissible explanatory chain, in which the source of belief
explains both the belief and the fact to which it refers (or it is explained
by that fact).

V

In explaining the significance of knowledge for knowing subjects,
Nozick argues that evolution or natural selection could be expected to
result in subjects not simply with (many) true beliefs, but with sensitivity of beliefs to (changing) facts (284). He takes this sensitivity to
consist in the ability to track facts. Thus he takes evolutionary theory

to support his analysis, which helps to show how the ability to know is an important achievement for the species as well as for the individual. Knowledge as tracking is the type of cognitive state that might be selected (or rather the ability to achieve such states might be selected). An analysis of knowledge should suggest why individuals and species benefit from its acquisition, and Nozick claims that his acount satisfies this desideratum.

But in fact tracking is not quite the relation we would expect between believer and fact as the result of natural selection. We would not expect or require this relation to propositions, if many propositions are false only in distant possible worlds. Survival is not enhanced by sensitivity to counterfactual occurrences in those worlds. In fact, as we saw from several earlier examples, sensitivity to such distant counterfactual situations might distract us from knowledge in the real world. On the other hand, facts must be (probabilistically) connected with beliefs across close possible worlds and not simply in the actual world. We must be sensitive to likely changes in empirical conditions that might falsify our beliefs in close possible worlds—that is, those that might well become actual. From this theoretical viewpoint too we require a connection weaker than Nozick's tracking, which takes us to distant worlds in many cases.

Nozick notes that knowledge as a significant cognitive state for subjects should fall somewhere between having beliefs that just happen to be true and having beliefs that vary with the facts to which they refer in all possible worlds (285–86). The reason why the latter is not required, however, is precisely that we need not connect to variations in facts in distant possible worlds, in circumstances very unlike our actual environments that are also very unlikely to occur. But his tracking requirement may demand just such connections when considering the falsity of our present beliefs. Nozick here suggests a fruitful criterion for a successful account of the connection between beliefs and facts that constitute knowledge. He also refers us to a spectrum of accounts differing in the strength of the modal relation they require. In my view he missed finding the right connection by just a short distance within that spectrum.

NOTES

1. E. Gettier, "Is Justified True Belief Knowledge?" *Analysis* 23 (1963): 121–23.

2. The classic attempt was Alvin Goldman, "A Causal Theory of Knowing," *Journal of Philosophy* 64 (1967): 357–72.

3. See Keith Lehrer, *Knowledge* (Oxford: Oxford University Press, 1974); Marshall Swain, *Reasons and Knowledge* (Ithaca: Cornell University Press, 1981).

4. See, for example, Alvin Goldman, "What Is Justified Belief?" in *Justification and Knowledge*, ed. G. Pappas (Dordrecht: Reidel, 1970): 1–25.

5. Robert Nozick, *Philosophical Explanations* (Cambridge: Harvard University Press, 1981), ch. 3; see also Fred Dretske, "Conclusive Reasons," *Australasian Journal of Philosophy* 49 (1971): 1–22.

6. Parenthetical references are to Nozick's book *Philosophical Explanations,* op. cit.

7. Similar problems for Nozick's account are raised by Robert Shope, "Cognitive Abilities, Conditionals, and Knowledge: A Response to Nozick," *Journal of Philosophy* 81 (1984): 29–48.

8. Compare Steven Luper-Foy, "What Skeptics Don't Know Refutes Them," *Pacific Philosophical Quarterly* 65 (1984): 86–96.

9. This move was suggested to me by Frederick Schmitt.

10. The example is now like one from Gilbert Harman, *Thought* (Princeton: Princeton University Press, 1974), 143–44.

11. Lehrer, op. cit., chap. 9.

12. This is a variant of an example in Robert Shope, *The Analysis of Knowing* (Princeton: Princeton University Press, 1983), 216.

13. Alan Goldman, "An Explanatory Analysis of Knowledge," *American Philosophical Quarterly* 21 (1984): 101–8.

six

TRACKING, CLOSURE, AND INDUCTIVE KNOWLEDGE

Jonathan Vogel

I. INTRODUCTION

One of Robert Nozick's chief concerns in *Philosophical Explanations* is to refute a classical argument for Cartesian skepticism. According to the skeptic, we don't know that we aren't victims of a massive illusion or deception. For that reason, we have little or no knowledge about the way the external world really is. Nozick concedes the first point, that we don't know that we aren't systematically deluded, but he rejects the legitimacy of the inference which takes the skeptic to his conclusion.

Nozick believes that, in making this inference, the skeptic at least tacitly assumes that knowledge is closed under known logical implication. In other words, the skeptic assumes that the following epistemic principle is valid:

> Closure Principle: Where S is a subject, and *p* and *q* are propositions, if S knows that *p* and knows that *p* entails *q,* then S knows that *q.*[1]

Nozick argues that this principle doesn't hold, and that the skeptical argument which depends upon it doesn't go through. His procedure is to present and defend an analysis of knowledge that explicitly provides for closure failures. If that analysis is really correct, then the Closure Principle doesn't hold, at least in its full generality.

A key feature of Nozick's analysis is a condition that he calls the tracking requirement. In this essay, I will examine the role of the tracking requirement in Nozick's analysis and attempt to clarify the relation between tracking and the Closure Principle. I will consider various problems with the notion of tracking, and argue that the tracking requirement is incompatible with a satisfactory account of inductive knowledge. My conclusion is that Nozick doesn't succeed in refuting the skeptic after all.

II. NOZICK'S TRACKING CONDITION

According to Nozick's distinctive account of knowledge, a knowing subject must satisfy an adherence condition (A) and a tracking condition (T). These requirements may be spelled out in a preliminary way as follows:

(A) If p were true, S would believe that p

(T) If p were false, S would not believe that p.

In this essay, I will be concerned with the tracking condition (T), and I will have little to say about (A) as such.

Nozick intends (A) and (T) to be read as standard English subjunctive conditionals. The most widely accepted theory of such conditionals analyzes their semantic properties in terms of a space of possible worlds, in which worlds are closer or farther from the actual world to the extent that they are more or less similar to that world. According to this analysis, due principally to David Lewis and Robert Stalnaker, a subjunctive conditional of the form $(t \to v)$ is true just in case v holds in the closest world (or worlds) to the actual world in which t is true.[2] Thus, (T) in particular says that S knows that p only if S doesn't believe that p in the closest possible world(s) in which not-p holds — that is, the closest possible world(s) in which p is false.[3]

However, (T) as stated cannot stand; there are clear cases of knowledge in which the appropriate instance of (T) is not satisfied. Alvin Goldman has illustrated this point with a nice example:

> Condition (3) also doesn't seem necessary for knowing. Consider this example. Oscar sees Dack the dachshund and believes there is a dog before him. If there weren't a dog before him, a hyena would be there instead, which Oscar would misclassify as a dog. Letting p = 'There is a dog before me,' condition (3) is violated; but Oscar still knows.[4]

To meet this difficulty and others like it, Nozick revises his original formulations to take into account the method by which a subject arrives at his belief. (T) is replaced by

(T)′ If p were false, it would not be the case that S would believe that p via method M (where M is the method S actually uses)[5]

This revised analysis escapes Goldman's "Dack the Dachshund" example. The problem for the original version was that, although Oscar knew there was a dog before him, he did not satisfy (T). But Oscar does satisfy (T)′, on a natural reading of it. (T)′ requires, in this case, that if there weren't a dog before Oscar, he wouldn't believe by *his actual method* that there was a dog before him. One way of characterizing Oscar's actual method would be something like 'If you seem to see a small, squat, elongated animal with short legs and floppy ears, that barks, etc., conclude that there is a dog before you.' Now, if there weren't a dog before Oscar, he would as it happens, believe that there was. However, his method would be roughly, 'If you seem to see a spotted animal, with short back legs and a bristly mane, that has a shrill cry, conclude that there is a dog in front of you.' This is not Oscar's actual method. So, it's the case that: if there weren't a dog in front of Oscar, he wouldn't believe by his *actual* method that there was. Oscar satisfied (T)′ after all.

This example points up how important the specification of a subject's method is to the success of Nozick's analysis. The concept of the method by which a person comes to believe something is not an immediately clear one; in the "Dack the Dachshund" example, there may well be better or more natural ways to describe Oscar's methods than the ones I gave. In fact, serious doubts have been raised as to whether any uniform construal of the notion of a method of knowing is suitable for Nozick's general purposes.[6] However, no resolution of this larger issue is needed in order to evaluate Nozick's views about skepticism and the Closure Principle. Rather, the following, more limited treatment is sufficient.

Nozick observes at one point that his view

> treat[s] the method he [the subject] uses as identified from the inside, to the extent that it is guided by internal cues and appearances. . . . The method used must be specified as having a certain generality if it is to play the appropriate role in subjunctives. This generality is set by the differences the person would notice; the methods are individuated from the inside. (*PE,* 232–33)

Let us say, then, that for (T)′ it is a *sufficient* condition for S's believing that *p* by the same method as S's actual one that: S's belief that *p* is based on exactly the same evidence and inference patterns (if any) as S actually utilized.[7] In other words, if it were the case, in some counterfactual situation, that S had the same evidence *e,* and believed that *p* on the basis of *e,* in that counterfactual situation S would believe that *p* by the same method S actually used.

The idea of (T)′ is that if *p* were false, S would not believe that *p* by the actual method S used to arrive at *p.* We just observed that if S had exactly the same evidence and believed *p* on that basis, S would believe that *p* by his actual method. (T)′, then, requires as a *minimum,* that if *p* were false, S would not believe that *p* on the basis of his actual evidence. This requirement is quite weak, since it is satisfied so long as S would have had different evidence, had p been false — regardless of what S believes in that situation. From now on, let (T)' mean this minimal condition.

III. NOZICK ON SKEPTICISM AND CLOSURE

It follows directly from Nozick's account of knowledge that none of us knows the various skeptical hypotheses to be false. That is, no one knows not-SK, where not-SK says of that person that he is not, for example, a systematically deceived brain in a vat. The reason why we do not know not-SK, on Nozick's account, is that each of us fails to satisfy the appropriate instance of (T)'. For Nozick himself, the instance of (T)' would run:

(1) Not-(not-SK) → not-(Nozick believes, on the basis of his actual evidence, that not-SK)

Less schematically:

(2) If Nozick were a brain in a vat, he wouldn't believe, on the basis of his actual evidence, that he wasn't a brain in a vat.

Surely (2) is false. If Nozick were a brain in a vat, the course of his experience would have been, by hypothesis, exactly the same as it actually has been. So, Nozick would have had the same beliefs and evidence he actually has, including the belief that he is not a brain in a vat. But (T)' requires that he not have that belief under the circumstances where he is a brain in a vat. So, (T)' isn't satisfied, and Nozick does not, by his theory, know that not-SK. He does not know that he isn't a brain in a vat.

Although the tracking requirement excludes knowledge that the skeptical hypothesis is false, it doesn't impair knowledge of various particular facts about the world. The example Nozick himself uses is that he still knows he is sitting in a chair in Jerusalem as he writes his book (206–7). The relevant instance of (T)' is:

(3) If Nozick weren't sitting in a chair in Jerusalem writing his book, he wouldn't believe, by his actual evidence, that he was.

(3) is true. If Nozick weren't sitting in a chair in Jerusalem, he would have been doing something else in Jerusalem, or perhaps gone somewhere other than Jerusalem. But in these counterfactual situations, he would have remained aware of where he was and what he was doing. So, he would not have held the erroneous belief that he was sitting in Jerusalem when he wasn't. A fortiori, he wouldn't have believed by his actual evidence that he was sitting in Jerusalem when he wasn't. In this

way, Nozick's belief about where he is does satisfy the tracking requirement, and is something he may know.

These examples show how the tracking requirement leads to violations of the Closure Principle for knowledge. In the situation described, Nozick knows that (J = 'Nozick is sitting in a chair in Jerusalem writing his book') entails (not-SK = 'Nozick isn't a systematically deceived brain in a vat near Alpha Centauri'). That is, for Nozick, J has not-SK as its clear logical consequence. But, as we just saw, on Nozick's analysis of knowledge, he may know that J while not knowing that not-SK.[8] Thus, the Closure Principle fails. This failure is due to the fact that the tracking condition itself isn't closed under known logical implication. For, despite Nozick's knowing that (J => not-SK), he satisfies (T)' for J but not for not-SK.

Now it seems reasonable to think that knowledge is closed under known logical implication only if its component necessary conditions are themselves so closed. If that is so, Nozick can establish that knowledge isn't closed just by showing that, in order to know, one must satisfy the tracking requirement. Questions arising in connection with other features of Nozick's analysis become irrelevant, so far as the closure of knowledge and skepticism are concerned.

However, the assumption on which this simplification depends is problematic. The view that knowledge is closed only if its component conditions are faces the following sort of counterexample.[9] Suppose that in order for S to know that p it is required that: K(1) S tracks p—that is, S and p satisfy the appropriate instance of (T) or (T)'; and K(2) S tracks all of p's logical consequences. Call the satisfaction of K(1) and K(2) 'contracking.' For the reasons just considered K(1) as identical to either (T) or (T)' is not closed, by itself, under known logical implication. But the point is well taken. If S 'contracks' p, S will 'contrack' all of p's logical consequences, and therefore S will 'contrack' the subset of those logical consequences that are clear to S. 'Contracking,' then, is closed under known logical implication, even though one of its component conditions is not.

It is easy to imagine the following reply from friends of Nozick's position. If knowledge *were* 'contracking,' it could be closed without having its component conditions severally subject to closure. But knowledge can't be 'contracking' or anything entailing it. For if S 'contracks' p, S must 'contrack' *all* of p's logical consequences, not just p's clear ones. So, if knowledge were 'contracking,' it would be a necessary condition for knowledge of p that a person know all of p's logical consequences. But no one can know all the logical consequences of anything that he knows; so, if knowledge were 'contracking' one could know literally nothing. And that sets the standard of knowledge too high even for the Cartesian skeptic.[10]

Another point worth noting is that, if closure holds despite the tracking requirement, Cartesian skepticism is inescapable. For, as the previous discussion indicates, belief in the falsity of the skeptical hypothesis fails to satisfy Nozick's tracking condition; thus, no one knows that the skeptical hypothesis is false. However, by the Closure Principle, we have to know that the skeptical hypothesis is false in order to know virtually anything about the external world. It follows, then, that we will have very little knowledge of the world if both the tracking condition and Closure Principle are valid. This outcome would be unwelcome to anyone who finds the Closure Principle intuitive and skepticism incredible.

It is clear, then, that the attempt to defend closure while granting that (T)′ may be necessary for knowledge is an approach which faces serious liabilities. An alternative line of thought, which I shall pursue, is to try to show that (T)′ is in fact *not* necessary to knowledge. If that is correct, then it is irrelevant, for my purposes, whether knowledge can be closed even if its component conditions are not.

IV. SOME PROPOSED COUNTEREXAMPLES

For the reasons just given we may grant the assumption that, if (T)′ is a necessary condition for knowledge, knowledge itself doesn't obey the Closure Principle. Such a result provides an important perspective on the large literature which has appeared in response to Nozick's book. Any number of counterexamples have been offered to refute Nozick's analysis of knowledge. Although many of them are controversial, some, I think, succeed. However, almost every counterexample offered aims to show that Nozick's analysis fails by being too *weak*; that is, the analysis is supposed to be defective because it fails to exclude cases which it ought not to count as knowledge. It is important to note, though, that counterexamples of that type do not undercut Nozick's case against closure, since they do not show that (T)′ is not necessary for knowledge.

Robet Shope, however, has argued against the validity of the tracking requirement. Shope maintains that some subject S can know that (C): 'It is true of some of those beliefs that S does have about beliefs that they might be otherwise; that is, that S might not have them.'[11] The tracking requirement would have us consider counterfactual situations in which (C) is false. Here, though, the limitation to beliefs about beliefs is cumbersome and implausible. If first-order beliefs could vary while second-order beliefs were fixed, in many cases S could believe that he believed that d, but not believe that d; also, S could believe that f, without believing that he believed it. It is problematic to characterize anyone subject to widespread incongruities like these as having beliefs at all, so Shope's example becomes difficult to grasp. For Shope's purposes, (C)′ would be better, where (C)′ is: 'It is true of some of the beliefs S has that they might be otherwise; that is, that S might not have them.

Shope's point can now be put this way: S may know that (C)′ yet S cannot satisfy (T)′ for (C)′. The appropriate instance of (T)′ says that if (C)′ were false, S would not believe (C)′ on the basis of S's actual evidence. But if (C)′ were false, all of S's beliefs would be fixed, including S's belief that (C)′ and all the beliefs, if any, upon which that belief depends. So, if (C)′ were false, S *would* believe that (C)′ on his actual evidence, making (T)′ *false*. Yet, it seems that (C)′ holds is the sort of thing we can and do know. So, (T)′ cannot be a necessary condition for knowledge.

There are still some mysteries about this example. It is clear that if S's beliefs were such that they could not have been otherwise, S wouldn't be an embodied, mobile person, with functioning senses, negotiating a normal environment — although that is what S would take himself to be. Shope suggests that "one can at least imagine a time at which an external power has forced on S those beliefs which S has about beliefs."[12] For (C)′ to be false, the "external power" would have to force all of S's beliefs upon him, and a great many of those beliefs would have to be false.[13] In short, (C)′ is the denial of a skeptical hypothesis of massive deception, and it would be perfectly consistent for Nozick to say that neither S nor anyone else knows (C)′.[14]

Actually, Shope's example can be seen as an especially baroque member of a family of examples which might be deployed against Nozick's analysis. If S knows that (C)′, S knows that he is not deceived in some crucial respects about the processes by which he arrives at his beliefs. On Nozick's analysis, it appears that it is impossible for anyone to know that he is not deceived about anything in particular. Imagine that I am looking at the statement I just received from the bank, and I believe my balance to be as it appears on the statement. I also believe that the bank is not deceiving me about how much money is in my account. Do I know that the bank isn't tricking me? If it were, I would be none the wiser, since by assumption I would be taken in. So, I do not satisfy (T)′ in this case; it is not true that if the bank were deceiving me, I would not believe that the bank was not deceiving me (on the basis of my actual evidence). The same line of thought can be applied to any claim by someone to know that he is not deceived in some way or other.

Presumably, Nozick would accept the result that we do not know ourselves to be undeceived by banks or anyone else. In effect, he would regard these as small-scale skeptical hypotheses. The counterintuitiveness of our not knowing ourselves not to be victims of small deceptions is mitigated for Nozick by the failure of the Closure Principle in these cases. For instance, suppose that, in the example just given, the bank is really honest. Even if I do not know that the bank is not tricking me, I do know what my balance is. If my balance had not been what it actually is, say $100, the bank, being honest, would have reported the different figure and I would not have believed that my balance was $100. In other words, I can satisfy (T)′ for my belief that my balance is $100, without satisfying it for the belief that the bank is not deceiving me. Consequently, I can know what my balance is, without knowing that the bank isn't deceiving me about my balance. This situation is analogous to the circumstances created by grand skeptical hypotheses postulating near-total deception.[15]

The possibility of defending (T)′ in this way raises a general methodological problem. Suppose an apparent counterexample to the tracking requirement is found, in which someone seems to know that p even though S doesn't satisfy (T)′ with respect to p. To make the counterexample legitimate, must it also be shown that p isn't the denial of what of what is, in some *extended* sense, a skeptical hypothesis? It is difficult to see what such a demand would really come to, or how it could be met. Still, as I will suggest, there are counterexamples to the tracking condition which seem to obey any reasonable version of this constraint.[16]

V. NON-CLOSURE AND THE PROBLEM OF INDUCTIVE KNOWLEDGE

I would like at this point to turn to Nozick's treatment of inductive knowledge. By inductive knowledge, I mean knowledge of some proposition on the basis of a limited sample, such that what one knows about the sample does not entail the truth of the proposition known. Inductive knowledge may be of general propositions (for example, 'All pure samples of silver are good conductors'). There is also inductive knowledge of singular propositions (such as, 'The next emerald you see will be green'). Nozick believes that inductive knowledge can be handled by his account to the extent that all genuine cases of inductive knowledge satisfy (T)′:

> Do we know that the sun will rise tomorrow, that the earth will continue to rotate its axis during the next 24-hour period? If the sun were not going to rise tomorrow, would we have seen that coming, would that alteration in the earth's rotation have been presaged in the facts available to us today and before? If so, then we do know the sun will rise tomorrow; our belief that it will tracks the fact that it will, by being based on facts that would have been different otherwise. But isn't it logically possible that everything was as it was until now, yet the earth will not continue to rotate tomorrow? Yes, there are such skeptical logical possibilities SK: the bread no longer nourishes us, the sun stops in the sky, an event of a

certain sort no longer continues to produce its usual effects. If they are elaborated suitably, so that everything we can detect up until now would have remained the same, then we don't know they do not hold. The skeptic about induction is right to say we don't know these possibilities do not hold, but he is wrong to deny we know those particular results of inductive inference whose falsity would have been reflected back and presaged in the facts upon which we base the inference. (PE, 222–223).

This approach leads directly to an odd consequence. Suppose that Nozick is right, and we can know in the way he describes that the earth will continue to spin. While we do know that the earth will continue to spin, we do *not* know that it won't *suddenly* stop spinning. That's because the relevant instance of (T)′ is false for the latter. That condition in this case reads 'If the earth were suddenly to stop spinning, you (or I) would not have believed on the basis of our actual evidence that the earth would not suddenly stop spinning.' But, if the change in the earth's rotation were to be sudden, we would have had no warning of it; we would have the same expectation we always have that the earth will keep going without stop, sudden or otherwise. Hence we would believe that 'The earth will not stop spinning suddenly' even if it were false, and thereby fail to meet the condition (T)′.

As the above quotation indicates, Nozick seems prepared to acknowledge that someone can know that 'The earth won't stop spinning at all,' yet, at the same time, not know that 'The earth won't stop spinning suddenly.' We could expect Nozick to explain the impression of anomaly here as due, once again, to an unreasoned commitment to the Closure Principle. For, it may be that we believe the earth won't stop spinning suddenly because we infer that from the wider belief that it won't stop spinning at all. In that case, the reason for thinking that we know the former would have to be some form of the Closure Principle. Even so, Nozick's treatment of this example is inadequate, if 'The earth won't stop spinning suddenly' is the sort of thing we do know. For then, there would be an instance of knowledge for which, as we saw, (T)′ doesn't hold.

More generally, if the inclusion of (T)′ in the analysis of knowledge has the consequence that we wouldn't know many of the singular propositions we do know by induction, then (T)′ has to be given up. Otherwise, Nozick is securing the failure of the Closure Principle, and, hence, freedom from Cartesian skepticism, at the cost of a strong kind of skepticism about induction. That hardly seems acceptable. It may be, though, that Nozick sees no *general* incompatibility between his tracking condition and inductive knowledge about particulars. He may think that conflicts arise only for a restricted, suspect class of propositions, one member of which would be 'The earth will not stop spinning suddenly.'[17] At any rate, I propose to give Nozick the benefit of the doubt about his case, and to see how his account handles other cases of inductive knowledge about particulars.

Let's turn to a fresh example. Imagine it's a hot day in August, say 95 degrees in the shade. Several hours ago, you left some ice cubes in a glass out in the direct sun, and since that time you've gone inside to get out of the heat. You think about the ice cubes, and it occurs to you that the ice you left outside must have melted by now. Despite the fact that you are not, at that moment, perceiving the shallow layer of water at the bottom of the glass, you know that the ice has melted.

If (T)′ is necessary for knowledge, then in this situation it has to be true that

(4) If the ice cubes hadn't melted, you wouldn't believe, on the basis of your actual evidence, that they had.

Now, I think, on a natural assessment, (4) comes out false. If the ice cubes hadn't melted, you would have been sitting inside thinking that they had, on the basis of all your past experience with ice, heat, and the like. The impression that (4) is false is bolstered by the fact that (5) seems true:

(5) If the ice cubes hadn't melted, you would have been very surprised to learn of their state.

Presumably, the reason (5) is true is that, even if the ice hadn't melted, you would still have your normal expectation that it had. If that is so, (4) will be false.

The intuitive grounds for holding (4) false in this situation are backed up by semantic theory. According to David Lewis's theory of counterfactuals, (4) is evaluated by considering the most similar world to the actual one where the ice cubes didn't melt. Lewis's theory further indicates that the most similar world is one which is identical to the actual world up until the time when the ice cubes actually begin to melt. Since the histories of the two worlds are identical up to that point, your evidence about ice cubes and your beliefs formed from that evidence will be the same in both worlds. Thus, in the nearest possible world in which the ice cubes don't melt, you do form the belief that they have melted, on the basis of your actual evidence. On Lewis's theory, then, (4) is false for the example given.

Nozick is conscious of the incompatibility of his account of inductive knowledge with Lewis's semantics, and he has a response. In order to discuss it, I have to introduce some terminology. A *forward conditional* is one in which the antecedent refers to a time that is earlier than, or contemporaneous with, the time described in the consequent. So, 'If Tom had gone to Denver yesterday, he would have been snowbound today' is a forward conditional. A *backward conditional* is one which says how things would have to have been before hand for some counterfactual situation to have come about; the antecedent refers to a time later than the time described in the consequent. An example is 'If Yale College had graduated 2,500 seniors in 1985, it would have to have been the case that they admitted over 2,000 freshmen in 1980.' Finally, a *backtracking compound* is a forward conditional treated as the combination of a backward and a forward conditional. Consider the forward conditional 'If I had played John McEnroe at the U.S. Open finals, I would have won a respectable number of points from him.' That may seem unlikely, in view of my lamentable tennis game, but, viewed as a backtracking compound, this counterfactual can come out true. For, we have the backward conditional 'If I had played McEnroe at the finals of the U.S. Open, I would have to have beaten other, very good players in the earlier rounds.' This combines with the forward conditional 'If I had beaten other, very good players in the earlier rounds of the Open, I would have won a respectable number of points from McEnroe in the finals.' Putting the two conditionals together makes it come out true that 'If I had played McEnroe in the finals, I would have won a respectable number of points,' where this conditional is taken as a backtracking compound.

Lewis's semantics excludes this kind of backtracking interpretation of conditionals, but such an interpretation is just what Nozick thinks he needs for his account of inductive knowledge. In a footnote, Nozick makes it clear that he wishes to reject Lewis's account of counterfactuals in favor of one that admits backtracking compounds:

> The relevant not-*p* world [that is, the one to be considered when determining whether the tracking conditional is satisfied] is not a world identical to the actual one until now, and then diverging so as to produce not-*p* . . . a more complicated theory will be needed; my hope is that any such theory can be plugged into the text above, producing only minor modifications in it. (*PE,* 223n).

Nozick makes some suggestive remarks about what a suitable theory might look like, but these give no guidance in treating concrete cases.

Still, it is clear enough what Nozick has in mind. In the ice cube example, the relevant instance of (T)' is to be treated as a backtracking compound. That is to say

(4) If the ice cubes hadn't melted, you wouldn't have believed, on the basis of your actual evidence, that they had.

is supposed to be true because a backward conditional like (6) holds:

(6) If the ice hadn't melted, it would have been the case that your previous experience was different in ways that would have led

you not to expect that the ice would melt under the circumstances.

My point is this: (6) is not clearly true at all. Who knows that your past
would have been like if the ice cubes hadn't melted? Perhaps, if there
were this one exception to the usual laws about the way ice behaves in
the heat, there would have been many others. These might, then, have
come to your attention beforehand, and led you not to expect the ice
cubes to melt in the sun. On the other hand, it could just as well have
been that the failure of the ice to melt on this occasion was a very rare,
even unique, exception to the ways ice normally behaves. In that event,
you would have had the same basis for expecting the ice to melt as you
actually did. (6) is, at best, indeterminate, because there is no reason to
favor one story rather than the other. Now, if (6) is indeterminate in
this way, and (4) is true only if (6) is, then (4) is itself indeterminate, if it
isn't false.[18] Because (4) is at best indeterminate, (T)′ would not be
satisfied in this case, despite the fact that you do know by induction
that the ice cubes have melted. (T)′, then, cannot be necessary for
knowledge.

   The problem here is a general one, and it has to do with the role
Nozick assigns to backtracking compounds. The backward conditionals they introduce are as a rule indeterminate.[19] As a result, a high degree of indeterminacy will characterize the relevant instances of (T)′
construed as backtracking compounds. So, if Nozick's approach to the
evaluation of the conditionals were correct, and satisfaction of (T)′
were necessary for knowledge, then attributions of inductive knowledge would themselves almost always be indeterminate (or false). Since
such indeterminacy doesn't exist, Nozick has to be wrong about the
status of (T)′.

   Let me summarize the criticisms I have offered. If instances of (T)′
are not taken as backtracking compounds, then (T)′ fails outright in
cases of inductive knowledge like the ice cube example. If, to avoid this
result, the crucial conditionals are taken as compounds, attributions of
inductive knowledge turn out to be, if not false, then highly indeterminate. The end result is that an account of knowledge which makes (T)′
a necessary condition will not adequately handle knowledge by
induction.

   In constructing these objections, I have been relying, in the first
place, on our intuitions about knowledge and about the truth-values of
various conditionals. My point can be put this way: an inconsistency
results from combining Nozick's tracking requirement, our intuitions
about counterfactuals, and out intuitions about inductive knowledge.
Under the circumstances, the tracking requirement ought to be given
up. Sometimes, it appears, it is philosophically desirable to sacrifice intuitions in favor of some theory. I see no reason why such a step would

be justified here. Moreover, rejecting the intuitions about counter-factuals in particular in order to save Nozick's epistemological theory would have a theoretical cost as well. For insofar as Lewis's theory of counterfactuals matches those intuitions, it too would have to be abandoned if the tracking condition is retained.[20]

VI. KNOWLEDGE AND NATURAL LAWS

My criticisms of Nozick in the previous section have been based on considerations concerning inductive knowledge of singular pro-positions. More specifically, I am claiming that, in a representative instance, Nozick's tracking condition is inconsistent with our knowing that unobserved exceptions to natural law don't occur. In this section, I want to take up an extended objection to the argument I just gave. The point of the objection is that, while some intuitions and Lewis's seman-tics do tell against the tracking condition, a revised semantic theory and perhaps some counterintuitions may be brought to support the tracking requirement.

Here is the objection: Let us reconsider the ice cube example. If, in the situation described, the ice cubes hadn't melted, there would have been a violation of the law that water melts at temperatures above 32 degrees F. The melting point of water, though, is determined by more basic physical laws. So, in the possible world where the ice cubes re-main frozen, the normal physical laws could not have been in force; the laws in force in that world would have to be quite different from the ac-tual ones. This difference, it might seem, would have shown up before-hand, in that world, in the previous abnormal behavior of water and many other things. In that event, your past experience would have been different from your actual experience in ways that would have been rel-evant to your belief about the state of the ice cubes on that particular afternoon. That is to say, there are reasons to think that (6) is probably true in this case:

> (6) If the ice hadn't melted, it would have been the case that your previous experience was different in ways that would have led you not to expect that the ice would melt under the circum-stances in question.

Moreover, if we are concerned with your belief about the ice cubes *after* the fact, as you sit inside without having looked, the appeal to backward conditionals like (6) can be dispensed with altogether. For, if the ice cubes hadn't melted after having been out in the sun for a long while, at that point at least, the normal physical laws would not be in force.[21] If they weren't in force, all kinds of strange things would be happening that you would surely notice. So, it is reasonable to assume that, in the face of all sorts of apparently impossible phenomena, you would not then be inclined to hold the belief that the ice cubes were melted.[22] This last counterfactual is not a *backtracking* compound; it combines the forward conditionals

> (7) If the ice weren't melted at time t, then at time t, the normal laws of nature wouldn't be in effect.

and

> (8) If, at time t, the normal laws of nature weren't in effect, you would be struck by the abnormal course of macro-level phenomena and not expect the ice to melt.

to yield the permissible forward conditional

> (9) If the ice cubes weren't melted at time t, you wouldn't expect the ice to behave as it normally does; that is, you wouldn't believe that it was melted.

On the face of it, though, this reply accomplishes little. It presupposes that if there were a local exception to the melting-point law, there would have to be widespread and noticeable exceptions to the more basic laws which underlie the law about the melting point. Why wouldn't the basic laws be broken only as they affect the ice cube at that time, leaving virtually everything — including your expectations — unaltered?

The proponent of (T)′ might answer as follows. One feature of the actual world is that it is governed by exceptionless physical laws that are invariant over space and time.[23] On this basis, it could be claimed that a possible world which has different, but unbroken and uniform physical laws more closely resembles the actual world than does a world governed by laws that admit exceptions. If similarity in this particular respect is given so much importance that it outweighs all other considerations, then the possible world(s) which determine the truth-values of the counterfactuals which concern us will be worlds governed by exceptionless laws. Specifically, the closest possible world to the actual one in which the ice cubes don't melt will turn out to be one where the basic physical laws permit ice to remain frozen at temperatures like 95 degrees F. Since these laws must be invariant over time and space, it is very plausible to think that your experience in that world would have been different enough, either before or at the time in question, to have led you not to expect that the ice left outside would melt. The key counterfactual 'If the ice hadn't melted, you wouldn't have believed that it had' comes out true, and (T)′ is satisfied here as Nozick requires.

Clearly, a working similarity ordering suitable for evaluating instances of (T)′ is not fully defined by the bare stipulation that possible worlds governed by uniform, exceptionless laws are closer to the actual world than worlds without such laws. It appears, then, that we ought to construe the argument of the previous paragraph as an argument in favor of modifying the standard similarity ordering for possible worlds given by Lewis. The modification consists in weighting complete conformity to invariant natural laws so heavily that it dominates all other criteria of similarity; otherwise, the criteria given by Lewis hold.[24] There will be substantial differences between Lewis's semantics and a semantics for counterfactuals built on the modified ordering. If the latter is taken as a *replacement* for Lewis's general theory of counterfactuals, an inferior semantics results. For example, on Lewis's account the following, apparently true counterfactual does come out true:

(10) If I changed dolphins into men, I would have performed a miracle.

The modified semantics makes this come out false.[25]

Despite the fact that the revised similarity ordering is inappropriate for a general semantics of counterfactuals, it remains open to the proponent of (T)′ to use that semantics to define a new modal connective "> > >." On this proposal, when S knows that p, S satisfies the relevant instance of [not-p > > > not-(S believes that p on the basis of S's actual evidence)]. Here, though, the resulting sentence is *not* to be read as a standard English counterfactual. Rather, it is to be evaluated according to the specifications given: it is true just in case the consequent holds in the nearest not-p world(s), where "nearest" means "nearest under the revised similarity ordering."

Now, even if we are willing to go this far in order to save (T)′, the effort will be unavailing. Consider

(11) The next emerald you see will not be "grue"

where "grue" means "green before the year 2,000 and blue otherwise."[26] Unless we succumb to skepticism about induction, we will say that (11) is something a person may know now. However, no subject can satisfy (T)′, even in its most recent transmogrification, for propositions like (11). (T)′ requires

(12) If the next emerald you see were "grue," you would not believe, on the basis of your actual evidence, that the next emerald you see will not be "grue."

(It is understood that this counterfactual is to be interpreted according to the revised nonstandard semantics). The existence of "grue" emeralds is inconsistent with actual physical law. By the revised semantics for (T)′, then, we must evaluate (12) by considering the nearest possible world with "grue" emeralds that is also governed by exceptionless, time-invariant physical laws — if such a world exists. Otherwise, we are to follow the other criteria Lewis gives for evaluating counterfactuals.

Now, any possible world in which "grue" emeralds are found is *not* a world in which the laws of nature are spatio-temporally invariant. Hence, we must fall back on Lewis's semantics in considering (12). The nearest world, on Lewis's rendering, in which the next emerald you see is "grue" is a possible world exactly like the actual one, except that the emerald you will encounter has a propensity to change from green to blue in a little more than a decade from now. In this possible world, there is no reason why your experience beforehand should be any different from your experience in the actual world. So, you would have up until now all the same beliefs as you actually have, including those upon which you base your belief that the next emerald you see will *not* be "grue." It turns out, finally, that if the next emerald were "grue," you *would* believe, on the basis of your actual evidence, that it wasn't "grue." (12), then, is false, and (T)′ fails for a genuine case of inductive knowledge. [27]

If this example seems too exotic, consider an alternative. Suppose two policemen confront a mugger, who is standing some distance away with a drawn gun. One of the officers, a rookie, attempts to disarm the mugger by shooting a bullet down the barrel of the mugger's gun. (I assume that the chances of doing this are virtually nil). Imagine that the rookie's veteran partner knows what the rookie is trying to do. The veteran sees him fire, but is screened from seeing the result. Aware that his partner is trying something that is all but impossible, the veteran thinks (correctly as it turns out)

(13) The rookie missed.

Now, I would way, in this sort of situation, the veteran might well know that the rookie had missed. But (T)′ requires

(14) If the rookie hadn't missed, the veteran would not have believed (by his actual evidence) that the rookie had missed.

where (14) is to be evaluated by considering the closest world, with invariant physical laws, in which the rookie does shoot a bullet down the barrel of the mugger's gun. It is possible, given the *actual* natural laws, for the rookie to succeed, although the likelihood of this is just about negligible. So, we may assume that the closest law-invariant world in which the rookie succeeds is one in which the actual laws hold; the invariance of those laws will do nothing to affect the veteran's reasonable expectation that the rookie will miss. As a result, in this world, the veteran believes the rookie will miss, and the consequent of (14) is false. However, as specified, the consequent of (14) is true, so the conditional as a whole comes out false. It emerges that (T)', even under its revised construal, is not satisfied in a case where someone would know.

VII. CONCLUSION

In the previous sections, I have been concerned to make clear how Nozick's denial of the Closure Principle rests on the claim that his tracking condition, (T)', is a necessary condition for knowledge. I argued that (T)' cannot be necessary for knowledge, because there are cases of inductive knowledge for which (T)' is not satisfied. If what was said on these points was correct, Nozick's case against the Closure Principle is unsuccessful. The skeptical argument which depends on that principle remains unrefuted.[28]

BIBLIOGRAPHY

Barker, S. F., and Peter Achinstein. "On the New Riddle of Induction," *Philosophical Review* 69 (1960): 511–22.

Bennet, Jonathan. "Counterfactuals and Temporal Direction," *Philosophical Review,* 93 (1984): 57–91.

Garrett, B. J. "Nozick on Knowledge," *Analysis* 43 (1983): 181–184.

Goldman, Alvin. Review of *Philosophical Explanations, Philosophical Review* 92 (1983): 81–88.

Goodman, Nelson. *Fact, Fiction, and Forecast,* 4th ed. Cambridge: Harvard University Press, 1983.

Lewis, David. "Counterfactual Dependence and Time's Arrow," *Nous* 13 (1979): 455–75.

———. *Counterfactuals.* Oxford: Blackwell, 1973.

Luper-Foy, Steven. "The Epistemic Predicament: Knowledge, Nozickian Tracking, and Skepticism," *The Australasian Journal of Philosophy* 62 (1984): 26 49.

McGinn, Colin. "The Concept of Knowledge," *Midwest Studies in Philosophy,* vol. 6, ed., French, Uehling, and Wettstein (Minneapolis: University of Minnesota Press, 1984).

Nozick, Robert. *Philosophical Explanations* (Boston: Harvard University Press, 1981).

Shope, Robert. "Cognitive Abilities, Conditionals, and Knowledge: A Response to Nozick," *The Journal of Philosophy* 81 (1984): 29–48.

Stalnaker, Robert. "A Theory of Counterfactuals," *American Philosophical Quarterly,* monograph no. 2 (1968): 98–112.

NOTES

1. The exact formulation of the Closure Principle is complicated by various psychological considerations that have to be taken into account. For example, it is conceivable that S might know some proposition *p* and also know that *p* entails *q,* yet fail to draw the conclusion *q* because S fails to "put what he or she knows together." The formulation given doesn't

cover all these complexities. Problems of this sort, however, don't affect issues connected with skepticism, where the logical relations among the relevant propositions may be taken to be fully explicit to the subject. In such cases, where there is no question about whether the Closure Principle would apply, I call the entailed proposition a *clear* logical consequence of the proposition known.

2. Here and throughout I will use the symbol '→' to stand for the subjunctive conditional; I use ' ⇒ ' to represent logical entailment. See David Lewis, *Counterfactuals,* and Robert Stalnaker, "A Theory of Conditionals" for a detailed discussion of subjunctive conditionals. Although Lewis and Stalnaker share a general approach, their analyses differ in important ways.

3. Nozick suggests that his theory may properly be viewed as a relevant alternatives account of knowledge. The application of the Lewis-Stalnaker framework to (A) and (T) provides a solution to the problem which plagues other relevant alternatives theories, viz. the problem of specifying which alternatives *are* relevant. For Nozick, the epistemically relevant situations, the ones in which S must be right about *p* in order to know that *p*, will be just those situations which must be considered in evaluating the subjunctive conditionals (A) and (T).

4. Alvin Goldman, Review of *Philosophical Explanations,* 84.

5. This formulation departs from the one given by Nozick (179), and incorporates certain refinements suggested by Steven Luper-Foy. Nozick's version of (T)′ requires that S not believe that *p* in the nearest possible world where *p* is false *and* S does employ method M. By contrast, Luper-Foy's rendering makes a requirement concerning the nearest possible world where *p* happens to be false; this world need not be one in which S employs method M. However, if S does employ method M in that world, Luper-Foy's version of (T)′ requires that S not believe that *p* by that method. See Steven Luper-Foy, "The Epistemic Predicament: Knowledge, Nozickian Tracking, and Scepticism," p. 28–29.

6. See particularly the essays by Shope, Luper-Foy, Garrett, and the review by Goldman.

7. Since, in the discussion that follows, particular inference patterns don't play an important role, I generally suppress the part of the condition which deals with them.

8. It isn't difficult to verify that Nozick's belief that *J* satisfies all the other conditions of his analysis, not just the tracking condition. Therefore, Nozick not only *can* know that *J*, but does know that *J*, despite not knowing that not-SK.

9. The basic point here is attributed to Klein by Luper-Foy, op. cit., 45n. The example is Luper-Foy's.

10. A more plausible proposal along the lines suggested might be that S knows that *p* just in case (1) S tracks *p*; and (2) S tracks all of *p*'s *known* logical consequences. However, knowledge so defined fails to be closed under known logical implication. To see this, suppose the following: (1) S tracks *a*. (2) S knows that ($a \Rightarrow b$). (3) S tracks *b*. (4) S knows that ($b \Rightarrow c$). (5) S doesn't track *c*. Because of (5), S can't know that *b*. But S may not realize that *c* is a logical consequence of *a* as well as *b*; in that case, (5) doesn't impair S's knowing that *a*. So S knows that *a*, but doesn't know its clear logical consequence *b*.

11. Shope, "Cognitive Abilities, Conditionals, and Knowledge," 41.

12. Shope, 41n.

13. Among S's false beliefs would have to be all those that entail that he is someone with normally functioning senses negotiating his environment in the usual manner. It is logically possible that, by a coincidence of cosmic proportions, S's other forced beliefs about the world might happen to be true. Thus, Shope's hypothesis, as modified, seems to be a somewhat weaker version of the usual brain-in-the-vat scenario.

14. Shope cites some passages which, he thinks, show that Nozick believes we do know that (C), and presumably, I would add, (C)′ as well; see Shope, 40. Unfortunately, Shope's citation is garbled, so his reading can't be verified. But, at any rate, if Nozick held the view Shope mentions, Shope's example shows that it was ill-considered.

15. Nozick might be expected to trace any resistance to this response back to devotion to the Closure Principle itself. Otherwise, what else could be counterintuitive about it? However, rejecting (T)′ as a necessary condition for knowledge because it conflicts with the Closure Principle is circular, if the rejection of (T)′ is supposed to be part of an argued defense of that principle.

16. Colin McGinn has offered a counterexample which, if acceptable, would show that tracking isn't necessary for knowledge. But as McGinn himself notes, intuitions about the

example conflict, so his criticism of the tracking requirement is, at best, not fully conclusive. See McGinn, "The Concept of Knowledge," 531–2. Also, I understand that Saul Kripke has advanced arguments against taking tracking as a necessary condition for knowledge, but these have not yet appeared in print.

17. Nozick might insist that 'The earth will stop spinning *suddenly*' is in some sense a "cooked-up" or skeptical hypothesis, the denial of which we really don't know.

18. The indeterminacy of (6) might make (4) outright false, if that indeterminacy means that you *might* have believed the ice cubes had melted when they hadn't. For if you might have believed that they were melted, it is false to say that you would not have believed that they were melted, in the situation described.

19. Lewis has observed that "Seldom, if ever can we find a clearly true counterfactual about how the past would be different if the present were somehow different." Lewis, "Counterfactual Dependence and Time's Arrow," 455.

20. Jonathan Bennett and others have criticized both Lewis's general approach to counterfactuals and his views about backward conditionals in particular. See Bennett, "Counterfactuals and Temporal Direction." I am not convinced by the objections raised against Lewis; also, it is my impression that the alternative accounts do not vindicate Nozick's epistemology.

21. There is a more complicated possibility, namely that the laws might have changed or ceased to be in effect temporarily, but returned to normal shortly before you reflected on the state of the ice cubes. This more complicated possibility could still be treated in the same way I treat the simpler situation in the text.

22. Since transitivity fails for counterfactuals, it isn't always permissible to combine them in this way. However, as I go on to claim, the real problem with this line of thought lies elsewhere.

23. This may not, as a matter of fact, be completely accurate since there is some reason to think that the values of basic physical constants change over time.

24. See Lewis, "Counterfactual Dependence and Time's Arrow," especially 472.

25. There is also a discrepancy between the two accounts as to the truth of (5) 'If the ice cubes hadn't melted, you would have been surprised by their state.' My sense is that Lewis's treatment, which makes (5) true, is correct.

26. See Nelson Goodman, *Fact, Fiction, and Forecast,* 74. I follow the interpretation given by Barker and Achinstein in "On the New Riddle of Induction." See 511.

27. It might be thought that there could be a world where it was a law, true at all times, that emeralds are "grue." In 1986, such a world would be indistinguishable to its inhabitants from actual world, and they would believe as we do that emeralds are not "grue." So, (12) comes out false anyway.

28. I wish to thank a number of people for helpful conversations on earlier drafts: Anthony Brueckner, John Martin Fischer, Harry Frankfurt, Steven Luper-Foy, Ross Mandel, and David Shatz.

part three

CRITICAL RESPONSES
Skepticism

seven

THE POSSIBILITY OF SKEPTICISM

Steven Luper-Foy

In this chapter I am going to elucidate the argument forms underlying the skeptical views discussed by Robert Nozick, G. E. Moore, Barry Stroud, and René Descartes.[1] We will see that the arguments they discuss are related in interesting ways. We will also see that these forms of skepticism should be rejected.

Let us begin with one of the oldest forms of skepticism, namely the sort discussed by Descartes.

I. CARTESIAN SKEPTICISM

Sitting in my home, staring at my newly purchased table, I would claim to know that a table is there before me. My present sensory information provides sufficient grounds for me to know that a table is there. Or does it? A typical skeptical argument to the contrary will begin with a sketch of a scenario such as the following: whereas there appears to be a table in my room, in fact there is no table there at all; instead, a hidden device is projecting an exact image of a table into my room. Clearly, skeptics point out, this is a logically possible situation. Yet in it, my sensory information would be misleading. Hence, they conclude, I do not know that a table is before me even though I see it there.

What has gone wrong here? Can the skeptic legitimately question my knowledge claim after establishing that the situation in which I am confronted with a hologram is possible? In order for the inference to go through, clearly a powerful assumption must be made about when it is that we can arrive at knowledge through our experiential sources. What is assumed by the Cartesian skeptic, I suggest, is that we know the truth of a belief of some sort by arriving at it through a given source (such as an inference based on a set of evidence) only if we would know the truth of that sort of belief in *any* situation in which we arrived at it through the same source. To know it through our source in one possible world, we would have to know it in any world in which we use that source. Let us state the Cartesian skeptic's assumption in the form of a principle:

> If a source were, in some situation, to yield a belief of a given sort without enabling us to know the truth of that belief, then it is for us never a source of knowledge of the truth of that sort of belief, no matter what the situation is in which it is used.

Call this the *Situation Principle*.[2]

Given this principle, the skeptic's conclusion goes through. I arrived at my belief that there is a table before me on the basis of the fact that there seemed to be one there. But there are situations in which that derivation would not put me in a position to know that there is such a table. If, for instance, I were to examine a hologram of a table projected into a room which contained no tables, then I would still seem to see a table there before me, and I might thereby be led to acquire the same belief. Given the Situation Principle, it follows that I do not know that a table is before me.

In the circumstances just sketched, I fail to know the truth of my belief because it is false. There are other situations in which I believe that a table is before me upon seeming to see one there, yet the truth of this belief is unknown to me even though I am correct. For example, suppose that I arrived at my belief by seeing the only real table in a room full of table holograms. Unlike the previous example in which I see a hologram, this is not a situation in which I fail to know because my belief is false. In this second example I fail to know because my belief might so easily *have been* false in spite of its source; because of my peculiar circumstances, I was very likely to be misled by my source and would have been had I seen one of the many holograms surrounding me. Although I am correct, I am right about my belief entirely by accident. In both situations, then, whether I am looking at the hologram or not, I would fail to possess knowledge. Given the Situation Principle, the existence of either situation is therefore sufficient to undermine my claim to know that there is a table before me on the basis of the fact that I seem to see one. No matter what my circumstances are, I cannot know the truth of that belief through that source.

According to the Situation Principle, then, we can undermine an individual's claim to know, through some source, that something is true by pointing out the existence of a certain sort of possibility. Let us use the term *skeptical scenario relative to S, p, and process P* to refer to a situation in which S arrives at the belief that *p* or a belief of the same sort as *p* via P, yet that belief is false or might be false given that S has arrived at it via P. The Situation Principle rules out knowledge in cases in which there are skeptical scenarios relative to the things we believe and the means through which we believe them. Only with difficulty will a true belief about a necessary truth be threatened by the Situation Principle since in no situation might a necessary truth be false. But beliefs about contingent truths do not fare so well. Given the Situation Principle, under no circumstances do we know that there is a table before us on the basis of seeming to see one because there is a skeptical scenario relative to that belief and its source.

Of course, the existence of just any skeptical scenario relative to my belief about my table does not show that I cannot know about tables in front of me. We have seen that the scenario in which I am confronted with a hologram eliminates all prospects for my knowing that a table is before me on the basis of my seeming to see one. But I can always adopt a new source for my belief. For example, I can base my belief not just on my seeming to see a table there, but also on my seeming to feel one there. The existence of a skeptical scenario relative to a belief based on visual information certainly does not entail that there is a skeptical scenario relative to a belief based both on visual and tactile information. My being confronted by a hologram of a table is a skeptical scenario relative to my visually based belief, but not relative to my visually and tactually based belief. Hence the existence of a skeptical scenario relative to a belief and its source does not entail that the truth of that belief is unknowable through any source. So, at any rate, says the Situation Principle.

Even more obviously, the existence of a skeptical scenario relative to my belief about my table and its source does not entail that I never arrive at knowledge on the basis of sensory information. Given the demands imposed by the Situation Principle on adequate sources of belief, many particular sorts of sensory information will fail to be adequate sources for particular sorts of beliefs about the world because of the existence of skeptical scenarios. But it does not follow that no sort of sensory information is an adequate basis for any sort of belief about the world.

However, the skeptic's arsenal of scenarios is extensive. With the right scenario, skeptics think that they can show that *no* sort of sensory information is *ever* a source of knowledge. That is precisely what Descartes tries to do in the *Meditations* with his dream and demon hypotheses. More modern skeptics prefer the hypothesis that I am a disembodied brain in a vat on a distant planet where alien scientists have stimulated my brain so as to give me my present misleading sensory evidence. The situation in which Descartes is being deceived by a demon about the beliefs he bases on his sensory information is a skeptical scenario relative to *any* sort of belief Descartes bases on *any* sort of sensory information. Hence if the Situation Principle is true, then Descartes knows nothing on the basis of sensory information. Since everyone else is in the same boat with Descartes, *no one* knows anything on the basis of sensory information.

In his own skeptical arguments, Descartes relied on rather global scenarios, ones designed to call large bodies of beliefs into doubt. But he need not have limited himself to global scenarios. It was not necessary for him to discover a single possibility that functions as a skeptical scenario relative to virtually all of his beliefs. He could have argued that relative to *each* of our beliefs and its available sources there is a skeptical scenario, though not necessarily the same one each time. If a skeptical scenario can be paired to each of our beliefs and its available sources, then none of them is known to be true, according to the Situation Principle. We have said that providing a scenario relative to a belief and its source does not show that the truth of our belief is unknowable since we can always find some *other* source for our belief, but this strategy fails if relative to *any* new source there waits yet another skeptical scenario. The scenarios used to cast doubt on our beliefs are, moreover, just as potent even if they are not compossible. Having pointed out that one situation is a skeptical scenario relative to one of our beliefs, so that we fail to know the truth of that belief according to the Situation Principle, nothing stops us from then adducing as a skeptical scenario relative to another belief a second situation which is inconsistent with the first.

Still, there may be a way to show that knowledge of the external world is possible in spite of the Situation Principle. Given this principle, we cannot know the truth of beliefs based solely on sensory information, but why should we say that processing sensory information is the whole of our source for beliefs about the world? Suppose we say that my belief about my table has as its source a causal chain beginning with light of a certain configuration striking my retinas which in turn send signals to my brain, providing it with sensory information which ultimately leads me to my belief. Notice that some global skeptical scenarios cannot threaten my belief given that this is its source. If, for instance, I were a disembodied brain being fed misleading sensory input by alien scientists, I could not be arriving at a belief through a causal chain involving retinas since I would not have any retinas. Of course, the skeptic could specify a skeptical scenario relative to this more inclusive source. Consistent with arriving at a belief through it we could be looking at a hologram projected into a tableless room. But what is to stop us from responding by revealing even more of the features of my belief source, insisting, for instance, that essential to it is the fact that light from a table in front of me has struck my retinas? If what I see were a hologram in a tableless room, then I could not have arrived at my belief through a causal chain involving light from a table in front of me since there would be no table. It is difficult indeed to find any skeptical scenarios relative to *that* source and my belief.

It is obvious that skeptics would remain unmoved by this strategy for resisting skeptical arguments. The trouble, they would say, is that there are skeptical scenarios relative to our means for arriving at *beliefs about the sources* for our beliefs. Arriving at a belief through a source relative to which there are no skeptical scenarios is well and good, but it is of no use to us if we must rely on a second source in order to determine that we used the first, and relative to the second source there *is* a skeptical scenario. That litmus paper has reacted in a certain way to a liquid is a good sign that the liquid is acid, but I am no closer to knowing that it is acid if I find out that the paper reacted as it did by asking Larry the Notorious Liar. Similarly, that my belief about my table has been produced by the detailed causal chain sketched above is a good indicator that it is true, but I can find out that I have used that source only by relying on certain sorts of sensory information, and relative to this sensory source there are skeptical scenarios. The image of a hierarchy is helpful here: the belief that I have relied on some source may in turn be derived from a second source which we can think of as being on the second level of a hierarchy. The belief that I have relied on this second-level source may itself be derived from a third source which we can place on a third level. Obviously the hierarchy must end; otherwise I could never get started in the business of knowing the things I believe.

The skeptic means to impose a requirement on the sources at each of these levels, starting with the highest: relative to none of these sources can there be a skeptical scenario if I am to know the truth of the beliefs I arrive at on the lowest level. Let us say that a belief which I have arrived at by using a hierarchy of sources which meets this requirement is *indubitable*. What skeptics mean to claim, then, is that in order for the truth of a belief to be known, it must be indubitable.

Notice that the hierarchical requirement which the skeptic has in mind is not that for each source I must have a second which allows me to verify to the skeptic's satisfaction that I have used the first. That requirement would be conceptually impossible to meet since it demands that we have not only a source for beliefs, but also a source for beliefs about that source, as well as a source for beliefs about that further source, and so on — an infinite regress of sources. A belief may be indubitable even if it is not acquired after working through an infinite series of sources each of which establishes that the next has been used.

Let me now gather the components of the skeptic's reasoning into a single argument:

(1) Relative to any belief arrived at solely on the basis of sensory information, there are skeptical scenarios.

(2) So beliefs arrived at entirely on the basis of sensory information are not indubitable. For a belief is indubitable if and only if there are no skeptical scenarios relative to any of the hierarchy of sources on which we have relied in order to arrive at that belief.

(3) But a belief must be indubitable in order to be known.

(4) Hence no beliefs arrived at solely on the basis of sensory information are known.

I suggest that something like this argument is behind what Descartes says in the early *Meditations*. It is, I think, a very plausible argument: not only is it valid, but each premise appears to be true. Nonetheless, it is flawed since, as I will argue later, dubitable beliefs can be known to be true.

Doesn't the requirement of indubitability threaten only *contingent* beliefs since relative to necessary truths there *are* no skeptical scenarios, no matter *what* the sources for those beliefs are? Any believed necessary truth seems indubitable since false in no situation whatever. However, there is a way for skeptics to challenge our knowledge of necessary truths such as $2 + 2 = 4$. Recall that our definition of 'skeptical scenario' is as follows: a skeptical scenario relative to S, the belief that p, and process P is a situation in which S has arrived at the belief that p *or a belief of the same sort as p* through P, yet that belief (p, or the belief of the same sort) is false or might be false given that S has arrived at it via P. Having adopted this definition, we can exploit the vague term 'sort of belief.' One way to classify my belief that $2 + 2 = 4$ is a mathematical belief. Construed as the latter, it falls into the same class as my (hasty and mistaken) belief that $23 + 31 = 64$. Hence I cannot know that $2 + 2 = 4$, according to the Situation Principle, since its source could yield a belief of the same sort without enabling me to know that it is true, namely my belief that $23 + 31 = 64$. Nor is my belief indubitable, given our willingness to include the italicized part of our definition of a skeptical scenario. It is true that one could distinguish between addition and correct addition, and insist that I know that $2 + 2 = 4$ after all, it being impossible to arrive at the belief that $23 + 31 = 64$ through correct addition. But the skeptic could reply that my belief that I have used correct addition must itself have a source, and somewhere along the way the possibility of false belief arises. Perhaps a demon has caused me to believe that I correctly added 23 to 31 in order to get 64. Even mathematical beliefs, then, are dubitable.

II. Nozick, Moore, and Stroud on Skepticism

Let us turn now to an examination of Nozick's reconstruction of the reasoning involved in skepticism. According to Nozick, skeptics begin by adopting part of his analysis of knowledge. They assume that in order for a person S to know that S's belief that *p* is true, the method M through which S actually believes that *p* must meet the following condition:

> If *p* were false and (S believed that *p* via M or S believed that not-*p* via M), then *S* would not believe that *p* via M.

Unfortunately, Nozick does not notice that this condition has a flaw, one that easily can be eliminated if the condition is altered slightly. The flaw is that it cannot deal properly with 'one-sided' methods of belief formation, that is, ones that, while capable of indicating that *p* is true, cannot ever recommend the belief that *p* is false. Such methods can *never* meet Nozick's condition. Its antecedent requires that S believe either that *p* or that not-*p* via M. In order to do so when using a one-sided method M, S *must* come to believe that not-*p*. And then S cannot meet the consequent of Nozick's condition.

This difficulty does not arise for the following condition:

> If *p* were false, S would not believe that *p* via M.

Let us therefore represent Nozick's skeptic as having adopted the assumption that:

> (a) Where M is the method via which a person S believes that *p*, S knows that *p* only if
> Were *p* false, S would not believe that *p* via M.[3]

Call this Nozick's *tracking condition*. And when a person S meets it vis-à-vis S's belief that *p*, let us say that S *tracks* the fact that (or truth of) *p*. On the strength of (a), skeptics conclude that we do not know we are not in a skeptical scenario. We do not, for example, know that we are not brains in vats on a distant planet near Alpha Centauri. For suppose that we have come to believe that we are not brains in vats on the basis of sensory information. In order for us to know that we are not brains in vats, the tracking condition requires that if we were in vats, our sensory information would not lead us to believe that we are not. But this requirement fails to be met.

> (b) S does not know that S is not a brain in a vat on a distant planet.

So far the skeptic has committed no error according to Nozick, who agrees with the skeptic's claim that we do not know that we are not in skeptical scenarios. But skeptics make a second assumption that is objectionable to Nozick. Namely, they assume the Principle of the Closure of Knowledge Under Entailment, or Principle of Entailment for short:

> (c) For any *p* and *q*, if S knows that *p* and S believes that *q* by deducing that *q* from S's belief that *p*, then S knows that *q*.

The rest of the skeptic's argument is a reductio against the claim that we know anything by processing sensory information. Take a claim that is incompatible with your being a brain in a vat on a distant planet but which you think you know by processing sensory information; for example, take the fact that you are on earth. You cannot be on earth if you are on a distant planet, so your being on earth entails that you are not a brain in a vat on a distant planet. Suppose that:

(d) S knows that S is on earth, and S believes that S is not a be-vatted brain on a distant planet by deducing the latter from the former.

Along with the assumption of the Principle of Entailment at (c), (d) entails that you know that you are not a brain in a vat.

(e) S knows that S is not a brain in a vat on a distant planet.

But you do *not* know this. That has already been established at (b) on the assumption of (a). So you do not know that you are on earth after all.

(f) S does not know that S is on earth.

More generally, the skeptic's point is that to be ignorant (as we are) of not being in a skeptical scenario is to be ignorant of being in any corresponding *anti*skeptical scenario, where an antiskeptical scenario corresponding to a given skeptical scenario is any situation that is incompatible with being in the skeptical scenario. (But this claim needs qualifying in view of the assumption, made at step (d), that we have seen the connection between skeptical and antiskeptical scenarios. At most, skeptics are entitled to claim that our ignorance of not being in a skeptical scenario precludes our knowing that we are in any corresponding antiskeptical scenario *when* our belief that we are in an antiskeptical scenario leads us to believe that we are not in the corresponding skeptical scenario. However, let us ignore this qualification.)

It is, of course, quite possible that people who have had skeptical inclinations have reasoned along the lines described by Nozick. If so, he thinks that a surprise is in store for them because the above reasoning is incoherent.

For Nozick suggests that skeptics are in no position to assume the Principle of Entailment once they accept the tracking condition. If, as Nozick and his skeptic suggest, the tracking condition is necessary for knowledge, then the falsity of the Entailment Principle is virtually assured. Hence, Nozick claims, the skeptic's argument is both inconsistent and based on a false premise.

The reason the Principle of Entailment is threatened (though perhaps not doomed) by the adoption of the tracking condition is that this condition itself is not closed under entailment. That is, it is possible to meet it with respect to your belief that p, arrive at your belief that q by deducing q from p, yet fail to meet the tracking condition with respect to q.

Consider the following example.[4] I am standing before a cage in a perfectly ordinary zoo and I arrive at the true belief that the one and only medium-sized animal in the cage is a zebra. This belief I base on the fact that I seem to see only one medium-sized animal in the cage, and it is one with stripes and other zebra-like features. I 'track' the fact that the animal in the cage is a zebra: in the situation that would arise if my belief were false, I would be confronted with an empty cage or with a cage with two medium-sized animals or the like, and I would not seem to see one medium-sized, zebra-like animal in the cage. However, my belief entails that the cage does not contain a mule that is cleverly disguised to look like a zebra. Yet I do not track this latter fact, even if I deduce it from my belief (whose truth I track) that the animal in the cage is a zebra. For if there were a cleverly disguised mule in the cage, I would still seem to see a zebra, and I would still be led to deduce that no disguised mule is in the cage. It is thus quite possible to track one belief without tracking a consequence we deduce from it. On the view that the tracking condition is necessary for knowledge, then, the Principle of Entailment appears to be false.

The reasoning involved in Nozick's account of skepticism makes the skeptic's position rather plausible — until and unless we become convinced that it is incoherent, as Nozick charges. Related accounts of skepticism have been offered as well, sometimes by skeptics, like Barry Stroud, and sometimes by antiskeptics such as G. E. Moore.[5] A key assumption made by the skeptic according to Moore and Stroud is that since we know little or nothing while we are dreaming (or while we are in some other skeptical scenario), then we must know that we are not dreaming if we are to avoid ignorance. Put in the form of a principle, the *Preconditions Principle,* the skeptic's key assumption is this:

If S knows that p, and S believes that q by deducing it from the fact that q is entailed by S's knowing that p, then S knows that q.

Consider how this principle may be applied by skeptics. Given our ordinary concept of knowledge, we can deduce that knowing the truth of anything on the basis of sensory information entails that we are not dreaming that information. So assuming that I am led to believe that I am not dreaming by deducing it from my belief that I know that there is a table in front of me, or from some other belief based on sensory information, then my ability to know that there is a table in front of me (or the like) depends on my knowing that I am not dreaming.

But as Moore and Stroud realize, the fact that it is incumbent upon us to achieve this goal is not in and of itself a threat. The goal threatens

our empirical knowledge only if it really is impossible for us to achieve
it. It is not enough for skeptics to convince us that we must know that
we are not dreaming if we are to avoid ignorance. They must also convince us that we cannot know that we are not dreaming even when we
are not dreaming.

Moore himself said that we *do* know that we are not dreaming since
our possessing this knowledge can be deduced from the facts that (a)
we know ordinary, sensorily based claims such as 'here is a hand,' and
(b) by the Preconditions Principle, we could know about our hands
only if we knew we were not dreaming. However, he showed signs of
being unsatisfied with this position, for he was not so sure that he *could*
know that he was not dreaming.[6] His doubts could have been due to
something like the Situation Principle. But it is not clear that anything
like the Situation Principle is behind *Stroud's* doubts that we know that
we are not dreaming (even when we are not). For on Stroud's interpretation, the key assumption made by the (Cartesian) skeptic is the following principle:

> If person S's circumstances were optimal for the accurate operation
> of belief-forming process P, yet P produced in S a belief of a given
> sort without enabling S to know the truth of that belief, then P is for
> S never a source of knowledge of that sort of belief, no matter what
> the situation in which it is used.

Call this the *Principle of Optimality.*

The Principle of Optimality is designed to focus our attention first
on our epistemic situation in optimal conditions; conclusions reached
here form the basis for a generalization about our epistemic situation
even in conditions that are far less than optimal. If we do not know in
optimal conditions we cannot know in ones that are less than optimal
either. And the goal of Stroud's discussion is to show that we do *not*
know in optimal conditions; even if we are in optimal conditions for
ascertaining we are awake (namely, ones in which we are awake), we
still do not know we are awake. Now, it is conceivable that the Situation Principle has led Stroud to the claim that we do not know that we
are not dreaming; it is clearly inconsistent with our knowing that we
are not dreaming.[7] But the strategy of adopting the Situation Principle
clashes with the strategy of adopting the Principle of Optimality. The
Situation Principle forces us to focus first on our epistemic situation in
minimal conditions, ones that are as unfavorable as possible for the reliable use of sensory experience. Conclusions reached here form the
basis for a generalization about our epistemic situation in optimal conditions. It would not be a mistake for Stroud to conclude that we do
not know in optimal conditions because we do not know in minimal
ones. But it would be absurd for him to go on to argue that we do not

know in minimal ones because we do not know in optimal ones. Continuing in this fashion would be entirely superfluous: if the Situation Principle is correct, then a demonstration of our ignorance in minimal conditions suffices to show that we do not know in any conditions, including optimal ones.

Rather than reasoning which directly involves the Situation Principle, Stroud seems to have rather different grounds for his view that we do not know that we are not dreaming even when we are in optimal conditions. His argument (one available to Moore as well) seems to be as follows:

(1) The only way we can know that we are awake is to possess evidence we would not have if we were dreaming.

(2) Unfortunately, sensory information is the only available basis for beliefs about whether or not we are awake, and any such sensibilia could be dreamt.

(3) Hence we are never in a position to know we are not dreaming.

A familiar pattern now emerges. Step (1) says that the only way we can be in a position to know that we are not dreaming is to have evidence which we would not have if dreaming. But why should we agree? The general principle behind this claim is presumably a version of Nozick's tracking condition: My knowing that a given statement p is true entails that if p were false then I would not have the evidence that led me to believe that p is true. Since any available basis for my belief that I am not dreaming is evidence I might still have if dreaming, then I do not track the fact that I am not dreaming, and hence do not know that my belief is true.

Given that Stroud is committed to the tracking condition, won't his argument be incoherent for reasons analogous to those Nozick adduced in his discussion of skepticism? Not necessarily. While Stroud presupposes that the tracking requirement is a necessary condition for knowledge, he never says anything to indicate that it is *sufficient*. It *is* true and important that the necessity *and sufficiency* of the tracking requirement entails that the Preconditions Principle is false. For the Preconditions Principle entails the Principle of Entailment. Hence the falsity of the Principle of Entailment implies the falsity of the Preconditions Principle. If we were to say that the tracking condition is both necessary and sufficient for knowledge, however, then we would have to reject the Principle of Entailment.

Stroud and other skeptics cannot say that the tracking condition is sufficient as well as necessary for knowledge, or else their argument *would* be incoherent. They would be forced to rely on an assumption which is inconsistent with the necessity and sufficiency of the tracking condition, namely, either the Principle of Entailment or the Preconditions Principle.

However, it is not clear that skeptics *would* say that the tracking condition is sufficient for knowledge. On the interpretation of Cartesian skepticism which I offered earlier, skeptics assume the Situation Principle, which entails that the tracking condition *and much else* is necessary for knowledge. In order for a method of belief formation to put us in a position to know the truth of a claim, that method must not lead us to adopt that claim in close worlds in which it is false. So says the tracking condition. But the Situation Principle is even stronger because it forbids our methods from leading us to adopt our claim in *any* world in which it is false. On the other hand, the tracking requirement is considerably weaker than the Situation Principle. It is easy for us to be so situated that given the source of our belief, we track its truth. For example, we can find ourselves in circumstances such that we would not believe that a table is before us on the basis of sensory information if no table were there. The existence of *remote* possible worlds (like brain-in-vat cases) in which our sensory information would mislead us about the presence of our table does not prevent us from tracking the truth of our belief about our table. However, the existence of these worlds *does* prevent our belief from meeting the Situation Principle.

If skeptics have adopted the Situation Principle, of course, then it is not terribly important to them whether or not the Principle of Entailment is true. If it were false, they could always fall back on the Cartesian argument for skepticism. However, it is quite possible that skeptics think that conditions much more powerful than the tracking condition are necessary for knowledge, and that once these are taken into consideration, the Principle of Entailment is true and therefore available for a skeptical argument. Earlier we said that it is rather difficult for knowledge to be closed under entailment unless each of its necessary conditions is as well. But it *is* possible for knowledge to be closed even when one necessary condition is not. Closure might be the result of the force of the *other* necessary conditions, perhaps acting jointly. An example will illustrate the point. Let us say that S *contracks p* if and only if:

S tracks *p and* S tracks every logical consequence of *p*.

Then knowledge construed as *contracking* sustains the Principle of Entailment. To obtain an account that sustains the Preconditions Principle, we need only construe knowledge as supercontracking, where S *supercontracks p* if and only if:

S tracks *p, and* S tracks every logical consequence of the fact that S tracks *p*, as well as the consequences of the fact that S tracks every consequence of S's tracking *p*, and so on.

If skeptics adopt the contracking or supercontracking analysis, they certainly can use the Principle of Entailment to reach their skeptical conclusion. Of course, they could as easily bypass the Principle of Entailment and rely solely on the Situation Principle, which is also upheld by the contracking and supercontracking accounts. So Nozick's, Stroud's, and Moore's reconstructions of skepticism could be seen as *sketches* of arguments whose full details are filled out along the lines of the Cartesian argument I laid out earlier.

However, committing ourselves to the Principle of Entailment is not to commit ourselves to the Situation Principle. There are accounts of knowledge which sustain the Principle of Entailment without sustaining the Situation Principle. Suppose we say that S *distracks p* if and only if:

(S tracks *p*) or (S tracks *q* and S believes that *p* because S has deduced it from *q*).

Then knowledge construed as distracking sustains the Principle of Entailment. But it does not uphold the Situation Principle. A belief source through which I distrack *p* in normal conditions may, if I am in a skeptical scenario, lead me to believe that *p* when *p* is false. Similarly, a weaker form of contracking (and supercontracking) will sustain the Entailment Principle without sustaining the Situation Principle. We need only say that S *weakly contracks p* just in case:

S tracks *p and* S tracks all of those logical consequences of *p* which S *believes by deduction from p or from p's consequences.*[8]

Even though the distracking analysis upholds the Principle of Entailment, skeptics cannot combine the distracking analysis with the Entailment Principle so as to defend their skeptical conclusion. To distrack, we need not track, and distracking the fact that we are not in a skeptical scenario such as being a brain in a vat near Alpha Centauri is as easy as deducing that we are not in such a scenario from some fact which we track, such as the fact that we are on earth. But skeptics could use the weak contracking analysis in combination with the Entailment Principle so as to reach their skeptical conclusion. And since the weak contracking account does not sustain the Situation Principle, skeptics need not commit themselves to this principle. Indeed, of analyses that require tracking, the weak contracking account might seem to give rise to the most plausible skeptical argument available. But this appearance is misleading. Adopting the weak contracking account would have intolerable consequences even aside from the support it might offer skeptics: assuming that I always assent to claims which, I see, follow from what I know, then whether I weakly contrack that I am a denizen of earth depends on my not noticing that my being here entails my not being a be-vatted brain near Alpha Centauri, for I do not track the latter. If we equate knowledge with weak contracking, then it *is* possible to know such ordinary things as that we are on earth, but *only if* (a) skeptics (and others — including *anti*skeptics) do not force us to *realize* that this knowledge entails our not being in skeptical situations, *or* (b) even though we *do* realize it, we refuse to believe these things that are entailed by what we know. But it would be absurd to claim that the possibility of knowledge requires ignorance of, or a stubborn refusal to believe, things that must be true if we know what we say we do, and a mistake to embrace an analysis of knowledge which forces us to.

III. SKEPTICISM REFUTED

We have seen that the skeptical arguments of Descartes, Stroud, Moore, and Nozick depend on the assumption that the truth of only tracked facts may be known. We have also seen that skeptics must supplement the tracking requirement with some stronger assumption, and that there are ways to do so which underwrite both the Principle of Entailment and the Situation Principle, as well as ways which sustain the former without sustaining the latter. It is time we looked more critically at the tracking requirement and Situation Principle, however. Neither of these assumptions is true, as I will now show. This I will do by pointing out that both are inconsistent with various facts about the way we ordinarily apply the term 'know.' I assume that in many (possibly hypothetical) situations it is clear whether the term 'know' is applicable; we have linguistic intuitions about the suitability of applying 'know' in many cases. These intuitions may be used as evidence for an account of the conditions under which knowledge exists. The strategy of adducing facts about usage in order to refute skeptical arguments may nonetheless appear to beg the question; I will attempt to dispel that impression in the last part of the essay.

Contrast two situations. In one, Norm is in a furniture store looking at a table. His circumstances are entirely normal: nothing out of the ordinary is going on. The lighting conditions are optimal, and Norm comes to believe that there is a table in front of him because he sees it there. I think that we would all agree that Norm knows that there is a table in front of him. Now consider a somewhat different situation. Imagine that, like Norm, Abnor has been led to believe that there is a table in front of him because he is looking at one. Unlike Norm's, however, Abnor's circumstances are very unusual. He has wandered into a building that has been disguised as a furniture store and is looking at the only real piece of furniture there. Although he is unaware of it, hundreds of holograms of tables are being projected into the room as well, and each is visually indistinguishable from the real thing. Abnor's belief, though correct, might so easily have been false given his circumstances; he is correct in his belief sheerly by accident. Hence we would all agree that Abnor's claim to know that there is a table before him is false.

If people really would describe the epistemic status of Norm's and Abnor's beliefs as I have suggested, then we may infer various things about the requirements for knowledge. For instance, it is obvious that the Situation Principle is false: Norm and Abnor have arrived at their beliefs through the very same source, yet Norm knows the truth of his belief while Abnor does not. Our willingness to apply the term 'know' in Norm's case but not in Abnor's is good reason to conclude that by our ordinary notion of knowledge the Situation Principle is false. Moreover, since Descartes' claim that only indubitable truths can be known entails the Situation Principle, then his indubitability condition cannot be necessary. Indubitability cannot be an essential feature of a belief that is known to be true.

What we are inclined to say about Abnor and Norm does not, however, establish that we need not track facts in order to know them. In the cases of Abnor and Norm, the tracking condition suggests exactly the results we want: Norm tracks the fact that a table is before him, while Abnor does not. Given his circumstances, any situation in which Norm would find himself if no table were before him is one in which he would not seem to see a table there. But Abnor is surrounded by table holograms: if no table were before him, he might well seem to see a table since he might so easily see one of the holograms.

Rather than presenting a difficulty for the view that only tracked facts are known, the cases of Norm and Abnor tend to help support this view. Whether a case can be made in favor of the tracking condition will ultimately depend on how well it handles clear intuitions about knowledge, intuitions like those responsible for the way we treat the cases of Abnor and Norm. Our intuitions about whether in optimal conditions we know that we are not dreaming, that we are not brains in vats, and that we are not being deceived by demons are troubled; they are too unclear to be useful toward showing that some condition is or is not necessary for knowledge.

In order to argue against the view that only tracked facts may be known, I will suggest a condition which adjudicates putative cases of knowledge in virtually the same way as the tracking condition; essentially, its implications diverge from those of the tracking condition only in unclear cases, such as situations in which the issue is whether or not we know that we are not be-vatted brains. The divergence is over whether or not we may know that extremely remote skeptical scenarios do not hold. The tracking condition says we cannot, while my alternative says we can know that these scenarios do not hold. If such an alternative to the tracking restriction exists, then we will be in a better position to reject the tracking condition. My alternative is not intended to be a complete analysis of knowledge,[9] only a condition which is as plausible as the tracking condition yet avoids skeptical difficulties.

Consider the contrapositive of the tracking condition: my knowing that a given statement p is true entails that if my evidence were to lead me to believe that p is true, then p would be true. When I meet this condition, let us say that I *contratrack* the fact that p. It turns out that I contratrack virtually everything I track; virtually the only exceptions are our beliefs that remote skeptical scenarios do not hold (assuming that they do not). Thus Norm contratracks the fact that a table is before him, while Abnor does not, and we have already seen that the tracking condition adjudicates these examples in the same way. Given his circumstances, in all of the situations which might confront Norm if he seemed to see a table before him, there would be such a table. That is, all of the close possible worlds in which Norm has his present sensibilia are worlds in which a table is in front of him. But Abnor's circumstances are different. In situations which might confront him if he were to seem to see a table before him, there might be no such table. One close possible world in which he seems to see a table before him when none is there is a world in which he is standing in front of one of the many holograms with which he is surrounded.

Consider the way the contratracking condition handles puzzling beliefs about remote skeptical scenarios. Unlike the tracking condition, the contratracking condition endorses my claim to know that I am not a brain in a vat. Suppose that I arrive at my belief as follows: I consult my sensory information and conclude that the most rational explanation for its features is that I am an ordinary embodied person living on the planet earth. Since this claim entails that I am not a brain in a vat on a distant planet, I conclude that I am not. This ordinary rational belief that I am not a disembodied brain counts as knowledge according to the contratracking condition, assuming that I am in fact an embodied person living on earth. Given my circumstances, the situations in which I might find myself if I were to have my present sensory information are ones in which I would be on earth and not a disembodied brain in a vat on a distant planet.

Adopting the contratracking condition as an analysis of knowledge helps narrow down the alternatives to our beliefs which we must be able conclusively to rule out in order to attain knowledge. To say we know that p is to say that we are able to rule out all alternatives to p which are *relevant*: it is to say that we can rule out each relevant alternative to p. That much is uncontroversial. What *is* controversial is when it is that an alternative is relevant; the tracking and contratracking conditions offer very similar assessments when alternatives are not remote, but diverge when alternatives are far out. Given his circumstances, the possibility that he is looking at a hologram is not a relevant alternative to Norm's belief that a table is in front of him. So say both the tracking and contratracking conditions. Similarly, both say that when we are in normal circumstances, the possibility that the bird in the cage in front of us is actually a cleverly disguised robot is not a relevant alternative to its being a canary; we can know that the bird is a canary without performing any test that conclusively proves that it is not a cleverly disguised robot. Only on the tracking account, however, is the possibility that I am a disembodied brain a relevant alternative to my true belief that I am not, and hence a possibility that must be ruled out if I am to know I am not a disembodied brain.

As these examples show, both accounts consider certain sorts of possibility irrelevant because extremely remote. That the bird is an ingeniously made robot is an irrelevant alternative to its being a bird according to both accounts. But the accounts differ when it comes to the negations of believed statements: on the tracking account, the negation of a statement is always a relevant alternative to that statement, no matter how preposterous that negation is, and hence a possibility that must be ruled out. That is why we are ignorant of the fact that we are not disembodied brains. The contratracking account, however, considers *all* extremely remote possibilities to be irrelevant alternatives to our beliefs. We may know the truth of what we believe without ruling out remote alternatives. We may even know that we are not brains in vats.

I have argued that the tracking and contratracking conditions virtually never diverge in their assessments of putative cases of knowledge except when applied to cases about which our pretheoretic intuitions are unclear. It may appear, then, that there is no way to choose between the two accounts. Fortunately, there is still a way to assess the relative merits of these two accounts. As Stroud's and Nozick's skeptical arguments show, the tracking condition taken in conjunction with the highly plausible Preconditions or Entailment Principles tend to threaten our ability to know the many things usage suggests that we know. The contratracking condition does not. Hence usage favors rejecting the tracking condition. Of course, adopting the tracking restriction as necessary *and* sufficient for knowledge would be no threat since then we would be forced to abandon the Preconditions and Entailment Principles. But even this strategy is unhappy, because the Entailment and Preconditions Principles are just too plausible. (Another way to lessen the threat would be to adopt the weak contracking account, but as we saw that analysis is too implausible to embrace.)

The contratracking condition, on the other hand, is entirely consistent with these principles; therefore, it is again the more plausible of the two restrictions. In fact, the contratracking condition clearly *sustains* the Principle of Entailment, as can be seen once we notice that the contratracking condition is a requirement not just on a belief p whose truth we know.[10] It is *also* a requirement on each consequence c of p, on everything entailed by p. For the contratracking condition requires that c be true in every possible world in which our belief source leads us to believe that p is true except those worlds that are remote. So if a given source enables us to contratrack p, and p entails c, then c also must be true in all of the near worlds in which we arrive at our belief that p through that source.

I have argued that facts about linguistic usage help show that the tracking condition should be abandoned, so that Stroud's and Nozick's skeptical arguments fail. Stroud, however, would resist this reasoning. According to him, "evidence from usage or from our practice will not establish a conclusion about the conditions of knowledge."[11] Typically we assume that people who make knowledge claims in various ordinary cases have a rough acquaintance with the conditions under which it is correct to apply the term 'know.' The fact that in such cases people are willing to claim knowledge would therefore seem to be good reason to infer that the conditions for knowing are met in those cases. But Stroud objects to drawing the conclusion that the conditions for knowledge are met in such cases since he thinks that there is always an alternative explanation of people's willingness to claim knowledge, one given which the conditions for knowledge are not met.

The alternative explanation Stroud gives relies on the distinction between the conditions under which we know and the conditions under which we justifiably claim to know. Consider a typical knowledge claim. When I am in my living room seated in front of my table and I see it there in front of me under clear lighting conditions, I am justified in believing that I know one is there, and will say as much. Can we infer that I do know what I say I know? We cannot, according to Stroud. All we can infer is that I am justified in claiming that I know there is a table before me. For, as other cases show, I would claim to know there is a table before me even when it is clear that I know nothing of the sort. If, for instance, someone were to remove my table and project in its place a table hologram, I would persist in claiming knowledge in spite of my obvious ignorance. Clearly, then, it is possible to meet the conditions for *claiming* we know without meeting the conditions for knowing. And since a sufficient reason for a person's claiming knowledge is the fact that she or he is justified in claiming knowledge, then a sufficient explanation for the fact that someone claims knowledge in some situation is that he or she is justified (but possibly mistaken) in claiming knowledge in those circumstances.

The fact that we are willing to claim knowledge in a given situation does not by itself constitute sufficient reason to conclude that the conditions for knowing are met on that occasion; Stroud is right to say that it might be an occasion on which we hold a justified but false claim to know. However, it would be a mistake to conclude that nothing about knowledge can be learned from available linguistic data. In particular, we may take advantage of (possibly hypothetical) knowledge claims that would be made by people who are fully aware of the circumstances they are in.

Consider the above example in which I held a justified, false claim to know that there is a table before me. What permitted me to hold a justified claim to knowledge in spite of my ignorance is that I held justified but mistaken beliefs about my circumstances. It is clear to anyone who is aware of my circumstances that my claim is false, and if I became apprised of them I myself would no longer be justified in claiming knowledge. But it is equally clear that there are countless cases of justified, true claims to knowledge. When I correctly and justifiably believe that I am seated before my table in normal circumstances, and I believe it is there because I see it, I will claim to know it is there, and my claim will be correct. My claim is not merely that I justifiably believe that I know that there is a table before me. That claim is true all right, but it is also the case that I *know* that there is a table there. Anyone familiar with this case will agree that I meet the conditions for knowing what I claim to know. This agreement is good evidence that we believe that all of the requirements for knowledge are met; in turn, this consensus is good reason to conclude that the requirements *are* met.

According to Stroud, the fact that most people claim knowledge in a certain situation is not a good enough reason to conclude that they *do* know in that situation. He is correct; they might be mistaken about their circumstances and hence ignorant while justifiably believing that they know. But we can still make good use of linguistic facts. The fact that most people who *take* themselves to be in a certain situation claim knowledge *is* good reason to conclude that they *would* possess knowledge in the situation in which they believe themselves to be. Facts about when it is that we attain knowledge can therefore be learned from an examination of situations in which people who claim knowledge believe themselves to be.

Even Stroud's own explanation of our willingness to claim knowledge on various occasions can succeed only if the requirements for knowledge really are met in the circumstances in which people normally take themselves to be. Stroud has reminded us that there are circumstances in which knowledge claims are justified but false, and suggests that all claims to knowledge may be false even if justified. He is right. But if the conditions for knowledge were not met in the circumstances which we *take* to be our own, then the knowledge claims we make there would be unjustified after all. For false, justified knowledge claims are ones we make when we justifiably but falsely believe that we are in a set of circumstances in which those claims would be entirely correct. To each justified, false knowledge claim is paired a set of circumstances that we (falsely) believe to be ours and in which all requirements for knowledge would truly be satisfied. Our knowledge claim is justified since there are circumstances in which it *would* be true, and we are justified in believing that we are in some such circumstances.

Notice how directly facts about usage can be used against the skeptic. Our collective willingness to claim knowledge in some situation in which we believe ourselves to be suggests, we said, that we do know in that situation. However, this situation which we believe is our own and in which all requirements for knowledge would be met *cannot* be one in which we can infallibly rule out skeptical possibilities such as holograms, dreams, and be-vatted brains, for we can *never* be in a position to do that. Nor are we so stupid as to think we can. So usage suggests that knowers need not possess the ability to infallibly rule out all of the skeptical alternatives. Yet Stroud is committed to the view that we really think we must rule out these alternatives. Otherwise he cannot reach his skeptical conclusion. But if he is correct in thinking that by our account of knowledge we must infallibly rule out all skeptical alternatives, then he cannot sustain his explanation of how skepticism can be true in spite of our willingness to claim knowledge. He cannot maintain that the admittedly justified knowledge claims we make over and over again are false. For if we really must infallibly rule out all alternatives in order to know the truth of our beliefs, then we are never justified in claiming knowledge.

Facts about usage neither prove nor presuppose that we actually know anything. But they are crucial to the defense of an account of the conditions under which knowledge exists. All we need assume in order to develop an analysis of knowledge is that when people are actually in situations *in which they take themselves to be when collectively believing that they possess knowledge,* they *do* possess knowledge. Since they could conceivably be wrong about their situation, they could conceivably fail to know. Hence there is nothing question-begging about using linguistic facts to arrive at an analysis of knowledge and then using the latter to discuss skepticism. Even the skeptic needs some way to arrive at an account of knowledge which is plausibly the one we all embrace. How would it be done if we did not rely on our own (and others', though that is no option for the skeptic) linguistic intuitions? Yet, using linguistic facts, we can conclude that the possibilities described by skeptics need not be conclusively ruled out in order for us to arrive at knowledge. Only if our actual situation really were one in which we are or might be seeing holograms or dreaming would these possibilities undermine our knowledge claims.

I believe that I have refuted the most common forms of skeptical arguments. But obviously there are other skeptical arguments waiting to be refuted. I have said nothing here, for example, about modes of skepticism which focus on rational (justified) belief rather than knowledge. That is, I have not dealt with arguments designed to show that we are not justified in believing things about the world. Pyrrhonianism is one example.[12] Consider another. Skeptics could argue that I am not justified in believing (say) that a table is before me when I see it by suggesting that the possibility that I am a brain in a vat on a tableless planet undermines any justification I might have. Now, of course the skeptic owes us some explanation of how the latter possibility undermines any justification I might have concerning my table. Thus they might suggest that in order for me to be justified in believing any given claim *p* on the basis of facts about my sensory information, it is necessary (but insufficient) that those facts would not still hold if *p* were false. Given this suggestion, they could conclude that I am not justified in believing that I am not a brain in a vat on a tableless planet. From here they could offer some version of the skeptical arguments we discussed above; e.g., assuming that I am justified in believing anything I believe by deduction from something else I am justified in believing, then since I am not justified in believing that I am not a brain in a vat on a tableless planet, then I am not justified in believing that a table is before me. Using similar reasoning, the skeptic could undermine our other beliefs about the world.

However, why should we grant that I am not justified in believing that *p* on the basis of facts about my sensory information if those facts would still hold if *p* were false? Instead, why not say that it suffices that those facts would hold if *p* were true? I do not claim that the latter is an adequate account of when it is that sensory information justifies us in believing something. But refinements of it are more likely to yield an adequate account than the requirement suggested by the skeptic at hand. Among other things, it upholds the principle that we are justified in believing what we believe by deduction from other things we are justified in believing, and refinements could retain the same virtue.[13]

To repeat: there certainly are modes of skeptical argumentation which I have not refuted, and dealing with one is not dealing with all. Thus to refute the Cartesian skeptical argument I sketched at the outset is not to refute all skeptical arguments which focus on justified belief. Of course, the reverse is true as well: even if we could show to our satisfaction that we *really are justified* in believing that we are confronted with tables and that we are not in vats, the Cartesian skeptical argument I sketched earlier would still arise. After all, knowing involves more than rational belief (I would argue that it *need not* involve rational belief), and skeptics could fasten onto the components of knowledge over and above the conditions for rational belief.

Obviously these other forms of skepticism must be addressed before it can be laid to final rest. There is, however, one claim about skepticism that deserves to be dismissed out of hand. Some people think that in order to refute skepticism it is necessary to show that there *cannot be* skeptical scenarios relative to what we believe by (say) processing sensory information. Such a refutation cannot be had since clearly there are such scenarios. Others think that a refutation requires an argument from premises the skeptic will accept to the conclusion that we are not in a skeptical scenario. This, too, is not forthcoming simply because the skeptic allows only premises arrived at through processes relative to which there are no skeptical scenarios.

That neither refutation is possible, however, is beside the point, which is that there is not a sound argument from the existence of skeptical scenarios to the conclusion that we do not know what we believe by processing sensory information.

NOTES

This essay includes an elaboration of my earlier piece "What Skeptics Don't Know Refutes Them," *Pacific Philosophical Quarterly* 65 (1985): 86–96. My discussion of Barry Stroud's style of skepticism was read at the 1986 meeting of the Pacific Division of the American Philosophical Association under the title, "The Insignificance of Skepticism." I thank Jane Duran for her helpful comments.

1. Nozick's discussion appears in his book *Philosophical Explanations* (Cambridge: Harvard University Press, 1981), section 3; Stroud's in *The Significance of Philosophical Skepticism* (Oxford: Clarendon Press, 1984); and Descartes' in *Meditations on First Philosophy,* Vol. 1. ed. E. Haldane and G. Ross (New York, 1955).

2. Elsewhere I gave a slightly different version of this principle the name *CH′*, and distinguished it from a weaker, related, one that I dubbed *CH*. The latter is a slightly different version of the following principle:

If a source were, in some situation, to yield a *true* belief of a given sort without enabling us to know the truth of that belief, then it is for us never a source of knowledge of the truth of that sort of belief, no matter what the situation is in which it is used (even situations in which the belief yielded is also true).

Here I adopt the name 'Situation Principle' since it is more suggestive than 'CH.' (See my "The Epistemic Predicament: Knowledge, Nozickian Tracking, and Skepticism," *Australasian Journal of Philosophy* 62, no. 1 (March 1984).

3. See Nozick's book *Philosophical Explanations,* chap. 3, and Fred Dretske's articles "Reasons and Consequences," *Analysis,* 1968, and "Epistemic Operators," *The Journal of Philosophy* #67, 1971, in which Dretske anticipates Nozick's approach to skepticism. Nozick coins the term 'track' to refer to the relation we have to a belief when we meet *all* of his conditions for knowledge, while I shall use the term to refer to the relation we have to beliefs when a version of Nozick's third condition is met.

4. Offered by Dretske in "Epistemic Operators," op. cit.

5. Moore's discussion appears primarily in "Certainty," *Philosophical Papers* (London: George Allen & Unwin, 1959).

6. Note Moore's floundering in the final paragraphs of "Certainty," and his confession that "there are bad mistakes in it which he cannot yet see how to put right" (see the Preface of *Philosophical Papers,* op. cit.).

7. More accurately, the requirement that a belief known to be true be *indubitable* (in the sense discussed in section I) is inconsistent with our knowing that we are not dreaming.

8. Adding the qualification embodied in this underlined clause to the definition of supercontracking will result in an account which sustains the Principle of Entailment but not the Situation Principle.

9. For a complete analysis, see my paper "The Causal Indicator Analysis of Knowledge," forthcoming in *Philosophy and Phenomenological Research,* in which I improve upon the account I offer in my paper "The Epistemic Predicament: Knowledge, Nozickian Tracking, and Skepticism," op. cit.

10. I ignore a trivial qualification which strictly speaking is necessary (see "The Epistemic Predicament," op. cit., 47).

11. Ibid., 64.

12. But see my essay, "The Dream Argument of Pyrrho and Sextus," *Contemporary Essays on Greek Ideas,* forthcoming.

13. For a discussion of the nature of rational belief, see my paper "Surviving Hume's Day," unpublished. In "The Reliabilist Theory of Rational Belief," *The Monist* 68 (1985), I discuss the relation between knowledge and rational belief.

eight

NOZICK'S CONCEPTION OF SKEPTICISM

David Shatz

While the dynamics of Nozick's development of his conditions on knowledge—his generation and treatment of examples and counter-examples in chapter 3, part I of *Philosophical Explanations*—ranks as an exciting and extremely important contribution to the post-Gettier problematic, the real distinctiveness, sweep, and interest of his account lies in the perspective that it provides on epistemological skepticism.[1] In this chapter I want to explore a basic question about the relationship between this perspective on skepticism and the account of knowledge that Nozick offers.

Consider the familiar pattern of antiskeptical and proskeptical theses that Nozick endorses: we know that p (where p[2] is some appropriate proposition about the existence and character of physical objects, about the sentient states of another person, about some past or future event, and so forth), but we do not know that not-SK (where SK is some suitable skeptical scenario). Broadly speaking, there are two ways in which one can conceive of the relationship between these theses and the account of knowledge.

(1) The pro- and antiskeptical theses are the fallout of the account; the account itself, however, down to its smallest details, is or can be motivated completely on extensional grounds that are independent of the skeptical problem.

(2) Because the theses strike Nozick as intuitive and right, he molds the account to yield those theses. In other words, the theses concerning skepticism motivate, if not the general thrust of the account, then certain crucial details of it.

My question is: which of these is Nozick's procedure?

The question is not about the context of discovery—which sequence did Nozick follow?—but about the context of justification. Does the account, independently motivated, justify or motivate the theses about skepticism or do the theses about skepticism justify or motivate the details of the account? The following remark made by Nozick about the context of discovery suggests, I think, a claim about justification:

> . . . the theory of knowledge that follows was not developed in order to explain how knowledge is possible. Rather the motivation was external to epistemology; only after the account was developed for another purpose did I notice its consequences for skepticism. . . . So whatever other defects the explanation [of how knowledge is possible] might have, it can hardly be called ad hoc. (169)

The pattern of pro- and antiskeptical results strikes Nozick as correct and perhaps provides *added* support for his account; but that is not what *has to* motivate or vindicate the account, according to the passage. It follows that even someone who is antecedently committed to the results can be brought around to embrace Nozick's analysis.

In the first part of this chapter I argue that this is not the case. True enough, the general contours of a tracking account can appear attractive independently of the account's results for skepticism. However, Nozick had available to him alternative accounts within the tracking view that would not have spawned the precise pattern of results that his account breeds. These modifications, moreover, are natural, compelling, and independently motivated; they will appeal to one who is not antecedently committed to Nozick's results. The argument for resisting these alterations can only be that to accept them is to give up the theses about skepticism. Ergo, one can be convinced to appropriate Nozick's particular version of tracking only if one is *already* committed to Nozick's theses about skepticism; commitment to a tracking account will not by itself produce a commitment to those theses. In particular, I shall argue that the proskeptical thesis that we do not know that not-SK can and should be resisted even within a tracking framework. Furthermore, I shall argue that Nozick misidentifies the nature and intuitive source of this proskeptical thesis and therefore gives the thesis more credence than it deserves.

In the second stage of my argument I move a step further. Nozick's conditions on knowledge, I maintain, do not satisfy some general intuition about where the skeptic is wrong and where the skeptic is right. For they do not yield any uniform, easily characterizable, and intuitive pattern of results vis-à-vis skepticism. Instead, the chips fall sometimes this way, sometimes that way; in particular, contrary to what Nozick sometimes suggests, where they fall does not depend on whether we are affirming a common sense proposition or instead denying a skeptical scenario. Because the results form no discernible pattern, because they are too much of a crazy quilt to allow us to say that as a whole they capture both the power and the weakness of skepticism, Nozick's theory cannot be made to rest on the results it bears for the skeptical problem. On the contrary, it may be rejected precisely because it generates those results.

I. TRACKING AND INFERENCE

Nozick's basic result, that we can know some commonsense proposition p while not knowing that not-SK, rests on the fact that, when p entails q, S may satisfy the variation condition for p (not-$p \rightarrow$ S does not believe that p via M) while failing to satisfy it for q.[3] Closure therefore fails. However, when applied to cases in which S knows that p and then infers q from p, Nozick's account seems to overlook something important. S's belief that q is not here arising in a vacuum, such that we might determine whether S knows that q solely by inquiring whether, if it were not the case that q, S would not believe that q. Nor is it arising solely from the experiences or evidence that give rise to the belief that p—that's only part of the method S is using. What S is doing is believing that q by inferring it from a proposition p that he tracks and knows. Surely S's use of inference from known p is of some relevance to whether he knows that q. If it were not of relevance, then knowledge could never be attained by proof. One could not infer, for example, $(Ex)Px$ from known Pa. In the skeptical case, S infers not-SK from a p that Nozick concedes S knows; surely that should help.

Nozick is at pains to block this response, and in this connection he makes two claims.

First, by straightforward application of the variation condition, S may know that q by the method of inferring q from p only if S satisfies the following condition: if it were not the case that q, S would not believe that p, or would not infer q from p. S's belief that p must track q. This condition is not satisfied where q = not-SK and p is, say, a singular physical object proposition (SPOP). It is satisfied, on the other hand, when S infers $(Ex)Px$ from Pa, so Nozick is not committed to denying that knowledge is ever transmitted by logical deduction (229 ff.)

Second, Nozick raises the objection:

> But can't we view the method of arriving at belief that q as: inferring q from p which is tracked, that is, known to be true? When p entails q, if q were false the person would not be using that method to arrive at a belief that q, and so would not believe q via that method.

His answer is this:

> The problem is that the method of inferring q from known p is indistinguishable by the person from the method of inferring q from (believed) p.

So, if the method M is defined as a combination of the method (M1) used to arrive at p and the method (M2) used to arrive at q (M2: logical deduction from p),[4] then S fails to satisfy the variation condition: not-q → S does not believe that q via M.

Methods have to be identified from the inside. For if they were identifiable from the outside,

> you needn't reach to inference to establish your knowledge that you are not floating in the tank on Alpha Centauri. You see you are not on Alpha Centauri, and via this method, externally specified, you track the fact you are not — even though if you were it would seem perceptually the same as it does to you now. . . Would even Dr. Jonson have said, "How do I know I am not dreaming? By seeing what is in front of me?" (233)

This is a striking and important passage. In the first place, it introduces an element of internalism that Nozick here and later acknowledges as such (233, 281), but which sits uneasily with his general externalist orientation. More critically, the argument hypothetically rejected "even" by Dr. Jonson is close to the kind of argument that G. E. Moore and, more recently, Peter Klein, use to answer the skeptic.[5] You know that you are not dreaming or not on Alpha Centauri not, perhaps, by seeing straight out that you are not, but by inferring that you are not from a known statement about where you are and what you are doing. Ultimately, Nozick's motivation for identifying methods from the inside, according to the passage, is that if you identified them from the outside, you could just see or infer from what you do see, that you are not being fed experiences on Alpha Centauri, not dreaming, and so on. Obviously, though, someone who liked the tracking approach yet wanted to resist the skeptical conclusion would resist this particular argument for identifying from the inside. Nozick's theses about skepticism seem to be shaping and pulling the account; the theses are not results of a tracking approach, but results of an antecedent commitment.

Nozick is correct that 'seeing' could not count as a method, albeit for reasons that are different from, and more persuasive than, his own. As Steven Luper-Foy observes, a person who is given a hallucinogenic drug but who happens to have a veridical perception of a hammer does not know that he is seeing a hammer. Yet, if the method were identified from the outside in terms of the chain of events involved in visual perception or just in terms of 'seeing,' then, if there were no hammer, S would not believe, via that method, that there is a hammer — S wouldn't be 'using' that method.[6] (Actually, a distinction between methods and processes would be helpful here, but I'll continue to talk of methods). All that this example shows, however, is that *some* methods, specifically the processes of visual perception, can't be allowed to figure in the subjunctives; it would not show that *all* externally specified methods must be ruled out, nor in particular that deductive inferential methods must be specified from the inside so that inferring q from known p has to be ruled out.

Nor can Nozick blanketly rule out *all* externally specified methods. Luper-Foy notes that knowledge can be acquired in cases in which a belief is induced directly by stimulation; in those cases, we say that S knows because were the beliefs false, S would not hold them via the stimulation. Here, there are no experiential states ('percepts') to include in specification of the method, so internal processes ('externally' specified) must be let in.[7]

A more compelling objection to counting 'inferring from known p' as a method is that doing so allows S to know that q by inference from p even if S has no good reason for making the inference (that is, for thinking that p entails q). If q were not the case, p would not be the case either and S would not believe that p; hence, S satisfies the conditions for knowing that q — clearly the wrong result. This objection is a good one, but it applies equally if the method is specified as 'inferring from p' rather than 'inferring from known p': the counterexample to counting the latter will work against counting the former. If my aim were to defend a tracking account, I would have to find a way of blocking cases in which S infers q from known p by using some absurd inferential rule. My aim, however, is not to develop a defensible version of the tracking account — I am confident there is none. Rather, while dissociating myself from the tracking account, I maintain that, if we go the tracking route, the method of 'inferring from known p' is at least as good a choice for specification of the method as 'inferring from p' unless we are already committed to Nozick's theses about skepticism.

Nozick might also object that once 'inferring from known p' is allowed to count as a method, 'inferring from *true p*' should be allowed to count as well, which would give us the absurd result that S can know that q by inferring it from p while failing to know that p. Isn't this a good enough reason for disallowing externally specified inferential methods? The answer, I think, is no. For one thing, as a perusal of the literature shows, Nozick in general lacks a principled way of specifying methods; the specification of method may have to be shaped in ad hoc fashion in order to yield the results desired in a particular example. Given Nozick's partial agnosticism about how methods are to be identified (184), it does not seem objectionable (1) to require S to satisfy only the conditions: S believes that q; it is true that q; S believes that q via inferring it from known p; if not-q were the case, S would not believe that q by inferring from known p and (2) to disallow 'inferring from true p' simply on the grounds that it is too liberal. However, in order better to motivate allowing 'inferring q from known p' to count as a method, let me set out a positive argument, an example in which specifying the method in this way yields a result that is far more intuitive than the results yielded by Nozick's specification of the method as 'inferring from p.'

Suppose that I come to know that (p) you did not attend the APA meetings, because you told me that you did not. From this I infer that (q) you did not attend an orgy that took place at the meetings. On Nozick's conditions, even though I know that p, I may not know that q. If you had attended an orgy (not-q), and I had used the combined method of hearing your testimony (with or without its evidential component specified) and inferring from it whether you had attended an orgy, I might have concluded that you did not attend an orgy — because under these conditions you might (or, even better, would) have been bent on covering up your attendance at the meetings, lest I go on to ask you whether you were at an orgy. I thus violate the condition on page 231: if it were the case that not-q, I would have believed p and would have inferred q from it. Yet, given that your actual denial of attendance at the meeting is in fact sincere, and that I know you weren't at the meetings, it seems absurd to say that I do not also know, by inference, that you were not at an orgy that took place at the meetings.

Here, saying that my method was inferring q (you did not go to an orgy) from *known p* gives the right result. Had you attended an orgy, I would not have believed, via the combined method of hearing your testimony and inferring from known p, that you did not attend an orgy; for had you attended an orgy, I wouldn't have known that p, and hence could not have used the method of inferring from known p. Of course, the example supposes that the fact that you would have lied had you been at an orgy does not affect the counterfactual, "if you had been at the meetings, I would not have believed via your testimony that you were not there"; that supposition is fine, however, since the counterfactual "if you had gone to the meetings, you might have gone to an orgy" may be false. This point holds regardless of whether there *was* an orgy that took place at the meetings.

Perhaps the only thing Nozick can say about this example is that it illustrates his point precisely. Your being at an orgy is a skeptical scenario that I cannot know not to obtain or not to be the real explanation of your testimony that you were not at the meetings. But what if, in the nearest of the faraway worlds in which you were at an orgy, you would have been hypnotized or drugged into believing that you weren't at the meetings? Does the truth of *this* counterfactual also imply that I don't know you weren't at an orgy via inferring it from your testimony that you were not at the meetings? Again, Nozick will say yes, it does imply that. Look at what is happening, though. We began by trying to build an account of knowledge that captures preanalytic intuitions, give or take a few peripheral ones (for example, the hologram example, 190).

We then apply the account to get the result that we don't know not-SK. We then take the sting out of counterexamples like the orgy example by comparing the q's in those cases to not-SK. Yet it would have been no worse methodologically to get a different result in the orgy example by specifying methods differently, and to then transfer that result to get a nonskeptical result about the SK's. That, in fact, is the course we would follow were we bent on first capturing intuitions and then moving to the skeptical problem.

Other examples of this type can be described. I know via M' that X is my natural mother, and infer from that that I am not an adopted child of X. Yet if I were adopted, I might have concluded that I am not, using the very same combination of M' plus inference. Again, Nozick may accept the conclusion that I know that X is my natural mother but fail to know by inference that I am not an adopted child of X; that, however, is not the conclusion that one would reach independently of a commitment to the proskeptical part of Nozick's theory. Nozick's conditions as they stand are a paranoid's delight.

Clearly, even if one accepts the general contours of a tracking account (which I do not), the only real motive for insisting that we can't conclude not-SK by inference is that this intuition is so obviously right that we should embrace it even if doing so commits us to accepting the result that I don't know, in my example, that you were not at an orgy. Not only are Nozick's preanalytic intuitions with the skeptic (197, 201–2); the account is tailored to fit those intuitions. Nonskeptics can therefore keep the tracking account by specifying the method as inferring from known p. The proskeptical theses are not *obligatory* for tracking theorists; rather, they are *available to* those who, like Nozick, want them and are prepared to live with parallel intuitions in cases like the orgy example.

At points, Nozick appears to offer a justification for his intuition that we don't know not-SK. An argument that could be constructed from some remarks of his is that, if we reject this proskeptical intuition, we can't account for the power of the skeptic's position (197). The proper reply to this, however, is that, yes, we can account for the power of skepticism; the power of skepticism lies in the fact that we have no argument that will persuade the skeptic that SPOPs are true or that we do track. Nozick concedes that we have no such argument (287), and I will say more about this concession later.

To sum up, there is a way to preserve closure within a tracking framework: count 'inferring from known p' as a method. Alternatively put: S's *knowledge* that p must track q. Only a prior commitment to the denial of closure can motivate rejection of this way of coming to know. Nozick's treatment of 'inferring from known p' certainly makes it appear that this is *his* motivation for rejecting the method specification.

Specifying methods differently and thus accepting closure is not the only way of avoiding Nozickian skepticism. A simpler emendation of Nozick's conditions will also block the skeptical result. Nozick himself points the way to the emendation:

> Granted that in all worlds close to the actual world the person would truly believe that p (when it is true) and would not falsely believe that p (when it is false), this last is satisfied if no situation or world close to the actual one is a not-p world. Why require in addition that in the closest not-p worlds, even when these are very far away, the person would not believe that p? (685, n. 25; see also 192, case (g); and 683, n. 15)

The amended condition would read:

Either not-p → S does not believe that p via M, or not-p worlds are very far away,

or:

In all not-p worlds that are not very remote from the actual world, S does not believe that p.

Although its results vis-à-vis closure are not immediately clear in every example,[8] this emendation would definitely block the skeptical result that we don't know not-SK. And interestingly, as in the case of his treatment of 'inferring from known p,' this is exactly the reason Nozick proffers for not allowing the emendation: "we take up these questions below, in part II on skepticism" (ibid.). Apart from nakedly invoking the skeptical thesis to shape the details of the account, Nozick here overlooks the fact that the emendation is well motivated. Suppose that the world is as we think it is, but with one catch: there is a demon or benevolent deity around, and were our world to undergo a cataclysm in which the physical objects that produce our experience were to go out of existence, this powerful being, whether out of benevolent or malevolent motives, would see to it that our sensory input remains intact. The counterfactual 'if the objects around me were to go out of existence, I would not believe that they exist,' is false. In fact, SK is the first subjunctive alternative to p. Yet our intuition is that we do still know that physical objects exist; so the variation condition is too strong.[9] Our proposed emendation will preserve the variation condition yet block this undesirable result; but it will also, as noted, allow us to know that not-SK when SK worlds are far away.[10] Once again, we conclude that a tracking account need not result in the proskeptical part of Nozick's theory. In fact, we can easily motivate a version of tracking that does not yield that result. Nozick is certainly entitled to resist the intuition I and others have about the 'demon in the bullpen' scenario; nevertheless, it is equally clear that he cannot persuade anyone who has the opposite intuition to reject an emendation that would accommodate the intuition and in the process allow knowledge of not-SK.

Nozick cannot here object that the suggested emendation should be resisted because it renders his subjunctives impure. For Nozick's subjunctives are not pure anyway. The method is held fixed in both the variation and adherence conditions, even though in some cases, if it were false that p, S would not be using the method (189); and as critics have noted, he probably has to hold e fixed in applying the adherence condition. (This should not be confused with the further point that Nozick may have to hold the evidence to be part of the method in both the variation and adherence conditions).[11] Next, he further adulterates the account with the condition that S does not believe that he does not satisfy the variation and adherence conditions, which he introduces to block Laurence BonJour's celebrated counterexamples (196; but see 266). (Nonphilosophers satisfy that condition trivially!) Hence the rationale for adopting his account over one that would inhibit us from considering any not-p world that is very remote cannot be that the extra condition is not in consonance with the spirit of the account, that is, cannot be read off in a 'pure' reading of the subjunctives. The rationale can only be a powerful intuition that the skeptic is right that we don't know his scenarios don't obtain. That intuition warrants great scrutiny given the weight it is being asked to bear; a possible source of the intuition will be explored later on.

Other writers have noted that Nozick's proskeptical results can be avoided by using the contrapositive of the tracking relation. What is required by them is that if S were to believe that p via M, p would be true.[12] I share the view that Nozick can have no objection to this new condition other than the fact that it thwarts his skeptical results. Nevertheless, if the arguments given in this section are persuasive, then an antiskeptical result about SK's can be secured even without altering the tracking condition in this particular way.

II. CLOSURE, TRACKING, AND RELEVANT ALTERNATIVES

In this section I want to show in a different way why a tracking theorist might have to allow not-SK to be known by inference from p, on pain of denying even knowledge that p. The point can be considered first in terms of a 'relevant alternatives' approach, to which Nozick's view clearly bears strong affinities. The variation condition may be viewed, says Nozick, as fleshing out a criterion for when an alternative is relevant: the criterion is whether the alternative might have obtained were p false (174–75; see 682, note 10, which is an emendation I will comment on).

I know that there is a computer screen in front of me. A computer screen rather than what? Rather than an empty table top, a journal, a mug, and so on. These are the relevant alternatives; to know that there is a computer screen in front of me, I need to know that the object in front of me is not any of these other things. Now, relevant alternative theorists accept a restricted closure principle to the effect that you know not-q for each q that is a relevant alternative. But how do I know that what is in front of me is none of these other things? Isn't it by inference — by knowing that it's a computer screen?

The point is that often knowing that *not-q* is not epistemically prior to knowing that p: the alternatives are ruled out just by seeing, or knowing, that something else — p — is the case, and inferring not-q from that.[13] Independent grounds (that is, grounds that do not include p) are not needed. This is not to say that S has to make the inference explicitly, but just to say that if he would infer not-q from p, he would thereby come to know that not-q. On any understanding of the relevant alternatives approach, it is too much to require that S have *explicitly* ruled out the relevant alternatives. That would leave too many relevant alternatives that have not been ruled out.

This observation about the use of p in inference leads to three other observations that threaten the relevant alternatives account.

First, the claim that, if S knows that p, S knows the falsehood of relevant alternative statements, seems, in some cases (I did not say *all*), to describe a *result* of S's knowing that p rather than a *precondition;* the claim now looks rather less interesting. Second, once *some* alternatives get to be ruled out by knowing that p, that is, once p, if known, is available as grounds for ruling out alternatives, we must wonder why *all* alternatives cannot get ruled out in this way, even the irrelevant ones. In fact, it should take more to rule out a relevant alternative than to rule out an irrelevant one. The relevant ones are supposed to be the real possibilities. If relevant ones can be ruled out by knowing that p, so can irrelevant ones. Closure holds. If I know that p, I do know that not-q for each counterpossibility q: I know that because I know that p.

As further support for this view, consider the clearly irrelevant alternative: the object in front of me is an aardvark. It would be bizarre to claim that, because this alternative is irrelevant, S cannot rule it out using p but instead requires independent grounds! Of course, it might be countered that, once S considers the aardvark possibility to the extent of making this inference, the aardvark possibility becomes relevant. But we then may say, by parity of reasoning, that once the inference to not-SK is drawn, so that SK becomes relevant, SK may be ruled out by inference just as the aardvark possibility was.

Third, some irrelevant alternatives clearly have to be known not to obtain even though they are irrelevant. The object's being an aardvark is an irrelevant alternative to its being a computer screen; yet surely if I do not know that it's not an aardvark, I would not know that it's a computer screen. However, once *some* irrelevant alternatives have to be known not to obtain for S to know that p, the question arises why *all* irrelevant alternatives should not have to be known not to obtain. If the question cannot be answered, we are left wondering why skeptical scenarios do not have to be known not to obtain. Here again, someone might argue that raising the aardvark possibility makes that possibility relevant; but the same could then be said about the skeptical alternative.

The upshot is that the compromise aimed for by the relevant alternatives view — we know that p but not that not-SK — cannot be achieved, for S cannot know that p without knowing of irrelevant alternatives that they do not obtain. And then, of course, there is no point to having the distinction between relevant and irrelevant alternatives.

Let us now relate all this to Nozick. In some respects Nozick is better off than the relevant alternatives theorist. For example, Nozick concedes (234-35) that where q^1 is the first subjunctive alternative to p — the 'most relevant' alternative — "the person who knows p need not know that not-q^1 independently of p." Rather, he may know that not-q^2 by inference from p, as we said; for, when q^1 is the first subjunctive alternative to p, and q^1 is not some skeptical possibility, then S's belief that p will track not-q^1 when not-q^1 is inferred from p. Thus, Nozick agrees with my basic observation that knowing that not-q^m may be a result of knowing that p rather than a precondition.[14]

Next, consider a q^m that is remote. May S know that not-q^m *only* by ruling out q^m independently? That is absurd. The possibility that the object in front of me here in the library is an aardvark is rather remote. Yet I can rule it out by inference from p, without independent grounds. Nozick has no trouble agreeing with this, because his conditions for knowing by inference are satisfied. Clearly, then, Nozick can agree that some remote alternatives are known not to obtain by inferring this from p; but whereas a relevant alternatives theorist will generally not be able to explain why I can't rule out *all* alternatives by inference, even SKs, Nozick can provide such an explanation in terms of his conditions for knowing by inference.

Thus, with respect to the first two of my observations about relevant alternatives theories, Nozick's account fares better than those theories. My third point, however, threatens his approach and the relevant alternatives view equally. If I do not know that the object is not an aardvark, I do not know that it is a computer screen. Again, I need not explicitly infer this; in fact, Nozick's formulation of the closure condition (203-4) says that if S *would* know that p and *would* know that p

entails *q,* then S *would* know that *q;* and given that formulation it certainly appears that the principle holds when *p* = *this is a computer screen* and *q* = *this is not an aardvark.* Acknowledging that, in this example, I cannot know that *p* without knowing (as a result) that *q,* threatens a basic principle Nozick has been using:

(N) If not-(q^m might have obtained were *p* false), then S need not know that not-q^m in order to know that *p.*

Once (N) has been repudiated, as it must be, given the aardvark example, the possibility is reinstated that, despite the remoteness of SK, S must know that not-SK in order to know that *p.* Nozick's compromise between common sense and skepticism has fallen apart. Surely Nozick could not reply that the aardvark possibility is different from SK because the aardvark possibility *can* be ruled out via inference given his conditions but the skeptical possibility cannot. For that is tantamount to saying that S *has to* know the falsehood only of those q^m's that he *can* know the falsehood of given Nozick's conditions. This principle is egregiously ad hoc; it has no inherent rationale.

In truth, there is a crucial fact that explains why we are ambivalent about the status of our belief that not-SK. That fact, however, is not that, in some contexts, SK is an irrelevant alternative, while in other contexts it is relevant because not-SK is the very proposition under consideration; nor is it that, in some contexts, SK would not have obtained were a given proposition (*p*) not the case, while in other contexts SK might or would have obtained were a given proposition (not-SK) not the case. The crucial fact, rather, is that there are two ways of 'ruling out' alternatives: one, by closure (deduction from *p*); the other, on independent grounds. We can by closure rule out many alternatives; we cannot, by closure, rule out those alternatives that must be ruled out on independent grounds. Our conflicting intuitions about whether we know that not-SK (by closure) or do not know that not-SK simply mirror the ambiguity in what is required to 'rule out' not-SK.

Now the claim that we know that not-SK by closure seems empty, insignificant, gimmicky; in Nozick's words, such claims "strike us as suspicious, strike us even as bad faith" (201). Somehow we think that not-SK, unlike the aardvark possibility, is the sort of thing that has to be known on independent grounds, by an argument whose premises do not include *p.* That's correct. But the reason that independent grounds are so important, the reason I should not be allowed to use *p* so as to get to not-SK, is, as Graeme Forbes has argued, that the problem of skepticism arises in a dialectical context.[15] The skeptic will not allow us to infer not-SK from *p* because, absent an argument for *p rather than* SK, he will not entitle us to *p.* Thus, the reasoning that grounds the intuition that we don't know *not*-SK could also be mobilized to support the view that we don't know that *p,* and the desired compromise between common sense and skepticism then falls apart.

Going a step further, the skeptic can grant Nozick even more than Nozick wants: he can concede that we know that not-SK by closure if the world is as we think it is. What he will not concede is that we have a dialectically effective argument for the claim that *p* or for the claim that the world is as we think it is. Let the skeptic say: "given that, on externalist conditions, I could have come to know that *p* just by tracking it, there is no reason for denying that I can come to know not-SK without independent grounds. But what I want here is an argument; and absent an argument that you in fact track *p,* you can't appeal to *p.*" This point *could* be framed as a point about a strong sense of 'know' in which knowledge requires argument; however, it is just as easily framed as the point that skepticism is not a problem about knowledge at all, but rather about *argument.*

Thus, Nozick's concession to skepticism, surprisingly, makes sense only if what is being required is an argument. I suspect, in fact, that Nozick can preserve his intuitions about skepticism only by shifting from one conception of skepticism to another. When he defends knowledge that *p,* he is thinking of the skeptic as arguing: you don't satisfy externalist constraints — you violate the variation condition. Nozick tells the skeptic that his externalist constraints are correct, but that he, the skeptic, does not know how to work with subjunctives. As we have seen, though, the variation condition can be accepted without denying closure or knowledge that not-SK, and I have argued in this section that any attempt to deny closure or knowledge that not-SK will be ad hoc. What does motivate Nozick to deny that we know that not-SK can only be a shift to a constraint on dialectically effective arguments. But this constraint should then result in skeptical conclusions about *p* as well; indeed, skepticism about *p* is what is leading to skepticism about not-SK.

III. HOW REFERENCE TO KNOWLEDGE OBSCURES THE SKEPTICAL PROBLEM

Earlier I implied that a skeptic need not be hurt if he grants the possibility that we know that not-SK by first satisfying externalist conditions for knowing that *p* and then deducing not-SK from *p.* Nor, a fortiori, need the skeptic be hurt by granting the possibility that we know that *p.* The skeptic's point is, rather, that we lack an argument for our view of things. True enough, skepticism, historically speaking, was framed as a problem about *knowledge.* This, however, was only because 'skeptics' had few of our post-Gettier worries about defining knowledge, blithely assumed that knowing entails having a good justifying argument, and adopted the formulation in terms of knowledge (rather than good argument) as a *façon de parler*. Had skeptics realized that externalist accounts of knowledge were available, they would not have phrased their claim in terms of knowledge. Accordingly, they can grant not just externalist knowledge of *p* but even externalist knowledge of not-SK; they are posing a different problem, the one about argument.

In this section I would like to do two things: first, to reinforce the claim that granting the possibility of externalist knowledge is not a significant concession on the part of the skeptic; second, to show that casting the problem of skepticism in terms of knowledge *obscures* the nature of the skeptical challenge.

Nozick is quite aware that the antiskeptical part of his thesis (namely the claim that we know that *p* if we satisfy his externalist constraints) is of limited force (197–98, 287–88). His aim seems to be not to *prove* that we know anything but to *'explain* to ourselves how knowledge is possible', in spite of our awareness of skeptical possibilities. (He states his own point incorrectly (197–98) when he says he is not *proving* to the skeptic that knowledge is possible. He *can* prove *that* — by proving that knowledge is tracking and that it is *possible* that we track. What he cannot prove is that we *do* track.)

The question, however, is whether Nozick's claim becomes so limited as to lose its significance for epistemology. I suggest it does.

(1) In the first place, if we strip Nozick's response of its technical casing, the response reduces to a claim that no skeptic ever thought of denying. The following, I think, is not an unfair synopsis of Nozick's point:

(A) Antiskeptical thesis: We have methods (or mechanisms or processes), identifiable from the inside, that are sensitive enough to distinguish tables from chairs, from cars, from other physical objects, and from empty spaces, albeit not from SKs.

(B) Proskeptical thesis 1: We have no methods (or mechanisms or processes), identifiable from the inside, that are sensitive enough to distinguish not-SK from SK.

No skeptic ever thought of denying (A). Consequently, it is hard to believe that affirming (A) could establish anything of real significance against the skeptic. Yet Nozick's variation condition basically expresses what (A) expresses. The only difference is that Nozick thinks that, because (A) is true, we can go on to claim something important: we can claim to know that *p*. I argue differently. Since (A) is innocuous, no significant points are won against the skeptic by making (A) the crucial entree to knowing commonsense propositions.

(2) If someone could defend a 'true belief' account of knowledge, that might show how knowledge is *possible:* our beliefs would constitute knowledge *if* the world is as we think it is. Yet nothing of epistemological significance would have been shown. We knew in advance that our beliefs *might* be true; defining knowledge as true belief cannot turn this innocuous point into something of significance.

(3) Suppose that someone believes the brain-in-the-vat hypothesis. We are wont to raise 'skeptical' objections to this hypothesis. Yet, given Nozick's strategy for responding to the skeptic, our 'brain in the vatter' could reply as follows: "If I am right now being caused to have this experience by the vat operators, and there being a table there isn't an alternative that might have obtained were I wrong (see 264), then I know that I'm being stimulated by the vat operator to have this experience." The point can be made more generally. Consider any two underdetermined hypotheses that compete with each other. If S believes H1 over H2, someone might raise 'skeptical' doubts about H1. Yet it is surely possible that S's belief tracks H1: for H1 might be true, and H2 need not be a nearby subjunctive alternative to H1. Indeed, competing hypotheses are not, typically, nearby subjunctive alternatives to each other. Yet the possibility that one competitor is true is precisely what generates skepticism about the other hypothesis. Even if we allow that S may know that *H1,* which Nozick might allow, we must not take the further step of saying we have undercut skepticism about *H1.* Skepticism about *H1* is generated by a competing hypothesis, even one that does not describe a close alternative to *H1.*

(4) If skepticism were a problem about (Nozickian) knowledge, then not only would it not be *necessary* to produce an argument in order to turn back skepticism about SPOPs, it would be *irrelevant* and *useless* to produce one in order to defeat skepticism about not-SK. For, whatever argument we use to show that our common sense explanation of our experience is superior to a skeptical one,[16] the fact remains that if an appropriate SK were true, where SK tautologically entails that you are mistaken in your reasoning[17], you would be going through the same reasoning. Yet surely production of an *argument* for the superiority of our common sense explanation has some bearing on the strength of the skeptical thesis that we do not know that not-SK.

Suppose, on the other hand, that SK is not taken to entail *tautologically* that we would be going through this same reasoning even if SK were to hold. Rather, take SK to be a detailed *hypothesis* — a scenario that is rich and detailed enough to count as a competing explanatory hypothesis or account. In that case, it is not clear that the skeptic is right: perhaps, were the scenario to obtain, we would not reason that the skeptical scenario has inferior explanatory power. However, if the issue is competing explanations, that issue should affect the status of *p* as well. For SK is an explanation that competes with *p*.

These points (1)–(4) establish, I think, that explaining how knowledge is possible does not have much bearing on the traditional problem of skepticism. As noted, Nozick is quite aware that his theses about skepticism are of limited power. What I have argued is that their power is so limited as to deprive them of epistemological significance.

Let me now turn to a second point, and that is that, by embedding the skeptical problem in the context of *knowledge,* Nozick masks the character of the problem. I provide two brief illustrations.

Consider first the following thesis:

(C) Proskeptical thesis 2: We have no methods (or mechanisms or processes), identifiable from the inside, that enable us to distinguish *p* from SK — to tell whether *p rather than SK.*

(C) expresses a perfectly intelligible version of skepticism about *p*, and a version that cannot be rejected without a dialectically effective argument. Furthermore, the truth of (C) has long plagued 'relevant alternative' responses to skepticism; for, once *SK* is introduced, as in (C), SK becomes a relevant alternative. In other words, relevant alternative theorists have to grant that there is *a* way of making SKs relevant: namely, introducing them explicitly as counterpossibilities. Not so Nozick. For Nozick, there is *no way* to make the demand for distinguishing *p* from SK pertinent to the epistemic status of *p;* even when SK is introduced explicitly as an alternative, it will not become a relevant alternative to *p* so long as it is remote. SK is a relevant alternative only to not-SK. Yet there is a perfectly clear sense in which (C) represents a version of skepticism *about p.* Nozick has no way of formulating this version of skepticism about *p* in terms of knowledge. Yet that should not make (C) any less unsettling.

The second illustration of how the skeptical problem is masked by reference to knowledge is more complex. It involves Nozick's emphasis on the closure argument. There are two objections to construing skepticism as a closure problem. One is that, since the Closure Principle stipulates in its antecedent that S knows that *p* entails *q,* one can make the skeptical problem go away by not knowing that *p* entails *q.* Nozick quietly defuses this objection by formulating the Closure Principle as a subjunctive: even if S *does not* know that *p* entails *q,* it is the case that if S were to know that *p* and *were* to know that *p* entails *q,* S would know that *q,* according to the skeptic. Thus, the first objection to construing skepticism as a closure problem falls away. The second objection, however, is this. Not all SPOPs entail the falsity of skeptical hypotheses. *There is a table* does not entail that S is not hallucinating, is not being stimulated by a demon, and so on (it may be that there is a table but that S is hallucinating). Surely these skeptical scenarios are no less effective against *there is a table* for not being usable in a *closure* argument. (The lack of entailment here need not affect my ability to know not-SK by inference frrom *other* proposition, e.g., *I see a table.*

The reason that these hypotheses are still effective is that skepticism is not a closure problem but rather a problem about underdetermination. Even if a hypothesis is not such that its falsehood is entailed by a particular SPOP, the hypothesis may show that the SPOP is underdetermined; for if the skeptic is right, then

(D) There is a hypothesis SK that would explain all our data just as well as our common sense or scientific hypotheses do.

I would suggest, furthermore, that turning the skeptical problem into a problem about knowledge obscures the importance of (D). For consider the following principle about knowledge:

(E) If S knows that *p* on the basis of R and there is a hypothesis *q* that, if true, would explain R just as well as *p* does, then S knows that *q* is false.

Given a tracking account, a skeptical argument based on (E), as distinct from one based on (D), does not *have* to be refuted by showing that (D) is false. It can be refuted by finding conditions for knowledge that allow knowledge that *p* to be had without knowledge that not-*q*. Yet this 'refutation' should not be allowed to obscure the truth, power, and unsettling implication of (D).

In sum, it should not be assumed that the antiskeptical part of Nozick's thesis seriously affects the traditional problem of skepticism. Rather, Nozick's way of considering the problem is capable of making us forget its real source.

IV. WHAT WE DO AND DO NOT KNOW

Suppose, contrary to the position I have been arguing for, that one were to find Nozick's compromise with skepticism attractive even when externalist knowledge is all that is at stake, and that one could show, again contrary to my view, that the tracking account leads to this compromise without ad hoc gerrymandering or a high cost in counterintuitive results. What is attractive about the compromise, I suggest, is that what we know and don't know gets sliced up so neatly. We know the common sense propositions we think we know; we don't know that exotic skeptical scenarios don't obtain.

Nozick seems to suggest that the division goes this way when he writes:

> Only by shifting his attention back to his relationship to the (different)
> fact that not-SK . . . can he [the skeptic] revive his skeptical belief and
> make it salient. . . . Only by fixating on the skeptical possibilities SK
> can he maintain his skeptical virtue. . . . [211]

This remark, however, is seriously misleading. The catalogue of what
we do and do not know on Nozick's account turns out to be far more
messy, complex, problematic, and unintuitive than this passage and
standard synopses of Nozick suggest. It is not true that Nozick
is a skeptic only about knowing the negations of SKs; nor is it true
that once SKs are raised we must be skeptics. Let me present some
examples.

   (1) Consider the conjunction: *p and not-SK*. Nozick affirms that we
know this conjunction (228). For if not-(p and not-SK), we would not
believe that (p and not-SK); in the nearer possible worlds in which
not-(p and not-SK), we would not believe that p, and so would not believe the conjunction (p and not-SK) either.[18] Furthermore, knowledge is closed under known logical equivalence; since p is logically
equivalent to *p and not-SK*, anyone who knows that p (an easy feat)
and recognizes the equivalence will know that (p and not-SK). Here we
fixate on a proposition that has not-SK as a conjunct, yet we know it.
Similarly, on the assumption that my being stimulated by a demon on
Alpha Centauri is a significantly more remote possibility than my being on Alpha Centauri without being subjected to this chicanery, I can
know that I am not on Alpha Centauri and am not being stimulated
there by a demon, even though I fail to know that I am not being stimulated by a demon on Alpha Centauri. The reason is that if not-(I am not
on Alpha Centauri and am not being stimulated there by a demon), I
would be on Alpha Centauri with my faculties not stimulated by the
demon and hence would not believe the conjunction. In general, one
may be able to assure knowledge of not-SK by framing not-SK as a
conjunction one of whose conjuncts is known to be true (for example,
'I am not in a vat, and my brain . . .').

   Does this answer to any intuition?

   (2) Consider knowledge that p where p is, again, an SPOP. If it were
not the case that p, I would not believe that p because I would not have
the same sensory experiences or the same evidence. Plainly, though, if
the experiential state or evidence were held constant, the counterfactual, 'if it were not the case that p (and S had the same experiences or
evidence), S would not believe that p,' would be false. Nozick says as
much: "given that e, I do not know that h" (226); but he points out that
we need not therefore conclude that we don't know that h (or that we
don't know that h given some proper part of e). Thus, whether the
skeptical problem arises is just a matter of how we understand the variation condition, of what we hold constant. You can know that p (on
the basis of e) without knowing that p, given e.

In this connection, it should once again be noticed that Nozick does not give his subjunctive not-$p \to$ not-(S believes that p) a 'pure' reading. Consequently, one cannot argue against holding the evidence constant by maintaining that this is how the subjunctives must be interpreted on a 'pure' reading, even assuming that the pure reading will not hold the evidence or experience fixed. Furthermore, the evidence needs to be held constant in the adherence condition if Nozick's treatment of the 'Jesse James' case (191–93) is to pan out;[19] and holding the evidence constant is one way of getting an intuitive result in the variant of the hologram example that Nozick handles in an admittedly counterintuitive way (190). Is there a better argument against holding e constant? Perhaps this: we should not fix what is held constant in a way that makes knowledge of common sense propositions impossible. Unfortunately for this argument, there turns out to be a common sense proposition that does not require us to "fixate on the skeptical possibilities" yet which we do not know on Nozick's account: not-(e and not-p). More importantly, there are certain common sense propositions whose interpretation may require us to hold e constant.

Consider a causal proposition: 'This experience is caused by a physical object of character C.'[20] Nozick tells us that "other linguistic devices such as demonstratives also fix things as constant" (225), a view that leads him to deny, for example, that I know that "this red Parker pen with [these and these characteristics] is the very pen my children bought me" (225–26). Consider, then, the following proposition, a slight reformulation of our original: 'this experience with these and these marks is the very experience that is now being caused by a physical object of character C.' If the experience were caused by something else, that something else would or might be a distorting process or mechanism. I thus know that there is an object of character C, but I do not know the proposition about the causation of my experiences. Here the skeptic gets his way *without shifting attention to the denial of skeptical scenarios.* That result, I suggest, does not answer to any antecedent intuition.

(3) 'I am awake.' Suppose that in the nearest possible worlds in which I am not awake I would be dreaming, and so would believe, by the method of attending to experiences, that I am awake. On Nozick's view I don't know that I am awake.[21]

It will not avail to argue that, if I were not awake, I would *later* come to believe that I was not awake. For by the same logic, I would always have to be said to know that I see a real fruit rather than an imitation, since I can disambiguate the situation later. And besides, the method would then not be held fixed. A better strategy for Nozick is to argue that the method in use is *inferring from these experiences;* if I were dreaming I would not be believing I am awake by *this* method — I'd be having *other experiences.* He in fact says that I can know that "I am not dreaming" without knowing that "I am not dreaming *this*" (219). However, my belief that I am awake does not really depend on my having *these* experiences — any will do; and we will shortly see that Nozick's thesis about dreaming is itself counterintuitive.

I am not sure how any theory accounts for our knowledge that we are awake. (What's the method? What's the reliable process? What's the justification?) However, for my purposes it is enough to show that, contrary to appearances, Nozick's account does not uniformly protect intuitively known common sense propositions.

(4) Robert Shope and Jonathan Vogel have shown that skepticism about induction is an ineluctable result of Nozick's account.[22] I do not know that the sun will rise tomorrow (Shope) and do not know that the ice cubes I left in the sun have melted (Vogel, perturbations in that fact would not affect my evidence.) Once again, the skeptical thesis that is established is about a common sense proposition that makes no reference to the skeptical scenario.

(5) Curiously, in considering whether I know that the desk exists now when no one is perceiving it, Nozick maintains that I can know this because of considerations regarding rebound rates (221–22). Since most of us do not rehearse such considerations before passing on the question of whether the desk exists unperceived, most of us would not know that the desk exists unperceived. (Incidentally, why not say that if it were not to exist now, I would not have had all the evidence I had previously? Is Nozick now holding the evidence fixed? cf. 222, lines 13–17.)

(6) There is a distinction, briefly flirted with by Nozick (219–20, 244–45), between exotic skeptical scenarios that imply large changes in the metaphysical character of the world, and skeptical scenarios that imply only local changes in the existence or character of specific objects or persons. For instance, the hypothesis that there are no objects and all the world's a dream, is exotic; the hypothesis that I am now dreaming (but am awake most of the time) involves local changes.[23] Other local hypotheses include (to borrow an example from Jonathan Vogel) the hypothesis that my bank is deceiving me when it tells me in my monthly statement that my account balance is B, the hypothesis that the liquid in this container is not real orange juice but an indiscernibly different imitation, and so forth; examples like the orgy example of section I also fall into this category, though here the SK does not *entail* that we can't detect it. Given Nozick's conditions, I may know that *p* but not know that *q* even where *q* is a negation of this *local* hypothesis. In some cases that follows trivially and tautologically: if I were not not-being deceived, I would obviously believe that I was not being deceived. (see 244–45)

I suggest that, if Nozick's original intuition that we don't know that not-SK was appealing, it was because SK was conceived as an exotic hypothesis, not as a local one. Denying knowledge of local skeptical hypotheses is not as attractive a move. Nozick states, for example, that, while I know that I am not dreaming (if I were dreaming, I wouldn't be having the precise experiences that led me to the belief that I am not dreaming), I do not know that I am not dreaming that I am writing (if I were dreaming *that,* I would believe that I am writing) (219).[24] Denying me knowledge that this last dream hypothesis isn't true is implausible even if denying me knowledge that 'all the world's a dream' isn't; and so on for other local skeptical hypotheses.

Incidentally, it can be argued that what is really wrong with the local hypotheses is that they cannot compete as hypotheses — full-blooded explanations that compete with other explanations — but only as theses that tautologically imply that we cannot detect their truth. As hypotheses, they are improbable relative to our background knowledge as to how things usually are. That Nozick does not take this line may reflect a tendency to take SKs as *by description* undetectable, in which case no reasoning on our part can make a dent.

Let's put all this together now. In any typical, everyday circumstance, in which I, say, see a table, I know that there is a table and I am not being deceived; but I do not know that I am not being deceived. I know that I am not in a vat and am not being fed beliefs by scientists, but I do not know that I am not in a vat being fed beliefs by scientists. On the basis of certain experiences, I know that there is a table, but given these experiences, I do not know that there is a table. Again, I know that there is a table there and perhaps that I see the table, but do not know that this experience is the very experience that is now being caused by a table. Through it all, I do not know that I am awake, even though I know that there is a table and I am not not-awake. Also, I know that I am not dreaming, though I don't know that I am not dreaming that there is a table there. Finally, I cannot know many propositions that intuitively are known on the basis of induction; and I may not know that the table exists unperceived until I examine rebound rates.

Is all this acceptable? Is it even intelligible? Here we need to separate out various sources of discomfort we may feel about these results. The first, and main, point is that, if we were enticed by Nozick's account, it was because it gave us our common sense knowledge while explaining the power of skepticism by saying that we don't know the denial of skeptical scenarios. Our intuitions got divided neatly and were systematized. What we now find is that the chips fall all over the place. Nozick takes the account wherever it leads him, and often we can't translate its results into anything like intuitive considerations.

The second source of discomfort is that the Nozickian results rob our knowledge of its coherence and its structure. Nozick himself recognizes coherence and structure as desiderata, but applies these constraints selectively.[25] He attempts to have knowing that *Pa* entail knowing that *(Ex)Px,* writing that "surely our knowledge that *p* does not stand in such splendid isolation from knowledge of other things so closely connected to *p*" (230). In a footnote early in the chapter, he notes: "our knowledge is not simply a bunch of separate items, it forms an interconnected network"; and he goes on to say that with the decline of foundationalism, questions about the connections "will receive more attention" (679, note 1). Given the results his own theory breeds, these remarks turn out to be rather ironic.

Third, if someone had presented a tracking account but did not spell out these consequences, and then Professor X were to come on the scene and show that with this account, you get these and these results, that would be taken as a reductio of the theory. But Nozick has managed to see at least some of these results before any critics of subjunctive theories did; so Nozick can swallow all these implications and simply claim squatter's rights: for him they are interesting results. As someone once remarked, Nozick's trick is to finish his *modus ponens* before his critics finish their *modus tollens.* One is tempted to ask: what pattern of results would Nozick allow to count against the theory?

Fourth, Nozick pays little if any attention to what his account means from the perspective of the first person. To begin with, it would be curious if someone said 'I know that *p* but not that *q,*' where *p* entails *q*;[26] yet anyone who has read Nozick will know that he or she does not know not-SK and so will be committed to this sort of odd assertion. In general, how do Nozick's results concerning knowledge translate into guidance for rational believers? Should I hesitate to infer *La* from *(x)Lx*? *Should* we draw the logical consequences of what we believe? Can we help doing so?[27]

Let me state, once more, the overarching point. We saw earlier that Nozick's tracking account will have a powerful appeal to someone who shares Nozick's intuitions about what we do and do not know. But as the theory is developed more fully, its results vis-à-vis skepticism exhibit a haphazard, crazy quilt pattern that either does not address our intuitions at all or runs contrary to them. Nozick's account can no longer be supported by the intuitive force of its results as regards skepticism. It must be supported on independent grounds. As we have seen, however, using independent grounds, that is, paying attention to antecedent intuitions about ordinary cases, won't produce a theory with the pattern of results vis-à-vis SK that Nozick's produces. Indeed, I would conclude with a stronger thesis. The crazy quilt is an irremediable defect in tracking accounts — I see little hope that modifications will help. Only an antecedent commitment to such bizarre results can justify continued acceptance of the theory, and that commitment, I trust, no one shares.[28]

NOTES

1. Although I focus here on skeptical arguments from closure and variation, Nozickian skeptics have a panoply of arguments at their disposal: the argument from adherence (212–13, and 690 note 54); the argument from the outweighing condition (213–14); the argument from small-scale hypotheses (244–45); the argument from deepest methods (216); the argument from unperceived existence (221); the KK-argument (245–47); the argument (against mathematical knowledge) from lack of a causal story (685, n. 23). Note also the discussion of "wider contexts" (220). An important additional argument is the argument from rigged circumstances discussed by Steven Luper-Foy in "The Epistemic Predicament: Knowledge, Nozickian Tracking, and Skepticism," *Australasian Journal of Philosophy* 62 (1984): 26–49.

2. Or, for those who prefer, that-*p*.

3. Throughout this paper I follow the reformulation suggested by Luper-Foy in "The Epistemic Predicament," 28–29. Roughly, we require not that in worlds in which not-*p* is the case and S applies M, S does not believe that *p*, but that in worlds in which not-*p*, S does not believe that *p* via M. Luper-Foy's emendation is essential if I am to develop the "orgy" example later in this section. However, Luper-Foy's argument for this change are completely convincing; moreover, Nozick himself appears to work with this formulation in the crucial passage on p. 232. cf. p. 189.

4. This reference to combined method, incidentally, is ignored by Nozick in his solution to a counterexample proposed by Eddy Zemach (189); the solution fails if the combined method is considered.

5. Klein, *Certainty: A Refutation of Skepticism* (University of Minnesota Press, 1981), esp. 82–92; on Moore, see Barry Stroud, *The Significance of Philosophical Skepticism* (New York: Oxford University Press, 1984), esp. 120–22. On the difference between Moore's closure principle and Nozick's, see Luper-Foy, "Epistemic Predicament," 43, note 37.

6. Luper-Foy, "Epistemic Predicament," 29–30. Note that this example as well as my "orgy" example, utilizes Luper-Foy's emendation in note 3. On the possibility that I would *see* that I'm not in *SK*, see note 13 below.

7. Ibid., 30.

8. The fullest discussion I know of ostensible closure failures is in Jonathan Vogel's dissertation at Yale University, 1986. His showcase example is: I know that my car is in location X where I parked it but don't know that it hasn't been stolen. See also Jeffrey Olen, "Knowledge, Probability, and Nomic Connections," *Southern Journal of Philosophy* 15 (1977): 521–25. Cf. Klein, *Certainty*. On the present suggestion, if *p* entails *q*, closure fails when the not-*q* worlds are within the cutoff point but are not worlds that might have obtained were *p* false.

9. Variations of this idea may be found in Colin McGinn, "The Concept of Knowledge," in *Midwest Studies in Philosophy IX: Causation and Causal Theories,* ed. Peter A. French, Theodore E. Uehling, Jr., (University of Minnesota Press, 1984), 529–54, at 531–32; and Richard Foley, "What's Wrong with Reliabilism?" *The Monist* 68 (1985): 188–202, at 192 (Foley is discussing rational belief, not knowledge). My own discussion follows McGinn's very closely.

10. To be sure, the emendation is problematic for a reason pointed out to me by Jonathan Vogel: it makes the variation condition almost trivially satisfiable when *p* states that a law L holds that in fact does hold. However, inductive knowledge is a problem for Nozick's account anyway (see section IV, example 4). Vogel has suggested to me that the conditions for knowledge may be a function of the type of proposition in question.

The amended account might seem to collapse the distinction between knowledge and true belief when *not-p* f is a "far-out" proposition: S can know that *p* just by virtue of (i) *not-p*'s being far-out and (ii) S's being right. However, I think that this result is analogous to ones that reliabilists have to live with anyway.

11. Graeme Forbes, "Nozick on Scepticism," *The Philosophical Quarterly* 34 (1984): 43–52, at 47–48; Robert Shope, "Cognitive Abilities, Conditionals, and Knowledge: A Response to Nozick," *The Journal of Philosophy* 81 (1984): 29–48, at 35–37; Alvin Goldman, review of *Philosophical Explanations, Philosophical Review* 92 (1983): 81–88, at 84–85. The key cases here are Nozick's Jesse James case, the Judy-Trudy case (191–93), and Gilbert Harman's newspaper case (197).

12. This particular naturalistic foil is close to the view that Nozick terms "reliabilism" on page 266. For details, see Luper-Foy, "Epistemic Predicament," and his essay in this volume.

13. After noticing this point about relevant alternatives some years ago, I found it made by David Sanford, in his penetrating paper, "Knowledge and Relevant Alternatives: Comments on Dretske," *Philosophical Studies* 40 (1981): 379–88. An issue can be raised here as to whether I need inference to get to the negated propositions, as opposed to seeing straight out that they are true or inferring from what experiences I don't have (as I certainly may when I can't identify what I do see but can say what I *don't* see). This is a formidable point, but (a) Nozick allows inference from p here (235); (b) inference is the right construal of *some* cases, such as those in which q is not considered during the act of perception. See also Sanford, op cit., 386 87.

14. In "Reliability and Relevant Alternatives," *Philosophical Studies* 39 (1981): 393–408, I argued that the relevance or irrelevance of an alternative cannot be read off from its closeness to or remoteness from the actual world. Suppose (to take a fresh example) that (1) physician H correctly diagnoses patient P as having disease D on the basis of symptom S; (2) If P had disease D', P would present the same symptom; however, (3) not-(if P did not have D, P might have had D'); (4) the doctor doesn't know this last fact; (5) if the patient did not have D, the patient would not have had S; (6) the doctor satisfies the adherence condition because he wouldn't think of D' in any of the p-neighborhoods or else would dismiss the possibility of D' dogmatically. All Nozick's conditions are satisfied, yet the case isn't one of knowledge; the D'-world is relevant though distant. Notice that if Nozick puts the weight on adherence and insists that H might have learned about or paid attention to D', then in any example in which a counterpossibility is nearby one can block the case from being one of knowledge by using adherence rather than variation. Just assume that somewhere in the p-neighborhood S learns about the counterpossibility and takes it seriously. But then the variation condition threatens to become superfluous, and knowledge would be closed because adherence is closed for true p (688, n. 51). Saying that the doctor must know on independent grounds that P doesn't have D' paves the way for requiring the same of SKs.

15. Forbes, "Nozick on Scepticism," 51–52. My ensuing claim that skepticism is a problem about lack of arguments, not lack of knowledge, amplifies remarks by Robert Fogelin in his review of *Philosophical Explanations, The Journal of Philosophy* 80 (1983): 819–23, 822–23.

16. See, for example, Laurence BonJour's argument in *The Structure of Empirical Knowledge* (Harvard University Press, 1985), 179–88. My distinction between a tautological skeptical thesis and a skeptical hypothesis roughly corresponds to his distinction between simple and elaborated demon hypotheses.

17. Nozick's treatment of evolution (283–87) is misleading here: because skeptical scenarios are characterized as scenarios that are undetectable, we know a priori that no mechanisms can detect them and don't need evolution to explain the fact that such mechanisms have not developed.

18. In lectures, Saul Kripke has noted that, for any true believed propositions q and p such that the former is not known but the latter is, one can Nozick-know (p and q) provided that not-p worlds, but not *not-q* worlds, might have obtained were the conjunction false.

19. See Shope, 35–37; Forbes, 48–51.

20. This sort of argument is raised by Anthony Brueckner in "Why Nozick is a Sceptic," *Mind* 93 (1984): 259–64, at 263–64. However, Brueckner does not raise the point about demonstratives; he assumes too quickly that on Nozick's conditions I do not know that I see a white wall. If Brueckner is right, though, my argument against Nozick is only enhanced.

21. This example was originally raised to me in conversation by Sidney Morgenbesser; subsequently I found it also in Brueckner, "Why Nozick is a Sceptic," 262–63. Cf. Nozick, 215 n.

22. Shope, "Cognitive Abilities, Conditionals, and Knowledge," 33–34; Vogel, essay in this volume.

23. Cf. Stroud, 264–72.

24. Nozick notes an odd exception: if I dream (and believe in the dream) that I am speaking in the House of Lords, and would not dream this if I were not speaking in the House of Lords, then I know, though dreaming, that I am speaking in the House of Lords (694, n. 75). This case reminds me of the hologram example (190).

25. Of course, the lottery and rational believer paradoxes raise doubts about coherence requirements. It is not clear, however, that the conjuncts in the lottery paradoxes are known as opposed to merely being rationally believed; hence closure might not be undermined for knowledge. Nozick, incidentally, accepts closure under adjudication (236).

26. Palle Yourgrau makes this point in "Knowledge and Relevant Alternatives," *Synthese* 55 (1983): 75–90.

In his contribution to this volume, Ernest Sosa points out that Nozick is committed to our believing that not-SK, since only if we attribute this belief can we attribute knowledge that p to ourselves and in that way explain how knowledge is possible (cf. Nozick 197–98). But then we are committed to 'not-SK, but I don't know that not-SK'. We believe that not-SK but believe that we do not know it. Sosa's point is also relevant to note 27 below.

27. Cf. Nozick, 688, note 49, where he seems to concede that a person believes the known logical consequences of what he knows. However, this principle needs to be restricted to cases where S makes the deduction and believes that q because of it, just as the Closure Principle for knowledge was hedged in these ways (203–4 cf. Forbes, 49–50). The principle about belief then becomes trivial. On the other hand, if S's knowing that p and that p entails q suffices for S to believe that q, then the principle about knowledge needed no hedges, and *no* person who knows that p and that p entails q could believe not-q. Thus, we would be *forced* to believe things which we know (from reading Nozick) that we don't know. See also 237–39, on the "conundrum" ascribed to Saul Kripke, where some hints about rational belief are found.

28. I have profited from long hours of conversation with Sidney Morgenbesser and Jonathan Vogel and from comments by Steven Luper-Foy.

nine

ON BEHALF OF THE SKEPTIC[1]

Peter Klein

I. INTRODUCTION

The purpose of this paper is to assess the adequacy of Robert Nozick's response to skepticism in his book, *Philosophical Explanations.*[2] Essentially, Nozick takes the skeptic to be arguing in the following way: Suppose that some skeptical scenario (call it 'SK') were true, for example, that I am a brain in the vat on Alpha Centauri and that I am having the same experiences that I am presently having. Since being in a room in New Brunswick entails not being on Alpha Centauri, if I know that I am in New Brunswick, then I know that I am not on Alpha Centauri. But I don't know that I am not on Alpha Centauri. Thus, I don't know that I am in New Brunswick.

According to Nozick, the skeptic appeals to the following general argument form ('K*p*' means that S knows that *p* and '→' stands for entailment):

K*p* & (*p* → not-SK), then K not-SK

not-K not-SK
$$\overline{}$$
∴ not-K*p*

Thus, the skeptic's general argument has two steps.[3] The first employs the so-called Closure Principle, namely, that knowledge is closed under entailment. The second is that S fails to know the denial of the skeptical scenario.

Nozick's response to the skeptic is that although S does not know that she is not a brain in the vat on Alpha Centauri, S can still know that she is in New Brunswick because the Closure Principle appealed to in the first premise is false. Knowledge is not closed under entailment.

I agree with Nozick that skepticism cannot be motivated by arguments employing the Closure Principle — but not for the reasons which he gives. I think Nozick's attack on the Closure Principle fails; but even if the principle were true, the argument employing it begs the question. Nevertheless, I want to show that skepticism remains an attractive view. Nozick's own account of knowledge lends itself to some skeptical worries; but, in addition, the ideal of knowledge envisioned by other skeptics is much richer than that portrayed by Nozick.

Before beginning my assessment of Nozick's response to the skeptics, it is important to make clear some of the limits of the argument in this paper. I will not *argue* that the Closure Principle is true. That would take us too far from the main purpose of this paper. Rather, I will merely attempt to show that Nozick's argument against that principle is not effective and *suggest* the basis for a defense of it. In addition, I will not claim that no skeptic ever appealed to an argument similar to the one cited by Nozick which employs the Closure Principle. Rather, I hope to show that two of the most historically important arguments for skepticism do not depend upon that principle in the way depicted by Nozick.

One type of argument, used by Sextus and Cicero, does not appeal to the Closure Principle in any way. The other type, used by Descartes, employs a principle much stronger than the Closure Principle. But arguments of that variety do not beg the question in the way in which the argument as delineated by Nozick does.

I hope that the attraction of the skeptic's view will become apparent, but I will not argue for its plausibility. In the final analysis, I don't believe that skepticism is plausible. But I won't argue for that here.[4]

II. NOZICK'S ACCOUNT OF KNOWLEDGE AND HIS DIAGNOSIS OF THE SKEPTIC'S CHALLENGE

Nozick's account of knowledge can be seen as a variety of reliabilism. S's belief that p, if true, is knowledge just in case it is reliably obtained. His account of the conditions under which a belief is reliably obtained is sufficiently well known that no detailed rehearsal of it is necessary. For our purposes, it will be necessary only to recall a few of its more important features.

The basic account is a fourfold set of necessary and jointly sufficient conditions:

S knows that p if and only if:

(1) p is true.

(2) S believes that p.

(3) If p were not true, S would not believe that p.

(4) If p were true, S would believe that p [Nozick, 175 ff].

Thus, for example, if S knows that there is a hand before her, then not only does she believe correctly that there is a hand, but, as Nozick puts it, she "tracks" the proposition that there is a hand. Were there not to be a hand before her, she would not believe that there was a hand before her. Further, were there to be a hand before her, she would believe that there was a hand before her. We can say that S *tracks p* just in case conditions (3) and (4) given above obtain. Tracking is Nozick's explication of the reliability condition.

Nozick modifies the basic account of knowledge in two ways which are important for our purposes. The first has to do with methods employed to arrive at beliefs; the second concerns the specific method employed when deducing certain consequences from known propositions.

The first modification is introduced by Nozick because, as they stand, the four conditions in the basic account are too strong. As he points out, it would be possible for S to use one method, say M1, to arrive at the belief that p, but if p were false, she would use another method, say M2, which would result in coming to mistakenly believe that p. Thus, condition (3) is not fulfilled because if p were false, S would still come to believe that p.

But as Nozick says, "the fact that [s]he would use another method [M2] of arriving at belief if p were false does not show that [s]he didn't know that p when [s]he used this method [M1]" (179). Thus, Nozick introduces a modification in the basic account which allows him to weaken it so that S knows that p just in case there is some method "via which S believes that p which satisfies conditions 1–4 [in the basic account], and that method is not outweighed by any other method(s), via which S actually believes that p, that fail to satisfy conditions 3 and 4" (182). Thus, in the case just considered, S would know that p because if S were to have used M1 in the situation in which p is false, S would not have come to believe that p.

In particular, Nozick modifies the basic account to allow for the use of various methods of obtaining belief as follows:

S knows that p via method M if and only if:

M1. p is true.

M2. S believes that p via method M.

M3. If p were not true and S were to use M to arrive at a belief whether (or not) p, then S wouldn't believe that p via M.

M4. If p were true and S were to use M to arrive at a belief whether (or not) p, then S would believe that p via M. (179).

The second modification of the basic account is required in order to allow for the fact that "sometimes we come to know something via a deduction or proof" (230). As Nozick says:

> Is knowledge closed under the inference of existential generalization, inferring from 'Pa' the statement 'there is an x such that Px'? Condition 3 can be satisfied for one yet not for the other. . . . But this apparent nonclosure result surely carries things too far. . . . Surely our knowledge that p does not stand in such splendid isolation from knowledge of other things so closely connected to p. (230)

Nozick adds the following condition to knowledge when that knowledge is the result of the inference of q from a known proposition, p:

> I: If q were false, S would not believe that p (or S wouldn't infer q from p). (231)

Since condition I is not fulfilled when q is the denial of the skeptical scenario, the general argument for skepticism is still not sound. As Nozick correctly points out, if I were envatted on Alpha Centauri, I would still believe that I was in New Brunswick.

Let us call conditions M3 and M4 the 'method tracking' conditions, and we can call condition I, given above, the 'inference tracking' condition.

Thus, Nozick has given a carefully constructed response to the skeptic which grants one of the central claims made by the skeptic — namely, that I do not know that any of the many skeptical scenarios is false. But even allowing for the modifications necessary for capturing those occasions when knowledge can be arrived at by deductive inferences, knowledge is not sufficiently closed to permit the skeptic to infer that we lack knowledge of those things generally believed to be known.

III. PRELIMINARY COMMENTS ON NOZICK'S ACCOUNT OF KNOWLEDGE

Much can be said in commenting on the adequacy of Nozick's account of knowledge, closure, and skepticism.[5] Of primary importance to this essay will be the reasons which the skeptic could advance for thinking that the conditions for knowledge proposed by Nozick are too *weak* — that they countenance many beliefs as knowledge which fall short of that ideal. Nevertheless, it will be worth noting reasons for thinking that the account is too *strong* because the reasons for thinking that the conditions are too strong cast doubt on Nozick's objections to the Closure Principle.

Let us begin by considering what we can call the 'Hit Rock Case.' Suppose that I believe that my gas tank is empty because the gauge reads 'empty.' And, let us suppose that the tank is, in fact, empty.

Supppose, further, that just moments before I looked at the gauge, the wire connected to the gauge had been disconnected because, unbeknownst to me, a rock kicked up by one of the tires loosened the wire from its connection to the gas tank. The gauge would then have read "empty" no matter how much gas was in the tank.

Two things are clear: (1) I do not know that the tank is empty; and (2) Nozick's method tracking condition (specifically, M3) is not fulfilled. For even if the tank were not empty, I might believe that the tank was empty. So far, so good.

But the following case shows that the method tracking condition, in particular M3, is too strong. Let us call the case the 'Missed Rock Case.' Almost everything is the same as before except that this time the rock just misses the connector. The rock does not affect the way the gauge is working. It is still working perfectly. Barring the skeptical worries to be considered later, I know that the tank is empty because the gauge is working properly and I correctly interpreted the gauge reading.

But now consider a near world in which the tank is not empty. Suppose that it is half full. The added weight of the gas in the tank changes the way the car is riding so that the rock, although having the same trajectory that it did in the actual world, now hits the connector, breaking the connection. In this situation, the tank is not empty but I believe that it is empty. Thus, if the tank had not been empty, I might still have believed that it was empty.

It is important to note that in the Hit Rock Case and in the Missed Rock Case the methods used by S to arrive at the belief that the tank is empty are identical. In the Hit Rock Case, S does not know that the tank is empty; whereas in the Missed Rock Case, S does know that the tank is empty. But from S's point of view, the method used to arrive at the belief that the tank is empty is the same in both cases. From the inside, so to speak, S would not be able to detect a difference between the two methods. The cases satisfy Nozick's strictures concerning the identity of methods. As he says,

> The notion of knowledge holds the method fixed . . . fixed enough only to exclude differences the person would detect, believing it to constitute a difference. The method used must be specified as having a certain generality if it is to play the appropriate role in subjunctives. This generality is set by the differences the person would notice; the methods are individuated from the inside. (232–33)

Thus in the Missed Rock Case the following are true: (1) Condition M3 given above is not fulfilled. In the very near possible world in which the tank is not empty and the gauge is not working, I would still believe that the tank was empty. The method employed in both cases is the same — look at the gas gauge and come to believe what the gauge says unless you have some reason to distrust it. (2) I do know that the tank is empty because in the actual world the rock missed the connector.

So, barring the skeptical worries which we will consider later, Nozick's suggested conditions are too strong. For there are cases which ought to be classified as knowledge but which are excluded by Nozick's method tracking condition.

As mentioned above, the reason for showing that Nozick's tracking condition, especially M3, is too strong is that by doing so we have already cast some doubt upon his objections to the Closure Principle. For, as mentioned above, those objections depended upon showing that S's inferred belief, say q, does not track q, even though S knows that p and p entails q. But since the tracking condition is too strong, the fact that S's belief that q does not track q cannot be used to show that S fails to know that q.

In addition, the general recipe for constructing counterexamples similar to the Missed Rock Case can be employed to show that Nozick's inference tracking condition, condition I, is also too strong. This is important since that condition was designed to portray a necessary condition of knowledge based upon inference. But as Nozick pointed out, that condition still blocks the Closure Principle.

The general recipe for cooking up counterexamples similar to the Missed Rock Case is this: Consider a two-stage process resulting in S's belief that q and make the 'output' of the first process the same as the 'input' of the second process which results in the belief that q. Now arrange the actual world so that there is a cause "waiting" to produce the same output of the first process even when the input is different. Thus, even if the input of the first process were different, S would still come to believe that q. In the gas gauge case, the world is such that even were the tank to be half full, S would believe that it was empty.

This general recipe can be used to show that the inference tracking condition is too strong. Consider what I will call the 'Taped Gauge Case.' Suppose that the gauge in S's car has some tape over the middle portion — the part that reads from '1/4' to '3/4' full. Thus, S cannot determine that the tank *is* half full by looking at the gauge. But, presumably, S could come to know that the tank is *not* half full by looking at the gauge and by inferring that it is not half full. That is, S could come to know that it is not half full by, for example, seeing that the gauge reads "empty" and inferring that it is not half full. Of course, the gauge would have to be working properly. Surely, knowledge that the tank is not half full *can* be acquired by such a process. But if the general recipe for constructing counterexamples used in the Missed Rock Case were employed here, S could come to know that the tank is not half full even though the inference tracking condition failed to hold.

In order to see that, let q be *the tank is not half full* and p be *the tank is empty.* The inference tracking condition requires that if S knows that *q* on the basis of inferring *q* from *p*, then if *q* were false, S would not believe that *p*. But if the tank had been half full, the rock would have hit the connector and S would have believed that the tank was empty. Thus, the inference tracking condition is too strong. Consequently, Nozick's attack on the Closure Principle fails.

But there is a deeper moral here which is directly related to the main topic of this essay, namely, Nozick's analysis of skepticism. From the skeptic's point of view our senses are like (unreliable) gauges which give us readings about our environment. Our senses 'read' colors, sounds, textures, smells, and so on. The 'testimony' of our senses provides the basis (albeit inadequate) for our general beliefs about our environment. Thus, I believe that I am in New Brunswick because of my sensory impressions. Further, since I believe that I am in New Brunswick, I can infer (deductively) that I am not in Boston. Similarly, I believe that I am not a brain in the vat on Alpha Centauri because I believe that I am in New Brunswick.

The situation is parallel to that in the combined Taped Gauge and Missed Rock Case. I know that the tank is not half full in that combined case because I know that the gauge reads 'empty' and I infer that the tank is not half full. I know that the tank is not half full even though were it to be half full, I would still believe that it was empty. Similarly, I could know that I am not a brain in the vat on Alpha Centauri on the basis of knowing that I am in New Brunswick, even though were I to be on Alpha Centauri, I would still believe that I was in New Brunswick.[6]

I want to *suggest* that Nozick's argument against the Closure Principle misses the crucial reason for thinking that the principle is, with some minor alterations, correct. Of course, the principle is false if knowing that *p* requires believing that *p*. Presumably, S could know that *p* and could even know that *p* entails *q*, but not believe that *q*. In addition, there are entailments which are extremely difficult to recognize and, given our limited capacities, we simply might not 'see' them.[7] But those concerns are what Nozick correctly confines to matters of 'detail' (206).

The issue could be put this way: If S knows that *p* and *p* entails *q*, is S in a position to know that *q*? The answer seems to me to be obvious. As Nozick said (see quotation above), our knowledge that *p* does not exist in "splendid isolation from other things so closely related to *p*." In the Taped Gauge Case, I am in a position to know that the tank is not half full because I can deductively infer it from some other known proposition. If this suggestion is correct, there is a perfectly general reason available to the skeptic for thinking that the Closure Principle is correct: S is in a position to know that *q* whenever S knows that *p* and *p* entails q because S has a perfectly reliable method of arriving at the belief that q, namely inferring it from p.

Nevertheless, even if this suggestion for defending the Closure Principle were accepted, the argument which Nozick attributes to the skeptic which employs the Closure Principle would not be effective. The reason is not, as Nozick would have it, that one of the premises is false. Rather, the argument begs the question. For, given the general reason which has just been presented for accepting the Closure Principle, the skeptic cannot defend the second premise in the argument without begging the question. The second premise is that S does not know that the skeptical scenario is false. But the skeptic has to grant that S could use p, were she to know that p, to deduce the negation of the skeptical scenario and arrive at knowledge that not-SK. Failing to grant *that* would undercut the general reason for accepting the Closure Principle, which is the first premise in the argument. Thus, in order to show that S does not know that not-SK, the skeptic would have to provide reasons for believing that there is nothing which S knows that entails the denial of the skeptical hypothesis. For it may be, as in the combined case, that the *only* means available to S for arriving at the belief that not-SK is through deduction from p or some other proposition about S's present environment.

In other words, the reason that the skeptic must show that S does not know that p in order to show that S does not know that not-SK is simply that the skeptic must grant that the process of deducing not-SK from p is a reliable one and could be the only way in which S could come to know that not-SK. Thus, since the skeptic must show that there is no reliable way to arrive at not-SK, the skeptic must show that S has no known proposition which entails not-SK.

Let me make clear that I am not claiming that every argument which has the form of *modus tollens* will beg the question. Consider a general argument form:

If p, then q
not-q
∴ not-p

Of course, if one offered a reason, say r, which entailed not-q, then r would entail not-p, since not-q entails not-p. Similarly, if the skeptic offered a reason which entailed that S did not know that the skeptical scenario was false, then S would have offered a reason which entailed that S did not know that p.

But my argument is that *if* knowledge is just true, reliably obtained belief, then in order for the skeptic to *show* that S does not know that the skeptical scenario is false, the skeptic would have to show as part of that very argument that S does not have any reliable way of arriving at that belief. That, in turn, requires showing that S does not know any proposition which entails the denial of the skeptical scenario.

In the general case of *modus tollens,* although r does entail not-*p,* one would not have to show that not-*p* in order to show that r. Whereas in the skeptical argument, one would have to show that S does not know any proposition (including *p*) which would entail the denial of the skeptical hypothesis.

Let me summarize the argument up to this point: Nozick's argument against the Closure Principle fails. But even were knowledge closed under entailment, that fact would be useless to the skeptic.[8]

IV. THE REAL GROUNDS FOR SKEPTICISM

Given that the Closure Principle is not a useful weapon in the skeptic's arsenal, what is the real basis of skepticism? I think that the answer is twofold. First, a skeptic could grant that knowledge is merely true, reliably obtained belief and argue that the tracking conditions do not obtain for most, if not all, of our beliefs about the world. Let us call this type of skeptic a Noskeptic (short for 'Nozickian Skeptic'). A second type of skeptic will be called a 'Cartesian Skeptic' for reasons which will become apparent shortly. Roughly put, the Cartesian Skeptic holds that knowledge is not just true, reliably obtained belief. Rather, knowledge is true, reliably obtained belief which is immune to legitimate doubt.

Let us consider the Noskeptic first. The Trudy/Judy and Grabit Twins have philosophical ancestors. Cicero wrote as follows:

> If therefore a person looking at Publius Servilius Geminus used to think he saw Quintus, he was encountering a presentation of a sort that could not be perceived, because there was no mark to distinguish a true presentation from a false one. . . . You say that so great a resemblance does not exist in the world. . . . let us grant by all means that it does not exist, but undoubtedly it can appear to exist, and therefore will cheat the sense, and if a single case of resemblance has done that, it will have made everything doubtful. . . . Therefore seeing that it is possible for Publius Geminus Quintus to appear to you, what reason have you for being satisfied that a person who is not Cotta cannot appear to you to be Cotta, inasmuch as something that is not real appears to be real.[9]

I take it that Cicero's point could be put this way: Twins could be unbiquitous. There is no 'mark' by which we can distinguish true from false appearances and, consequently, our senses are unreliable guides to the world. Nozick's method tracking conditions of knowledge are not fulfilled. Things could be different than they in fact are, but we would not believe that they were different because our sense impressions lack internal marks by which we can tell which impression is an accurate one. Put another way, there are near worlds in which twins are much more plentiful than we think (but do not know) that they are in ours.

Similar arguments can be found in Sextus Empiricus.[10] He points to case after case in which our senses cannot be giving us accurate information about the world because their 'testimony' is either confused or contradictory. Towers which appear round at a distance appear square when we are close to them (I.32, I.118). When we are asleep, the impressions which we have are so different from those which we have when awake that neither can accurately portray the world about us (I.104). He draws this conclusion from the examples which he has given:

> Consequently we are unable to say what is the real nature of each of these things, although it is possible to say what each thing at the moment appears to be.[11] (I.93)

Return to the Rock Cases again. We saw that in those cases, knowledge depended upon two things — the accuracy of the gauge and the ability to interpret it. Similarly, the validity of the Closure Principle depends upon the fact that it implicitly points to a two-stage process: (1) The process which produced the knowledge that p, and (2) the process of inferring q from p. We could imagine the first process being the acquisition of knowledge through the means of the senses. As mentioned earlier, our senses gauge the world, so to speak. The second step is the acquisition of knowledge via deductive inference. If the first process is unreliable, then even though deduction is a reliable method of acquiring beliefs, it could not produce knowledge if the initial process were not, so to speak, on track. Thus, not only would the senses be unable to provide us with knowledge of the world, but inferences based upon the 'testimony of our senses,' although deductive and, hence, reliable would not produce knowledge.

Of course, the disagreement between a Noskeptic and his/her critic turns on how one should delineate the *conditions* which determine the 'nearness' of possible worlds. Both the Noskeptic and his/her critic require that our senses track. Both agree that in the world in which twins are ubiquitous, we would have many false beliefs. The Noskeptic takes *that* world to be near — or, near enough. That is, the Noskeptic thinks it appropriate to test the subjunctive conditional, M3, by determining what obtains in that world. (I think that this is clear from the passage cited above by Cicero.) On the other hand, his/her critic does not think *that* world is an appropriate one in which to test the subjunctive conditional.

My point here is *not* that one or more of these considerations succeeds in establishing the Noskeptic's claim that our beliefs fall short of knowledge. In fact, as we will see, Descartes thought these considerations do not show that we lack all knowledge of the world about us. Rather, the point here is that a Noskeptic does not appeal to the Closure Principle. Such skeptics could accept Nozick's account of knowledge and simply deny that the method tracking conditions obtain. Our senses are not such that they track the 'real nature' of things. They would argue that Nozick's method tracking conditions provide fertile ground in which to plant the seeds of skepticism.

But Descartes does not accept the Noskeptic's reasons for skepticism. His skepticism is rooted in a different and much richer soil.[12] Descartes considers and rejects reasons like those given by Sextus and Cicero for withholding ascent to beliefs based upon the testimony of the senses. As he says, even though our senses do sometimes, or even often, deceive us, it does not follow that they are not ever trustworthy. We can distinguish those circumstances when they can be trusted from those when they are unreliable. Looking at something like a tower from a great distance or in bad light, for example, is not a reliable way to obtain beliefs.[13] He considers the possibility, raised by Sextus, that in dreams our experience does not accurately portray reality. But he replies that even in sleep, the "simples" which appear in dreams are "representations" of what is real and are "counterparts of something real and true" (146).

Descartes argues that even if one were to grant the premise of the Pyrrhonian arguments, namely that there is no clear *internal* mark which distinguishes accurate from inaccurate impressions, it does not follow that our senses do not ever reliably picture some important features (the simples) of the world. And, consequently, if knowledge were true, reliably obtained belief, then the fact that our senses have misled us on occasion is not sufficient to show that we lack knowledge on all occasions. Put another way: One could add the belief that our senses are often unreliable to our other beliefs and still be justified in believing many of the things which we do believe. That is, the recognition of the fact that our senses are sometimes unreliable is not a grounds for doubting everything which we once believed that we knew.

Nevertheless, there is, he thinks, a good argument for the skeptical claim that we have little or no knowledge about the world. The argument is designed to show that given his present beliefs he is not justified in denying that his senses are *inherently* unreliable.

Now, I do *not* want to examine his argument which shows that he is not justified in denying that his senses are *inherently* unreliable.[14] My point here is merely to present his argument for skepticism in order to show how it differs from that presented by the Noskeptic. After giving his reasons for thinking that he is not presently justified in denying that his senses are inherently unreliable, he says:

> To these reasons I have certainly nothing to reply, but at the end I feel
> constrained to confess that there is nothing in all that I formerly believed

to be true, of which I cannot in some measure doubt, and that not merely
through want of thought and levity, but for reasons which are very powerful and maturely considered; so that henceforth I ought not the less
carefully refrain from giving credence to these opinions than to that
which is manifestly false, if I desire to arrive at any certainty . . .
(147–48)

Further, in commenting about the conclusion of his skeptical reasoning, he says of the "ancient and commonly held opinions" that they all
fall short of "right knowledge" even though there are more reasons to
believe them than to deny them:

> . . . nor will I ever lose the habit of deferring to them [the ancient and
> commonly held opinions] as they really are, i.e., opinions in some meas-
> ure doubtful, as I have just shown, and at the same time highly probable,
> so that there is much more reason to believe in than to deny them. (148)

Here is a much richer concept of knowledge than that envisioned by the
reliabilists. I take it that Descartes' point could be put this way: Even
though my former beliefs are more reasonable to believe than deny and
even if they were obtained in a reliable fashion, they are not beyond
doubt. Only beliefs which are beyond doubt are certifiable as "right
knowledge." Thus, we do not have right knowledge or genuine
knowledge.

The tasks remaining for this paper are: (1) To make some initial attempt to clarify what makes a belief immune from doubt[15] and (2) to
show that the argument which employs this concept of doubt to motivate skepticism does not beg the question in the way in which the argument employing the Closure Principle does.

I think it is clear from Descartes' rejection of Pyrrhonian grounds
for skepticism and from his own positive account that a proposition
provides legitimate grounds for doubting that p for S just in case (1) it
is one which S is not justified in denying and (2) it is one which if S were
to add to his/her beliefs, S would no longer be justified in believing
that p. And, in order for a belief to be certifiable as knowledge, it must
be immune from all doubt. For example, even were Descartes to add to
his beliefs that he is now dreaming, his beliefs about "simples" would
still be justified. So the proposition that he is dreaming is not one
which provides a ground for doubting his beliefs about the simples.

The general argument strategy employed by the Cartesian Skeptic
can be put this way:

If S knows that p, then S is justified in denying all grounds for doubting p.

S is not justified in denying all grounds for doubting p

∴ S does not know that p

If we use 'Jp' to mean that p is justified for S, 'Jp' to mean that p is not justified for S, and '$q ⊕ B$' to mean that q is added to S's set of beliefs, we can put the necessary condition of knowledge employed by the Cartesian Skeptic in the first premise as follows:

Immunity Principle   If Kp and [($q ⊕ B$) → Jp], then J not-q.

Now, it should be noted that the Immunity Principle is much stronger than the Closure Principle and virtually implies it. It is stronger because a proposition, say q, could provide the grounds for doubting that p without its negation being implied by the purportedly known proposition. Specifically, propositions other than those equivalent to one of the skeptical scenarios can provide grounds for doubt. Consider the proposition that there is a hand before me. Presumably, the proposition that my senses are inherently unreliable would satisfy the second condition in the antecedent of the Immunity Principle, but the proposition that there is a hand before me does not entail the negation of the proposition that my senses are unreliable.

But the Immunity Principle does entail the Closure Principle *if* knowledge is true, justified, immune belief. Consider any of the many skeptical scenarios, SK. If SK were added to S's beliefs then S would no longer be justified in believing that p. For the evidence for p would be overridden by SK. Thus, the second condition in the antecedent of the Immunity Principle is satisfied. Hence, if Kp, then J not-SK. Now if p is true, not-SK is true. And finally, if not-SK were not immune from doubt, neither would p be immune from doubt, since p → not-SK. For any grounds for doubting not-SK would be equally good grounds for doubting p. Hence, if Kp and (p → not-SK), then K not-SK. The argument just given could be generalized to cover any pair of propositions, (p, q), such that if Kp and p → q, then Kq. I take it that this argument provides another reason, independent of those given earlier which depended upon realiabilist intuitions, for thinking that the Closure Principle is correct.

Let me hasten to add that this argument for Cartesian Skepticism does not beg the question in the way which the argument employing the Closure Principle does. Evidence for the second premise in the argument for the skepticism employing the Closure Principle must include that S does not know that p — since p, alone, provides an inferential path to not-SK. The Cartesian argument given above can be stated as follows (where 'p' stands for the proposition that there is a hand before S; and 'q' stands for the proposition that S's senses are inherently unreliable):

If Kp and [($q ⊕ B$) → Jp], then J not-q.
not-J not-q
_____
∴ not-Kp

Evidence for the second premise in this argument, not-J not-q, need not include that S does not know that p, since p, alone, is not evidence for not-q.[16] The fact that there is a hand before me does not justify the proposition that my senses are inherently reliable. In other words, one would not have to show that not-Kp in order to show that not-J not-q because p, alone, is not a proposition which can be used by S to come to know that not-q.

It is tempting, here, to begin a more detailed investigation of the argument for Cartesian Skepticism. For example, what restrictions apply to the addition of beliefs to belief sets? (Surely when some beliefs are added, others must be subtracted if we are to maintain a set of justified beliefs.) What arguments can be developed to substantiate the Immunity Principle? (Many philosophers have argued that such a principle is too strong.) And finally, are there propositions which provide the necessary grounds for doubting most, if not all, of our "ancient and commonly held" opinions? (That is, is Cartesian Skepticism plausible?) Tempting though these questions are, they take us far beyond the scope of this paper.[17] Here, the point is merely that there is an *apparently* attractive argument for skepticism which depends upon a conception of knowledge much richer than that envisioned by Nozick's reliabilist account.

V. CONCLUSION

If the arguments in this paper are sound, Nozick's assessment of the skeptic's position is defective in various ways. Nozick thinks that skeptics employ the Closure Principle and that the principle is false. To the contrary, Nozick's argument against the Closure Principle fails; but even were the principle true, it would be useless to the skeptic. Nozick's own proposed necessary conditions provide the basis for one form of skepticism. But another form of skepticism, one which regards knowledge as more than true, reliably acquired belief and one which has a philosophical pedigree extending back at least to Descartes, can be developed. That form of skepticism cannot even be addressed by Nozick's account of knowledge.

NOTES

1. I would like to thank Ann Jaap Jacobson and Steven Luper-Foy for their help with earlier drafts of this paper. In addition, my wits were sharpened — or at least made somewhat less dull — by discussing some of the issues raised in this paper with Richard Foley.
2. Robert Nozick, *Philosophical Explanations* (Cambridge, Massachusetts: Harvard University Press, 1981).
3. The argument tacitly assumes that $p \rightarrow$ not-SK.
4. For a more extended treatment of some related issues, see Peter Klein, *Certainty* (Minneapolis. University of Minnesota Press, 1981).

5. It is this section of the essay which owes much of its final form to the comments I received on earlier drafts by Anne Jaap Jacobson and Steven Luper-Foy.

6. Of course, I do not mean to imply that the skeptic would believe that I know that I am in New Brunswick. Rather, I am claiming that the skeptic would endorse the hypothetical claim that if I know that I am in New Brunswick, then I am in a position to know that I am not on Alpha Centauri.

7. There is another related issue which should be mentioned. To say that knowledge is closed under entailment could mean that the set of known propositions is closed under entailment. That is a stronger principle than the one being discussed here. That principle would require that if S knows that p and S knows that q, then S knows that (p and q). The principle which is being discussed here does not entail that conjunctive principle.

8. For a more detailed treatment of these points, see *Certainty*, especially 82–87.

9. Cicero, *Academica* 2 (Lucullus), Rackham translation, 26. 84–85.

10. Sextus Empiricus, *Outlines of Pyrrhonism*, translated by R. G. Bury (Cambridge, Mass.: Harvard University Press, 1976) I.32, 118.

11. Sextus, of course, presents additional arguments to show that we cannot rely upon "proof" as a method of producing reliably obtained beliefs (I.60, 116, 123 and especially, II.143ff). But an examination of them would take us too far afield.

12. Obviously, what I am referring to here is not the nonskeptical position which is Descartes' eventual position in the *Meditations*. Rather I am referring to the skeptical argument given in the first "Meditation." All references to the *Meditations* will be to the translation by Haldane and Ross, Vol. 1 (New York: Dover Publications, 1931), 148.

13. Of course looking at some things at great distances and in bad light is a reliable way to obtain beliefs. Consider beliefs about the phases of the moon.

14. Here is what I take that argument to be: (1) Either my senses were created by a perfect cause or they were not. (2) If they were created by a perfect cause, then there is (at least at present) no explanation of how error could ever arise. (3) Error does arise. (4) If the senses were created by an imperfect cause, then "it is clear that the greater will be the probability of my being so imperfect as to deceive myself ever, as is the Author to whom they assign my origin the less powerful." (5) Therefore, I am not presently in a position to deny that my senses are inherently defective (147).

15. I attempt to develop the notion of legitimate doubt in my paper "Immune Belief Systems," *Philosophical Topics*, Spring 1986, 14.1: 259–80.

16. As in the argument given by Nozick which employs the Closure Principle, this argument tacitly assumes that $[(q \oplus B) \rightarrow Ip]$.

17. See Klein, "Immune Belief Systems," cited above for an attempt to answer some of these questions.

ten

CONDITIONALS AND SKEPTICISM

Stephen F. Barker

Robert Nozick's *Philosophical Explanations* is a massive, rambling, high-spirited work, which makes stimulating contributions to many central problems of philosophy. Its third chapter treats epistemology. In the earlier part of that chapter Nozick presents an analysis of knowing which he works out in light of his distinctive metaphor of 'tracking.' Then later in the chapter he uses this analysis in order to propose a resolution of the problem of skepticism. In opposition to the skeptic, he holds that one can know many things, for example, that one is sitting in a chair reading a book. However, somewhat surprisingly, he agrees with the skeptic that one cannot know some other basic things, for example, that one is not a brain in a vat receiving systematically misleading sensory stimuli. To those who believe that one can know things of the former kind only if one also knows things of the latter kind, this stand of Nozick's will seem paradoxical. But he states his position firmly, declaring, with regard to things of the latter kind, that all attempts to show that we do know them "leave us suspicious, strike us even as bad faith." (201)[1]

There is much to admire in what Nozick has to say in this chapter about knowing and skepticism. The vigor and ingenuity of his discussion are most impressive, and much of his doctrine is surely on the right track. However, I believe that his view that we cannot know things of the latter kind makes more of a concession to the skeptic than Nozick's own view of knowing should require. Running the risk of being in bad faith, I want to disagree with Nozick's account of why we cannot know things of the latter kind — for example, that we are not brains in vats being systematically deceived. The criticism that I want to present here will have to do with the way in which Nozick expresses and understands the conditional statements that are central to his analysis of knowing. I propose to lead up to this criticism by first noting what I take to be the basic elements of Nozick's position concerning this matter.

I. NOZICK'S ANALYSIS OF KNOWING

In developing his analysis of what it is to know, Nozick aims to formulate a set of necessary conditions for knowing which, taken together, will constitute a sufficient condition. That is, he seeks a set of conditions such that 'S knows that p' (for any interpretations of 'S' and 'p') will hold true if and only if these conditions all are satisfied.

The first condition laid down by Nozick is that one can know only what is true (*PE* 170, 172).

(1) p is true.

This condition is hardly controversial.

The second condition has to do with belief. Most twentieth-century philosophers who have sought to analyze what knowing is have held that it is a species of believing. Nozick agrees with the majority, and lays down as the second provision of his analysis that one can know only what one believes (*PE* 170, 172, and 180, note 6).

(2) S believes that p.

This requirement is slightly controversial. Cook Wilson[2] and Prichard[3] were significant dissenters from what has come to be the majority view. Presumably inspired by Plato's passage on the divided line[4], they held that knowing and believing are mutually exclusive states of mind, and hence that believing is a sufficient condition for *not* knowing. Their view has won few recent adherents, however, for it seems to flout ordinary usage too much. Provisio (2) seems to be correct, in that to whatever extent one knows, one must to that extent also believe.

During the middle of this century, a good many philosophers followed the lead of Russell[5] and held that the analysis of knowing can be completed by adding to the first two provisos a third to the effect that S's belief in p is justified (or based on good reasons,[6] or on adequate evidence[7]). This analysis of knowledge as justified true belief was decisively refuted by Gettier's counterexamples.[8] Nozick avoids it.

Instead, he seeks to complete his analysis by appeal to the idea that what is involved in knowledge, over and above true belief, is that the person's state of belief 'tracks' the truth. This metaphor needs some explaining, however It is drawn originally from the field of hunting, of course. The hunter literally tracks his quarry by following its traces while continually keeping alert to adjust his own direction of travel in response to any change which the traces indicate has occurred in the direction taken by his quarry. His aim is to reach the quarry, and if he is a good tracker he will modify his own direction whenever further traces of his quarry indicate that doing so will best keep him on its track.

A metaphorical extension of this way of speaking occurs in connection with electronic warfare, where missiles guided by radar which they carry are said to 'track' their targets in order to reach and destroy them. Here the pursuer does not rely on mere traces which the quarry has left behind, but detects it more directly by bouncing radio waves off it. The pursuing missile tracks its target by altering its own direction in response to any evasive maneuvers of the latter, thus maintaining a collision course. If the tracking is good, the pursuer will actually zero in on its target; but in addition it will be the case that if the target had made rather different evasive maneuvers instead, the pursuing missile would have zeroed in on it all the same.

A less aggressive form of 'tracking' occurs when a microwave antenna on earth moves so as to stay focussed on the radio transmissions of a passing satellite. Here the tracker does not approach the object tracked, but merely adjusts its own orientation continuously so as to maintain maximum signal strength. The system controlling the antenna adjusts it so that signal strength actually is maintained and in addition would turn the antenna in other rather different ways were the motion of the satellite to make that appropriate.

In all cases such as these, the tracking, whether it occurs in a literal or metaphorical sense, involves movement by the tracker in close response to the movement of its target. What is the notion of tracking supposed to mean, however, if we stretch it considerably further to cover a relationship between belief and the truth, where change of place is not in question? Here Nozick's suggestive idea is that we may speak of tracking when a person's state of belief about some matter reliably adjusts itself to conform to the truth about that matter. This person's state of belief does and would change to suit varying situations, so that correspondence is and would be maintained between what is believed and what is the case. In this sense, the person's state of belief is analogous to the antenna which rotates so as to stay locked in on its target: each is 'tracking' something, in that each alters as is required in order to maintain a certain conformity between itself and what it, so to speak, tracks.

For example, consider an old salt who, whenever he feels a certain ache in his bones, believes that it will rain the following day; when he feels no such ache, he does not expect rain. Suppose that his way of forecasting actually is reliable; in the long run the beliefs about the weather on the morrow to which it leads him are generally true ones. Moreover, suppose that if he were to use this method of forecasting in circumstances that were somewhat different (for example, in other seas and other ports) this reliable correspondence between his belief and the truth still would be maintained. Then his beliefs about rain on the morrow can be said to track the truth. This type of tracking of the truth is what Nozick regards as knowledge.

Nozick does not propose to complete his analysis of knowing by adding a third proviso to the effect that S's belief that *p* tracks whether *p* is true. Clearly he could not regard such an analysis as misrepresenting what knowing is, but apparently he would regard it as somehow unworkmanlike. Instead, he seeks to express this relationship of tracking in other terms.

He undertakes to do this by using conditional statements. To complete a first version of his analysis he lays down the following two provisos:

(3) If *p* were not true, then S wouldn't believe it.

(4) If *p* is true, then S believes it.[9]

Nozick calls these 'subjunctives'; I shall comment presently on his doing so and on his wording of the latter one. For now, let us merely note that for a certain range of cases (those in which S is not using any specific method or way of forming beliefs), Nozick intends these two conditions to express the idea that S's belief that *p* tracks whether *p* is true. The idea is of a relationship between S's believing that *p* and the truth concerning *p*, such that S's state of belief both actually and potentially conforms itself to what is the case.

Here (3) and (4) are to be factual statements, in order to convey the idea of tracking. Provisos (1), (2), (3), and (4), taken together, are to constitute a necessary and sufficient condition for 'S knows that *p*' for a certain range of cases—those where S does not employ any specific method or way of forming his belief that *p*.

Where S does employ a specific method or way of forming his belief, Nozick supplants the simpler analysis which has just been discussed by a somewhat more elaborate one. He says that then 'S knows that *p*' is true if and only if:

There is a method M such that

(1) *p* is true;

(2) S believes, via method M, that *p*;

(3) if *p* were not true and S were to use M to arrive at a belief about whether *p*, then S would not believe, via M, that *p*;

(4) if *p* is true and S uses M to arrive at a belief about whether *p*, then S believes, via M, that *p*;

and all other methods via which S believes that p and which do not
satisfy conditions (1) to (4) are outweighed by M (179–82).[10]

Here for M to outweigh other methods means that when its outcome
conflicts with theirs, S will rely on M rather than on the others; that is,
he will believe what M indicates for him to believe rather than what
they do.

This is Nozick's analysis of knowing. Before we discuss how he
applies it to the problem of skepticism, let us consider further the character of the conditional statements that figure as provisos (3) and (4) in
the analysis.

II. CONDITIONALS

How are Nozick's conditionals to be understood? Let us first note
some familiar aspects of conditionals generally, in order to lay a basis
for further discussion of this issue.

Every conditional can be regarded as having the form 'If q then r'
and as expressing the thought that q (the antecedent) is true only in case
r (the consequent) is true also. Thus the truth of a conditional always is
incompatible with its antecedent being true while its consequent is
false.

A strictly minimal interpretation of what a conditional statement
means would equate it simply with this denial that the antecedent is
true while the consequent is false. On this interpretation, 'If q then r'
will be strictly equivalent to 'Not both q and not-r.' Such a conditional
says nothing more than that the combination of true antecedent with
false consequent is not the case. A conditional understood in this minimal way is truth-functional, in that the truth values of its components
suffice to determine the truth value of the conditional.

However, conditionals as they typically occur in ordinary discourse
are not truth-functional. Consider the conditionals 'If Rex is a dog,
then Rex is an animal' and 'If you drop that vase, it will break.' Suppose we establish that Rex is both a dog and an animal, and that the
vase is not going to be dropped and is not going to break. This by no
means suffices to establish whether these conditionals are true or false,
though it would have to suffice for this if they were truth-functional
conditionals. Conditionals of this nontruth-functional character are
used to affirm some more appreciable sort of connection between antecedent and consequent than is conveyed by a truth-functional conditional.

Coming back to Nozick's analysis, what does proviso (3) mean when
it speaks about what S's state of belief would be were the truth otherwise than it is? This is a contrary-to-fact conditional, and such conditionals have long been a source of concern to analytic philosophers.[11]
Nozick suggests an account of this in terms of possible worlds (PE

173-74).[12] According to this account, proviso (3) invites us to consider possible worlds in which it is not the case that *p*, and to focus on those of them close to the actual world (or if all are remote, then we are to focus on the less remote among them). Proviso (3) says of these possible worlds that in them S does not believe that *p*. Analogously, (4) asks us to consider possible worlds in which it is the case that *p* which are close to the actual world; and it says that in them it is true that S believes that *p*.

Some philosophers consider this talk about possible worlds to be highly illuminating as an analysis of conditionals like these. Nozick, however, does not heavily commit himself to such talk, apparently regarding its value as open to question. Certainly one does not obtain a *false* account of these conditionals by explaining them this way in terms of possible worlds. This account will be misleading, though, if we imagine that it adds precision and rigor to our understanding of what these conditionals say. It does not do that, for we possess no understanding of possible worlds which enables us to define in any clear or precise way what it is for one to be 'closer' to the actual world than another is. To be sure, if we were to characterize possible worlds by using a totally artificial language whose predicates and singular terms were highly regimented, we might then be able to define with some exactitude the idea of comparative distance between possible worlds; but such a definition would have little bearing upon those possible worlds which we characterize in natural language. The danger which attends reliance upon this talk about possible worlds is that it may lead us to suppose that the factual content of conditionals such as (3) and (4) is much more definite than it is.

For those of us who do not find talk about possible worlds especially illuminating, there is an alternative approach. We can give a general account of the purport of conditionals that are not truth-functional if we say that always the point of affirming such a conditional is to claim that its consequent can legitimately be inferred from its antecedent. In some cases where a relation of inferability exists it will be deductive, while in other cases it will be nondeductive. This allows us to divide conditionals that are not truth-functional into two types.[13]

The conditional 'If Rex is a dog, then Rex is an animal' is an example of the first type. Here we take for granted that the name 'Rex' refers to a unique individual and that the various terms involved are being used literally and in their normal senses. Under these circumstances this conditional must necessarily be true, since its consequent will be deductively inferable from its antecedent.

Conditionals of this first type may be contrasted with the type of conditionals that are contingent. Consider 'If you drop that vase, it will break.' To evaluate the truth of a conditional such as this, we must think of ourselves as first of all taking inventory of what we know about the situation. Call all this our data. Now we add to our data the information contained in the antecedent. If the antecedent in some way conflicts (deductively or inductively) with part of our data, as of course it will if the conditional is contrary to fact, then we alter our data in as minimal a way as we can so as to avoid incoherency. In making such alterations we consider changes in statements about particular individual things to be more minimal than otherwise similar changes in statements expressing laws of nature.[14] Then we must determine whether the consequent would be probable relative to this body of information consisting of (modified) data plus antecedent.

Applying this strategy to our example, we think over what background data we have about the situation; we add to our data the assumption that the vase is dropped, making changes in the data if doing so is needed in order to preserve coherency, but keeping these changes as minimal as possible; we then determine whether, relative to this basis, it follows with probability that the vase will break. Here, if the consequent does follow, it will follow inductively, rather than deductively,[15] from the assumptions made. The conditional as a whole, if true, will be a contingent truth, to be arrived at by inductive thinking grounded upon empirical considerations.

It is an important aspect of Nozick's analysis of knowing, I believe, that it requires provisos (3) and (4) to be contingent conditionals, grounded in this way upon empirical considerations.

III. SUBJUNCTIVES

There is a problem concerning the grammar in terms of which Nozick formulates the conditional statements in his analysis. His provisos (3) and (4) are conditionals, and he calls them 'subjunctives,' wording them in the subjunctive mood. Here he is carrying further a practice begun by previous writers.[16] However, by doing this he is expressing the belief that both these conditionals are contrary to fact. In English we do of course use the subjunctive mood in cases where we are assuming that the antecedent of a conditional is false ('If I were you, I wouldn't do that'). This is appropriate for the third proviso of Nozick's analysis, because in the third proviso the antecedent of the conditional must be considered false, since it is the negation of what the first proviso declares to be the case. The fourth proviso cannot be regarded as contrary to fact, though; the truth of its antecedent has already been affirmed by the first proviso. Thus it is inappropriate to use the subjunctive mood in wording the fourth proviso, and inappropriate to call it a subjunctive.

Nozick's handling of this grammar becomes especially awkward when, in regard to provisos (1), (2), and (4), he writes, "Not only is *p* true and S believes it, but if it were true he would believe it." (PE 176)

Here in a single remark he combines together the asserting of a conditional, worded as though he assumed its antecedent to be false, with the asserting of its antecedent. That is, in the first clause of his remark he says that *p* is true, while in the remainder of his remark he expresses the assumption that it is not true. This is too close to inconsistency to be a happy way of formulating proviso (4).

Presumably Nozick is trying to word both the conditionals that occur in his analysis in the same way in order to underline how alike they are and how far they are from being mere truth-functional conditionals. That is, he is perhaps trying to word each of them so as to emphasize how it conveys the thought that a relation of inferability holds between antecedent and consequent, regardless of whether the antecedent is true. Since this is the crux of the conditional in the fourth proviso just as much as it is of that in the third, he tries to word them both in the same way, and employs the subjunctive mood for this purpose.

Now, to be sure, in the English of past centuries the subjunctive mood was used in conditionals to indicate that the antecedent was regarded as a mere supposition, a contingency which might or might not arise (for example, "Or what man is there of you whom, if his son ask bread, will he give him a stone?"[17]). Because of this, Nozick's use of the subjunctive mood in proviso (4) does have a certain archaic half-plausibility. However, that old usage would call for the present subjunctive in (4), not the past subjunctive. In any case, in modern English the use of subjunctives is not the way to convey this sense of mere possibility.[18] One simply uses indicative conditionals, reserving the subjunctive mood for those cases where the antecedent is assumed to be contrary to fact.

If special wording should be needed to emphasize how much the conditional of proviso (4) is like the conditional of proviso (3) and how far they both are from being truth-functional, then use of the auxiliaries 'should' and 'would' will permit a better formulation. We can word proviso (4) as 'If *p* should be true, then S would believe it' and proviso (3) as 'If *p* should not be true, then S would not believe it.' These versions are genuinely conditional but they avoid expressing any assumption one way or the other about whether the antecedent is contrary to fact. However, in general the type of statement that is called for here is simply the conditional.

IV. NOZICK'S RESPONSE TO SKEPTICISM

Skepticism about whether we can have knowledge of the external world has been the most striking and influential form of skepticism in modern philosophy. The skeptic who attacks our claim to possess such knowledge may argue along the following lines. If anyone were a brain in a vat receiving sensory stimuli which misleadingly suggest that he has a body and is normally situated in the world (these stimuli would be selected by a malicious psychologist), then he would believe he was not a brain in a vat. Therefore, no one can know that he is not a brain in a vat receiving such stimuli. Furthermore, there is a large group of one's ordinary beliefs based on sense experience, each of which obviously entails that one is not a brain in a vat (such as one's belief that one is sitting reading a book). If one does not know that one is not a brain in a vat, one cannot know any of these things. Here the principle is that if I am aware that q entails r and I do not know that r, then I do not know that q either. If no belief which entails that one is not a brain in a vat can be known, then all or most of the rest of what we suppose ourselves to know on the basis of sense experience is indirectly undermined as well. The skeptic thus reaches his conclusion that we know nothing, or almost nothing, on the basis of sense experience.

Nozick's reply to this line of thought involves disagreeing with the skeptic by affirming that one can know one is sitting and that one is reading a book, while granting to the skeptic that one does not know that one is not a brain in a vat. This position involves rejecting the principle that things cannot be known which one knows entail things one does not know.

From Nozick's point of view, you can know that you are sitting, because your belief to this effect can perfectly well track the truth. If we regard reliance on the senses as a method of knowing, then Nozick's more elaborate analysis has to be invoked, but its provisos can readily be satisfied. Replacing 'p' by 'You are sitting', 'S' by 'you', and 'M' by 'sensory observation,' we find that according to Nozick's more elaborate analysis you know by sensory observation that you are sitting if and only if:

There is a method of sensory observation such that

(1) You are sitting;

(2) you believe by this method that you are sitting;

(3) if you were not sitting and were to use sensory observation to arrive at a belief about whether you were sitting, then you would not believe, via sensory observation, that you were sitting;

(4) if you are sitting and you use sensory observation to arrive at a belief about whether you are sitting, then you will believe, by this method, that you are sitting;

and all other methods by which you believe that you are sitting and which do not satisfy (1) to (4) are outweighed by the method of sensory observation.

Here everything is in order. Provisos (3) and (4) are appropriately contingent conditionals. Since the various provisos all can be true, we indeed see, according to the analysis, that you can know that you are sitting. Thus, Nozick's analysis provides us with a philosophical explanation of the possibility of such knowledge, despite the cavils of the skeptic.

However, one's belief that one is not a brain in a vat cannot meet the requirements of the analysis, according to Nozick. There seems to be no method by which one believes that one is not a brain in a vat, so it seems best to fall back upon the simpler version of the analysis.[19] But here, Nozick holds, proviso (3) fails to be satisfied. If it is not the case that one is not a brain in a vat (that is, if one is a brain in a vat), one would still not believe this. The analysis therefore classifies the belief that one is not a brain in a vat as not a case of knowing.

V. INAPPROPRIATE CONDITIONALS

Under most interpretations that we are likely to make of the letters '*p*' and 'S' in Nozick's schematic analysis of knowing, provisos (3) and (4) will become conditional statements of the sort appropriate to expressing tracking. We obtain such statements in the example discussed above concerning whether you know that you are sitting. In that example, as in other straightforward examples, both conditionals will be contingent in character, and empirical evidence will have to provide the basis on which we judge whether they are true or false — in other words, whether their consequents are inferable from their antecedents.

However, the analysis does not work so smoothly in every possible case. Certain special interpretations of '*p*' and 'S' can be selected under which (3) and (4) do not both become contingent empirical statements. Then (3) and (4) will not be appropriate to express tracking, and Nozick's analysis will have difficulty coming to bear.

For example, suppose that we are interested in whether Socrates (who claims to know nothing) knows that he believes at least one thing. No method seems to be involved, so we use the simpler schema of analysis. Replacing '*p*' by 'Socrates believes something' and 'S' by 'Socrates,' we find that according to the analysis 'Socrates knows that he believes something' is true if and only if:

(1) Socrates believes something;

(2) Socrates believes that he believes something;

(3) if Socrates did not believe anything, then he would not believe that he believes something;

(4) if Socrates believes something, then he believes that he believes something.

Here provisos (1), (2), and (4) are straightforward and give no trouble. However, with (3) a problem arises. Proviso (3) is not a contingent conditional that makes an empirical claim about Socrates' state of belief. Instead, it is a truism, a trivial necessary truth, which says nothing informative about his state of belief.[20] Consequently, (3) makes no proper contribution toward saying that Socrates' state of belief tracks the truth. Because (3) is an inappropriate conditional for our purposes. combining it with (4) does not succeed in this case in capturing the desired idea of tracking. The analysis consequently fails as an elucidation of what it would mean to assert that Socrates knows he believes at least one thing.

Let us remember the idea of tracking as we considered it in connection with a radio system which tracks a satellite. We considered that to be tracking because the system does and would rotate the antenna in varying circumstances so as to maintain maximum signal strength. When the system does indeed track a satellite, that it does so has to be a contingent empirical fact about the system. If we are to characterize this fact by means of a pair of conditional statements of the form that Nozick uses, conditionals that are to express two necessary conditions of the tracking relationship, then these conditionals both should be contingent empirical statements. To let one of them be a necessary truism would short-circuit one of the necessary conditions that our analysis needs to contain. This would deprive our analysis of an essential part of what it ought to be saying and would make it inadequate to the thought we were trying to capture.

Similarly, the idea that someone's state of belief tracks the truth is the idea that what he believes does and would adjust itself in varying circumstances so as to conform to what is the case. When someone's believing does indeed track the truth, this must be a contingent empirical fact about him. If we are to characterize this fact by means of a pair of conditional statements which are supposed to express two necessary conditions for it, then we must employ conditionals both of which are contingent and empirical. Neither can be a necessary truism, for, if one of them were, this would emasculate our analysis by suppressing one of the necessary conditions which it needs to include.

In our example about Socrates, even though Nozick's four-part analysis proves unsatisfactory, we still can revert to the idea of tracking in order to clarify the statement under discussion. We can ask whether Socrates' state of belief about how much he believes would tend to change in conformity with the truth about how many beliefs he holds and how strongly he holds them. if Socrates' beliefs were to increase in number or in strength, would his belief about how much he believes alter correspondingly? By means of questions such as these we can give sense to the idea of tracking in this case, and thereby we can illuminate the meaning of 'Socrates knows that he believes at least one thing,' even though Nozick's four-part analysis fails here because proviso (3) in this case cannot do its normal job.

This indicates that the metaphor of tracking has a broader application than does Nozick's four-part analysis. Conditionals (3) and (4) together do not succeed in capturing what tracking is for every last case. In an eccentric case like this where they fail to do so, we should fall back upon the underlying metaphor of tracking; it can make us think about conditional possibilities other than those made explicit in the four-part analysis, thereby serving to elucidate what knowing is.

Finally, let us come back to the vexed issue of whether one can know that one is not a brain in a vat. Nozick's position is that this cannot be known, because proviso (3) will come out false. Taking 'p' as 'One is not a brain in a vat' and 'S' as naming oneself, proviso (3) requires that if it were not the case that one is not a brain in a vat (that is, if one were a brain in a vat), then one would not believe one was not in that situation. But this is false, Nozick holds, since, under the supposed circumstances, one would believe one was not.

What sort of conditional is this, however? It is not a normal contingent conditional, for in judging it to be true one does not bring to bear empirical background data about oneself, about brains in vats, or about malicious psychologists. There are not and could not be any physiological or psychological studies which would tend to confirm or to disconfirm the conditional in question. How then do we judge that the conditional is true?

The antecedent of this conditional asks one to suppose that one is a brain in a vat, but not just in any kind of vat. One is to suppose specifically that one is a disembodied brain receiving sensory stimulation that is systematically misleading. The malicious psychologist, acting according to his program of deception, provides stimuli which one finds completely indistinguishable from those one would have had if one had had a body and were normally situated. This elaborate supposition is built into the antecedent of the conditional. It is from this supposition and from it alone that the consequent of the conditional follows. It follows simply because, by definition, the misleading stimuli are indistinguishable to one only if one fails to distinguish them from normal stimuli. Hence, the consequent is a truistic deductive consequence of the antecedent; no body of background data is invoked, no inductive reasoning is required.

Thus this conditional is a necessary truth, not a contingent one. Its consequent merely spells out a part of what has been put, by hypothesis, into the antecedent, and which follows deductively from the antecedent. For the reasons already given, such a conditional cannot appropriately serve in an analysis of tracking. Here we have a second and philosophically more important case in which Nozick's four-part analysis fails to apply satisfactorily. The analysis does not work for the particular choice of 'p' and 'S' that we encounter in this example, and hence resort to the analysis does not yield us any acceptable answer to whether this is a case of knowing.

However, this does not mean that Nozick's approach cannot contribute toward the understanding of whether there can be knowledge in this type of case. Setting aside the four-part schema of analysis as inapplicable here, we may fall back on Nozick's basic metaphor of tracking. It can shed light on what it would be for there to be knowing in this case.

In general, when we view knowing in terms of the metaphor of tracking we are going to translate questions of the form 'Does S know that p?' into questions of the form 'Does S's state of belief concerning p track what is the case about p?' To deal adequately with questions of this latter form, we must not focus our attention narrowly on the actual situations of S and on p alone. That would not suffice to capture the idea of tracking, which has to do with potential situations even more than with actual ones. Rather, we should take into account a *range* of different possible situations which S might be in, and, correlated with them, a range of statements more or less akin to p. Of each such situation we should ask whether in it S's state of belief concerning the relevant statements would conform to what is the case. If the range of possible situations has been appropriately chosen, then to say that S's belief concerning p tracks the truth will be to say that S's belief would thus conform to the truth throughout this range of situations.

The question we are considering is whether one knows that one is not a brain in a vat being systematically misled by deceptive sensory input. Let us translate this into the question whether one's belief that this is not the case tracks the truth. In dealing with this issue we ought not to focus solely upon the one extreme situation which the skeptic imagines. To say that someone's belief tracks the truth is to make a claim about how his belief would conform to the truth in a range of possible situations. What range is appropriate here? We must consider a range of situations asymptomatically approaching the one extreme situation that the skeptic imagines. In this range of possible situations, would the subject be able to penetrate the deception? In other words, if one were to become more nearly disembodied in various ways and were to receive various sensory inputs that were rather carefully calculated to deceive, would one's state of belief about whether one was in that situation alter so as to accord with what would then be the case?

Of course this question does not yet have any definite answer, as the 'scenario' is so vaguely defined. How is it supposed to have come about that one's degree of embodiment has become so reduced? What types of deception are being practiced, by what kinds of persons, and for what purposes? These are material details, because they may well make a difference as to whether the subject will be able to penetrate the deception. Background assumptions will have to be made concerning the empirical facts before any conclusion can be reached about whether the subject's belief tracks the truth. Nevertheless, despite the utter vagueness of the question as initially posed, by making judicious assumptions we can turn it into an empirical question to be investigated inductively.

When the issue is framed in this way, naturally there need be no universal answer to the question whether one's belief that one is not a brain in a vat tracks the truth. Perhaps some subjects would be able to penetrate the deception in the relevant range of situations, while others would not be able to do so. Whether a given individual could do so has to depend not only on the detailed facts about the situation, but also on facts about his own psychology—on how skeptical he is, and on how shrewd at interpreting small clues.

Suppose that someone is the sort of shrewd individual who is able to see through such deceptions, even when they become extreme; that is, his belief about the degree to which he is disembodied and is subject to misleading sensory input would reliably conform to the truth under varied circumstances of near-disembodiment and of extensive sensory deception. Then it begins to be proper to say of him that his belief *tracks* the truth in this matter. This sort of requirement is not impossible to meet. Therefore, our conclusion should be that it is possible (though perhaps not easy) for a person's belief to track the truth about his degree of disembodiment. And if his belief tracks it, he knows it.

Thus I conclude that when Nozick says that no one knows whether he is a brain in a vat, Nozick is making more of a concession to skepticism than is called for. He does this because he relies too heavily upon his four-part analysis of knowing, trying to apply it to a case in which it does not work. I suggest that his metaphor of tracking be invoked to make up for the inapplicability to this case of his four-part analysis of knowing, and that the metaphor can show us the way toward an understanding of the case.

NOTES

1. *Philosophical Explanations* (Harvard. 1981), 201.
2. J. Cook Wilson, *Statement and Inference* (Clarendon Press, 1926), especially vol. 1, 34–47.
3. H. A. Prichard, *Knowledge and Perception* (Clarendon Press, 1950), especially 85–91.
4. *The Republic*, Book VI.
5. Bertrand Russell in his widely read book, *The Problems of Philosophy* (Home University Library, 1912), at the beginning of chapter 13 wrote about the conditions of knowing

in a way that would have suggested this view to many readers, even though Russell did not explicitly adopt it.

6. See for example Norman Malcolm's discussion of what he calls "the weak sense" of knowing in his "Knowledge and Belief," *Mind* 51 (1952): 178–189.

7. See for example Roderick Chisholm, *Perceiving* (Ithaca, N.Y.: Conrnell University Press, 1957), 16.

8. Edmund L. Gettier, "Is Justified True Belief Knowledge?" *Analysis* 23 (1963): 121–123.

9. Here I have slightly simplified Nozick's versions of (3) and (4). He uses an arrow symbol for the kind of 'if-then' connective involved here. Later, as a further refinement, he modifies (4) so that it reads "If *p* is true, S believes it and does not also believe not-*p*". See *PE*, 172–176 and 178.

10. I have slightly altered Nozick's wording of proviso (4).

11. Two early treatments of this issue were Roderick Chisholm, "The Contrary-to-fact Conditional," *Mind* 55 (1946): 289–307; and Nelson Goodman, "The Problem of Counterfactual Conditionals," *Journal of Philosophy* 44 (1947): 113–128.

12. Semantical accounts in terms of possible worlds owe their modern popularity to Saul Kripke's use of such semantics for modal logic; see his "Semantical Analysis of Modal Logics, I," *Zeitschrift Für mathematische Logic und Grundlagen der Mathematik* 9 (1963): 67–96. Discussion of possible worlds in relation to contrary-to-fact conditionals has been much influenced by David K. Lewis's *Counterfactuals* (Cambridge, Mass.: Harvard University Press, 1973).

13. The distinction between these two types is vague, of course, to the extent that the distinction between deductive and nondeductive inference is vague. It is important to insist, however, that a distinction can be useful and sound even though it is rather vague.

14. David K. Lewis in his *Counterfactuals* presents a set of guidelines for assessing the comparative 'closeness' of possible worlds. These can equally well be interpreted as guidelines for judging whether one sort of alteration in the data is more minimal than another. They are not at all precise rules, but they bring a little order into an otherwise chaotic matter.

15. Here of course I am rejecting the doctrine, introduced by Russell and since maintained by many logicians, that all inference is deductive. See Bertrand Russell, *Our Knowledge of the External World* (New York: Norton, 1914), Lecture I.

16. For example, John L. Pollack in his *Subjunctive Reasoning* (D. Reidel, 1976) speaks of what he calls 'subjunctive statements' in a way which indicates that he does not mean by this merely statements that are worded in this subjunctive mood; he clearly is trying to use this terminology to mark off a special philosophical category of statements, to which certain kinds of statements will belong regardless of the grammatical mood in which they are formulated. Thus he declares that laws of nature and causal statements are really all subjunctive statements—this despite the fact that they are commonly worded in the indicative mood. This terminology is hardly felicitous, even if there are sound points which those who write this way are trying to convey.

17. *Matthew* 7:9.

18. One modern guide to usage declares, "The subjunctive mood has almost disappeared from English . . . . The . . . indicative mood suffices for supposition, contingencies, and the like." Wilson Follett, *Modern American Usage* (Hill and Wang, 1966), 313.

19. Even if one tried to argue that one knows this via the method of sensory observation, and so invoked the more elaborate schema of analysis, this would not seem to yield any less skeptical a result.

20. The present argument takes for granted that we can recognize proviso (3) in this example to be a statement substantially different in character from those which figured as third provisos in our preceding examples. However, this argument does not need to commit us to the assumption that we have any clear understanding of a universal distinction between analytic and synthetic statements, and certainly need not commit us to embracing all that has been said about that distinction by its traditional advocates.

eleven

NOZICK, EXTERNALISM, AND SKEPTICISM

Laurence BonJour

The avowed purpose of Nozick's epistemological account in *Philosophical Explanations*[1] is to provide an answer to skepticism by showing how it is possible for knowledge to exist in spite of various familiar skeptical possibilities, such as the possibility that my experiences might be produced by a Cartesian demon or the possibility that I might be a brain in a vat whose experiences are produced by artificial stimulation of some sort. The theory that is intended to accomplish this result is one version of an *externalist* theory of knowledge: that is, it holds that the conditions required for knowledge in addition to true belief concern facts about the relation between belief and world which need not (and normally will not) be within the cognitive grasp of the believer; thus such a believer can have knowledge without having any reason for thinking that his belief is true (or even likely to be true). The contrast is with an *internalist* theory according to which it is a requirement for knowledge that the believer have a grasp of such a reason.[2]

My purpose in the present paper is to explore these two aspects of Nozick's position: its externalist character and its attempted response to skepticism. I will argue (1) that externalism is intuitively implausible as an account of knowledge, (2) that Nozick fails to provide an adequate answer to one of the deepest and most troubling kinds of skepticism (and that this failure is in part a result of the externalist character of his view), and (3) that the price paid for a relatively weak response to skepticism, namely the denial that knowledge is closed under known entailment, is alarmingly high.

One preliminary point needs to be mentioned. One feature of Nozick's overall position is a metaphilosophical position which eschews, or at least purports to eschew, the use of arguments in support of the views which he advances (4–7). The motivation (not argument, of course) advanced for this view is quite unconvincing, at least to me: Nozick views arguments primarily as heavy-handed attempts to coerce belief in others and objects to such coercion on something like moral grounds. But arguments are surely to be viewed at least as much as attempts to justify one's own beliefs, to make a case to the reader and, even more importantly, to oneself that more than personal idiosyncrasy is involved, that there is reason to think that the views in question are *true*. The point for the moment, however, is that since I do not know how to take Nozick's views on knowledge seriously other than by looking for arguments for and against them, this is what I will do. (In fact, as one might suspect, there are arguments or at least hints of arguments to be found in Nozick, the main consequence of his metaphilosophical view being only that they are often less clearly identified and developed than one might want.)

I

I begin with a look at the broad outlines of Nozick's position. Though his view of knowledge is very different from the pre-Gettier conception of knowledge as justified true belief, Nozick agrees with that view that the presence of a true belief is a necessary condition for knowledge, i.e. that for a person S to know that *p* requires that the following two conditions be satisfied:

(1) *p* is true.

(2) S believes that *p*.

In place of the familiar requirement of justification, however, Nozick's view requires instead, in first approximation, that the following two further conditions be satisfied:

(3) If *p* weren't true, S wouldn't believe that *p*.

(4) If *p* were true, S would believe that *p*.

As the wording suggests, these two conditionals are to be interpreted as subjunctive rather than material conditionals, so that, for example, (4) is not made true simply by the truth of (2).[3]

Where (3) and (4) are both satisfied, S's holding or not holding the belief that *p* will be directly correlated with the truth or falsity of *p* (in appropriately "close" possible worlds): if *p* is true, S will believe it; and if *p* is false, S won't believe it. Nozick expresses this subjunctive correlation of belief and truth by characterizing a situation in which conditions (1)–(4) are satisfied as one in which the belief in question *tracks* the truth.[4] Knowledge, for Nozick, is thus "a particular way of being connected to the world: tracking it" (178). The reason that this is an externalist requirement is that the knower need have no inkling at all that conditions (3) and (4) are satisfied and thus may well have no reason at all for thinking that his belief is true.

The foregoing account is only an initial approximation, however, for it is easy to see that it is too demanding to be plausible. Even if the particular cognitive procedure or "method" via which S arrived at his belief that p guarantees a perfect correlation with the truth, in the sense captured by (3) and (4), this would obviously not preclude the possibility that S might have employed some other, less satisfactory method or might simply have failed to employ any suitable method at all. The first of these possibilities could falsify (3), since the use of an alternative method could produce a belief that p even if p were false; while either of them could falsify (4) in an analogous way.[5] (For example, I believe that my copy of Nozick is on my desk because I see it there, and this seems to be a case of knowledge. But no matter how trustworthy my vision may be, I still might have arrived at such belief in some other way — for example, by remembering — or might simply not have noticed at all; memory might have yielded such a belief even when it was false, and either reliance on memory or simply not noticing might have led to my having no such belief even though the proposition in question was true.[6]) But it seems intuitively incorrect that the status of S's belief as knowledge should be affected in this way by the mere possibility of methods other than the one which was actually used.

Thus the account needs to be relativized to a particular method or cognitive procedure, yielding the following revised versions of conditions (2)–(4):

(2) S believes, via method or way of coming to believe M, that p.

(3) If p weren't true and S were to use M to arrive at a belief whether (or not) p, then S wouldn't believe, via M, that p.

(4) If p were true and S were to use M to arrive at a belief whether (or not) p, then S would believe, via M, that p. (179)

If condition (1) and the revised versions of (2)–(4) are satisfied, then S knows via method M that p. Knowledge via a specific method is not, however, sufficient for knowledge simpliciter; the latter also requires that the method in question *outweigh* any other method via which S also believes that p, where one method outweighs another, roughly, if its verdict would always be accepted by S in cases where the two methods conflict (182).[7]

One obvious question to ask at this point is how such cognitive procedures or "methods" are to be individuated. Nozick does not attempt to offer a complete discussion of this point, but what he does say is somewhat surprising. The main point is an appeal to experience:

> Usually, a method will have a final upshot in experience on which the be-
> lief is based, such as visual experience, and then (a) no method without
> this upshot is the same method, and (b) any method experientially the
> same, the same "from the inside", will count as the same
> method. . . . (184–85)

Obviously this is fairly vague, and it is easy to imagine cases where it
would be difficult to apply. But the reason it is surprising is that such
an appeal to internal appearances does not seem to agree at all well
with the general externalist trust of Nozick's position. Suppose, for example, that there are two modes of belief production which are quite
different in terms of the causal mechanisms involved but which have
indiscernible experiential "upshots"; suppose further that one of them
satisfies conditions (3) and (4) for some belief p while the other does
not. On the foregoing account, these two modes of belief production
will together constitute one method, one which fails to satisfy (3) and
(4) for the belief in question, so that a belief that p which results from
the reliable mode will be impugned by association with the unreliable
one and hence will not constitute knowledge. And while this result is
obviously correct from an internalist standpoint (since the believer
would have no way of telling the difference between the two modes of
belief production and hence no reason within his grasp for trusting the
beliefs resulting from either), it is not clear why an externalist like
Nozick should accept it.

II

Though Nozick's position is a form of externalism, it differs significantly from most other versions of externalism. The most standard
externalist theories are versions of *reliabilism*: they hold that the main
condition required for a true belief to constitute knowledge is that it be
reliably produced; that is, roughly, that it be a law of nature that a belief with that content produced in those conditions will be true (or, perhaps, is highly likely to be true).[8] In order for a belief that p to constitute knowledge, the reliabilist thus requires that something like
following subjunctive conditional be satisfied:

> (R) If S were to believe that p under the conditions which actually
> obtain, then p would be true.[9]

Some reliabilist theories construe (R) as a condition for epistemic justification which then fits into something like a standard justified true belief conception of knowledge, while others repudiate the justified true
belief conception and construe (R) directly as a requirement for
knowledge.
Nozick's view differs in a variety of ways from these reliabilist ac-

counts. One difference, already mentioned above, is his way of individuating cognitive methods: while the reliabilist appeal to conditions is intended to capture the specific way in which the belief is causally produced, and thus corresponds approximately to Nozick's idea of method, it would be contrary to the main thrust of reliabilism to appeal to the inner experiential "upshot" in the way that Nozick does, and no reliabilist view that I know of does this.

Another difference, the most obvious, is that while the reliabilist views require that the belief in question be sensitive to the truth in one way, namely that such beliefs would only occur, under those conditions, when they would be true (corresponding roughly to Nozick's [3]), they typically do not require that the belief be sensitive to the truth in the opposite direction (corresponding to Nozick's [4]). They say nothing, that is, about whether such a belief will occur (or is to any degree likely to occur), under the specified conditions, when it would be true if it did occur. Thus such a reliabilist view would count as knowledge a belief which is produced in a way which nomologically guarantees that it will be true if it occurs, even if the causal mechanism in question often or even usually fails to produce such beliefs even when they would be true. An example here would be the visual beliefs of a weak-eyed person whose vision is very erratic with regard to how far he can see clearly, and who is very cautious about trusting his vision: such a person will often fail to see and hence fail to believe many true things about his surroundings which he might have seen and believed at some other time; but when he does have such a belief, we may suppose, it is sure to be true. For the reliabilist, such a person's occasional true visual beliefs count as knowledge; while for Nozick they do not, because condition (4) is not satisfied for the method in question.

Though the issue is tangential to the main concerns of this paper, it is quite doubtful that Nozick is correct on this point. While the sort of cognitive virtue which is enshrined in condition (4) is very important — especially in the context of testing a general view or theory by checking to see if its consequences are satisfied — it is hard to see why its failure to obtain for a particular method means that the method fails to yield knowledge even on the (perhaps rare) conditions when it succeeds (so long as [R] or [3] is satisfied): why, for example, the poor-sighted man fails to know even on those occasions when he succeeds in discerning something clearly enough to arrive at a belief about it. Thus the inclusion of condition (4) as a requirement for knowledge appears to be a mistake even from an externalist perspective.

Nozick's main rationale for introducing condition (4) is to deal with a version of the familiar brain-in-a-vat case in which the person's brain is artificially stimulated so as to produce the belief that he is a brain floating in a vat. In such a case, condition (3) is apparently satisfied: if the person weren't a brain in a vat, he wouldn't have come to believe *in that way* that he was; but clearly the belief is not knowledge. Nozick's diagnosis of this case is that the belief in question is not knowledge because it is not sensitive to the truth in the way required by (4) (176–77). But the obvious difference between this case and that of the weak-sighted person is that although (3) is satisfied for the belief in question, the belief that the person is a brain in a vat, it fails to be satisfied for all sorts of very similar beliefs, including even more specific versions of this one (such as the belief that the person is a brain in a red vat); whereas in the case of the weak-sighted person, (3) is satisfied for similar beliefs as well. My suggestion is that some condition in this direction, which I will not pause to formulate exactly, is a more plausible way of ruling out the vat-person's belief as a case of knowledge, so that (4) is not required for this purpose.[10] On this point, then, the more standard externalist view seems preferable to Nozick's.

A more subtle difference between Nozick's position and the reliabilist's concerns condition (3). I have spoken so far as though condition (3) and the reliabilist's condition (R) amounted to more or less the same thing, but this is at least not obviously correct. Look again at (R) and at the version of (3) which is relativized to methods:

(R) If S were to believe that p under the conditions which actually obtain, then p would be true.

(3) If p weren't true and S were to use M to arrive at a belief whether (or not) p, then S wouldn't believe, via M, that p.

If we treat the reference to conditions in (R) and the reference to method in (3) as amounting to the same thing (though we have seen that this is not quite true), then (3) is roughly the contrapositive of (R). And since contraposition is not in general valid for subjunctive conditionals,[11] the two conditions are not equivalent. The difference is that (R) looks at all the "close" counterfactual situations in which S has a belief that p which results from the method in question, stipulating that p is true in all such situations; whereas (3) looks at all the "close" counterfactual situations in which p is false and S employs that method, stipulating that no belief that p results (cf. 266) (R) could be true and (3) false if worlds in which p is false are sufficiently less "close" to the actual world to include worlds in which S, using the method in question, believes p anyway, even though p is true in all "close" worlds in which S believes that p. But while it would be possible to envisage circumstances which would produce this result for particular instances of p, I can see no reason for thinking that it obtains at all widely. Thus it seems safe to treat the two conditions as amounting to at least approximately the same thing.

III

Though it differs from more standard externalist views in the ways discussed, Nozick's view seems vulnerable to the same sorts of objections which apply to those other views. I have argued elsewhere that externalist conditions fail to be sufficient for either epistemic justification or knowledge,[12] and others have argued that such conditions are also not necessary for justification or knowledge.[13] Here I will concentrate on the former sort of argument.

The fundamental idea behind the objection to be developed here is that whereas, from an intuitive standpoint, knowledge is supposed to be a quintessentially *rational* state of mind, in contrast to mere guesswork, prejudice, and the like, a belief which satisfies purely externalist conditions like Nozick's (3) and (4) may in fact be quite irrational. Since the believer need not have any inkling that the external conditions in question are satisfied, he need have no reason at all for thinking that his belief is true or likely to be true, and hence may be quite unreasonable and irresponsible, from an epistemic standpoint, in accepting it.

To provide an intuitively clear illustration of this point, it is necessary to select examples which are somewhat removed from the traditional fare of epistemology. Cases of ordinary perception and introspection will not work, since the intuition that beliefs derived from these sources are in *some* way reasonable or justified is strong enough to override everything else. What is needed are cases for which one can stipulate in an intuitively effective way that *only* the externalist conditions are satisfied, that nothing else of epistemological significance is involved. Previously I have used clairvoyance as an example for this purpose, but in the present paper I will focus instead on telepathy, the alleged psychic power of knowing what is going on in the mind of another person without relying on behavioral cues or other evidence deriving from normal channels of information.

Consider then the following case:

Case I. Leroy is, in his own view at least, very close to his parents and other close relatives and friends, though he rarely calls or writes to them. He regards such communication as unnecessary, because he firmly believes that one can at any time, with only a little effort, achieve a telepathic awareness of the mental states of one's loved ones, though he has no reason, general or specific, for this belief. Leroy believes that he frequently achieves such states of awareness in relation to all of these people, and frequently muses at great length, both to himself and to others, about their fears, joys, hopes, and so on. He has, however, never attempted to confirm the beliefs thus arrived at through more ordinary channels of information. Now, as it happens, Leroy is an extremely reliable telepath in the sole case of his mother: when he is in the right mental set, which we may suppose to be phenomenologically distinctive, his beliefs about her mental states are extremely accurate and complete. But in the case of his father and the others, no such telepathic awareness exists; his beliefs about them, though arrived at in the same phenomenologically distinctive way, are pure fantasy, bearing no relation to the truth. On a certain day, Leroy believes via his supposed telepathic power that his mother is happy. The belief is true and does result from telepathy.

For this belief about his mother, we may suppose that Nozick's conditions (3) and (4), as relativized to the telepathic method, are satisfied (and that there is no other method involved), so that Leroy *knows,* according to Nozick's account, that his mother is happy.

Is this an intuitively plausible result? Clearly Leroy has no reason at all for thinking that his belief about his mother is true, but this in itself will obviously not bother an externalist like Nozick. There are, however, other ways of motivating the intuition that something is seriously amiss with Nozick's account at this point. One way is to compare Leroy's belief about his mother with an analogous belief about his father:

> *Case II.* As in case I, except that Leroy this time arrives at a belief that his father is happy, again thinking that the belief results from his telepathic power. This belief happens, by pure chance, to be true, but it does not result from telepathy.

It seems clear that there is nothing positive to be said about this latter belief from an epistemic standpoint: it is not knowledge on any account and seems to be thoroughly irrational, in spite of being true. But is there enough difference between this belief and the one in Case I to make it plausible to regard the former belief as knowledge while condemning the latter as irrational? Admittedly, it is in an obvious way not an accident that the former belief is true, a way which is captured by Nozick's (3) and (4). But *from Leroy's standpoint,* it is just as much of an accident, a fortuitous coincidence, that (3) and (4) are satisfied for his belief about his mother as that his belief about his father is true, and it is hard to see why the one coincidence should make any more difference to the rationality of the belief than the other. On the contrary, it seems clear that the difference between the two beliefs, whatever other significance it may possess, has nothing to do with rationality or reasonableness or what we might call epistemic responsibility. Thus Nozick's account, like any externalist view, is committed to divorcing knowledge quite completely from the idea of reasonable or rational belief, a result which I take to be highly implausible.

A further way to elaborate the same basic intuitive objection is to have Leroy act on his belief:

Case III. Leroy's sister is worried about their mother, who has lately been quite depressed, even occasionally suicidal. She suggests to Leroy that he telephone her in order to cheer her up and check on her state of mind. (Leroy is her favorite child.) Leroy takes the suggestion seriously, but before actually making the call, he achieves a state of what he believes to be telepathic insight, comes to believe in that way that his mother is already quite happy on that day, and so decides not to bother with the call. The belief is genuinely produced by his telepathic ability and is accordingly true.

Suppose that Leroy's filial duties to his mother are reasonably strong, and consider whether he is *morally* justified in not making the call. Clearly in an analogous case involving his father, which I will not pause to formulate, he would not be justified, but would on the contrary be behaving quite irresponsibly in risking the well-being of a loved one by relying on a psychic ability which he has no reason to think that he possesses. But does the difference between the cases, whatever its epistemic significance may turn out to be, make any difference as to the moral responsibility or irresponsibility of Leroy's behavior? I suggest that it is intuitively clear that it does not, that Leroy is being morally just as irresponsible, and for precisely the same reason, in Case III as in the envisioned analogue.

There is, however, an obvious justification that Leroy can offer for his behavior in Case III, a justification which *seems* as though it should be more than adequate: he can say that he didn't call his mother because he *knew* that she was happy and did not need the call. What assessment are we to make of this response? Assuming as I shall that the foregoing intuitive assessment of the case was accurate, i.e. that Leroy's behavior was not morally justified, there are only three possibilities. The first is that the claim to know, though correct, provides no moral justification for Leroy's action, which amounts to saying that one can know and yet not be morally justified in acting on one's knowledge. This seems obviously unacceptable: if knowledge does not justify appropriate action, then it becomes very hard to see what it is good for or why one should seek it.[14]

The second possibility is that the claim of knowledge is correct and would provide adequate justification if Leroy were in a position to offer it, but that he is not in such a position because, although he knows, he does not know that he knows. This response also does not seem to work, however, even apart from worries about whether it would mean that only knowing that one knows, not knowledge simpliciter, can justify action. For if Leroy has arrived at the true belief that he knows that his mother is happy by reflecting on the phenomenological character of the telepathic experience and if Leroy's telepathic beliefs about his mother satisfy (3) and (4), then his belief that he knows that his mother is happy also satisfies (3) and (4), as relativized to the method of reflection: if he didn't know, he wouldn't believe in that way that he did; and if he did know and used that method, he would know that he did. Thus if Nozick's general account is correct, Leroy does know that he kows.

If the foregoing is correct, then only the third possibility remains: Leroy's claim to know, though it would provide an adequate moral justification if it were true (and perhaps if also he knew that it were true), and though it would be true (and he would know that it was true) if Nozick's general account were correct, does not provide such a justification because it is not true — which means that Nozick's account must be mistaken.

The foregoing intuitive objection to externalism, though it could undoubtedly use more elaboration, seems to me to be overwhelmingly compelling — so much so, indeed, as to make externalist views like Nozick's unacceptable whether or not a viable internalist alternative can be found. But because it is an intuitive objection, it is always open to the externalist to simply bite the bullet and reject the opposing intuitions. I will argue in the final section of this paper, however, that even if we concede Nozick his account of knowledge, he will still be unable to provide a satisfying answer to one of the most important varieties of skepticism.

IV

As already noted, Nozick's discussion of skepticism focuses on those versions of skepticism which appeal to global skeptical hypotheses, such as the possibility that all of my beliefs and experiences are produced by a Cartesian demon or that I am a brain in a vat whose experiences and beliefs are produced by artificial stimulation.[15] He considers two importantly different ways, both of them taking off from his own account of knowledge, in which such possibilities might be thought to generate a skeptical conclusion.

The first skeptical argument claims that, in virtue of such skeptical possibilities, condition (3) of Nozick's account of knowledge is not satisfied for most or all of the ordinary things that we think we know. Suppose that I believe that I am sitting in a chair and typing on a computer. The skeptic points out that if his favorite hypothesis (for example, that I am a brain in a vat) were true, then I might well still believe (via the same method, as individuated by subjective "upshot") that I am sitting in a chair and typing on a computer, even though this would not then be true. Thus it is not the case that if the proposition in question were false, I would not (using the same method) believe it (198–99).

Nozick's response is that this argument depends on a serious misunderstanding of what is claimed by a subjunctive conditional like (3). Properly understood, (3) does not claim that in any situation in which *p* is false, S doesn't believe that *p*, but only that in those non-*p* worlds which are in the neighborhood of the actual world, the worlds which would obtain if *p* were false, S doesn't believe that *p*. Since the skeptic has no way of showing (and obviously cannot just assume) that the possible worlds which realize his favored hypothesis are close enough to the actual world, he has not shown that (3) is false, so that this argument fails (199–200). (Notice, however, that it would also be question-begging to assume, as Nozick seems to at one point [200] that the skeptic's possible worlds are *not* in the neighborhood of the actual world.)

The second skeptical line of argument begins with the claim that we do not know that the skeptical possibilities do not obtain, for example, that we are not brains in vats. Many philosophers would obviously reject this claim, but Nozick is in no position to oppose it, since its truth is a straightforward consequences of his own account of knowledge. For the specific case of knowing that a certain skeptical hypothesis *h* does not obtain, Nozick's condition (3) says that if it were not the case that *h* did not obtain, i.e. if *h* did obtain, the subject S would not believe that *h* did not obtain. Clearly this condition will not be satisfied if *h* is a skeptical hypothesis which has been chosen with reasonable care, for the whole point of such an hypothesis is that if it did obtain, the subject would still have his ordinary common-sense beliefs, which might well include the belief that *h* does not obtain (though this would not always be so, since many subjects have never even considered such hypotheses). Hence no such subject knows, on Nozick's account, that *h* does not obtain (201).

Given this initial premise, the skeptic, according to Nozick, proceeds to reason as follows. The proposition that, for example, I am sitting in a chair and typing on a computer entails that the skeptical possibilities do not obtain, for example, that I am not a brain in a vat, and moreover I know that this is so, namely that *p* entails not-*h*. But if I know that *p* entails not-*h*, then if I knew that *p*, I would also know that not-*h*, which we have just seen is not the case. Assuming that my knowledge of the entailment is beyond question, it follows that I do not know that *p*. The principle which underlies this argument is the principle that knowledge is closed under known logical implication: that is, the principle that if I know one thing and know that this first thing entails a second thing, then I also know the second thing.[16]

One thing to notice at this point is that, contrary to what Nozick seems to suggest (203–4), it is not immediately obvious how the general skeptical conclusion that we know almost nothing is supposed to follow from the foregoing argument. What does seem to follow is that each individual knows almost nothing about his own nonmental personal history. But the extension of this conclusion to propositions about the inanimate physical world or even about other people is not immediate, since these other claims do not entail in any straightforward way that I am not a brain in a vat. I do not wish to claim that there is no way to generalize the argument in this way, but I at least have not succeeded in finding one which remains within the externalist framework. And if the argument cannot be generalized, then Nozick's claim to have given an accurate account of the skeptic's reasoning is seriously impugned, since clearly the typical skeptic who employs one of these skeptical hypotheses wants to claim that a general skepticism results.[17]

Nozick's response to this form of skeptical argument is a straightforward denial of the principle of epistemic closure which underlies it.[18] For the principle to hold, given Nozick's account of knowledge, an analogous principle of closure would apparently have to hold for each of his four conditions of knowledge.[19] But while such a principle of closure obviously holds for condition (1) and may perhaps be assumed to hold for condition (2), at least where the issue of whether q is true has been raised, it does not, Nozick argues, hold for conditions (3) and (4). While the details are complicated, the main point is that while these two conditions as applied to p look to close possible worlds where p is false or true, the conditions for q look instead to close possible worlds where q is false or true. Since these possible worlds need not and in general will not be the same, the fact that a condition is satisfied for p does not in any way guarantee that it will be satisfied for q (206–209). The basic point here is the same one made in the discussion of the first skeptical line of argument: the reason given there to show that the skeptical possibility does not falsify (3) as applied to an ordinary claim (for example, that I am sitting in a chair and typing on a computer) does not extend to (3) as applied to the denial of a skeptical hypothesis (for example, the denial that I am a brain in a vat). Thus this second skeptical argument is also unsuccessful.

How adequate is Nozick's response to skepticism? I will conclude this paper by considering two general difficulties which seem to me to be very serious. The first of these concerns the force and extent of the response itself, while the second concerns the high price paid for this response, namely the denial of epistemic closure.

First, Nozick's response to skepticism, even in relation to those versions of skepticism to which it is intended to apply, is very weak, perhaps too weak to be of very much interest. He does not show or even purport to show that the skeptic is mistaken in claiming that "we know very little or nothing of what we think we know," nor still less that the weaker claim merely that this skeptical position "is no less reasonable than the belief in knowledge," which he offers (197) as an alternate version of skepticism, is mistaken. His thesis is merely that knowledge is *possible* in spite of the fact that the skeptical hypotheses are also possible, and indeed, as it turns out, in spite of the fact that we do not know that they are not true. Thus it is incompatible with only a very strong, perhaps unreasonably strong version of skepticism, one which claims that knowledge is impossible as long as the skeptical hypothesis is even possible.[20]

To be sure, this relatively weak result is one which Nozick himself recognizes and indeed insists upon. In keeping with the general metaphilosophical stance described earlier, he insists that his aim is only to "explain to ourselves how knowledge is possible, not to prove to someone else that knowledge is possible" (198) — that is, not to refute someone else who is inclined towards skepticism. Thus the idea seems to be that even though "we" who believe in knowledge cannot force the skeptic out of his position (and should not, by Nozick's lights, even want to), the skeptic equally cannot force "us" to give up our belief in knowledge. But what this rather chummy first-person-plural formulation overlooks is the possibility that some of "us," unlike Nozick, might not be content to rest comfortably in our common-sensical conviction that we know, given only that it cannot be actually refuted — that we might instead want to find reasons for believing that our supposed knowledge is actual, not merely possible, where the point of finding such reasons is not so much to coerce an imagined skeptic into agreeing as to convince ourselves. For someone who wants to adopt an essentially Socratic stance toward his own conviction that he knows, who is willing (like Descartes) to be in effect his own skeptic, Nozick's discussion is unlikely to be very satisfying. (My suggestion would be that the most compelling and fundamental epistemological issues are precisely those which arise from this Socratic-Cartesian standpoint.)

Moreover, in addition to giving only a very weak response to the versions of skepticism which he does consider, Nozick fails to offer any response at all to other versions of skepticism which arise from the very same skeptical hypotheses. One very natural way to derive a skeptical conclusion from the hypothesis, for example, that I am only a brain in a vat is to point out that a brain in a vat might have the very same putative experiential *reasons* (in the internalist sense) as I do for thinking that its various beliefs about the external world were true, even though those beliefs would be totally false. But, the skeptic now argues, if my experiential reasons could just as well have arisen in a situation in which the beliefs which they seem to support are false, then they do not

give me any genuine reason for thinking that those beliefs are true—
and this is so even if I am in fact not a brain in a vat, even if my experiences are in fact caused in just the way that I think they are. The principle which underlies this argument is that evidence which could have arisen just as well from the truth of either of two competing hypotheses provides no reason to think that one as against the other is true (assuming that the two hypotheses are equally likely prior to the consideration of the evidence). To a skeptical argument of this sort, Nozick, like any externalist, has nothing to say at all.

This variety of skepticism arises most naturally, of course, in the context of an internalist conception of knowledge which makes it a requirement for knowledge that one possess reasons, in the internalist sense, for thinking that one's belief is true: if correct, it would show that the beliefs in question are not knowledge as understood by that conception. I submit, however, that it remains a significant and threatening form of skepticism even if Nozick's externalist conception of knowledge is conceded, for the sake of the argument, to be correct. For it is still alarming and difficult to accept, from both a theoretical and practical standpoint, that we possess no reason at all (in the internalist sense) for thinking that our cherished beliefs about the world are true or even likely to be true—even if we are assured by Nozick that in spite of this we may still have knowledge if the appropriate subjunctive conditionals should happen to hold. Indeed, it is very hard to imagine anyone seriously in the grip of such a skeptical argument finding any comfort at all in Nozick. What I am suggesting is that many at least of the most fundamental, intuitively perplexing, and intellectually disturbing issues in the vicinity of skepticism have to do primarily with the rationality of our beliefs, in more or less the externalist sense, and only secondarily, if at all, with whether or not they may properly be described as "knowledge"—in which case, the controversy between the internalist and externalist conceptions of knowledge may turn out to have substantially less importance for issues of this kind than is often thought.[21]

Second, the price paid for this relatively puny response to skepticism is very high, (though Nozick himself seems not to appreciate fully how devastating his denial of closure is from the standpoint of the intuitive conception of knowledge). One problem is that knowing something does not allow one to reason from it via a known entailment to some further conclusion and thereby know the result, then what, one might well ask, is the point of having knowledge in the first place? In particular, if we infer from our knowledge that a particular course of action is the best choice in a particular situation, we will not thereby know that it is best, leaving it quite unclear how knowledge can serve the crucial role of guiding action.[22]

But though this is serious enough, the main problem with the denial of closure lies deeper still. It arises when we stop to ask what it is that we know when we know that some particular proposition p is true. What, that is, is the *content* of such knowledge? There is, of course, a tautological specification which is readily available: what we know when we know that p is true is simply that p is true. But if we are not content with this, surely the natural thing to say is that the content of our knowledge that p consists, in first approximation, in a knowledge of the truth of the various things entailed by p together with the falsity of the various things whose denials are entailed by p.[23] If Nozick is right, however, this natural answer will not do, for we do not know all of these things merely in virtue of knowing p, and this leaves it quite obscure what we do thereby know.

Some examples draw from Nozick's own discussion may help to illustrate the problem. In the course of discussing skepticism concerning other minds (a narrower version of skepticism which is nevertheless quite parallel to the more general versions discussed above, relying in the same way on a skeptical hypothesis), Nozick makes the astonishing claim that though he knows that his children are at various times happy, sad, proud, embarrassed, or frightened, he does not thereby know that they are not cleverly constructed automata that have no feelings at all (218–20). But does such a view even make coherent sense? What possible content or meaning can the proposition that a particular child is happy at a particular time have for him if it does not even exclude its being such an automaton? Similarly, what content can the known proposition that I am sitting in a chair and typing on a computer have for me if the knowledge in question does not exclude my being a brain in a vat? I can find no intuitively satisfactory answer to questions such as these, none which does not destroy the plausibility of the claim that I genuinely know the propositions in question.

The temptation in the face of such examples is to say that what we know is not the original proposition p, but rather some weaker proposition which entails only that subset of the things entailed by p which can be known by knowing p and knowing the entailment. But apart from the problem that there is no general way to specify which of the things entailed by p fall into this subset, the problem would merely repeat itself for the new proposition. It is surely very tempting to regard this difficulty as a *reductio ad absurdum* of Nozick's whole conception of knowledge.[24]

My conclusion is that Nozick's account of knowledge is inadequate, both because of its externalist character and because of the further consequence that the denial of closure makes it seemingly impossible to give a coherent account of what it is that we are supposed to know. In addition, even if the account of knowledge were acceptable, the response to skepticism which emerges (and which seems to provide the main motivation for the view) seems inadequate in both strength and extent.[25]

NOTES

1. Robert Nozick, *Philosophical Explanations* (Cambridge, Mass.: Harvard University Press, 1981), ch. 3. References in the text are to the pages of *Philosophical Explanations*.

2. Unless, of course, having a reason for thinking that a belief is true is also given an externalist construal. (Nozick does offer externalist accounts of the related notions of evidence and justification.) But if the issue between externalism and internalism is not to be obscured by verbal legislation, some locution in this vicinity must be reserved for the internalist; in this chapter "having a reason to think that a belief is true" will play that role. For a general discussion of externalism and an implicit contrast with internalism (though that term is not employed) see my book, *The Structure of Empirical Knowledge* (Cambridge, Mass.: Harvard University Press, 1985), ch. 3.

3. Nor is (4) to be made true simply by the fact that S holds contradictory beliefs; I will not bother here, however, with the reformulation needed to avoid such a result. According to David Lewis's account in *Counterfactuals* (Cambridge, Mass.: Harvard University Press, 1973), a subjunctive conditional is true whenever its antecedent and consequent are both true, so that the truth of (1) and (2) in the actual world would suffice for the truth of (4). Nozick rejects this result, holding roughly that the truth of a counterfactual requires that its consequent be true throughout the "neighborhood" of the actual world in which the antecedent is true, where this "neighborhood" will always include more than just the actual world itself, even if the antecedent is true there. Cf. 680–81, n. 8.

4. It would be more natural to use the term 'tracking' to describe the situation in which (3) and (4) are satisfied, whether or not (1) and (2) are also satisfied; this is in fact what Nozick occasionally does later on, e.g. at p. 249, but not in the passage where the term is first introduced.

5. This account is too simple, for such a possibility is only relevant if it would have occurred in some appropriately "close" counterfactual situation. Nozick spends a substantial amount of space on the subtleties of the possible worlds account of subjunctive conditionals, but the issues involved are largely beyond the scope of the present discussion.

6. As this example suggests, "methods" need not involve anything which is deliberately methodical; any way of arriving at a belief will count, for Nozick, as a use of some method (184).

7. Here again I am ignoring some qualifications and refinements which do not matter for present purposes.

8. For an example of such a view, see D. M. Armstrong, *Belief, Truth and Knowledge* (London: Cambridge University Press, 1973). A similar view, differing from Armstrong's in requiring only high rather than perfect reliability, is offered by Alvin Goldman in his paper "What is Justified Belief?" in *Justification and Knowledge* ed. George Pappas, (Dordrecht, Holland: Reidel, 1979), 1–23. Though they are not entirely clear on this point, both Armstrong and Goldman seem to accept something like the justified true belief account of knowledge, and hence to offer reliabilist accounts of justification rather than directly of knowledge.

9. Obviously the conditions in question must be delimited so as not to include the truth or falsity of the belief. Just how this can be done is a difficult issue, but fortunately one which is beyond the scope of this paper.

10. A second case which (4) is supposed to handle is Harman's example of the political assassination which is first reported and then officially denied in a way which would convince anyone who heard the denials; an isolated individual who chances not to hear the denials and thus continues to believe that the assassination took place does not seem intuitively to possess knowledge, even though the belief in question might seem to satisfy (3) (177). (See Gilbert Harman, *Thought* [Princeton: Princeton University Press, 1973], 142–54.) In this case, however, it is not clear that (3) is satisfied, and hence not clear that (4) is needed to rule out this belief as a case of knowledge.

11. See, e.g., Lewis, *Counterfactuals,* 35.

12. See *The Structure of Empirical Knowledge,* ch. 3. An earlier version of this argument appeared in "Externalist Theories of Empirical Knowledge," *Midwest Studies in Philosophy* 5 (1980): 53–73.

13. See, for example, Richard Foley, "What's Wrong with Reliabilism?" *Monist* 68 (1985): 188–202.

14. We will observe below a further reason for doubting the relevance of knowledge, as conceived by Nozick, to the justification of action.

15. Nozick seems to suggest and may well want to claim that all varieties of skepticism are of this general sort (though some may appeal to narrower skeptical hypotheses, e.g. the hypothesis that the apparently injured person who is writhing on the ground is only acting). Such a claim seems to me obviously false, but I will not discuss it here.

16. Indeed, Nozick seems to suggest (204) that all skeptical arguments depend on this principle. But it is very doubtful that this is the case: Nozick's first skeptical argument, discussed above, seems to provide one counterexample; others will emerge later.

17. As already noted, Nozick does discuss later on how other sorts of beliefs can be challenged by narrower forms of the same skeptical move: e.g., the belief that the individual writhing on the ground is in severe pain may be challenged by appeal to the skeptical possibility that what I am observing is a programmed automaton (281–20). But this does not affect the point made in the text.

18. Nozick also notes that the principle as formulated above is very likely too simple, that an adequate formulation would involve not only first-level knowledge but also the second-level knowledge of such knowledge (205–6). I will, however, follow him in assuming that these complications do not affect the main issue and will accordingly ignore them here.

19. "Apparently," because this assumes that the satisfaction of, e.g., condition (3) for *q* where *p* is known to entail *q* would have to follow, if at all, only from the satisfaction of condition (3) for *p* (together with the knowledge of the entailment), rather than somehow depending also on the satisfaction for *p* of one or more of the other three conditions. But this assumption seems reasonable enough.

20. Such a version of skepticism is, of course, at least part of what troubled Descartes (and many others). But there it seems to depend essentially on a definition of knowledge which demands logical certainty or infallibility, relative to one's evidence; since Nozick, like most recent philosophers, clearly would not accept such a definition even apart from his particular conception of knowledge, he does not need that conception to handle Descartes's problem.

21. My own view is that the sort of skeptical argument just discussed can be answered only by showing either: (1) that the experiential evidence in question, though it could have been produced in the way suggested by the skeptical hypothesis, is substantially less likely to have been produced in that way than in the way suggested by the nonskeptical alternative; or (2) that the skeptical hypothesis is less likely to be true from an a priori standpoint. In fact, it seems likely that some skeptical hypotheses can only be dealt with in the first of these ways, while others can only be dealt with in the second — and also that the plausibility of skepticism derives in substantial part from a failure to specify skeptical hypotheses fully enough to make clear which of these approaches is applicable. For a tentative attempt at a refutation of skepticism along these lines, in the context of a coherence theory of epistemic justification, see *The Structure of Empirical Knowledge,* ch. 8.

22. It should be noted that Nozick's view is not that we never know things by virtue of the fact that they follow from things we know via known entailments. He holds rather that inference of this sort sometimes yields knowledge and sometimes does not, and even offers some discussion of which formal rules always preserve knowledge (existential instantiation, addition, and conjunction) and which do not (universal instantiation and simplification). But this does not seem to help very much in meeting the problems discussed in the text, especially since very many actual entailments fail to fall neatly under formal rules.

23. An adequate version of this view would have to exclude at least necessary truths and the denials of necessary falsehoods and also various complicated, purely formal entailments. But it seems very unlikely that such refinements would affect the sorts of cases which matter for present purposes, such as the examples considered in the text.

24. And of many other accounts as well, since, as Nozick (following Dretske) points out, any account which relies on subjunctives in a similar way will also yield nonclosure.

25. I am grateful to Ann Baker and David Haugen for helpful comments on an earlier version of this paper.

twelve

OFFTRACK BETS AGAINST THE SKEPTIC

Ernest Sosa

Philosophical Explanations tries to explain how various things are possible, which is argued to be a main task for philosophy. Our focus here will be the part on epistemology, where the question is how we can know despite skeptical arguments. The explanation in this part tries to defuse the arguments of the skeptic through a novel account of knowledge.

Nozick's reasoning is attractively imaginative, as indeed it has to be for the novelty it attains in so old a field. The literature gathering around it has spotted a number of problems, some of which appear rather formidable. They do not consign the view to early oblivion, however, since it can remain an attractively simple and interesting alternative to be retained at least within peripheral sight. Philosophy conceives many possibilities, and many can deserve attention at any given time even if some then look inferior to others. Though I agree with Nozick on that point of metaphilosophy, I cannot be sanguine about his proposals in epistemology. Anyhow I hope we can do better, for they are not entirely trouble-free. This has been explained at some length already or is about to appear, so I will not delay over it for any twists of my own.[1] What follows will focus instead on a certain consequence whose importance, which strikes me as high, is nicely matched by its neglect to date.[2]

Part I will present Nozick's preferred account of knowledge, Part II will present his use of that account in responding to the skeptic, and Part III will examine that response.

I

According to Nozick's Tracking Account, to know that p requires that one correctly believe that p, and either that one's belief "track the truth" with regard to the question whether p, if one's belief was formed by means of no method, or else that one's belief track the truth given employment of the method actually used in forming that belief. More explicitly (where '$p \to q$' abbreviates 'If it were the case that p then it would be the case that q'):

S knows that p if and only if
    (1)   it is true that p

    (2)   S believes that p; and either

    (3a) S uses no method to form his belief that p, and both

         (i)   not-$p \to$ not-(S believes that p), and

         (ii) $p \to$ S believes that p; or else

    (3b) S uses a single method M to form his belief that p, and both

         (i)   (not-p and S uses M to form belief on the question whether p) $\to$ not-(S believes that p), and

         (ii) (p and S uses M to form belief on the question whether p) $\to$ (S believes that p)

(Actually, some further embellishments are added to that sketch, but these will not be relevant to our discussion.)

II

Nozick's account of knowledge has the important virtue of enabling an explanation of how we can possibly know so much of what ordinarily we take ourselves to know, despite the powerful arguments deployed by skeptics. His discussion is focused more specifically on recurring skeptical reasoning that takes the following argument form:

    (1) S knows that p.

                                          Assumption

    (2) S deduces that q from the premise that p.

                                          Assumption

    (3) If S knows that p and S deduces that q from the premise that p, then S knows that q.

                                          Assumption

    (4) It follows that S knows that q.

                                          From 1, 2, 3

    (5) But in fact S does *not* know that q.

                                          Assumption

In his reasoning the skeptic affirms (2), (3), and (5), drawing from these the conclusion that S does *not* after all know that *p*. Here is a concrete example.

(1) S knows (*P*) *that he is sitting before a fire.*

Assumption

(2) S deduces (*Q*) *that there is no Cartesian demon who is deceiving him into thinking falsely that he is sitting before a fire by giving him the appropriate sensory illusion of sitting before a fire* from premise *P* (above).

Assumption

(3) If S knows *P* and deduces *Q* from premise *P*, then S knows *Q*.

(4) It follows that S knows *Q*.

From 1, 2, 3

(5) But in fact S has no way of knowing *Q*.

Assumption

And here the skeptic goes on to argue from the affirmation that one cannot know oneself not to be the victim of a Cartesian demon (5) by *reductio* to the conclusion that S does not after all know himself to be sitting before a fire (by *reductio,* therefore, to the negation of [1]). In his *reductio* the skeptic hence affirms not only (5) but also (2) and (3).

Granted success in such a case, the skeptic quickly spreads his attack to cover all supposed perceptual knowledge. Nozick is willing to grant the skeptic something — in keeping with his doctrine's appeal down through the ages — but not nearly everything. Indeed, Nozick's own account of knowledge bears out the skeptic's assumption that one cannot know oneself to be safe from the Cartesian demon. Though the skeptic be granted that much, yet we need not follow him all along his radical way, nor even so far as to deny with him the very possibility of perceptual knowledge. How then can perceptual knowledge be possible, however, if we cannot rule out the demon? The explanation is said to lie in our mistaken assumption that one always knows whatever one deduces from the already known to one (assumption [3] above).

It is indeed Nozick's view that though we cannot rule out, with knowledge, skeptical hypotheses of a Cartesian demon (or the like), it is yet a fallacy to deny on that basis the very possibility of perceptual knowledge. We can indeed know the colors and shapes of things around us, even if we cannot know ourselves safe from the demon.

And the reason is of course that we *can* track the colors and shapes of things around us even if we *cannot* track the presence or absence of a demon who deceives us.

III

Nozick makes a very persuasive case, to my mind conclusive, that on his account of knowledge one does not necessarily always know what one deduces from the already known. The basic reason is of course that deduction does not preserve tracking. Indeed he also shows that though in general we fail to know the falsehood of skeptical hypotheses like that of the deceiving demon, yet this does not on his account preclude much ordinary knowledge. All this is shown about as conclusively as it is possible to show anything within the bounds imposed by crucial use of the subjunctive and of the notion of a "method" for forming beliefs.

If the main philosophical task were simply to show how various things are possible, the demonstration of how ordinary knowledge is possible despite the skeptic would be philosophically a paramount virtue of the Tracking Account of Knowledge. And it *is* often important to explain how something is possible when we know the thing in question to be thus possible. What we seek in such explanation seems in fact nothing more remarkable than the traditional philosophical and scientific ideal of more comprehensive coherence in our view of things (in the face of skeptical challenge). But the skeptic is challenging not only the claim that it is *possible* for us to have perceptual and other ordinary knowledge. The skeptic challenges also our claim that we do *in fact* have such knowledge. Accordingly, we should like the possibility of our knowledge to be shown coherent with our account of knowledge, true enough, but we want the *actuality* of such knowledge also to be shown coherent — all in view of relevant skeptical challenges, like the challenge that we can't know ourselves to be safe from the Cartesian demon.

What again is required by the Tracking Account for one to know oneself to sit before a fire? — that believing oneself to be thus seated track the corresponding fact. Therefore: if I accept the Tracking Account and believe myself to know I sit before a fire, I must think my belief that I so sit to track its object. But then for comprehensive coherence I must also believe myself free of the deceiving demon. What is more, for coherence my degree of conviction in this latter belief must match the degree of my conviction in the former. The robustness of our conviction in the reality of our ordinary knowledge therefore requires in coherence that we believe ourselves free of the deceiving demon with comparably robust conviction. For coherence the Tracking

Account hence requires us to be sure that we are free of a deceiving demon — about as sure as that we know the colors and shapes of objects presently perceived, et cetera. This is required for two reasons: first, because from the believed proposition, that p, it follows logically that no one is making us *falsely believe that p*; and, second, because if our minds are under the control of a Cartesian demon, then even if he is not deceiving us on the particular question whether p, even if on this particular question he does allow us correct belief, yet our belief that p does not track the truth, for what we believe then depends not on the truth about the matter in question but rather on the whims of the Cartesian demon. What is more, the Tracking Account also requires us to think that for all we know at all we are *not* free of a deceiving demon. The Tracking Account therefore exacts the following combination of commitments: (a) conviction on one's part that one *is* free of the deceiving demon, and (b) conviction on one's part, at the very same time, that one has no knowledge at all as to whether one is or is not free of the deceiving demon. And that falls somewhat short of perfect coherence. In fact, I myself regard it as a form of incoherence. Not that it is incoherent for S to be quite convinced that p without knowing that p. No, that much happens all the time. No absurdity is entailed. All it takes is a simple mistake. What strikes me as incoherent is rather any case where someone is fully convinced that p while yet admitting that for all he knows *at all* it's actually false that p: 'I am quite certain there is no demon fooling me *but,* for all I know at all, there really is one.'

In discussion I have encountered two responses on behalf of the Tracking Account, and these I have found to be evenly matched in number of adherents and in degree of plausibility, but they are actually in polar opposition. According to the first response, though the denial of various skeptical hypotheses does follow from our robust self-attributions of ordinary knowledge, and though such denial if comparably robust would fail to cohere with our recognition that our robust denial is no knowledge at all, still in the face of that it would be best to avert our eyes and turn away: to disregard and never make any of the denials that we see so clearly to follow from our robust commitments.

The reasoning behind our objection to the Tracking Account assumes the following (or the like):

(C) If a given degree of conviction that p is appropriate for S and S deduces that q from the premise that p, then a comparable degree of conviction that q is appropriate for S.

Thus, appropriateness of conviction is said to be preserved through deduction. But, developing now the 'first response' (above) to our objection, might one not resist assumption (C) with the following two thoughts?

(a) It might be urged, in the first place, that coherence has to be assessed by considering the relation of a belief to a network. Recall moreover that we have already allowed, for the sake of argument, that knowledge is not preserved through deduction (when we allowed the rejection of Assumption 3 in the skeptic's argument above). Hence it might now be urged further that simple coherence requires allowing also that appropriateness of conviction is not preserved through deduction either.

(b) Besides, rejecting the claim that deduction preserves appropriateness of conviction also coheres better with our belief that, in allocating conviction, one should be guided by one's opinions as to whether one *knows*. We do ordinarily look askance at people with too high a degree of confidence in something they can see to lie beyond their ken.

Against such a twofold response it must be said that if deductive reasoning fails us not only as a sure source of knowledge but even as a guide to belief, one has to wonder what detectives, scientists, lawyers, and philosophers are supposed to be doing. What are we doing right here and now? Why adduce (a) and (b) if any reasoning from them will have no bearing on the degree of assurance appropriate for the conclusion? And the same goes for the reasoning that takes place *within* (a) and (b). Or are we to suppose that deductive reasoning can *sometimes* guide allocation of degree of assurance, but cannot always be allowed to do so. The implication is then of course that (i) the reasoning that leads to the negation of the deep skeptical hypotheses does *not* preserve degree of appropriate conviction, whereas (ii) the reasoning with (a) and (b) and from (a) and (b) to (i) *does* preserve degree of appropriate conviction. Here again I can't help sensing more than a whiff of incoherence. At a minimum we would need an explanation of just what distinguishes the cases in which deductive reasoning does preserve degree of appropriate conviction from the cases in which it does not.

That concludes our discussion of the first response. According to the second response, the Tracking Account can even more easily handle the objection. For if one adopts *that* account, one could be quite convinced of one's freedom from any deceiving demon, yet easily admit that one does not *know* oneself to be free of any such demon. Surely one can be quite convinced of one's freedom from any demon, while willingly conceding that one fails to track that fact. The two attitudes are by no means incompatible.

This second response strikes me as unpersuasive. One might as well respond to Gettier by insisting that if by knowledge one just *means* justified true belief, one is then entitled to disregard that whole literature (perhaps with a sigh of relief). What our objection holds incoherent is the combination of full conviction on some matter along with denial that one has any knowledge at all about it; and knowledge here should be presumed to mean knowledge as commonly understood, unless we are shown sufficient reason to attribute ambiguity to the ordinary word "knowledge," or to introduce a 'reforming definition,' or the like. It is true that according to the Tracking Account there is no incoherence, but from this one might reasonably conclude not that our sense of incoherence is an illusion but rather that the Tracking Account is inadequate. The difficulty raised here is certainly not advanced as any kind of knockdown argument; and that not because aggressive figures are offensive in philosophy,[3] but more importantly because philosophy has little if any room for any such absolute proof, deductive or other. The difficulty is rather a consequence worth pondering, along with the more weighty consequence that if knowledge is tracking then deduction fails to transmit knowledge since it fails to transmit tracking.

The Tracking Account saves us from incoherence on the possibility of much ordinary knowledge despite granting the skeptic his general skeptical scenarios like that of the deceiving demon, and his claim that we can't know ourselves safe from them. But the Tracking Account leads us into incoherence on the actuality of much ordinary knowledge, and for that reason we may well find against it. It is an interesting account, of course, and not one to be dumped from our basket.[4] But there had better be alternatives higher up the plausibility ranking.

To its credit the Tracking Account does explain to us a *possible* way in which one might have knowledge despite conceding to the skeptic one's inability to rule out with knowledge his deep skeptical hypotheses (evil demon, brain in a vat, et cetera). But the Tracking Account also presses upon us two unwelcome consequences. First, it implies that even the simplest and most obvious deduction from the already known yet needn't yield knowledge in turn, as has been widely lamented. Nozick himself takes note of this consequence and tries to turn critical weakness into spectacular strength by using precisely that consequence for a novel response to the skeptic. But that very response itself depends crucially on the second unwelcome consequence. For it requires that we who consider the skeptic's radical hypotheses must *reject* them about as robustly as we attribute to ourselves our various instances of ordinary knowledge. But every such robust denial of a radical skeptical hypothesis must also be linked — incoherently, as it seems to me — with the further belief on our part that, for all we know, that radical skeptical hypothesis is in fact true. (That is, it must be so linked just as soon as we both consider the question whether we do or do not know about the radical skeptical hypothesis, and also perceive the consequence of the Tracking Account for that question.) The reflective Nozickian is hence constantly forced to deny the radical hypotheses of the skeptic, but his denials are always mere bluster, never knowledge, since they never track the truth. They are offtrack bets against the skeptic, nothing more, and yet we are forced to accord them the conviction appropriate to secure knowledge, while fully assured that they are nothing of the sort.[5]

NOTES

1. Robert Shope, "Cognitive Abilities, Conditionals, and Knowledge: A Response to Nozick," *The Journal of Philosophy* 81 (1984) 29–48. Graeme Forbes, "Nozick on Scepticism," *The Philosophical Quarterly* 53, no. 134: 43–52. Steven Luper-Foy, "The Epistemic Predicament: Knowledge, Nozickian Tracking, and Skepticism," *The Australasian Journal of Philosophy* 62 (1984); and "What Skeptics Don't Know Refutes Them," forthcoming in *The Pacific Philosophical Quarterly*. Also, in volume 43 (1983) of *Analysis:* Raymond Martin, "Tracking Nozick's Sceptic: A Better Method," 28–33; Crispin Wright, "Keeping Track of Nozick," 134–40; B. J. Garrett, "Nozick on Knowledge," 181–84 (replying to but also supplementing Martin's critique of Nozick). In volume 44 (1984): David Gordon, "Knowledge, Reliable Methods, and Nozick," 30–33 (a reply to Martin and Garrett); Jonathan Dancy, "On the Tracks of the Sceptic," 121–126 (supplementing Wright's critique); B. J. Garrett, "Nozick and Knowledge – A Rejoinder," 194–96 (a rejoinder to Gordon). And in volume 45: Anthony L. Brueckner, "Losing Track of the Sceptic," 103–4 (a reply to Dancy).

2. In fact the consequence follows already from Fred Dretske's presentation of a similar view in three articles of fifteen to twenty years ago: "Reasons and Consequences," *Analysis* 28 (1968); "Epistemic Operators," *Journal of Philosophy* 67 (1970) 1007–23; and "Conclusive Reasons," *Australasian Journal of Philosophy* 49 (1971) 1–22.

3. "Why are philosophers intent on forcing others to believe things? Is that a nice way to behave towards someone? . . . So don't look here for a knockdown argument that there are no knockdown arguments, for the knockdown argument to end all knockdown arguing." (*Philosophical Explanations,* 5.)

4. "Even when one view is clearly best, though, we do not keep only this first ranked view, rejecting all the others. Our total view is the basket of philosophical views, containing all the admissible views." (*Philosophical Explanations,* 21–22.)

5. My thanks to Steven Luper-Foy and Robert Shope for their comments.

BIBLIOGRAPHY

Below are selected works pertaining to the following topics: those directly concerned with Nozick's epistemology, those dealing with the transmission of justification or of knowledge through entailment, and ones dealing with subjunctive conditionals. For works discussing naturalistic theories of knowledge, see Frederick Schmitt's bibliography in *Naturalizing Epistemology,* ed. H. Kornblith (Cambridge: MIT Press, 1985), 269-301.

I. ARTICLES THAT DISCUSS NOZICK'S EPISTEMOLOGY

Brueckner, Anthony L. "Why Nozick is a Sceptic." *Mind* 93 (1984): 259-65.

———. "Losing Track of the Sceptic." *Analysis* 45 (1985): 103-4.

Burnyeat, M. F. "The Matter of Fact Omelette Eater." *Times Literary Supplement,* October 15, 1982.

Dancy, Jonathan. "On the Tracks of the Sceptic." *Analysis* 44 (1984): 121-26.

Ellis, Anthony. Review in *Mind* 93 (1984): 450-55.

Fogelin, Robert. Review in *The Journal of Philosophy* 80 (1983): 819-25.

Foley, Richard. "What's Wrong with Reliabilism? *The Monist* 68 (1985): 188-202.

Forbes, Graeme. "Nozick on Scepticism." *The Philosophical Quarterly* 34 (1984): 43-52.

———. "A Reply to Mazoué and Brueckner." *The Philosophical Quarterly* 35 (1985): 196-99.

Garrett, B. J. "Nozick on Knowledge." *Analysis* 43 (1983): 181-84.

———. "Nozick and Knowledge – a Rejoinder." *Analysis* 44 (1984): 194-96.

Goldman, Alvin. Review in *Philosophical Review* 92 (1983): 81-88.

———. "An Explanatory Analysis of Knowledge." *American Philosophical Quarterly* 21 (1984): 101-8.

Gordon, David. "Knowledge, Reliable Methods, and Nozick." *Analysis* 44 (1984): 30–33.

Harrison, Ross. Review in *Ratio* 26 (1984): 205–7.

Holland, R. F. Review in *Philosophy* 58 (1983): 118–21.

Johnsen, Bredo. "Nozick on Skepticism." *Philosophia,* forthcoming.

Kirkham, Richard L. "Does the Gettier Problem Rest on a Mistake?" *Mind* 93 (1984): 501–13.

Luper-Foy, Steven. "The Epistemic Predicament: Knowledge, Nozickian Tracking, and Skepticism." *The Australasian Journal of Philosophy* 62 (1984): 26–48.

———. "What Skeptics Don't Know Refutes Them." *The Pacific Philosophical Quarterly* 65 (1984): 86–96.

Martin, Raymond. "Tracking Nozick's Sceptic: a Better Method." *Analysis* 43 (1984): 28–33.

Mazoué, James G. "Nozick on Inferential Knowledge." *The Philosophical Quarterly* 35 (1985): 191–93.

McGinn, Colin. "The Concept of Knowledge." *Midwest Studies in Philosophy, vol. 9, Causation and Causal Theories,* ed. Peter A. French, Theodore E. Uehling, Jr., and Howard K. Wettstein. Minneapolis: University of Minnesota Press, 1984.

Schmitt, Frederick. "Knowledge as Tracking?" *Topoi* 4 (1985): 73–80.

Shope, Robert. "Cognitive Abilities, Conditionals, and Knowledge: A Response to Nozick." *The Journal of Philosophy* 81 (1984): 29–48.

Swinburne, Richard. Review in *Australasian Journal of Philosophy* 61 (1983): 303–7.

Wright, Crispin. "Keeping Track of Nozick." *Analysis* 43 (1983): 134–40.

II. BOOKS THAT DISCUSS NOZICK'S EPISTEMOLOGY

Dancy, Jonathan. *Introduction to Contemporary Epistemology.* Oxford: Basil Blackwell, 1985.

Stroud, Barry. *The Significance of Philosophical Scepticism.* Oxford: Oxford University Press, 1984.

Ziff, Paul. *Epistemic Analysis: A Coherence Theory of Knowledge.* Dordrecht: Reidel, 1984.

III. ARTICLES DEALING WITH TRANSMISSION OF JUSTIFICATION OR KNOWLEDGE THROUGH ENTAILMENT

Adler, J. "Skepticism and Universalizability." *Journal of Philosophy* 78 (1981): 143–56.

Bogdan, Radu J. "Cognition and Epistemic Closure." *American Philosophical Quarterly* 22 (1985): 55–63.

Brueckner, Anthony L. "Epistemic Universalizability Principles." *Philosophical Studies* 46 (1984): 297–305.

———. "Skepticism and Epistemic Closure." *Philosophical Topics* 13 (1985): 89–117.

_____. "Transmission for Knowledge Not Established." *The Philosophical Quarterly* 35 (1985): 193–96.

Carrier, L. S. "Skepticism Disarmed." *Canadian Journal of Philosophy* 13 (1983): 107–14.

Dretske, Fred. "Epistemic Operators." *Journal of Philosophy* 67 (1970): 1007–23.

_____. "Conclusive Reasons." *Australasian Journal of Philosophy* 49 (1971).

_____. "The Pragmatic Dimension of Knowledge." *Philosophical Studies* 40 (1981): 363–78.

Hooker, Michael. "In Defense of the Principle for Deducibility of Justification." *Philosophical Studies* 24 (1973): 402–5.

Hempel, Carl. "Studies in the Logic of Confirmation." In *Aspects of Scientific Explanation*. New York: Free Press, 1965.

Johnson, Bredo. "Skeptical Rearmament." *Canadian Journal of Philosophy* 15 (1985): 507–9.

Luper-Foy, Steven. "The Epistemic Predicament: Knowledge, Nozickian Tracking, and Skepticism." *Australasian Journal of Philosophy* 62 (1984): 26–49.

_____. "The Causal Indicator Analysis of Knowledge." *Philosophy and Phenomenological Research,* forthcoming.

Olen, Jeffrey. "Knowledge, Probability, and Nomic Connections." *Southern Journal of Philosophy* 15 (1977): 521–26.

Sanford, David H. "Knowledge and Relevant Alternatives: Comments on Dretske." *Philosophical Studies* 40 (1981): 379–88.

Saunders, John Turk. "Thalberg's Challenge to Justification via Deduction." *Philosophical Studies* 23 (1972): 358–64.

Shatz, David. "Reliability and Relevant Alternatives." *Philosophical Studies* 39 (1981): 393–408.

Shuger, Scott. "Knowledge and Its Consequences." *American Philosophical Quarterly* 20 (1983): 217–26.

Stine, Gail. "Dretske on Knowing the Logical Consequences." *Journal of Philosophy* 68 (1971): 296–99.

_____. "Skepticism, Relevant Alternatives and Deductive Closure." *Philosophical Studies* 29 (1976): 249–60.

Thalberg, Irving. "In Defense of Justified True Belief," *Journal of Philosophy* 66 (1969): 798–803.

_____. "Is Justification Transmissible Through Deduction?" *Philosophical Studies* 25 (1974): 347–56.

Vinci, Thomas. "Review of Klein's *Certainty.*" *The Canadian Journal of Philosophy* 14 (1984): 125–45.

Yourgrau, Palle. "Knowledge and Relevant Alternatives." *Synthese* 55 (1983): 175–90.

IV. BOOKS DEALING WITH TRANSMISSION OF JUSTIFICATION OR KNOWLEDGE THROUGH ENTAILMENT

Dretske, Fred. *Knowledge and The Flow of Information.* Cambridge, Mass.: MIT Press. See also Open Peer Commentary, *Behavioral and Brain Sciences* 6 (1983): 63–82; and Dretske's Response, "Why Information?" 82–89.

Klein, Peter. *Certainty: A Refutation of Skepticism.* Minneapolis: University of Minnesota Press, 1981.

Goodman, Nelson. *Fact, Fiction and Forecast.* Indianapolis: Hackett, 1979. Ch. 3.

Scheffler, Israel. *The Anatomy of Inquiry.* Indianapolis: Bobbs-Merrill, 1963. Part 3.

Unger, Peter. *Ignorance.* Oxford: Oxford University Press, 1975.

V. SUBJUNCTIVE CONDITIONALS: ARTICLES

Bennett, Jonathan. "Counterfactuals and Possible Worlds." *Canadian Journal of Philosophy* 4 (1974): 381–402.

———. "Counterfactuals and Temporal Direction." *The Philosophical Review* 93 (1984): 57–91.

Bigelow, John. "If-Then Meets Possible Worlds." *Philosophia* 6 (1976): 215–35.

Chisholm, Roderick M. "The Contrary-to-Fact Conditional." *Mind* 55 (1946): 289–307.

Davis, Wayne A. "Indicative and Subjunctive Conditionals." *The Philosophical Review* 88 (1979): 544–64.

Downing, P. B. "Subjunctive Conditionals, Time Order, and Causation." *Proceedings of the Aristotelian Society* 59 (1958–59): 125–40.

Fine, Kit. Review of Lewis's *Counterfactuals. Mind* 84 (1975): 451–58.

Goodman, Nelson. "The Problem of Counterfactual Conditionals." *Journal of Philosophy* 44 (1947): 113–28.

Jackson, Frank. "A Causal Theory of Counterfactuals." *Australasian Journal of Philosophy* 55 (1977): 3–21.

Lewis, David. "Counterfactual Dependence and Time's Arrow." *Nous* 13 (1979): 455–76.

Parry, William Tuthill. "Reexamination of the Problem of Counterfactual Conditionals." *The Journal of Philosophy* 54 (1957): 85–94.

Slote, Michael A. "Time in Counterfactuals." *The Philosophical Review* 87 (1978): 3–27.

Stalnaker, Robert C. "A Theory of Conditionals." *American Philosophical Quarterly,* monograph no. 2 (1968): 98–112.

VI. SUBJUNCTIVE CONDITIONALS: BOOKS

Adams, Ernest. *The Logic of Conditionals.* Dordrecht: Reidel, 1975.

Kvart, Igal. *A Theory of Counterfactuals.* Indianapolis: Hackett, 1986.

Lewis, David. *Counterfactuals.* Cambridge: Harvard University Press, 1973.

Pollock, John. *Subjunctive Reasoning.* Dordrecht: Reidel, 1976.

NAME INDEX

SUBJECT INDEX